WOMEN IN THE BARRACKS

philippa strum

Women
in the
Barracks

The VMI Case and
Equal Rights

University Press of Kansas

Published by the University Press of Kansas (Lawrence, Kansas 66049),
which was organized by the Kansas Board of Regents and is operated and
funded by Emporia State University, Fort Hays State University, Kansas
State University, Pittsburg State University, the University of Kansas, and
Wichita State University

Library of Congress Cataloging-in-Publication Data
Strum, Philippa.
    Women in the barracks : the VMI case and equal rights /
Philippa Strum.
       p.   cm.
Includes bibliographical references and index.
    ISBN 0-7006-1164-9 (cloth : alk. paper)
    ISBN 0-7006-1336-6 (paper : alk. paper)
    1. United States—Trials, litigation, etc.   2. Virginia Military Institute—
Trials, litigation, etc.   3. Educational equalization—Law and legislation—
United States.   4. Sex discrimination in education—Law and legislation—
United States.   5. Military education—Law and legislation—United States.
6. Women—education—Law and legislation—United States. [1. Sex
discrimination in education—Law and legislation.]   I. title.
    KF228.U5 S77 2002
     344.73'0798'0269—dc21   2001005180

British Library Cataloging in Publication Data is available.

Printed in the United States of America

10 9 8 7 6 5 4 3 2

The paper used in this publication meets the minimum requirements of
the American National Standard for Permanence of Paper for Printed
Library Materials Z39.48-1984.

Contents

Photographs appear following pages 154 and 296.

Acknowledgments

The idea of writing a book about *United States v. Virginia* occurred to me in 1998, when I lived for a while in northern Virginia, lectured in southern Virginia, and heard the Virginia Military Institute gender integration case discussed all around me. I became curious about VMI and, doing some preliminary research about its past, was so intrigued that I began to delve more deeply. That led to other avenues for exploration, such as the development of women's higher education in the South and the anthropology of male bonding rituals. Each of the new paths I traveled is reflected in this volume, and I am extremely grateful to have found knowledgeable guides for every one.

The plaintiff in the case remains anonymous and, unable to talk with her, I began instead with her attorneys. My thanks go to Judith Keith, Michael Maurer, and Jessica D. Silver of the Department of Justice's Civil Rights Division. They were patient during interviews and supplied me with otherwise unobtainable copies of some of the documents in the case.

I then spoke with Robert Patterson and Anne Marie Whittemore, VMI's lawyers in the case, who were equally kind in answering my questions. So were a number of attorneys who filed amicus curiae briefs: Isabelle Katz Pinzler, Marcia Greenberger, Joan Bertin, and Eileen N. Wagner. Eileen also searched her files for useful information and filled me in on some of the intricacies of Virginia politics.

My next step was two visits to VMI. I owe a major debt of gratitude to the people there who were generous and forthcoming, however skeptical they may have been and still may be about the result of my labors. General Josiah Bunting III spoke at length about his view of the case and gave me the better of the deal when we swapped books, because he merely got one of mine but I received a volume of Thucydides. Colonel Norman Bissell shared his recollections and views during a delightful chat that made it apparent why VMI alumni remember him so fondly. Dr. Laura Brodie and Professor Rose Mary Sheldon enabled me to see the case through the eyes of women who were there. Erin Claunch and Kendra Russell, two members of the first class of women cadets, were kind beyond the bounds of duty when they took time from studying for finals to speak with me. Other women cadets, faculty, and staff members chatted informally about their reactions and perceptions, and while they prefer that I not use their names, I am very grateful to them. Diane B. Jacob, the expert VMI archivist, located documents and stayed me from egregious error. Colonels Blair Turner and Cash Koeniger permitted me to sit in on their classes. Sean Collins was my gracious cadet escort for a parade on the VMI post, and Colonel Chuck Steenburgh found photos for this volume. But above all, I thank Colonel Mike Strickler, who helped arrange meetings and interviews, answered questions in person and through a stream of e-mails, dug out statistics, and gave me a tour of the post, all with unflagging good humor.

Dean Heather Wilson of Mary Baldwin College graciously furnished documents about the creation of the Virginia Women's Institute for Leadership, and Brenda Bryant, VWIL's director, took time in the middle of a hot Virginia day to answer innumerable questions. Page Miller, a fine scholar who attended Mary Baldwin, and Professor Gordon Bowen of that college each supplied important background information. Nicole Simmons, at Mary Baldwin, and Carole Green, at VMI, helped with e-mail inquiries.

Other people whom I did not know and had no particular reason to be interested in this project were nonetheless extremely helpful. I would not have identified Eileen Wagner or Andrew Kurt Clark, a recent VMI graduate who shared some of his memories and pictures with me, without the good offices of Professor John Paul Jones of the University of Richmond. Professor Quentin Kidd furthered my education in Virginia politics; Dr. Joan I. Biddle discussed the lives of women in the U.S. military and let me read her dissertation about military wives. Professors Mary Anne Case and Susan Gluck Mezey gave me their articles on VMI and gender integration. Dr. Gordon Davies, formerly of the Virginia Council of Higher Education, shared his recollections and views of the case. Linda Greenhouse, the *New York Times'* superb Supreme Court reporter, used the notes she took when the Court heard oral argument in the case to help me identify the recorded voices of the justices.

Professor Scott Keeter, a colleague during my short stint at Virginia Commonwealth University, filled me in on public reaction to the case. Professor Serena Nanda, a colleague at City University of New York, introduced me to some of the anthropological literature on bonding rituals while giving me the benefit of her own knowledge of the subject.

My special thanks go to Supreme Court Justice Ruth Bader Ginsburg, who has permitted me to interview her over the years and has been supportive of this project in many ways. I am also grateful to her assistant, Linda O'Donnell, who has the knack of doing a difficult job with elegance, and to Lisa Beattie, who worked on the VMI case as a clerk in Justice Ginsburg's chambers. Justice Antonin Scalia was very kind indeed to speak with me about the operation of his chambers and his interpretation of the Constitution's equal protection clause. Judge Diana Gribbon Motz located and gave me permission to use a paper she wrote about Justice Ginsburg.

I was blessed with two wonderful research assistants as I worked on this volume. I met Lika Miyake when she was my intern at the Woodrow Wilson International Center for Scholars and was able to keep her on, as well as to travel to interviews, through a City University of New York Faculty Research Award Program grant. The travel and research funds I received from the Wayne State University Law School paid for trips to other interviews and, best of all, permitted me to hire Laura Sheets as a research assistant. My files are filled with material that Lika and Laura turned up that I would never have found by myself.

Any manuscript of this length is bound to contain stylistic blunders, confusing prose, and factual errors, especially in draft. If the number of errors that no doubt remain has been minimized, that is due entirely to colleagues who read through and commented on various versions. Judith H. Stiehm brought her expertise to bear on the chapters about the military, Isabelle Katz Pinzler annotated the chapters about the litigation, and Marjorie Heins critiqued the entire manuscript. I was fortunate to enlist once again the fine intelligence and scrupulous editing of H. N. Hirsch, Peter Rajsingh, and Melvin Urofsky. Above all, Jill Norgren provided the kind of thoughtful and painstaking reading that every author should have but rarely does, and she was unstinting as well with encouragement and support.

I have been delighted by the University Press of Kansas since it published one of my books back in 1993. As always, thanks to Fred Woodward, Michael Briggs, and Susan Schott and, in addition, to Melinda Wirkus, the senior production editor for this volume.

Additional thanks to Nathan Beck and to Sam Dean and the *Roanoke Times and World News* for permitting me to use their extraordinarily revealing photographs of VMI without fee, and to VMI and the Supreme Court Historical Society as well. I am also grateful to Andrew Alonso for the use of his good pictures.

Emily Altman and Michael Kahan, two very dear friends, were endlessly supportive of this project. Michael, in fact, was nothing less than a bulwark of my life for almost thirty years. He was discovered to have cancer while I was writing *Women in the Barracks,* and in spite of the brave battle he and Emily waged, he died before the book could be published. I dedicate it to Emily, and to the memory of Michael, with love and admiration for their ability to meet adversity with courage and grace.

Introduction: A Fantasy and a True Story

The fantasy belongs to a tall man named Josiah Bunting. He and a petite woman named Ruth Bader Ginsburg meet somewhere in the vicinity of Washington, D.C., to sit and chat over a glass of wine. During their conversation, Bunting invites Ginsburg to the Virginia Military Institute so that she can see for herself what VMI is all about.[1]

Bunting and Ginsburg have, in fact, never met. He is the general who runs VMI and had to implement the U.S. Supreme Court's 1996 order that VMI admit women as students, something that he had opposed vociferously; Ginsburg is the Supreme Court justice who wrote the decision in that case.

It is intriguing to imagine the six-foot-four military man and the tiny feminist justice strolling through the enclave in the western Virginia mountains that is VMI, which carefully excluded women for a century and a half. The VMI citizen-soldier and the women's rights advocate, watching the stiffly saluting cadets, would no doubt have seen quite different things. And each set of perceptions would have reflected the wars over values that were taking place in the country they both served and loved.

The true story, the one that goes by the name *United States v. Virginia,* has another man and another woman as bookends. John Logan of Virginia was the first student to sign the VMI register when the all-male Institute opened in 1839. In 1997 Beth Ann Hogan of Oregon added her name to the 16,000 signatures in the Institute's leather-bound ledgers and went off with the other members of the class of 2001 to get her head shaved.[2] She was the first woman to enroll at VMI, and as she did so, local shops were selling T-shirts and bumper stickers that protested, "Save the Males."[3]

In between these two scrawled moments lies a long tale. Although Bunting and Ginsburg and Logan and Hogan are characters in it, the larger story is not really about them. It is, instead, about the changes in women's—and men's—roles during more than 150 years of American history, particularly in the second half of the twentieth century. It reflects the place of the Supreme Court in American political life and the way the justices both stamp societal change with the legitimization of the Constitution and help shape further change. It tells of the way women finally became generals and lawyers and Supreme Court justices and how some men helped them get there, while other men—and many women—said that the changes were all wrong.

It is a tale of change, but it is also about tradition. One part of the story recounts the dramatic participation of VMI cadets in the Civil War and the way that memory illuminates the rituals and thinking of the Institute to this day. Another concerns the history of VMI men such as Stonewall Jackson and George C. Marshall, proud servants of their country whose continued presence is visible to every VMI student and visitor. The story makes sense only if one knows something about the history of VMI.

As the chapters that follow indicate, another aspect of the story is the generations-long assumption that citizenship meant one thing for women and another for men. The mid-twentieth-century women's movement led to basic alterations in that assumption and in the legal status of women, which is where Ginsburg and a large cast of other female lawyers come in. The country's attitude toward women as it was expressed in the fight to keep women out of the military is yet another crucial piece of the story, because it helps explain why women were irrelevant when VMI was created in the nineteenth century and why it was still so difficult in the 1990s for VMI administrators to imagine that women could succeed in a tough military school. Then there is the South and its myths and realities, including both its particular image of women and its deep vein of suspicion about the folks up north in Washington.

The outline of the story is short. In 1989 the U.S. Department of Justice began investigating the fact that VMI, a publicly funded college, would not accept women. The Justice Department believed that this was a violation of the Constitution. VMI refused to change its admissions policy, and the matter went to court—to a number of courts, in fact, because there would be a trial, an appeal to a higher court, a second trial, a second appeal, and, eventually, a hearing before the U.S. Supreme Court. The Court declared that VMI could not continue as a public institution if it persisted in excluding women, and VMI decided, however grudgingly, to let them in.

But that is just the outline, and like most outlines, it barely begins to explain what happened. To tell the whole story and explain the fantasy, then, one must journey to Lexington, Virginia, where it all began.

1

A Crowd of Honorable Youths

Many bad subjects were sent here to be reformed, and,

although it was by no means a desirable thing to be in any

sense a Reformatory School, or "House of Correction," we started

with the idea that we would admit such bad subjects, and try

and see what could be done with them.

—Francis Henney Smith, first superintendent of VMI

There is no airport in Lexington, Virginia, population a little over 4,000. If you want to get to the Virginia Military Institute by air, you land in Roanoke and rent a car for the hour's drive north to Lexington. There, you find yourself on streets that rise sharply before they descend into the center of town, following the contours of the hills. Lexington is nestled in the valley of Virginia, between the Blue Ridge and Allegheny Mountains, and has the feel of a mountain enclave. Its brick shops, restaurants, and churches seem to beckon to the visitor in a friendly, small-town fashion from up the hill. It is a world away from urban America.

You turn off Route 11 onto Letcher Avenue, named for a former governor of Virginia who was also the father of a VMI cadet. Straight ahead lies the campus of Washington and Lee University, where General Robert E. Lee and his horse both lie. In keeping with the small-town Southern feel of the town, the campus is gracious, its lawns rolling gently to white pillared buildings. Another turn, a moment's drive, and the welcoming hills disappear. You have arrived at the Virginia Military Institute—another world.

The first sight to greet the traveler is the neo-Gothic gray Barracks that looms straight ahead, on the opposite side of the flat, no-nonsense, nine-acre parade ground. All VMI students live in the Barracks' two connected wings. Although its massive five-story walls and parapets evoke a castle, it is not the romantic kind in which a fair, brocade-clad princess is serenaded by lutes while she awaits her Prince Charming. VMI's castle seems more a relic of the Dark Ages, designed to repel nonbelieving hordes. It would take a George C. Marshall rather than an Errol Flynn or an Antonio Banderas to scale those walls—and indeed, Marshall began his career at VMI. The Barracks' parapets, which have remained much the same since they were built in 1850, seem to dare the visitor to violate their stern sense of mission. The building has been described as "forbidding"; it is certainly formidable.

The inside of the Barracks immediately brings to mind the setting for every bad penitentiary movie ever made, and there are times, particularly during the students' difficult first year, when the comparison must ring all too true. It is Charles Dickens come to Virginia. On all four sides rise tiers of cell-like bedrooms, fronting on open balconies that surround the courtyard. The windowed doors provide a sight line that extends to each room's back window. Anyone standing in the center of the courtyard, where there is a sentinel box, has total knowledge of the cadets' comings and goings. An imaginative visitor might gaze up at the tiers and picture inmates banging on tin dishes and calling for the warden. VMI alumni remember the Barracks with the sense of accomplishment and relief that comes only from having, unexpectedly, survived.[1]

VMI does not have a "campus." It is a military school, and the grounds are called "the post." In 1974 the federal government designated the entire post, which lies in the heart of Lexington, a national historic district. Its libraries and museums are open to the public, and tourists can be seen gawking at the buildings and the students' immaculate uniforms. But even when school is out of session, and the cadets are not marching to classes in their stiffly pressed uniforms, VMI would not be mistaken for a civilian college. The Barracks looms, and the post is dotted with military statuary.

The Barracks' main entrance is guarded at all times by a marble embodiment of General Stonewall Jackson. The general taught at VMI before the Civil War, and his remains were buried off post in Lexington. His horse's hide, however, resides at VMI permanently and can be found, mounted, in the basement of the museum. It is perhaps indicative of the pre-1997 culture of VMI that it rigorously excluded women while giving the general's dead horse a place of honor. All first-year students—known as "rats"—are required to salute General Jackson each time they walk by. A few yards away stands the seven-foot bronze statue of General Marshall, VMI class of 1901, resting solidly on an eight-foot stone base. Next comes the hexagonal Citizen-Soldier Cincinnatus Monument, commemorating the man described in a VMI publication as "the Roman patriot generally recognized as the citizen-soldier role model." In front of Smith Hall, named for first superintendent Francis Henney Smith, stands a model of that gentleman, a diploma in his right hand and a Bible in his left.[2]

The only woman similarly displayed on the post is, tellingly, both civilian and idealized. She is called Virginia Mourning Her Dead. The statue was created by VMI alumnus Moses Ezekiel to commemorate the Confederate fallen. Clad in chain mail, she signals the end of hostilities by holding her lance in a reversed position; one foot rests on a broken cannon covered with ivy. At her feet lie the graves of six VMI cadets (more about them later).

The parade ground, a grass-covered field shaped a bit like a U with a straight line running across the top, is circled by a drive. The Barracks is on one side of the U-shaped field, and at the bottom there are six imposing houses, two of them dating from the 1850s. They echo the architecture of the Barracks and are home to VMI's superintendent, its commandant, and a few other faculty and staff members. Trees behind them partially hide the rifle range, the tennis courts, and the baseball, soccer, and lacrosse fields. The buildings along the other side of the U, facing the Barracks, are the Marshall Library and Museum, where the general's papers and memorabilia are stored; Smith Hall; and an alumni center. A number of buildings march across the straight top of the U: the Science Building, the Preston Library, the Nichols Engineering Hall and its annex (Virginia Mourning Her Dead is there, facing the parade ground), and Jackson Memorial Hall.

Jackson Memorial Hall serves as VMI's chapel and assembly room. If it is true that a community's character is reflected in its religious institutions, the impressive hall deserves careful examination. It was built in 1915 to match the external architecture of the Barracks. Inside, however, the aesthetics are more forgiving. The chapel, which seats over 1,000, soars up to a balcony and beyond. Overhead hang the flags of the twenty-six states that belonged to the Union when VMI was founded. Bibles and hymnals stand in the racks attached to the wooden pews. The entire space is dominated by an enormous oil painting at the rostrum, produced by another alumnus, that depicts cadets in a Civil War battle that has become central to VMI's ethos. Portraits of Robert E. Lee and Stonewall Jackson flank the rostrum. Downstairs is VMI's museum and, even further down, a boxing room connected underground to the five-story school gym.

Along the road behind the Barracks are classroom buildings and the VMI hospital. A Federal cannonball, a reminder of the destruction of much of VMI during the Civil War, rests on a concrete base at a corner of the parade ground. It is, as the *Bullet* (the student handbook) boasts, "the only piece of 'Yankee' property on the Post."[3] A number of cannon stand guard near General Jackson.

Behind Nichols Hall, down the hill that pauses briefly to accommodate U.S. Route 11, is the 173-foot-high football stadium that was built in 1920 with funds subscribed by alumni. It has been expanded and now seats 10,000. When the home Kaydets take the field against visiting teams, they are greeted with a loud salute from "Little John II," a three-fifths scale replica of a 1750 howitzer used in the Revolutionary War. Little John roars into life again whenever the Kaydets score.[4]

All told, there are twenty-three major buildings on VMI's 134 acres. (VMI also owns a 160-acre maneuver area and tank course three miles away and another 160-acre tract, New Market Battlefield Park, seventy-five miles north of Lexington.) Many of them would not exist without the contributions and intensive fund-raising of VMI's grateful and unusually devoted alumni.

Next to Smith Hall, for example, stands the large and elegant William L. Moody, Jr. (class of 1886) Hall, opened in 1969 and the product of a gift from Moody's daughter. It holds meeting rooms for faculty and alumni and some overnight rooms for alumni and VMI guests. The gift was solicited in 1964 by Robert H. Patterson, Jr. (class of 1949), then serving as alumni association president and the same Patterson who would be VMI's chief attorney in *United States v. Virginia*.[5] The gym, the six-lane swimming pool, the building that houses the student center and bookstore, the 227,184-volume open-stack library, the glee club, the debating team—none would exist without the generosity of VMI's alumni, in spite of the substantial amount of money the school receives from the commonwealth of Virginia.[6] VMI refused to admit women in large part because of alumni pressure, and the post provides a striking visual reminder of their clout.

A visitor retracing her steps along the short street that separates VMI and its parade ground from Washington and Lee University passes a number of modest houses, a few serving as homes to faculty and others now used as administrative offices. One of them is Pendleton-Coles House, which was built in 1876 and now contains the admissions office. It became the residence of

Colonel Edmund Pendleton—graduate of VMI's first class (of 1842) and later president of the alumni association and member of VMI's Board of Visitors, and ancestor of a twentieth-century VMI graduate and Rhodes scholar.[7] The colonel's granddaughter, Elizabeth Coles, was married in the house to George C. Marshall a few months after Marshall graduated from VMI.

That was the way VMI kept its women for over 150 years: off center stage, permitted into the cast only as mother, wife, daughter, or idealized statue. VMI was a male preserve and, as a faculty wife wrote, "a deliberately anachronistic Southern institution."[8] It was a place where the demands of adolescent testosterone were kept in rigid check, a gentleman's code dictated the courtliest of behavior in mixed company, and community was defined as fraternity. It was only fathers and nephews and sons who went to VMI, their learning process untainted by the distracting persons and ideas of the "other" sex.

That was changed by *United States v. Virginia*. An institution-sized fraternity was, however, precisely the goal VMI set for itself when it was created in 1839.

SOME TWO DECADES EARLIER, as the War of 1812 came to a close, the commonwealth of Virginia found itself with a problem: how to store securely the 30,000 muskets and other arms amassed for the war effort.[9] Virginia's answer involved some of its young militiamen.

Militiamen were citizen-soldiers: men who were not professional soldiers but who would leave their civilian lives and become temporary members of a military force when the exigencies of the times necessitated their doing so. Male Native Americans were citizen-soldiers long before Europeans arrived on these shores, although the term was not used by or about them. White Americans became citizen-soldiers as soon as they arrived on these shores, again without using the term. The tradition flourished during the years leading to the American Revolution and the writing of the U.S. Constitution.

The Framers' distaste for potentially rebellious armed services was reflected in the constitutional provision that there would be no standing army and that appropriations for the young nation's armed forces would be made for no longer than two years at a time. Fearing centralized power, the states insisted on maintaining their own militias as well, and all the states had laws providing for them.[10] Article I, Section 8 of the Constitution empowers Congress "to provide for organizing, arming, and disciplining the Militia . . . reserving to the States respectively, the Appointment of the Officers, and the

Authority of training the Militia according to the discipline prescribed by Congress." Article II, Section 2 declares the president to be commander in chief "of the militia of the several States, when called into the actual Service of the United States," as well as of the federal army and navy. The Second Amendment to the Constitution reads, "A well regulated Militia, being necessary to the security of a free State, the right of the people to keep and bear Arms, shall not be infringed."

These were the clauses under which Congress acted in 1792, when it passed a statute establishing a uniform militia that would consist of all white male citizens, each of whom would provide his own arms.[11] The law proved both expensive for individual citizens and productive of a spotty supply of arms, and in 1808 Congress decided to appropriate annual funds for distribution to state militias on the basis of their size. In 1855 the allocation was changed to reflect representation in Congress.[12] State militias were so important that they were supported by federal money, back in the days when there was relatively little federal money to spend.

Local militias were extensive throughout the South from the earliest days of the United States; by 1852, at least eight were based in Richmond alone. Virginia law required that they muster a minimum of four times a year. The musters and parades became important social occasions, with the local population frequently turning out as an audience. Militias were a source of status as well as protection and entertainment. It sometimes seemed that every white male Virginian sought to become an officer. John Hope Franklin reports that "the architect Latrobe had the feeling that everyone he met in the South was either a captain, colonel or general"; although there were twice as many men in the New York militia, there were 84 percent more officers in Virginia.[13]

The Virginia militia was not a plaything, however. In the early days of nationhood it was counted on to repel Indians, but it quickly became equally vital in putting down slave insurrections.[14] Southern militias thrived on the fear of slave rebellions and were a key element in the preservation of the South's "peculiar institution." One Virginia company, in fact, kept its horses saddled and bridled every night for three weeks during the Nat Turner rebellion.[15] As the slave population grew, so did fears of its turning against the whites, and an early version of military preparedness was created. Along with it came an emphasis on the military as an expression of patriotism. Service in the country's wars was a particular source of pride for Southern men, who were disproportionately present in the War of 1812 and again during the Mexican War. By the time of the Civil War, the South would lay claim to being the

most martially inclined part of the country: it took credit for being the training ground for the nation's soldiers and the producer of its best treatises on
the science of war.[16]

So it was logical in 1816 for Virginia, faced with the munitions assembled
during the War of 1812, to establish three arsenals and staff them with members of the militia. One of the arms depots was the Lexington Arsenal, located
on 7.7 acres amid the courthouse, homes, churches, hotels, and small fac-
tories that made up the town.[17] The twenty Virginia militiamen detailed there
had little to do beyond routine drills; in fact, their leisure-time antics became
distasteful and threatening to the townspeople. They were, a VMI historian
reported, "an undesirable element in the social economy of aristocratic Lexington" and "of such a low social order as to be objectionable to the thrifty
people of Lexington."[18]

Among the citizens distressed by the young men's rowdiness were the
members of the Franklin Literary Society, one of the town's most influential
institutions. It was an incorporated literary and debating body made up of
lawyers, physicians, merchants, and mechanics; its wealth and standing in
the community were reflected by the fact that it possessed its own brick building. In December 1834 the group devoted two discussions to the topic,
"Would it be politic for the State to establish a military school, at the Arsenal,
near Lexington, in connection with Washington College, on the plan of the
West Point Academy?" A vote was taken at the conclusion of the second
evening's discussion, and there was unanimous agreement in favor.[19] The
next step was to develop a consensus in the community.

To that end, three articles signed "Cives" were placed in the *Lexington
Gazette*. They were almost certainly written by a young Lexington attorney
named John Thomas Lewis Preston, a grandson of Edmund Randolph,
George Washington's second secretary of state. The first article, published on
August 28, 1835, stated: "The object is to supply the place of the present
Guard, by another, composed of young men, from seventeen to twenty-four
years of age, to perform the necessary duties of a guard, who would receive
no pay, but, in lieu, have afforded to them the opportunities of a liberal education."[20]

The men would be taught by a tutor, who would be responsible for the
classics; a professor, who would teach science; and a captain, who would
serve as an officer and instructor in military arts. "We would have the whole
Guard or School under military discipline, not only to secure the object of the
State in establishing this military post, but likewise that industry, regularity,

and health might be promoted," the article declared. Showing a solid sense of what might appeal to the state's legislators, the writer proposed that each state senator be entitled to nominate one student from his district. The article continued with a description of "the healthful and pleasant abode of a crowd of honorable youths pressing up the hill of science, with noble emulation, a gratifying spectacle, an honor to our country and our state, objects of honest pride to their instructors, and fair specimens of citizen-soldiers, attached to their native state, proud of her fame, and ready in every time of deepest peril to vindicate her honor or defend her rights."[21] These words would later be engraved in bronze at the entrance to the VMI Memorial Garden.

Ninety-four citizens of Lexington signed a petition in favor of the proposed school; so did eighteen citizens of nearby Fairfield.[22] Preston and his allies began lobbying members of the Virginia House of Delegates, and on March 22, 1836, the legislature approved an act creating a military school. It would be run by a Board of Visitors consisting of four members plus the state adjutant general, serving ex officio, and would be annexed to nearby Washington College. The governor appointed the first board in May 1837.[23] The makeup of the board has changed since then: two of its now fifteen members are required by law to be non-Virginians, and the governor almost always chooses new members from a list submitted by VMI's alumni association. Nonetheless, the Board of Visitors essentially remains today what it was in 1837: the body with sole and complete power over VMI's physical property and governance. It was a late-twentieth-century version of the Board of Visitors that resolutely refused to admit women to VMI, thereby setting the stage for *United States v. Virginia*.

But that was all in the future when VMI was first planned. The local residents were pleased by the idea that the militiamen would be withdrawn and were reassured by the connection with Washington College (renamed Washington and Lee University in 1881), which dated back to 1749 and boasted an endowment from George Washington. The link gave the fledgling institution immediate prestige.[24] Washington College had not been consulted about these arrangements, however, and apparently was sufficiently miffed to delay the opening of the school.[25] The planners returned to the drawing board and created an entity less tied to the college, with the consent of the legislature. Preston and four other Lexington residents, all of them graduates of Washington College, were appointed to the board, and planning went forward.[26]

Preston gave the new institution its name, writing later, "The object was not to fit the graduate for a single profession exacting in its demands . . . but to prepare young men for the varied work of civil life. . . . The military feature, though essential to its discipline, is not primary in its scheme of education."[27] Leadership of the school, however, quickly passed from Preston and his friends into the hands of two other men. One, VMI's first commandant (roughly equivalent to dean of students), was Claudius Crozet, a French immigrant whose credentials included an education at the elite Ecole Polytechnique, service in Napoleon Bonaparte's army, and appointment as professor of engineering and math at West Point.[28] The second was superintendent Francis H. Smith.

Smith, the twenty-six-year-old scion of an aristocratic Tidewater family and a West Point graduate, brought an autocratic style, a strong sense of discipline, and a firm piety to the new institution. It was he who established mandatory attendance at church and Bible classes on Sundays and, finding the local Presbyterian and Methodist churches not to his liking, founded the Episcopal Grace Church (later renamed Robert E. Lee Memorial Church). Smith's practice of giving each graduate a "beautifully bound" copy of the Bible along with a diploma upon graduation has been revived by superintendent Josiah Bunting.[29] As the *Bullet* says, "religion plays an important part in the education and life of a cadet."[30] Compulsory attendance for Protestant cadets at Sunday religious services was abolished only in 1973, meaning that the first captain no longer barked at Sunday morning formation, "All Catholics, Jews, and nonbelievers fall out."[31]

Smith employed religion as a tool of pedagogy and discipline, as well as one of spiritual enhancement. He was faced with a student body that apparently was only a minor improvement over the young militiamen who had manned the arsenal. "From the beginning," he wrote later, "I had to rely upon discipline as a means of forming and developing individual character. . . . Many bad subjects were sent here to be *reformed,* and, although it was by no means a desirable thing to be in any sense a Reformatory School, or 'House of Correction,' we started with the idea that we would admit such bad subjects, and try and see what could be done with them. The *military* organization of the institution had a tendency to fascinate such unruly spirits, who might be made valuable men by the military pride which promotion to the military offices of the school held out to them."[32] He found military training the "most important element of discipline," as his charges were "just at an age when *waywardness* is the only fully developed trait in their character."[33]

From its earliest years, then, VMI's military component was primarily a means rather than an end. The goal of the Institute was to guard Virginia's arms while utilizing military discipline as a way of turning particularly unruly boys into men. Relatively few of those men would become professional soldiers. VMI's young citizen-soldiers would guard the arsenal while the school produced the next generation of civilian leaders, all of them ready to spring to their country's defense when needed. Unlike the nation's federal military academies, VMI was never intended to be a pipeline for a professional army.

The new students would be educated and whipped into shape through a curriculum adopted by the Board of Visitors in 1839. It would not be an easy one, and the board's first book order was for forty copies each of La Croix's *Arithmetic,* Davies's *Algebra,* Davies's or Brewster's *Geometry,* Berard's *French Grammar* and *French Lessons,* Nugent's *Dictionaries,* and *Gil Blas.* The students would study infantry tactics and military policing, mathematics, English language and literature, French and German, topography and architectural drawing, natural and experimental philosophy (astronomy, chemistry, mineralogy, geology), the science and practice of artillery, and civil and military engineering—all to be mastered in three years.[34] VMI would be the first school in the South to teach engineering and industrial chemistry, with engineering quickly emerging as the core of its studies.[35] The board requested 100 muskets and equipment from the federal government, and with textbooks and armaments at hand, VMI was ready for business.

ON NOVEMBER 11, 1839, the flag of Virginia was raised over VMI as twenty-three of the commonwealth's young white male citizens, all investigated for character and stability and chosen from more than seventy applicants, inscribed their names in the matriculation register. (Five additional students arrived two days later.) Each young man was, as required, between sixteen and twenty-five years old, at least four feet nine inches tall, and unafflicted "with any disease or infirmity which would render him unfit for military service; or . . . any disorder of an infectious or immoral character." Every student brought shoes, underwear, bed linen, towels, and "1 foul clothes bag, made of ticking"; each was expected to join with his roommates to purchase "one looking glass, one wash stand, one tin wash pan, one pitcher, one pail, one broom, and one scrubbing brush." They were forbidden to use "wine, porter, or any other spirituous or intoxicating liquor" or tobacco on post; possess playing cards; or gamble.[36]

John B. Strange, the first cadet sentinel, was ordered to mount guard in the arsenal courtyard, thereby relieving the military guard. He and the other young men were outfitted with long, gray, caped surtouts, or overcoats, and kepis—French-type military caps like those that would be worn in the Civil War. Each was supplied as well with a gray coatee (jacket), a gray winter vest, two white summer vests, gray winter trousers, white summer trousers, and fatigues. Their uniforms were modeled on those worn at West Point, but theirs bore the proud insignia of Virginia, and they were required to wear them at all times. They would drill for at least an hour every day except Saturday and Sunday, parade in dress uniform each evening, and stand inspection every Saturday morning.[37]

VMI was the country's first state-sponsored school of military education.[38] Today, many of the original features are still in place: the cadets dress in uniforms similar to those worn by the first class, they are all given identical haircuts, they are forbidden to make unnecessary conversation, they are assigned to live four in a room and have surprise room inspections, they drill and march to and from class, and they grumble about the Spartan conditions.[39] History and continuity are central to the VMI ideology and would be invoked repeatedly in *United States v. Virginia*.

The new cadets quickly got into the spirit of things, adopting an honor code against lying, cheating, stealing, and failing to report violations to an Honor Court. The code is still in force.[40] Their military supplies seem to have been late in arriving, for military instruction began only in the spring of 1840. By June, the Board of Visitors was able to began its annual examinations at what was quickly dubbed "the West Point of the South." The Virginia legislature granted commissions in the state militia to VMI's professorial staff, and the enterprise gained such immediate respect that neighboring South Carolina decided to open two military academies of its own. One of them was The Citadel.[41] In 1842 the first VMI cadet flag, a white banner inscribed with the motto "Virginia Fidem Praesto" ("I am true to Virginia"), joined the Virginia flag flying overhead.[42]

Something of that first year is apparent in the oldest known extant letter from a VMI cadet, dated November 30, 1839. Valentine Saunders told his parents, back home in Leesburg:

> I have just returned from exploring the dusky halls of the old Arsenal. There are deposited in this arsenal at which we are stationed fifty six thousand stand of arms including a vast number of old rifles, muskets, pistols, and dragoon swords. . . .
>
> At a particular hour we are marched in squads at the beat of the drum to the recitation room where we are examined individually by Major Smith. . . . [He] is a man of the nicest discrimination and shrewdness I ever knew. I will defy anyone

to fool or dupe him, for one can't get along here otherwise than doing his duty. . . .

We are drilled every day by the Major. . . . Our present course of instruction includes [Mathematics]. . . . We also progress rapidly in the study of French. . . .

Our service here is very hard.[43]

The first annual appropriation made by the Virginia legislature for VMI was a little over $6,000. Money was tight, as the "state cadets" nominated by state senators received free tuition, room, "board, washing, fuel, bedding and books," subject to two years' subsequent service.[44] Teachers had to be paid: Preston, VMI's first teacher of languages, earned $700 a year. In 1842 the cadets journeyed to the grounds of the state capitol in Richmond, impressing the legislators with their prowess at parading and answering questions about their studies. The legislature responded as hoped, enacting a law that recreated VMI in part as a "normal school" charged with training teachers. To that end, the statute both increased VMI's funding and required state cadets to teach for two years after graduation unless they were excused from doing so by the Board of Visitors.[45] VMI thereby became Virginia's first normal school, as well as its first public military college.[46]

When the *Lexington Gazette* reported on VMI's first graduation in 1842, it described VMI's functions as "send[ing] forth accomplished soldiers to impart skill and discipline and a military spirit to her [Virginia's] militia; and in giving to her common schools gentlemen who are educated, and capable to instruct the youth of our State."[47] An 1881 survey of VMI graduates found that 175 of them had become professors and teachers, and 135 had become civil and mining engineers.[48] Although the combination of military and teacher training may seem strange today, it made sense in the South of the 1840s. As John Hope Franklin noted, much of the white male population in the South during the first half of the nineteenth century was uneducated and violence prone, and young Southerners were "accustomed to disregarding law and order."[49] Men rather than women were the instructors of choice, given the region's unruly young male population and the fact that teachers in small rural schools had to cope with a variety of ages. Seventy-five percent of the South's public school teachers through the 1870s were men, but even they found it rough going. In the years between the founding of VMI and the Civil War, the South therefore turned increasingly to military education, creating more and more schools modeled on VMI and drawing on its graduates to fill posts as teachers.[50]

What would become VMI's powerful alumni association also grew out of its first class. The day after graduation, the new alumni organized themselves as the Alumni Military Association. It became the Society of the Alumni a decade later, began raising money for scholarships, and was incorporated as the VMI Alumni Association in 1919.[51]

Neighboring Washington College was unimpressed by VMI's early success and remained uneasy about its forced relationship. Initially, the Washington cadets were drilled jointly with those from VMI. When the Washington students took to calling those from VMI "rats," the latter responded by labeling the Washington students "minks . . . because they were so mean and sly in their contacts with cadets."[52] Washington administrators were more concerned with what they considered to be Superintendent Smith's excessive sectarianism, and the two institutions severed all formal ties on February 22, 1846.[53] The appellation "rats," however, would be adopted by VMI students themselves sometime in the 1850s, as a term for new cadets.[54]

By then, the rigorous VMI curriculum was firmly established. Freshmen studied natural philosophy and chemistry, rhetoric and English literature, and the engineering of science and war. Second-year students took mathematics, which consisted of calculus, analytical geometry, and descriptive geometry; French and Latin (the latter having been substituted for German); and drawing. Third-year math consisted of algebra, geometry, analytical geometry, and descriptive geometry; students also continued their studies of French and Latin. Fourth-year students went on with math and French, in addition to English and geography.[55]

The new Barracks building, built in 1850 to house the increasing number of students, is still in use today. State cadets had been joined by "pay cadets"—Virginians who had not been nominated by senators but were eager for the VMI experience. It was feared that the presence of cadets whose families could afford to pay their way, in addition to those who presumably relied on state scholarships, might create distinctions of wealth and class. The school therefore developed an early ethos of equality, turning a consciously blind eye to the students' social status outside the institution and insisting on equal treatment within its walls. Life within the Barracks, with its four "stoops," or floors, was deliberately kept Spartan for everyone.[56] The notion of equality, however, was not intended to apply to nonwhites, and the superintendent was expected to purchase enough slaves to maintain the cadets' quarters. They were referred to as "stoop niggers."[57] Two Negro musicians were turned over to the Institute by the former arsenal guard.[58] A Washington College professor hired out one of his slaves to be a waiter at VMI, later selling him to the Institute.[59] VMI was very much a part of the Old South.

The recession that swept the nation in 1857 created vacancies in VMI's ranks, and the Institute began turning to out-of-staters for additional income.[60] The school enjoyed what one of its historians called a "flood of applications" from young men in other states who wanted the benefits of VMI's emphasis on scientific and technical training. Although most of the newcomers were from other Southern states, VMI had begun the process of becoming a national institution. Pay cadets from Virginia, however, continued to be given preference over those from out of state.[61]

In 1851 VMI hired a West Point graduate named Thomas Jonathan Jackson—better known to history as Stonewall—as its professor of natural philosophy (that is, science) and artillery tactics. He had left West Point to fight in the Mexican War and had distinguished himself in that conflict, so he arrived at VMI with some fanfare. The students, however, were less than impressed with his highly regimented rule in the classroom, where he reportedly attempted to replicate the tight discipline of the military hierarchy and generally demonstrated that he was better suited for the army than for academia.[62] Finding him both moody and eccentric, they nicknamed him "Tom Fool" Jackson or "Old Tom Jackson."[63] A cadet damned both Jackson and VMI, poetically, in an 1856 letter:

> The V.M.I. O What a spot
> In winter cold, in summer hot
> Great Lord Al—what a wonder
> Major Jackson Hell & Thunder[64]

The Society of the Alumni made an unsuccessful attempt to have Jackson's teaching methods formally investigated, but it was the Civil War that would end Jackson's classroom career.[65]

JACKSON'S REPUTATION AT VMI took a distinct turn for the better when hostilities erupted between the North and the South. Anticipating the Civil War, the Board of Visitors had announced in the 1850s that every VMI cadet was in state military service and under command of the governor, whose authority took precedence over parental control.[66] The object was to make them legally ready for service in what would become the Confederacy, and the war found them well prepared.

Some of them were pressed into service even before war was formally declared. Fear of a slave rebellion in the nearby town of Buchanan caused the cadets to be put on alert in 1856, with Jackson sitting awake in the guard room all night.[67] In December 1859 Jackson led a detachment of eighty-five cadets to Charles Town (Harpers Ferry) to help keep order at the execution of John Brown. Some of the cadets seem to have found the proceedings emotionally fraught. One of them, a member of the Preston family, rushed to the scaffold crying, "So perish all such enemies of Virginia. All such enemies of the Union. All such foes of the human race." His professor was more restrained: the devout Jackson remained in his place, praying for Brown's soul.[68]

Although the South in general and Virginia in particular had its share of men trained by and serving in the military, it, like the North, had to take rapid steps to prepare even more soldiers once the war began in earnest. The well-drilled cadets of VMI were enrolled in the effort, following receipt of a Confederate army order:

> Richmond, April 20th, 1861. Send courier to Majr Preston immediately to send Corps of Cadets to Richmond. Let inefficient cadets remain to aid as guard and get volunteers from Lexington to aid as guard. Bring down all the ordnance and ordnance stores with full supply of ammunition. Majr Gilham and Mr. Catlett will report here without delay. Wm. H. Richardson, Adjt. Genl"[69]

Orders to send 10,000 muskets to Richmond and other ammunition to Harpers Ferry were received the next day.[70]

Three hundred cadets out of a total student body of 348 promptly left for Richmond's Camp Lee under Jackson's command to drill and instruct Confederate recruits. The newly published manual they used had been written by William Gilham, West Point class of 1840, who arrived at VMI in 1846 as the first commandant of the VMI Corps. His *Manual of Instruction for the Volunteers and Militia* became the Confederate army's official guidelines.[71]

There was a sharp culture clash between the young cadets and the estimated 15,000 to 20,000 recruits they drilled over the next eight months.[72] Many of the volunteers reported with makeshift weapons such as squirrel rifles, shotguns, butcher's knives, and ancient horse pistols, and the cadets mocked both the weapons and the recruits' unkempt hair and scraggly beards. The recruits, in turn, looked on the cadets as dandies: too wide awake, too clean, too white gloved, too young.[73] Many of the older cadets left Camp

Lee to enlist in the Confederate army. There they joined the 1,796 VMI graduates (94 percent of VMI's alumni) who were in Confederate uniform at
some time during the war—as were at least fifteen others who fought with
the Union armies.[74] Nine of the sixteen men who graduated in VMI's first
class served; one of those killed in battle was John Strange, the first sentinel.[75]
Meanwhile, students from the University of Virginia and other state institutions traveled to VMI, which set up a military science course concentrating
on drill.[76]

VMI cadets soon were called into more active service. Detachments of
them followed Jackson in the 1862 battle of Manassas and were engaged in
three 1863 battles at Goshen and Rockbridge Baths, as well as in Lynchburg
in 1864. VMI alumni fought alongside Jackson in the battle of Chancel-
lorsville on May 2, 1863. Surveying the battlefield before the fighting began
and noting the number of VMI men mustered there, Jackson commented,
"The Institute will be heard from today." Those words are inscribed on the
statue of Jackson that now guards the Jackson Arch entrance to the Barracks.
Jackson's favorite classroom maxim, "You may be whatever you resolve to be,"
appears on the arch.

Jackson died as a result of wounds he received that day. The coffin of the
once-mocked professor, taken to Lexington by boat, lay in state overnight in
his old lecture room at VMI. It was then escorted to burial by his former
students.[77]

Exactly a year later, another battle that would have a lasting impact on
VMI's history, ethic, and reputation took place. It was fought eighty miles
away from VMI, at New Market.

General Ulysses S. Grant had ordered the Union forces led by General
Frank Sigel to cut the supply routes from the Shenandoah Valley to General
Robert E. Lee's army. Lee gave the job of defending the supply routes to General John C. Breckinridge, a former vice president of the United States who
commanded the Southern forces of about 4,500. His numbers were too few,
and on May 11, 1861, 241 VMI cadets left to provide reinforcement. Fewer
than two dozen remained behind, rather disgusted at being ordered to guard
the school rather than prepare for battle.[78] The young cadets—aged fifteen
to twenty-two, with an average age of around eighteen—marched north
under rainy skies for four days, carrying the colors not of the Confederacy but
of VMI. Among them were sons of Governor John Letcher and former governor Henry A. Wise; nephews of Lee, General Jubal Early, and Secretary of
War James A. Seddon; two cousins of General Breckinridge; and a descen-

dent of Chief Justice John Marshall. One of the cadets was future U.S. senator Thomas S. Martin; another, a future uncle of Douglas MacArthur.[79]

The cadets were greeted as heroes as they marched into Staunton on May 12 and were feted at dances the town had quickly arranged,[80] but as they continued their trek during the next three days, the mood was somewhat more solemn. (We will revisit Staunton, an important site in our story, later on.) They began passing Virginians escaping from the Union advance with their livestock and other possessions; here and there, they could see a wounded Confederate soldier or a group of Union prisoners.[81]

Before they broke camp on the morning of May 15, Captain Frank Preston, the Latin professor whose empty sleeve was a souvenir of an earlier battle, gathered them for prayer. Shortly thereafter they reached New Market and immediately marched into battle, still carrying VMI's colors—the only student body of an American college ever to fight as a unit. The young men charged the Union lines, taking prisoners and capturing a cannon. When the first commander of the cadets was disabled by a shell burst, he was immediately replaced by young VMI professor Henry A. Wise (class of 1862), a son of the former governor. Another son, class of 1866, was wounded. The Confederate regulars, some of whom had been ready to break after the first Union charge, rallied at the sight of the "baby soldiers" in their parade dress. The Union forces were beaten back.[82]

For VMI, however, the price of victory was high. Ten VMI cadets died or were fatally wounded in the clash, and forty-seven others were injured. The morning after the battle, Moses Ezekiel, the young Jewish cadet who would win world renown as a sculptor, brought one of his wounded schoolmates from the rudimentary field hospital to the home of Mrs. Eliza Clindinst Crim. Ezekiel had persuaded Mrs. Crim to take in the casualty, sixteen-year-old Thomas Garland Jefferson. Remaining at Jefferson's bedside, Ezekiel nursed him, read to him from the New Testament, and watched him die.[83]

The events of the day had a lasting effect on VMI. A battle streamer of gray and blue, embroidered "New Market," still hangs from VMI's regimental colors. An enormous painting of the event by a VMI alumnus dominates VMI's chapel. The bodies of six of the dead cadets still lie at the foot of Ezekiel's statue of Virginia Mourning Her Dead, which bears the names of all the New Market cadets; four tablets commemorate those buried elsewhere in the state. On May 15, 1887, in a ceremony similar to one that had been sponsored by Napoleon in 1800, cadets in several companies were assigned to represent those killed at New Market. As the name of each of the dead was called, the cadet representing him stepped to the front, saluted, and proclaimed, "Died on the field of honor." A version of the ceremony is performed each year, and every year VMI freshmen parade and charge at New Market as their predecessors did.[84]

The VMI alumni who fought in the Army of the South included 3 major generals, 15 brigadier generals, 95 colonels, 65 lieutenant colonels, 110 majors, and 310 captains.[85] Among them were the four Patton brothers who had attended VMI, along with some of their cousins. One commanded a battalion at New Market and later served VMI as a professor of civil engineering. Together with their three non-VMI brothers, the Pattons commanded eleven different infantry regiments.[86] General George Patton of World War II fame, one of their descendants, began his military education at VMI but transferred to West Point. One of Patton's sons, a major general in the army, would refer to the seventeen relatives who had graduated from VMI in a vitriolic letter he wrote in 1991 protesting the idea of gender integration.[87]

The tradition of VMI as a family institution was well established by the time of the Civil War, and it would continue. A son and nephew of John Strange would attend VMI, as would the brother and nephew of another member of the first class and a great-grandson of a third.[88] Captain Cary Breckinridge, for example, had one son each in the classes of 1857, 1858, 1860, and 1867; two of them died in the Civil War.[89] The families of Governor Wise and his brother John Cropper Wise would produce, to date, fourteen VMI graduates over three generations, including a number who wrote histories of VMI.[90]

Most of the VMI students who had not enlisted after their stint of training recruits did so in 1862, after the battle of Manassas, and the school closed temporarily.[91] VMI had indeed become the West Point of the South.

The institution itself did not go unscathed. Union General David H. Hunter and his troops shelled and burned VMI in 1864, sparing only two buildings, in one of which lay the superintendent's ill daughter. Despite having no authority to attack property lacking a military function, they pillaged and destroyed or stole nearly 10,000 books, leading Congress to make partial restitution fifty years later.[92] There are still three black cannon shells jutting from the walls of Old Barracks, embedded there when Union gunboats on the Maury River attacked VMI.[93] The Barracks itself, in ruins except for its stone and brick walls, was determinedly rebuilt after the war.

Students returned to VMI in October 1864. When the war ended, Robert E. Lee was elected president of Washington College; his oldest son, General

G. W. Custis Lee, was named to a professorship at VMI.[94] One of Robert E. Lee's gifts to the college was his supervision of the building of its graceful chapel, where he attended daily worship services with the students and would be buried; twentieth-century VMI cadets would be expected to salute when they passed by. A letter from a cadet to his mother described the scene after Lee's death in 1870, suggesting that the spirit of New Market was very much alive:

> All duties, military and academic suspended at the Institute, and all the black crape and all similar black material in Lexington, was used up at once, and they had to send on to Lynchburg for more. Every cadet had black crape issued to him, and an order was published at once requiring us to wear it as a badge of mourning for six months. The battallion flag was heavily draped in black. . . . The Institute has been hung all around with black. . . . The morning after his death we marched up and escorted the remains from the house to Washington College Chapel, where they lay in "state" until the burial yesterday morning. . . . Myself and four other cadets with Gen Smith's permission sat up all night with the corpse on Friday night. . . . It was considered a great honor to be allowed to sit up with the remains.[95]

As the Civil War closed, then, VMI could look back at almost three decades of existence as a bastion of Southern white manhood, given a militaristic twist. It embodied the values of patriotism and machismo, tradition and fraternity, and it knew in its collective heart that white men were superior to everyone else. It had developed a stern sense of honor that entailed fidelity to VMI's standards, however brutal, and disdain for the part of the world that had not gone to VMI—which was, of course, most of it. Its students and alumni had proved themselves by fighting valiantly to maintain the Old South. Like much of the South, VMI would celebrate the war by turning its face resolutely toward the past, acknowledging the present in its academic subjects but insistently promulgating the mythology and values of an era that was rapidly fading.

Yet, oddly enough, it was the legislators sitting in Richmond, the still-proud capital of the Confederacy, who would challenge VMI's continued right to exist.

From the Civil War to
the Civil Rights Era

We think the things we did in 1890 and 1930 are still valid today.

—Josiah Bunting, thirteenth superintendent of VMI

As Robert E. Lee surrendered his sword to General Ulysses S. Grant at Appomattox, Virginia's economy lay in ruins, and the state had to decide where it could trim costs. One result of the subsequent examination of expenditures was an 1868 legislative committee's order to Superintendent Smith to show cause why VMI should not be closed. Smith lobbied hard and ultimately convinced the Assembly that VMI's technical know-how would help rebuild the state and, perhaps more importantly, that it would do so without public funds. He had toured a number of European technical and military schools back in 1858, and his report, *Scientific Education in Europe,* now became the basis of a new curriculum for VMI.[1] One aspect of the new VMI would be the surrender of its identity as a normal school.

During the war, when the men were away fighting, women had gradually taken over many of the South's teaching jobs. They remained in them as the men came home and began rebuilding the economy. Even more women joined the workforce with the advent of peace, as husbands returned to find their income-producing farms in ruins and wives and widows necessarily sought paid employment. Teaching was a respectable choice. The number of women schoolteachers quickly doubled, and by the late 1880s, they would constitute a majority of Southern teachers.[2] In order to train them, the South created women's normal schools,[3] which had the unanticipated effect of leading increasing numbers of women to view college as an ordinary part of life—

a phenomenon that would have an impact a century later in *United States v. Virginia*.

In 1868, however, that could scarcely have been foreseen. Smith nonetheless looked ahead and, abandoning VMI's incarnation as a normal school, prepared to transform it into a scientific and technical college.[4] The school essentially reinvented itself, raising admissions standards, increasing and developing its academic offerings, and upgrading its faculty (although still preferring to hire its own alumni, as would remain the case through the twentieth century). It became an element in the evolution of a new Southern leadership, a managerial and professional class. VMI created ties to the national military and saw its graduates serve as officers in the Spanish-American War and the war in the Philippines.[5]

Although the curriculum changed, VMI's ethos of strict egalitarianism did not; yet it, too, was threatened at the Civil War's end. Three cadets who were disgruntled with Reconstruction formed the selective Sigma Nu fraternity in 1869. It became one of many at the Institute. Alpha Tau Omega also had its roots at VMI, and chapters of at least half a dozen other national fraternities were established there in the postwar years. VMI eventually banned fraternities as too rambunctious.[6] They are warmly remembered, however. There is a plaque on the Sigma Nu meeting house, and a fountain and two benches donated by Alpha Tau Omega grace the lawn in front of Preston Library. The phenomenon is interesting in light of VMI's insistence throughout *United States v. Virginia* that life at the Institute had always been exactly the same for every cadet.

VMI's egalitarianism did not extend to Virginia's black population; there were no black students at the Institute. The black faces there belonged to the mess hall waiters and the two black musicians, who, in addition to "chopping wood, hauling water and attending to the other wants of the Institute," played fife and drum for reveille and taps and other daily routines.[7]

The postwar period did bring another change: the institutionalization of a practice that would grab the attention of the nation as *United States v. Virginia* was litigated and would be used as a reason for keeping women out. That practice was the hazing of "rats."

HAZING HAD GROWN RIFE AT VMI in the 1850s, when, for the first time, a cadet was dismissed for abusing a newcomer. Freshmen were regularly terrorized by a practice known as "company room," in which they were forced to perform rapid sets of exercises and were subjected to corporal punishment, and by "sweat parties," the equivalent of "company room" in a steam-filled shower room. They were expected to maintain a rigid posture called "straining" and to undertake "fagging," or serving upperclassmen.[8] Moses Ezekiel remembered hazing in 1862:

> At that time it was customary for every newcomer at the Institute to be called a "rat," and any old cadet had the right to exact any service from a "rat" and also, on meeting him, to order the "rat" to hold up his right hand, when the old cadet would take hold of it and twist his arm until it was almost out of joint, declaring that he was impudent. If the "rat" made any resistance, he was taken to a room in the barracks, his hands were bound together over his knees, and he was turned over on his face and bucked with a bayonet scabbard, his name being spelled on his back side with a lick for every letter, and Constantinople for a middle name.[9]

The custom of calling freshmen "rats" survived the Civil War, as did hazing. One of the gawkier and less promising rats who arrived at VMI at the beginning of the 1898–1899 year was the younger brother of a recent VMI graduate and descended from a family that had settled in Virginia before the Revolution. George Catlett Marshall, still recovering from a case of typhoid when he reached VMI, almost ended his military career there as a result of hazing. Upperclassmen made him squat over a bayonet as a test of his endurance. Weakened by his illness, he slipped, injured himself, and spent several days in the hospital. He refused to tell VMI authorities who was responsible for the incident, and his relieved tormentors rewarded him by exempting him from the rest of the rat line.[10] The bayonet incident did nothing to minimize Marshall's strong devotion to VMI, where he achieved the honor of becoming first captain of the Corps of Cadets.[11]

Marshall, of course, went on to become a five-star general, army chief of staff, creator of the famed post–World War II Marshall Plan, secretary of state, secretary of defense, and the only American career military figure to win the Nobel Peace Prize. After the war, Marshall served on VMI's Board of Visitors and as the first chairman of the board of the VMI Foundation.[12]

Marshall remains VMI's most renowned graduate, and his career epitomizes what the Institute thought it was fighting to save in *United States v. Virginia*. Its alumni were and are an impressive group, achieving distinction in the military, politics, business, and the arts. The first class at VMI produced four farmers, five teachers, three doctors, six lawyers, two lawyer/teachers, a dentist, and a clergyman. Later, Governor Harry F. Byrd, Sr., and Supreme

Court Justice Tom Clark attended VMI; so did actors and authors, a chief curator of the Corcoran Gallery of Art, Rhodes scholars, thirty-nine college and university presidents, numerous federal and state governmental officials, and many corporate executives across the country. The *New York Times* considers VMI to be "heavily linked to future business success" in Virginia and the nation; *Virginia Business* magazine, counting the number of chief executive officers of publicly traded Virginia-based companies, calculated that VMI produces more of them than any other college in the state.[13]

The VMI of Marshall's era also began to build an international reputation. Its first foreign cadets, from China, were admitted in 1904.[14] (By the time *United States v. Virginia* began, there would be twenty-nine students from twelve countries in residence.)[15] Some modifications were made for the foreigners. The rat line was still so harsh that it was feared that hazing Chinese students might cause an international incident.[16] As a result, the Chinese were exempted from the worst of it. In return, they ran a laundry for the more senior cadets.[17] The new cadets scarcely threatened Virginia's domination of the student body, however. Whether as a matter of largesse or because someone found the influx of non-Virginians unsettling, in 1910 the Virginia legislature created the classification of "Virginia cadet": any VMI student from Virginia who had not been chosen by a state senator as a "state cadet" would be entitled to free tuition.[18]

It was nonetheless the commonwealth itself that raised the next threat to the Institute's existence. The context was the report of a commission appointed by the state legislature in 1927 to survey all state-funded education. Although the commission members included "several pillars of the Virginia Establishment," it was headed by a professor from the University of Wisconsin—an institution soon to be denounced by the head of VMI's Board of Visitors as a 'hotbed' of postwar pacifism."[19] The commission concluded that VMI should be closed.

Its 1928 report acknowledged VMI's "long history of distinguished service." It nonetheless found that "the conditions in the nation have so changed that the peculiar type of education afforded by V.M.I. is no longer needed" and that "the military needs of the nation that can be met only by a four-year collegiate education are adequately met by West Point." The report also raised a question that would resurface toward the end of the century, when some commentators on *United States v. Virginia* would ask what the connection was between military-style training and VMI's goal of producing leaders for civilian life. The report declared:

> The survey staff have been told that the chief benefit to be derived from train-
> ing at the Virginia Military Institute today concerns obedience and discipline. It
> has been impressed upon the staff that military training is essential for the devel-
> opment of respect for and compliance with authority. The survey staff believe that
> this position cannot be maintained. . . . The excessive number of hours given to
> military theory and practice impinges greatly upon the time that the student should
> give to real intellectual or vocational preparation for his work in life.[20]

VMI was not cost-effective, because "the work in liberal arts which is being
done at V.M.I. can be done in a more efficient way at the University of Virginia and the College of William and Mary. The engineering courses there can
be conducted more efficiently at V.P.I. [Virginia Polytechnic Institute] . . . military training for men is provided at the Polytechnic Institute and it could be
provided for and required of men at the University of Virginia and the College of William and Mary."[21] In addition, because "there are children in Virginia of elementary age who are growing up in illiteracy because there are not
adequate provisions for their education, *and so long as the State is not making adequate provision for the higher education of women,*" it was unacceptable to expend public monies on VMI.[22] The commission therefore recommended the immediate discontinuation of scholarship aid and appropriations
for capital outlay. If alumni or others were not interested in running VMI as
a private institution rented from the state for $1 a year, it should be converted
"as speedily as possible" into "an institution providing for vocational work and
preparation for professional courses."[23]

Economic considerations were no doubt of major importance to the commission, but it also may have been influenced by the hazing that was still endemic at VMI. The report noted the "brutal hazing" and "disrespect for authority, the likes of which was unknown in any other state-supported
institution of higher education."[24] There had been some particularly virulent
hazing at the time the commission was carrying out its work, most notably an
incident in which a rat was so severely beaten by upperclassmen that he suffered an attack of appendicitis. A number of cadets were dismissed as a result, and the students went out on strike in protest. In fact, the state legislature was moved to enact a law against hazing, partly because of its concerns
about VMI.[25]

The commission's report caused a furor. VMI's influential alumni, including Governor Harry F. Byrd, were heard from, and VMI was kept intact.[26]
("Of all the rats," Byrd would say later with pride, "I was beaten more than
anyone else.")[27] In fact, far from being consigned to the wastebasket of his-

tory, VMI was about to gain national fame as a cultural icon. Two cadets in the class of 1932, encouraged by their senior professor of English, wrote a comedy about cadet life. George Abbott produced the play on Broadway in 1936, it was published as a book in 1937, and Warner Brothers decided to turn it into a movie. Filmed at VMI with Ronald Reagan, Wayne Morris, and Eddie Albert playing the leads, *Brother Rat* premiered in October 1938.

Having beaten back its detractors, VMI continued to adapt itself to the gentler norms of the twentieth century. The rat line underwent a number of changes, each making it marginally less strenuous, and each greeted with lamentations by alumni. "Finning out"—the mandatory rat posture consisting of a "stiffly erect stance with hands at trouser seams with the palms facing front"—was replaced in the mid-1930s by the slightly less exaggerated "strain," or a stiff, full-attention stance.[28] "Bloody Sunday"—forced exercise done to the point of collapse from exhaustion, followed by revival with buckets of liquid filth—and the practice of upperclassmen throwing heavy water tumblers at rats during meals were superseded by "running the gauntlet" of flailing cadets, which in turn was abolished at the end of the 1940s.[29] Rats still had to "run the stoops," fighting their way up to their quarters on the fourth floor of the Barracks over stairs covered with mattresses and manned by hostile upperclassmen.[30] In the 1950s the absolute rule against liquor was modified to permit cadets to imbibe off post in the company of their parents. Illicit use of alcohol was no longer automatic grounds for dismissal, and more weekend leaves were granted.[31]

VMI had maintained its tradition of providing men for the military during World War I. More than 2,000 VMI alumni served in the war, 1,200 of them as commissioned officers. That, according to VMI's calculations, amounted to more than 82 percent of all VMI students and alumni between the ages of seventeen and forty.[32] The tradition was upheld in World War II, with George Marshall the highest ranking VMI graduate in uniform. Two other VMI alumni were four-star generals, five were lieutenant generals, eleven were major generals, and thirty-two were brigadier generals. Six of the navy's rear admirals were VMI alumni, as were eleven captains, twenty commanders, and sixty-two lieutenant commanders. In all, there were 3,252 VMI alumni in the army, 532 in the navy, and 254 in the marines. Four of China's major generals and three of its lieutenant generals in that war were also VMI alumni.[33]

Some of the students who interrupted their studies at VMI to fight in World War II were married by the time they returned. They were joined by

newcomers, many of them also married, who could now afford a college education as a result of the GI Bill. Other veterans were uninterested in returning from battle to live in a dormitory with youngsters, so VMI broke its
historic tradition of insisting that cadets be unmarried and live on post. After
World War II and again following the Korean War, VMI gave married as well
as unmarried veterans with two years' VMI experience the option of living off
post and participating only in academic work.[34] Thus, VMI did *not* always insist that all students be treated exactly alike, and it did not necessarily shrink
from change—major contentions of VMI in *United States v. Virginia*—as long
as VMI was able to suggest the changes and do the differentiating itself.

VMI had adopted the Reserve Officers' Training Corps (ROTC) system instituted under the National Defense Act of 1916, and after World War II, enrollment in ROTC became a requirement for all VMI students.[35] The requirement was waived for foreign cadets.[36] In 1957 VMI introduced a special
program for superior new cadets. The following year it established a remedial
reading course, staffed by specialists from a private firm, that was later turned
into a developmental reading laboratory for new cadets with inadequate reading skills. A "cadet waiter program" was begun in 1952 so that students who
needed to earn money could do so, which also alleviated the problem of insufficient help in the mess hall. By 1975, twenty-one cadets were earning a
total of $15,000 in wages as waiters.[37]

In 1965, faced with an impending visit by a committee of the Southern
Association of Colleges and Schools, VMI conducted its first self-study. Among
the resulting recommendations was the inclusion of non-alumni on the Board
of Visitors. Three "outsiders" were appointed shortly thereafter.[38] It was a remarkable step for an institution that cherished its private rituals and language
and had long insisted that it could not be understood by anyone but a cadet
or alumnus. At about the same time, a decision was made to extend VMI's
services to the community, in part by opening up its summer session to students other than cadets with failing grades. Women were admitted to summer school in 1966, although they did not live in the Barracks.[39]

Clearly, VMI was able to absorb change, even if its mythology held otherwise. Equally clearly, in spite of the rhetoric of total equality and its largely
successful attempt to ignore class background, VMI had the sense to treat students with different needs differently from one another. It did so most dramatically when African Americans who were neither slaves nor servants were
finally allowed through its doors.

LIKE EVERY OTHER SOUTHERN INSTITUTION, VMI was affected by the civil rights movement and the Supreme Court's desegregation decisions of the 1950s and 1960s. And, as was the case with most Southern institutions, it was brought into the new era kicking and screaming. In 1956 the Board of Visitors added a paragraph to VMI regulations, stating that if the Admissions Committee had any doubt about any applicant, he bore the responsibility of obtaining letters of recommendation from three alumni.[40] It was a fairly transparent device to ensure that no student of doubtful racial pedigree gained admission. A few years later, funding agencies such as the Ford Foundation announced that they would no longer grant money to segregated institutions. The response of the VMI board was a declaration that it would not accept funds from any source that attempted to "dictate" VMI's policies.[41]

In the late 1960s, however, the Department of Health, Education, and Welfare threatened that Virginia would lose federal funds if its public colleges did not end segregation. VMI dropped the three-alumni requirement for admission. In 1968 five African American Virginians were admitted to the class of 1972. The institution that had begun in a slave society was about to change dramatically—but only under outside pressure.

Unsurprisingly, the transition was not easy, in spite of VMI's recognition that new socialization was required. The president of the senior class, himself the son of an alumnus, held meetings with groups of students to stress that the newcomers were to be treated with the equality on which VMI prided itself. "There was a minority, a small minority, who had a strong negative reaction," he would recall, "and they were rather strident and not very tactful in the way they expressed their opinion. But there were no incidents."[42]

That depends on what one calls "incidents." When the media asked one of the new cadets if he was receiving equal treatment while experiencing the horrors of the rat line, he reportedly replied, laughing, "This is the most equal place I ever heard of. Here they treat everybody like a nigger."[43] Harry W. Gore, Jr., one of the African American cadets, became managing editor of the college newspaper; another, Philip L. Wilkerson, Jr., was elected a cadet captain in his senior year and reputedly was called the Institute's finest soldier by the commandant.[44]

The three later said that they had decided to attend VMI before learning that they would be the ones to integrate the Institute.[45] Once they arrived, they discovered the need for coping strategies. Harry Gore was a drummer in the regimental band, which had a role in the annual New Market ceremony.

The ceremony included a moment when the entire student body saluted the Confederate flag while the band played "Dixie." Gore and African American cadet Richard Valentine simply refused to salute the flag, which was flown at all VMI sports events, and Gore stopped playing whenever the band broke into "Dixie." Ironically, Valentine, a cadet lieutenant during his senior year, had to give the order to salute the flag to his company. He ignored it himself. Whenever a ceremony was to take place, Gore and Valentine tried to switch assignments with other cadets so that they would have guard duty and would not be present, thereby evading the flag salute. VMI also required cadets to salute when passing the Lee Chapel on the Washington and Lee campus—the place where Robert E. Lee was buried. The two men avoided the chapel as well, and VMI looked the other way.[46] (Gore went on to a twenty-four-year career in the air force, retiring as a lieutenant colonel. Wilkerson became the first black VMI graduate to make the rank of army colonel.)

Four more African Americans enrolled in 1969, and during the following years, there were between twenty and thirty black cadets in the corps. In 1969 some cadets, both African Americans and whites from Northern states, ignored the Lee Chapel salute; VMI dropped it as mandatory (but continued to recommend it).[47] The school also gave up playing "Dixie" at athletic events.[48]

In 1972, however, when the original group of black cadets was due to graduate, they were ordered to revoke the trade they had made for guard duty and fall in for the New Market ceremony. They refused, and when they were reported for the serious infraction of direct disobedience, the superintendent intervened, imposing a relatively minor penalty and permitting them to graduate.[49] The following year the African American cadets threatened to go absent without leave (AWOL) rather than attend the ceremony, thereby forcing the student body, the administration, and the alumni to confront the issue. The students discovered that the Confederate flag had not been carried by the cadets at New Market, and it had not become part of the memorial ceremony until the 1950s. They voted narrowly to eliminate the flag and "Dixie" at the ceremony—and were promptly overruled by a unanimous vote of the Board of Visitors. The alumni then, as in the 1990s, were adamant about keeping the school as it had been during their years there.[50]

The alumni, however, did not live on post with the African American students, and those who did chose another path. Ignoring the board, VMI eliminated "Dixie," and in 1974 it altered the school calendar so that the New Market ceremony was held after graduation. That had the effect of making attendance voluntary. By the late 1970s, VMI had given up the flag entirely, and the New Market ceremony was conducted without Confederate symbolism.[51] When *United States v. Virginia* began, there were eighty-four African American (6.7 percent), one Native American, nineteen Latino, and forty-one Asian American cadets at VMI.[52]

Women also began to appear regularly on the VMI campus in capacities other than as cadets' dates. In fact, most of them took on a job almost tailor-made for the perpetuation of stereotypes. Women students from Southern Seminary Junior College joined what became a coeducational cheerleading squad in 1971.[53] VMI also integrated its faculty: its first full-time female faculty member was employed as an assistant professor of chemistry during the 1974–1975 academic year.[54] But the idea of women in the corps was another matter.

In 1985 VMI adopted a long-range academic plan that would take it through the year 2000. The plan was preceded by a self-study. It included an examination of the possible admission of women to VMI, and it did so for two reasons. The first was the Supreme Court's decision in the 1982 case *Mississippi University for Women v. Hogan*.[55] The majority opinion written by Justice Sandra Day O'Connor would prove to be the first chapter in what might be called the tale of "VMI Meets the Women's Movement."

Hogan involved the decision by the state-supported Mississippi University for Women to exclude men from its School of Nursing. It and the cases leading up to it are explored in chapters 4 and 5. The relevance of the case to VMI lay in Justice O'Connor's declaration that state discrimination on the basis of gender was subject to scrutiny under the Constitution's Fourteenth Amendment and that in justifying such discrimination, the state would have to show an "exceedingly persuasive justification" that served "important governmental objectives."[56] The Court found that the exclusion of men from the School of Nursing failed to meet that test.

The question for VMI was the implication of the holding for VMI's men-only tradition. The Board of Visitors appointed an ad hoc committee to study VMI's mission and charged it in part with evaluating the men-only admissions policy.

In January 1985 four committee members traveled to the U.S. Naval Academy (USNA) at Annapolis to be briefed by its superintendent, Rear Admiral Charles R. Larson, and other USNA officials. There had been no particular disciplinary problems since women had been admitted to the USNA by a federal statute in 1976, the visitors were told. Annapolis had made only minimal changes to accommodate women, and they performed as well as the men. A woman had been the top-stand midshipman in 1984. The male cadets were more or less accepting of the women, and the academy's alumni had accepted the change. Committee members who visited West Point some months later heard much the same thing. West Point officials explained the doctrine of "comparable training," telling the visitors that physical education requirements were the same for women as for men, except that self-defense training, grappling, and striking skills were substituted for wrestling and boxing.[57]

Over a total of five days, committee members also met with Virginia Secretary of Education John T. Casteen III, who called the University of Virginia's experience with coeducation (instituted in 1972) a "very positive" one, and President John D. Wilson of Washington and Lee University, which had begun accepting women in 1984. In addition, they visited the all-male Citadel in South Carolina.[58]

The committee produced its final report on May 16, 1986. "It is the mission of the Virginia Military Institute to produce educated and honorable men," the report said, "prepared for the varied work of civil life, imbued with love of learning, confident in the functions and attitudes of leadership, possessing a high sense of public service, advocates of the American Democracy and free enterprise system, and ready as citizen-soldiers to defend their country in time of national peril." The committee's findings were:

1. The admission of women into the Corps of Cadets would alter the mission of VMI.

2. The presence of women at VMI would not adversely affect the academic program.

3. Given the experience of the U.S. Service Academies, demand among women for admission to VMI is and can be expected to remain so low as to produce only a token number of female matriculants.

4. In any institution, and particularly at VMI, the chances of success of less than a critical mass of women, estimated at no less than ten percent of the Corps, would be severely limited and would be unfair to them.

5. The committee found no information that would warrant the change of VMI status as a single-sex college.

THEREFORE, on the basis of these findings, the committee recommends that VMI should continue to adhere to its mission as an all-male institution.

The "Findings" section and the following one, "Explanatory Remarks," took up less than two pages. The remarks contain the gist of what would become VMI's case in *United States v. Virginia:*

The number of potential female cadets who possess the necessary combination of academic and physical qualifications required for entrance to VMI or the Service Academies has been found to be small. To compete for these female students against the Service Academies would not only place a heavy burden upon VMI's limited recruiting staff but could threaten a lowering of academic and physical standards. . . . There would have to be some adjustments made in the military and physical demands made upon male cadets. Because many of these demands contribute to the ethos of which the Virginia Military Institute is proud and which, it is firmly believed, contributes to the unity of the Corps, there is doubt that the same spirit could be maintained at the same level and in the same way if women were introduced into the Corps.[59]

VMI would hold the line. There would be no women parading in front of the statue of Stonewall Jackson.

WHAT THE BOARD OF VISITORS DID NOT put in its report was that by the late 1980s, VMI was having trouble finding enough students, in spite of its modest requirements. A young man who wanted to attend VMI had to be between sixteen and twenty-two, unmarried, and in the top half of his high school class. Prospective transfer students had to have at least a C average.[60] As detractors pointed out, accepting students who ranked no higher than in the top half of a high school class or who had only a C average at another college scarcely made VMI highly selective; in fact, it accepted 76 percent of its applicants. By comparison, the University of Virginia accepted roughly 30 percent of its applicants; Virginia's George Mason University, 50 percent; Harvard University, 18 percent; and West Point 10.5 percent.

Applications had nonetheless fallen dramatically as a result of the anti-military sentiment that resulted from American involvement in the Vietnam War. Mark S. Sandy, VMI's associate dean for enrollment management, told the press that back in the 1960s, "when a lot of kids came from farms and didn't have cable TV and all that," VMI was appealing. By the last decade of the century, however, "with MTV and Nintendo and all that, kids aren't used to getting up early working all day and being deprived of things."[61]

The truth was that, for whatever reason, VMI was not attracting the cream of the crop. And even with its high admission rate, enrollment was plummeting. The Board of Visitors voted on January 27, 1990, to drop the requirement that VMI graduates accept a commission in the armed forces. The stated reason was that the U.S. military had cut back the number of troops on active duty and no longer needed such high levels of manpower. It appeared, however, that the services were able to find enough qualified recruits and had raised their standards; they could no longer be counted on to offer commissions to all VMI men. The board recognized that the commission requirement had discouraged some applicants and apparently eliminated it in the hope of attracting more.

Even without the commission requirement, the 1987 Council of Higher Education's Virginia Plan for Higher Education described VMI's primary purpose as "the thorough education of young men within a framework of military discipline," with the military atmosphere contributing "to the Institute's philosophy of a broad and sound education," which included "self-reliance and self-discipline." VMI's catalog stated that "the challenging military portion of the VMI program is a distinctive aspect of the VMI college experience," and "the military system characterizes and distinguishes life at VMI."[62] That would become a major issue in *United States v. Virginia* when the commonwealth quickly created a substitute "parallel" program for women, but one without a "military way of life."

In spite of its emphasis on military discipline, only about 18 percent of VMI's graduates became career military men. VMI's goal, as described in its 1989–1990 catalog, was, instead, the production of a citizen-soldier, "a man prepared to take his place in civilian life but ready to respond as a combat leader in times of national military need." VMI faculty and staff set the model by being commissioned in the Virginia militia, which was the source of the title "colonel" for most.[63] The Institute offered twelve degree programs: civil engineering, electrical engineering, mechanical engineering, economics, English, history, modern languages, mathematics, physics, biology, chemistry, and computer science.[64]

VMI's difficulties in attracting students was ironic in light of the Institute's extraordinarily solid financial base. As of the 1990–1991 school year, according to the Council of Higher Education, VMI's annual budget was $25.9 million, of which only $9 million came from the state.[65] Its endowment of $86.7 million worked out to almost $66,000 for each of its roughly 1,300 cadets—the highest amount of any public college in the country.[66] It is true that no college ever has "enough" money; ambitions grow with income, and college presidents spend a large amount of their time raising funds. Still, simply stated, VMI was rich. The major reason for this was its alumni.

The alumni association had organized the VMI Foundation in 1936 and incorporated it the following year with the stated purpose of building an endowment. Forty years later, it had $8 million in assets, and that was after giving VMI almost $6 million over the years.[67] The separate Board of Visitors endowment fund underwrote a multiplicity of cadet activities, from the chemistry club to the Commanders, its dance band, as well as faculty leaves.[68] When the alumni spoke, VMI, like many colleges, responded—but it necessarily responded with even more alacrity than most. That fact, too, would be important to *United States v. Virginia,* as the organized alumni proved resistant to gender integration at their alma mater.

Their resistance to change in general and to the prospect of women at VMI in particular was reflected in the 1986 Board of Visitors' decision. "VMI Runs Rear-Guard Action Against Admitting Women," the *Washington Post* trumpeted after the board endorsed the committee's report on May 30.[69] George P. Ramsey, Jr., the board's president, told the media, "You keep your fingers crossed, and you hope that it will never happen. I would hope that a female would not want to disrupt the uniqueness of VMI."[70]

One of the people who clipped the article was Judith Keith, a lawyer in the Justice Department's Civil Rights Division.[71] Dismayed at what she saw as flagrantly unconstitutional gender discrimination, Keith would become the government's lead lawyer in *United States v. Virginia.* The Institute's history was about to change. It would do so, however, over the fervent objections of Josiah Bunting, class of 1963, one of its most distinguished alumni.

3

Brother Rat

Were it not for the existence of the "rat line," VMI would be
just another military school.

—*The Bullet* (VMI student handbook)

VMI's 1989 mission statement read:

It is the mission of the Virginia Military Institute to produce educated and honorable men, prepared for the varied work of civil life, imbued with love of learning, confident in the functions and attitudes of leadership, possessing a high sense of public service, advocates of the American democracy and free enterprise system, and ready as citizen-soldiers to defend their country in time of national peril.

It might have been written to describe Josiah Bunting (class of 1963), the man who was VMI's superintendent during the last stages of *United States v. Virginia.*

Bunting was born in 1939 to a Philadelphia Main Line family. His father was a real estate developer; one grandfather was a Quaker minister. The young Bunting, however, did not follow the direct route to status and respectability that one might have expected. After his parents' marriage ended, he and his mother moved to Litchfield, Connecticut, where he distinguished himself primarily by being asked to leave one private school after another. The schools apparently found his propensity for boyhood pranks less than endearing. One finally permitted him to take his last high school exams at home. Then, in 1957, he joined the Marines.

"In those days, in the late 1950s," he remembered, "there was a fair amount of that going on. It was between Korea and Vietnam. A lot of young guys would join the Marines—a kind of thing you would do if you had something to prove to yourself."[1] He went through basic training at Parris Island and served with an infantry unit in the Mediterranean, picking up a tattoo of the Marine Corps emblem on his right forearm. When a fellow marine suggested that Bunting consider VMI at the end of his two-year stint, the only thing Bunting could recall about the Institute was that at Dwight Eisenhower's 1953 inaugural parade, his father had commented that the VMI unit marching in it looked better than the one from West Point. He applied anyway. VMI was unimpressed by his academic credentials but decided to give the tall, athletic marine a try.[2]

Bunting found himself at the Institute. He majored in English and graduated third in his class. He was captain of the swimming team and an editor of the school newspaper, as well as a member of the music society (he is a classical pianist). The former prankster was chosen for VMI's student Honor Court, which tries and punishes infractions of regulations, and as first captain of the Corps of Cadets. His yearbook called him a student to be emulated.

His next stop was Christ Church College at Oxford University. Bunting had won a Rhodes scholarship, the prestigious award based on a college student's scholarly and athletic achievements and continuing potential. After receiving another bachelor of arts degree and a master's degree in English history at Oxford, he fulfilled the army commission he had accepted upon graduation from VMI and signed up for advanced infantry school. From there, he went to Fort Bragg, North Carolina, and into combat in Vietnam in 1967. After commanding the 505th Infantry, he left Vietnam with a Bronze Star with two oak-leaf clusters, an Army Commendation Medal, a Vietnam Honor Medal, a presidential unit citation, and parachute and combat infantry badges.[3] By 1972, he was a major and told the *New York Times* that he thought he had an 80 percent chance of becoming a general.[4]

Bunting had developed into the paradigmatic VMI alumnus: highly educated, cultured, athletic, family oriented (he and the Sorbonne student he married while at Oxford would have four children), bedecked with military honors. He took his credentials to West Point and began a successful career as an educator, thereby maintaining VMI's early incarnation as a normal school.

Bunting became an assistant professor of history and social sciences at West Point and reportedly was one of its most popular social studies instructors. In keeping with his wide-ranging interests and his ability to do many things at once, he also wrote a novel based on his Vietnam experiences. It depicted an infantry operation in the Mekong Delta during which a high-ranking officer's politically motivated decisions result in the needless deaths of troops. *The Lionheads*, published in 1972, was an immediate best-seller.[5] The Book-of-the-Month Club made it an alternate selection, *Time* called it one of the ten best novels of the year, and it eventually would be translated into fifteen languages.

The military, not surprisingly, was far less enthusiastic about the book and gave Bunting unmistakable encouragement to end his army career. He, in turn, was increasingly dissatisfied with what he saw as the military's "massive, leaden inertia."[6] So, in 1973, after a six-year military career, the soldier became a civilian. He did not, however, renounce leadership.

Instead, Bunting accepted the position of president of Briarcliff College. In addition to fulfilling his presidential duties, he commuted from upstate New York to Columbia University, completing a fellowship in history. He also published a second, less well received novel. His four-year stay at Briarcliff was highly successful, and one consequence was his being offered a new job back in Virginia, just a two-hour drive away from VMI.

Hampden-Sydney College, an all-male school that opened in 1776 and included Patrick Henry and James Madison on its first Board of Trustees, chose Bunting as its president in 1977. The school was in poor shape. Its enrollment was down to 600, and it was essentially resting on laurels earned decades earlier. By the time Bunting left Hampden-Sydney ten years later, enrollment was up to 970, and his name was being mentioned as a possible Republican candidate for senator or governor.[7]

Bunting had defined himself as an educator, however, and so had academia. He was approached by a number of universities when he was ready to leave Hampden-Sydney, but he turned them down to become headmaster of the Lawrenceville School in New Jersey. Interestingly enough, given his future role in the gender integration dispute at VMI, he arrived at the all-male Lawrenceville School right after its trustees had made the decision to open its doors to women.

Lawrenceville, situated five miles from Princeton, is a boarding school that has functioned as a feeder for Princeton University since the nineteenth century. The trustees had considered and rejected coeducation a number of times in the 1970s and 1980s. By the time of the final vote in 1985, however, both the Board of Trustees and the faculty were overwhelmingly in favor of gender integration. The school could no longer recruit the national cross section of students it had once attracted. As Bunting would say, a fifteen-year-old California boy of the 1980s had no desire to travel to the East Coast to attend an all-male institution. And young women were inquiring about Lawrenceville, perhaps because of its academic standards and its Princeton connection.[8] Bunting would preside over their arrival, taking in stride the unhappiness of alumni—the same kind of people who would be the fiercest opponents of gender integration at VMI—and some of the senior faculty.

Bunting thought that gender integration at Lawrenceville was "very successful, immediately successful," but the circumstances were "entirely different" from those at VMI. There was the enthusiasm of the trustees and many faculty members, as well as the existence of a large pool of female potential students. Recalcitrant faculty changed their minds once women were in their classes. "You had these kind of crusty old Tory boarding school masters—they're wonderful educational people, usually men in their fifties and sixties—and they were quite won over after about six months." When Bunting watched the U.S. women's soccer team win the Women's World Cup in 1999, its members—"so ardent, like female Frank Merriwells [the dime novel hero of the early 1900s who combined physical and mental prowess]"—reminded him of the first coeds at Lawrenceville, whose enthusiasm and achievements had converted the faculty holdouts.[9]

But he was certain that the same thing would not—and should not—happen at VMI. To understand why Bunting and other VMI alumni felt that way, one has to look at VMI as it existed for Josiah Bunting, student. Although Bunting graduated in 1963, he would tell journalists three decades later, "We think the things we did in 1890 and 1930 are still valid today."[10]

EACH NEW STUDENT AT VMI is presented with a 3½-by-6-inch pamphlet formally called *The Bullet* but better known by its subtitle, *The Rat Bible*. It is prepared by the senior class and must be carried by each rat (freshman) at all times. The number of pages varies from year to year, but whether it is sixty or eighty, it must be memorized in its entirety by all rats.

The Rat Bible includes basic information about VMI: its history, physical layout, student government, insignia, school-year calendar, colloquial terms and abbreviations, clubs, and publications. Two things are always near the beginning: a few paragraphs addressed "To the Rat," and a letter from the president of the student Honor Court.[11]

"Within your first five minutes at VMI you will realize that you have entered a new world," is how "To the Rat" begins. "You are a Rat . . . you know little of the VMI system, and it remains for you and your class to prove your-

selves capable of accepting and carrying out the responsibilities of a VMI cadet."
The 1990 "Regimental Commander's Letter" added, "VMI, however, is not a
place for individuals"; the emphasis was on community and cooperation.

A rat, by definition, is subject to the rat line, and "were it not for the existence of the 'rat line,'" the *Bullet* says, "VMI would be just another military
school." The rat line, or "adversative system," is specifically described as "the
heart of the military system" as it is found at VMI.

Another key part of the VMI method is the Honor Court, composed of
roughly two dozen students from the senior and junior classes. It is charged
with enforcing the honor code that was written back in 1839: "A cadet does
not lie, cheat, steal, nor tolerate those who do." There are no locks on bedroom doors; the honor code renders them unnecessary. A cadet who violates
the code is expelled.

VMI students are expected to be responsible members of a community.
Until 1997, that meant a community of gentlemen. One of the lines in the
Bullet's "Songs and Yells" section is, "I'm a Southern gentleman." Supreme
Court Justice Antonin Scalia would be so taken by "The Code of a Gentle-
man," as found in the 1990 *Bullet,* that he would quote it in his opinion in
United States v. Virginia. It reads, in part:

> The honor of a gentleman demands the inviolability of his word, and the incor-
> ruptibility of his principles. He is the descendant of the knight, the crusader; he
> is the defender of the defenseless and the champion of justice. . . .
>
> A Gentleman . . .
> Does not discuss his family affairs in public or with acquaintances.
> Does not speak more than casually about his girl friend.
> Does not go to a lady's house if he is affected by alcohol. . . .
> Does not mention names exactly as he avoids the mention of what things cost.
> Does not borrow money. . . .
> Does not slap strangers on the back nor so much as lay a finger on a lady. . . .
> A Gentleman respects the reserves of others, but demands that others respect
>   those which are his.
> A Gentleman can become what he wills to be.

The experience that the *Rat Bible* hinted at was one in which young men
were isolated from the people and customs they knew. They were subjected
to a deliberately harsh regime designed to strip them of their values and
imbue them with a new ethic, forged in the kind of communal suffering and
endurance that would forever differentiate VMI men from the rest of the
world. The community created at VMI would set the Institute's graduates

apart from other men, whom they would lead. The ethic that VMI graduates shared included a sharp delineation of the absolute boundaries between men and women.

CULTURAL ANTHROPOLOGISTS HAVE WRITTEN extensively about male bonding rituals, which can be found in cultures around the world. As psychoanalyst Nancy Chodorow explains, children identify with the mothers who provide most of their early nurturance. Girls continue to identify with mothers as they grow older; boys, however, must learn to differentiate themselves from their mothers and the female role models they provide. Masculinity, then, is not a given but is achieved only when a boy is able to separate himself psychologically from his mother.[12] As Margaret Mead wrote, "The little boy learns that he must act like a boy, do things, prove that he is a boy, and prove it over and over again, while the little girl learns that she *is* a girl, and all she has to do is refrain from acting like a boy.'"[13] Or, as Norman Mailer put it:

> Masculinity is not something given to you, something you're born with, but something you gain.
>
> Nobody was born a man; you earned manhood provided you were good enough, bold enough.[14]

Mailer's comment that masculinity is earned through boldness could have been written about VMI. So could legal scholar Kenneth L. Karst's observation that "a boy becomes a man chiefly by differentiating himself from women."[15] Anthropologist David D. Gilmore, looking at cultural concepts of masculinity around the world, noted that they invariably include "a stress on hard work and effective enterprise and a parallel belief that this work ethic must be artificially inculcated in hesitant or passive males." "Manhood," he writes, "is problematic, a critical threshold that boys must pass through testing."[16]

Daughters have mothers to define their identities. Boys, however, are faced with the challenge of creating their own. It is a challenge whose "heroic quality lies in its self-direction and discipline." Boys are turned into men through what Gilmore calls "tempering and toughening."[17] They also become masculine to the extent that they differentiate themselves from those who are feminine. Females are the "other"—the entities against whom real men can measure themselves. Men, according to these scholars, are not-women. The obvious question, then, is this: if masculinity is not a matter of biology but of differentiation from women, and if women can do the same things as men, how are men to define themselves? It is a question that resounds loudly in the context of VMI's passionate fight to continue excluding women.

Part of the traditional answer has been found in the process by which malehood is achieved. Gilmore describes the transition as a test:

> To be socially meaningful, the decision for manhood must be characterized by enthusiasm combined with stoic resolve or perhaps "grace." It must show a public demonstration of positive choice, of jubilation even in pain, for it represents a moral commitment to defend the society and its core values against all odds. So manhood is the defeat of a childish narcissism that is not only different from the adult role but antithetical to it.[18]

Karst adds that although masculine identification initially requires separation, it is subsequently reinforced by activities in male peer groups.[19]

Restated in the context of VMI, manhood is the willingness of a VMI cadet to subordinate his own desires to the needs of his class; of the VMI graduate, when called, to set aside his usual pursuits and serve his country as a citizen-soldier. Ethnologist Arnold Van Gennep described the passage into manhood as tripartite, involving separation from society, transformation, and reintegration.[20] As the *Rat Bible* adjures:

> Forget your past successes and failures; they are of no consequence now. Everyone of you will start at the same place: the bottom. From there you will have to work long and hard to prove that you are ready to become a class. How will you do this? You will do it by abandoning individualism and adhering to a doctrine based on unity, enthusiasm, sacrifice, and respect to authority. . . . You will face many hardships, some of which you will not understand, but remember that there is a purpose in your struggles. Do not quit. Do not falter. Each time you are set back charge forward even harder.[21]

"Manhood ideologies," Gilmore tells us, "always include a criterion of selfless generosity, even to the point of sacrifice. Again and again we find that 'real' men are those who give more than they take: they serve others. . . . Manhood ideologies force men to shape up on penalty of being robbed of their identity."[22] It would be so easy for boys to remain feminized. Strong measures are needed to turn them into men—a process that is necessary, after all, for their own good. As Bunting wrote, when a student enters VMI, he and his fellow cadets are "thrown exclusively upon their own resources of determination, guts and wit." Each day is "impossibly long"; "privacy and leisure" are "practically nonexistent." To Bunting, what differentiates VMI from other col-

leges with similar traditions is its character training, the "essential foundation" of undergraduate education. Its "crowding array" of daily academic,
physical, and military requirements is deliberately overwhelming, challenging students to push themselves to new limits.[23] But those requirements,
however strenuous and ineluctable, do not constitute the heart of the VMI
discipline. That, referred to at trial as the co-curriculum, takes place primarily
in the Barracks.

THE VMI METHODOLOGY—the adversative system—was de-
scribed at length in *United States v. Virginia* by Colonel Norman M. Bissell,
VMI's commandant of cadets. It begins with the rat line.

> Q: Could you define the term rat?
> A: A rat is a term we affectionately tied to the classmen that come to VMI, re-
> ferred to as probably the lowest animal on earth and part of our humbling experi-
> ence where we try to bring everybody into a basic commonality, everybody is very
> spartan, very—they are all treated exactly alike and the rat term kind of defines
> that very appropriately. They are referred to as a rat through about seven months,
> until such time as they break out of the rat line in the March time frame and then
> they become fourth classmen.[24]

Rats at VMI would be called freshmen elsewhere. Their new status is
made graphically real to them as soon as they enter VMI: the first time they
look in a mirror thereafter, they see a bald head peering back. Their heads are
shaved—a fast way to begin stripping them of their individuality. Then they
assemble for their first ceremony, at which they are less participants than the
laboratory animals that will be the latest fodder for VMI's ongoing experiment
in depersonalization and resocialization.

The rats are lined up on two sides of the courtyard in facing lines. A drum
beats slowly and ominously; glowering upperclassmen march in at a pace of
ninety steps a minute, dressed in their uniforms of gray blouses and white
duck trousers. One of them parades to the center of the second tier of the
Barracks and proclaims, "This is your cadre. They represent the essence of
VMI. From these men, you will learn everything you will need to know to survive here. You will not fail them. They will teach and you will learn."

The ceremony lasts for eight minutes. Then the upperclassmen attack.
Charging into the ranks of the rats, they scream, bellow, threaten, insult. The
spittle flies as upperclassmen surround a hapless rat, all yelling at once: "I
said stand at attention. You call that attention? Get your chin in. Further,

idiot! Put your shoulders back. Look smart, Dumbo. Who ever told you *you* were VMI material, rat?" The stunned rats finally are released to race up the stairs, double time, to their new quarters on the fourth floor.[25]

Any upperclassman can order any rat committing any alleged infraction to drop down for penalty push-ups. Any rat passing a classmate so engaged must join his classmate, in order to build community spirit. At any hour, day or night, upperclassmen can come barging through a bedroom door, screaming, demanding push-ups in the room, in the communal showers while water pours down; anywhere. Rats must walk at rigid attention outside their rooms, eyes straight ahead, chins tucked into their collarbones. The orders upperclassmen bawl out at them may be less than consistent. One journalist listened to a hapless rat, attempting to get to the shower, being ordered simultaneously by different upperclassmen, "To the showers, rat! To your room, rat!"[26] A perceived infraction of the rules can send a rat to the rat disciplinary committee, which has the power to impose penalties of fifteen minutes of marching or twenty minutes of calisthenic exercises. Throughout the day rats are in danger of being "flamed": required to recite verbatim from the *Rat Bible*. The penalty for failure? More push-ups.

There is no privacy. Until 1997, the four-student bedrooms had doors with shadeless windows and a sight line to the back window that had to be unobstructed by furniture. Bathrooms are communal; again, until 1997, they boasted no partitions or stalls.[27] All rooms are subject to random inspection, and there is a total white-glove inspection once a week. The norm of college life, where one's room is a haven and the classroom is a place of tension, is reversed at VMI; the classroom and the library are the only places a rat can relax. There, upperclassmen are not in charge.

Even without the threat of interrogation and punishment, the new cadets' "home" lacks certain amenities. Each room has one bed per cadet, one wall locker per cadet, one clothes rack per cadet, one sink. There can be one clock per table or desk. Each locker must be organized with the regulation number of each item, hung or placed in exactly the correct order. Each bed frame must be stacked precisely against the wall each morning, with the mattress rolled up and secured—almost a necessity, given the size of the rooms. There are no carpets, no telephones, no pictures on the walls, no television sets, no air-conditioning. As a witness would tell the court in *United States v. Virginia:*

> To say that the barracks are spartan does them excessive credit. They are extremely crowded. As many as four cadets share rooms of less than 300 square feet.

Temperature control is poor. Some of the furniture in an adjacent museum appears to be of more modern vintage (or at least in better condition) than some that is currently in use by fourth classmen [rats].[28]

The day begins at 6:30 A.M.; lights out is at 11 P.M. There are sit-ups, pull-ups, and a mile and a half run before breakfast. Classes last from 8:00 to 3:30 five days a week. After classes, rats run in double time for several miles in military formation, wearing their fatigues and carrying their rifles. Twice a week they go through "Rat Challenge," an endurance test of ropes courses, wall climbing, and obstacle courses in a nearby field. Rats spend their seventeen-hour days in an exhausted daze. It is common for them to fall asleep in the relative sanctuary of the library.[29]

The 1989 VMI catalog stated that the rat line was "equal and impersonal in its application, tending to remove wealth and former station in life as factors in one's standing as a cadet, and ensuring equal opportunity for all to advance by personal effort and enjoy those returns that are earned." Colonel Bissell testified at the trial that the rat line "literally dissects the young student that comes in there, kind of pulls him apart" in a practice that "has far more dramatic, more pressure, more stress than boot camp or basic camp."[30] Bunting told a journalist, "If you are able to survive with grace and efficiency in a system which is very tough, you are brimming with confidence to undertake anything else in life."[31]

The women who had family connections with VMI and were willing to speak out against its exclusion of women—not a common phenomenon, given VMI's social and economic power in Virginia and the loyalty many felt toward it—characterized the rat line rather differently. A writer who was a daughter, granddaughter, sister, and niece of VMI graduates saw its purpose as being "to break down the 18-year-old male, inducing utter disorientation and uncertainty, and then slowly to build him up again, to make him proud of himself and his unsuspected capacity for survival."[32] The coordinator of the Virginia National Organization for Women, whose husband was a VMI alumnus, was quoted by the *St. Louis Post-Dispatch* as saying, "The amount of state dollars going into supporting an exclusive club that's based on sadomasochistic bonding rituals is appalling."[33] Even one of VMI's expert witnesses would add at the trial:

It is an experience that is designed to strip away from the individual who comes in, or challenge everything that they have ever been led to believe that it's accurate and correct. It's a fundamental leveling process that simply challenges all values, all forms of behavior as a sort of prerequisite to instill the values and behaviors for which VMI exists, and so the new cadet system centered in the barracks involves the indoctrination process . . . it involves sort of rituals in the way that people walk the rat line, which is a way of getting from one place to another, the very minute regulation of individual behavior, the frequent punishments, both individual and en masse, the use of privileges to support behaviors that are perceived as headed in the right direction. . . . It is very odious.[34]

Eventually, the rat line ends, and its survivors officially become the "fourth class." When *United States v. Virginia* began, the transition from rat to freshman occurred during a ceremony known as "breakout" that had been instituted in 1982. It was a ritual that became the focus of much attention at the trial and in the media.

The date of the ceremony was chosen by the senior class, which decided when the rats were ready to become men. It always took place sometime around March, when wintry temperatures prevail in western Virginia. Physical preparations for breakout began with the Lexington Fire Department, which arrived to hose down a steep thirty-foot incline behind the Barracks until it was transformed into a hill of mud. Colonel Bissell, who had put himself through breakout in 1991 (it had not existed when he graduated from VMI in 1961), told the trial court what happened as rats attempted to scale the hill:

A: The formality consists of breaking the class into approximately five waves, if you will, equally breaking them down into five groups. . . . It is here that they actually go through a process where a hill and a low flat are prior to the hill, approximately 25, 30 yards across, totally wetted down, if you will, and made into a very much of a mud quagmire. . . .

Very briefly, about the first 25 to 30 yards it is just totally a mud area—about four to five inches of mud that literally—you get no grip on things, you just kind of slide along and try to move the best you can. . . . Once you reach the end of that level ground, you then have a very steep incline, I would say 40 to 50 degrees, perhaps 14 to 16 feet high that also is totally wet down to the point where there is no traction, there is no grip, there is no way of getting up. . . .

Q: Colonel Bissell, what type of physical strength is required to complete the break out?

A: . . . I had a tremendous amount of problem being able to reach up and pull myself up when the upperclassmen held down their arms, their leg, extending it, literally you have to pull yourself up and pull yourself over there. . . . You are carrying probably equal to half of your body weight again in mud in your pants and shirt when you are going up there, trying to get up that hill. . . .

As you can imagine, as you are going through this mud and slop, people are climbing over each other, entangled with each other. I would say the body language and the interactions is very close, very much like wrestling might be, where you are in close contact with each other, you are working with each other, in some cases hanging onto each other, as you are moving up that cliff and moving across. . . . Frequently . . . there is a lot of exposure to bodies where clothes are ripped, as you can well imagine from pulling and tugging, there are a lot of body exposure factors that go on there.[35]

Colonel Bissell characterized the ritual "as kind of a graduation ceremony" in which the rats learned that they needed one another and the help of the seniors if they were to get through it.[36] Rats were warned to keep their eyes shut to prevent their becoming filled with mud, so they went through breakout blind as well as cold and wet and covered with slime. The sophomore and junior classes did their best to make it impossible for the rats to climb up. Then, after the rats had suffered sufficiently, seniors reached down a saving arm or leg that the rats could grab and use to hoist themselves up. The following paragraph of Bissell's description should be read with the male coming-of-age ritual in mind.

> But then to me, there is another unique experience, is when you get halfway up that hill and that is about as far as you really can get unless you really have a very cooperative class, you will find that an upperclassman will dangle down a leg or arm and that is the kind of thing a rat can grab and pull himself up that arm or leg. To me it's the symbology of that arm or leg, kind of the upperclassman saying, "hey, you have made it, son, you are now part of the upper class system, you are part of us, we will help you." It is kind of climbing over that last bit and then be taken by a first classman or some other classman to wash down your face and so forth, that really just brought it altogether to me, a very meaningful, a very physical and very memorable experience for rats, probably the most so in the rat year.[37]

It was a graduation into manhood, and manhood meant membership in a fraternity as well as individual status. Breakout turned the separate human beings who had arrived at VMI seven months earlier into a club, each of its members distinct for all time from outsiders. It represented "the fine cementing, the bonding, that brings together the whole brotherhood of the class system," Colonel Bissell said. "They suddenly realize, I have to depend on my brother rats, we can't do it alone."[38]

Each VMI rat is assigned a *dyke*—a senior who monitors the rat's performance and is supposed to protect him. The word comes from the crossed belts, or "cross dykes," on the front of the cadets' dress uniforms. It is almost impossible to adjust the belts oneself; the rat's duties include doing that for the senior, or dyking him out, as well as cleaning the dyke's shoes and shining the brass on his uniforms. The rat is thus guided through the rituals of VMI and the process of becoming a man by a mentor.

A dyke is a rat daddy. Anthropologist Abigail E. Adams, who was permitted to study VMI and its breakout, noted that the dyke of one's dyke is one's granddyke. VMI is serious when it refers to the VMI "family"; it is a multigenerational one. Adams suggests that dykes serve as surrogate parents, and she calls the VMI method "a unique patrilineal descent system." Rats are reborn at VMI, she notes. Their identity is stripped away in the rat line, and they begin life over again, finally emerging into the world as men. It is a system of reproduction without women.[39]

Taking responsibility for junior cadets is as much a part of the VMI ethos as is breaking them down so they can be reconstituted. VMI's class system, another part of the co-curriculum, gives increasing responsibilities and increasing privileges to each group of students as it moves into a higher class. Seniors, members of the first class, run much of the students' life outside the classroom, including the important Honor Court, which bears the primary responsibility for disciplining those who break the rules. The juniors, or second class, organize the Ring Figure weekend, at which cadets are permitted to put on the rings that many of them will wear for the rest of their lives. VMI believes that learning how to take responsibility is a precondition of leadership. "We give upperclassmen a broad range of responsibility and autonomy," Bunting says, "and see what they do with it."[40]

Some of the rats will never exercise that responsibility or emerge into VMI's world of men. Four percent of them leave during the first week. Almost 25 percent leave before the end of the first year—more than twice the attrition rate of the service academies.[41] Many of those who remain consider themselves comrades for life in an elite society that until 1997 was all male.

Bunting believed that it had to remain that way. And when the federal government asked the courts to order VMI to admit women, Bunting was appalled.

"THE VERY CULTURE OF VMI LIFE would be changed radically, irretrievably, by the admission of women," Bunting wrote to the *Richmond Times-Dispatch* in 1995.[42] That was the year he was chosen as VMI's superintendent. "I am a convinced partisan of VMI as an all-male place," he told reporters when he began his new job. "I think that is our history, that is our future, and we're good at that."[43]

Bunting delights in a worldview based on that of Edmund Burke, the conservative eighteenth-century Anglo-Irish statesman and political thinker.

Burke believed that institutions that have proved themselves should not be subjected to radical tinkering. VMI, Bunting notes, works. It has consistently produced highly disciplined, educated young patriots—in the best sense of that word.

> I come finally to the . . . Burkean argument . . . that these little platoons which have functioned successfully over a number of generations and whose graduates appear to have the kind of skills that are needed from generation to generation—that those cultures should not be tampered with. Beethoven's Fourth Piano Concerto gave as much pleasure to you last week as it gave in 1880 to somebody who heard it at that time. . . . By going to these places and saying, "Now you must become coeducational," you are putting at hazard something which clearly has worked very well.[44]

One reason VMI worked very well, he believed, was that it was all male. "If there were a single college or school in our country that would seem to have depended for its efficiency . . . upon being a school for one gender only, VMI was it," he would tell the National Press Club.[45]

His argument, and that of other opponents of gender integration at VMI, went like this: There are undoubted benefits of single-sex education for women. Even the brightest teenaged girls are self-conscious and afraid to answer questions in front of their male counterparts; this stage lasts until they are around sixteen and is an argument for all-girls high schools. They may be more poised by the time they reach college, but the crucial element in single-sex institutions, according to Bunting, is "the very large number of women professors and administrators, the majority of whom are very successful, very active, very verbal, very impressive people." It is important for young women to be in the presence of that kind of accomplished, empowered woman. Citing studies of women who have gone to single-sex colleges, Bunting notes:

> Everybody knows that one out of twenty-five Wellesley graduates goes onto a corporate board . . . the culture understands that there are demonstrable proved benefits that accrue to girls who have gone to girls' schools and women who have gone to women's colleges. There is a body of literature; there are data.[46]

But there are no comparable studies of boys' schools and men's colleges, "so that single sex in effect becomes a slipshod synonym for girls' schools and women's colleges. The whole controversy that swirls around the issue of single-sex education is rhetorically a nonstarter when it comes to boys and men." The "average intelligent professional man" will agree that women's colleges are beneficial; the "average intelligent woman and most intelligent men" are not persuaded by the argument that the same is true for boys' and men's schools. And yet, looking back at his student days at VMI and his experience as president of Hampden-Sydney, Bunting speaks of "a certain unself-consciousness and ease of learning—of camaraderie, if you will—which is helpful and beneficial in helping them [young men] focus intellectually on the things that they should be looking at."[47]

As the case progressed, Bunting expressed his certainty that VMI's "superb tradition of academic and teaching excellence" could be shown, "compellingly, to be largely a product of the fact that only men live in that place."[48] What made VMI's "lessons, academic and moral, stick to the ribs of its graduates" was "the intensity—the ferocity, even"—of its ethos.[49] That would be destroyed by gender integration: "The very culture of VMI life would be changed radically, irretrievably, by the admission of women."[50]

The culture was bound up in the lack of privacy that VMI men considered crucial to the Institute's egalitarianism. No one could be expected to withstand VMI's rigors—to embrace them—unless he was certain that everyone else was experiencing the same trial by fire. The only way to ensure that was for everyone to be subjected to exactly the same requirements and to be able to see everyone else at all times. Then, in the knowledge that they were all enduring together, the necessary bonds would be forged. The result would be a sense of community so strong that each man would feel responsible for all the others. And that sense of responsibility, VMI believed, was a crucial component of leadership. It was VMI's mission to produce citizen-soldiers prepared not only to follow their country but also to care enough about their country to want to lead it.

To Bunting, as to other VMI men, the advocates of gender integration were either ignorant or malicious. Retired army major Lillian A. Pfluke, the top physical education graduate in her 1980 West Point class, an engineer, a military parachutist, and the author of *Breast-feeding and the Active Woman,* wrote a 1995 op-ed column entitled "VMI Should Follow West Point's Lead" for the *Richmond Times-Dispatch.* In it, she called VMI and The Citadel "dangerously out of touch with the very mission they pride themselves on: educating leaders for our country and our society." The armed forces were gender integrated in both training and battle, she noted. "The questions that should be stressed in this debate therefore should include the following: Why should federal taxpayers' money support ROTC programs antithetical to the climate of concerned and caring teamwork and leadership that today's Armed Forces are developing so well?"[51]

Bunting's letter in reply emphasized that "those most determined to force coeducation upon us have never visited VMI, seen the barracks, watched and understood the character of the lives we live here. . . . They know not the nature of the school and they presume to judge." He added that the proponents of such "profoundly radical . . . social engineering" failed to understand that "they would be depriving more than 1,200 young men of *their* choice: to attend a men's college," for the sake of "a *tiny* cohort of young women."[52]

That was the charitable view of VMI's adversaries, its defenders felt: as uncomprehending outsiders. VMI cadets, alumni, and faculty referred frequently to the VMI "family," which uses a private familial language of acronyms and practices rituals and rules that are unknown to the outside world. Outsiders could not understand that admitting women would destroy the Institute's basic ethos. The complete equality based on lack of privacy and identical treatment would be gone. Women would need privacy. (Proponents of admitting women expressed skepticism that the absence of bathroom stalls was an integral component of institutional spirit or educational methodology.) Male cadets would not treat women rats with the same mercilessness they ladled out to men. (Critics wondered how what they perceived as cruelty, rather than a relentless insistence on perfection, contributed to character building and leadership skills.)

Proponents of an all-male VMI were as incredulous as Bunting at critics' unwillingness to come to VMI and see for themselves. Familiarity would result in sympathetic understanding, they believed. Lack of an on-the-premises attempt to understand could only indicate malice. In a hearing before the trial, VMI's chief lawyer invited Judge Jackson L. Kiser to tour VMI's campus, "to be there for reveille . . . to go through a day in the life of VMI." Kiser, who had gone to law school at neighboring Washington and Lee, said, "I'm pretty familiar with it unless it's changed dramatically," and commented, "I went to law school with a guy who had a saber scar across his chest. He said he got it from leaving the Rat Line, when the rats revolted against the upperclassmen."[53]

At various times, the federal government's suit was perceived as yet another attempt by a tyrannical bureaucracy to impose its power on the states and as a federal effort to dictate a Southern state's values. VMI would contend in court, as Bunting did, that the number of women who would want the VMI experience was infinitesimal and that to force a destructive change on an institution that was working well for the sake of so few potential students made no sense. The assertion might have been more convincing had the Institute championed the commonwealth's provision of a truly equivalent educational opportunity for women elsewhere.

IT MAY WELL BE THAT NO ARGUMENT against gender integration would have convinced VMI's opponents. Advocates of admitting women to VMI reiterated that there were no VMI activities that could not be completed successfully by women. To VMI, that was not the point. VMI could not make its real point persuasively, however, because it did not articulate it, even to itself. The idea of VMI as all male was an end in itself. When Bunting published a novel describing his model twenty-first-century college, he depicted what seemed like a VMI with higher academic standards. In what was perhaps a nod to the inevitable, the school was coed, but the school song was entitled "Once to Every *Man* and Nation."[54]

Like the Boy Scouts, VMI prided itself on turning boys into men. It could not reasonably argue, however, that boys cannot be turned into men in coeducational settings, or that coeducational colleges have failed to produce male citizen-soldiers or male leaders.

What VMI was attempting to protect was a four-year-long male bonding ritual whose very essence was differentiation from women and those things perceived as feminine. Could the argument be made that for *some* boys, that kind of ritual, that kind of temporary separateness, might be necessary or wise or desirable? That a setting in which the male bonding ritual was central rather than peripheral to the educational experience worked better for some boys than any other could? That what was being defended so passionately was not the only or even necessarily the best method of producing male leaders but the best method for *some* young men? And that, as Bunting believed, so few women would be attracted to the VMI regime that they would always remain a tiny minority, singled out for that reason and therefore destructive of the school's cohesion through no fault of their own?

Even if such a claim had any merit, of course, it did not obviate the federal government's charge in *United States v. Virginia* that in keeping VMI all male, the commonwealth was providing a publicly funded military college for men and none for women. Virginia's doing so reflected a belief that men and women were destined for very different roles in life. And that was precisely the kind of thinking that Ruth Bader Ginsburg had made it her life's work to change.

The Advocate

"Feminist" simply means believing that women should have a fair chance in the world to do whatever their talent enables them to do.

—Ruth Bader Ginsburg

Ruth Bader did not know much about the law when she was a little girl growing up in Brooklyn during the 1930s and 1940s. Her mother took her to the library regularly and encouraged her to read, and the daughter used what she read to such good effect that she was chosen to speak at her high school graduation. A less perceptive young woman might have gotten the impression that women were equal in the United States. But of course they were not, and that inequality had been fully endorsed and encouraged by the Supreme Court on which she would sit decades later. As of the 1950s, when Ruth Bader graduated from college, no woman had ever sat on the nation's highest tribunal.

Few girls expected to become lawyers during those middle years of the twentieth century. Back in 1873, when Myra Bradwell was denied a license to practice law in the state of Illinois and asked the Supreme Court to declare that she had a constitutional right to do so, the justices had expressed dismay at the idea.[1] Her lawyer reminded the Court that it had said only seven years earlier:

> The theory upon which our political institutions rest is, that all men have certain inalienable rights—that among these are life, liberty, and the pursuit of happiness; and that in the pursuit of happiness all avocations, all honors, all positions, are alike open to every one, and that in the protection of these rights all are equal be-

fore the law. Any deprivation or suspension of any of these rights for past conduct is punishment, and can be in no otherwise defined.[2]

Justice Samuel F. Miller's opinion for the Court said simply that the matter lay within the power of the states and was not controlled by the U.S. Constitution. Justice Joseph P. Bradley's concurrence went further and would be quoted in most subsequent cases denying equality to women. It was true that there were inalienable rights, Bradley believed, but *women* could not lay claim to all of them.

> Man is, or should be, woman's protector and defender. The natural and proper timidity and delicacy which belongs to the female sex evidently unfits it for many of the occupations of civil life. The constitution of the family organization, which is founded in the divine ordinance, as well as in the nature of things, indicates the domestic sphere as that which properly belongs to the domain and functions of womanhood.

"The paramount destiny and mission of woman," Bradley continued, "are to fulfil the noble and benign offices of wife and mother. This is the law of the Creator."[3] It was neither the first nor the last time that God would be invoked to deny women equal opportunity.

The Supreme Court had in fact handed down one decision after another that endorsed and contributed to the status of women as second-class citizens who had no role to play outside the home. During the nineteenth century it asserted vigorously that married women had to live where their husbands chose, that their citizenship was derived from that of their husbands, and that husbands owned their wives' property.[4] Even after the Fourteenth and Fifteenth Amendments guaranteed male ex-slaves the right to vote, the Court held that women's citizenship gave them no similar right.[5] When, toward the end of the century, attorney Belva Lockwood asked to practice before the bar of the Supreme Court, it turned her down. Lockwood had to push a bill through Congress before the Court finally admitted her in 1879, and it was not until 1880 that she became the first woman to argue before the nation's highest court.[6] The Supreme Court was no friend of women throughout most of its history.

Women had nonetheless won the right to practice law by the time Ruth Bader Ginsburg (her married name) went to law school in the 1950s, but the Supreme Court's thinking about women had not changed drastically. In 1961, when the justices unanimously sustained a law giving women an absolute exemption from jury duty, the reason would be couched in secular language but would otherwise be the same as Justice Bradley's. Gwendolyn Hoyt, accused of murdering her husband, had no right to anything other than an all-male jury, because "woman is still regarded as the center of home and family life" and could not be available to serve on juries.[7] It was one of the decisions that Ginsburg would later fight to overturn.

A few years before the Hoyt case, the Supreme Court had contributed to a civil rights revolution by declaring that segregated public schools were unconstitutional. The Fourteenth Amendment's equal protection clause ("No state shall . . . deny to any person within its jurisdiction the equal protection of the laws") meant that any state-provided service had to be made equally available to everyone eligible. In *Brown v. Board of Education,* the Court held that forcing African American children to go to separate schools left them with a sense of inferiority that impeded their ability to learn.[8] By being excluded, the children were being denied the equal protection of the laws.

Brown and its progeny helped make Americans aware of the damage that could be done by policies of exclusion. Exclusion stigmatized; exclusion denied equal opportunities for employment and participation in civic life, as well as for education. Southern resistance to court-ordered integration, coupled with the civil rights movement, culminated in passage of the federal Civil Rights Act of 1964, which banned discrimination on the basis of race, color, religion, or national origin. While it was still being debated in Congress, Representative Howard W. Smith of Virginia, determined to demonstrate how foolish such a statute would be, slyly offered an amendment to add "sex" to the illegal bases for discrimination in employment. In doing so, Smith underestimated the persuasive power of the National Woman's Party, which had been lobbying for just such an addition, as well as that of the House's few women members. To his dismay, but to the delight of women already involved in the early stages of the women's liberation movement, the amendment became part of the laws of the United States.[9]

Their success scarcely meant that women—or people of color, for that matter—would henceforth be treated equally in the workplace or elsewhere. Achieving equality would come only with a great deal of organizing and political activism.[10] It would also require turning to the courts for recourse. That was where Ruth Bader Ginsburg was prepared to help.

RUTH BADER'S MOTHER DIED after a four-year bout with cancer, the night before her daughter's high school graduation in 1950. The grieving daughter went to Cornell, where there was one woman in the school of arts and sciences for every four men. As was the norm for college women in those days, she was expected to aspire no higher than school teaching—a field in which women were welcome and that would enable her to support herself.[11] But thanks to the encouragement of Robert Cushman, her constitutional law professor, and her husband, she applied to law school.[12]

Ruth Bader and fellow Cornell student Martin Ginsburg were married upon graduation, and they wanted to attend graduate school together. He was interested in studying at Harvard Business School, but it did not admit women. Instead, they went to Harvard Law School, which had opened its doors to women in 1950.[13]

At the law school, Ginsburg was one of nine women out of a class of about 500. She made law review and wanted to take her mother-in-law to the annual banquet, but she could not because it was held at the Harvard Club in Boston, which would not lift its men-only rule for anyone other than the two women students on law review.[14]

She also was invited to the dinner that Dean Erwin Griswold held every year for the female students. Each young woman was assigned a faculty member as an escort—it never occurred to Griswold that a female student might be married or, as Ginsburg was when she arrived at Harvard, the mother of a fourteen-month-old child. Her escort was Herbert Wechsler, a distinguished Columbia Law School scholar who was visiting Harvard for the year. "I was in awe of him," Ginsburg recalled. "I worried that he would find me gauche, not worth his time."[15]

After dinner, they all retired to the Griswolds' living room. Ginsburg was seated next to her escort, and she nervously held their joint ashtray on her lap. Griswold's habit was to ask each of the women "why were we in law school, occupying a seat that could be held by a man." (He later told Ginsburg that the reason was to have a supply of good answers when the male faculty demanded to know why the school was admitting women.)

> I rose when called on, and there went the cigarette butts, spread about the rug in front of me. It was one of those moments in life you never forget. If only I had a button to push, so I could vanish through a trap door! I didn't know whether to get on my knees and clean up the mess. I mumbled something about my husband being in the second-year class and how important it was for a wife to understand her husband's work. I didn't mean to say that, but that's what came out.[16]

Another woman told the dean, perhaps with tongue in cheek, that the male-female ratio made the law school a great place to find a husband.[17]

Martin Ginsburg was a year ahead of his wife. When he graduated and got a job in New York, she—not wanting to be a single parent—transferred to Columbia Law School. She was one of about twelve women in a class of roughly 300 and the only woman in her class on law review.[18] But her high grades at two of the country's top law schools made no difference when she got her degree and tried to find a job.

It was and is common for the country's best law students to gain experience and prestige by clerking for a judge after graduation, but most judges in 1959 were loath to take on a woman. None of the firms to which she applied would hire her, although she "signed up for every interview I could get"—an experience that paralleled that of Sandra Day O'Connor.[19] Professor Gerald Gunther finally talked Judge Edmund L. Palmieri, of the federal district court in Manhattan, into giving her a chance.[20] The following year, when one of her former professors at Harvard recommended her to Supreme Court Justice Felix Frankfurter, the justice's response was that he certainly was not ready to take on a woman as his law clerk.[21]

Ginsburg spent two years as Palmieri's clerk and another two working on a book about Swedish civil procedure, for which she had to learn Swedish and travel to Sweden.[22] Her months there coincided with the revival of the Swedish women's movement and led her to think seriously "about women's right to control their life's course, to be men's full partners," as did her reading of Simone de Beauvoir's *Second Sex*.[23] She was then offered a job teaching at Rutgers Law School, where the dean saw nothing wrong with paying her less than a man would have received. The school administrators knew that Ginsburg had a child, but she feared that her year-to-year contract would not be renewed if they realized that she was pregnant and would soon be the mother of a newborn as well, so she hid her pregnancy by wearing her mother-in-law's larger clothes.[24]

School officials throughout the country considered it inappropriate for pregnant women to be in the classroom, and the New Jersey affiliate of the American Civil Liberties Union (ACLU) asked Ginsburg to handle the cases of pregnant schoolteachers who had been forced out of their jobs. There were other sex discrimination cases, as well as interest among some of her women students (and a few men) in taking a course on women and the law.[25] Ginsburg created one in the early 1970s and, surprised at the paucity of materials for the course, accepted an invitation from Herma Hill Kay and Kenneth M. Davidson to put together the constitutional law section of what became the first casebook on sex-based discrimination.[26] She later credited the ACLU cases and her Rutgers students, along with her experience in Sweden, with educating her about gender discrimination.[27]

The students' interest in studying women and the law, and perhaps even Ginsburg's job at Rutgers, resulted from the women's movement that had begun in the 1960s. Women who had been active in the civil rights movement of the 1950s and 1960s confronted the fact that even there, in the midst of a drive for equality, they were treated as inferior.[28] Women active in party politics, women labor leaders, and women educators were dismayed that the Equal Employment Opportunity Commission (EEOC) established under the 1964 Civil Rights Act was giving short shrift to complaints filed by women. Their distress was a major reason for the creation of the National Organization for Women (NOW) in 1966 and, subsequently, a variety of women's legal action groups. Many women read Betty Friedan's *The Feminine Mystique,* published in 1963, which became a best-seller and sold more than 3 million copies.[29]

What was happening inside these groups, and among Rutgers students, reflected larger societal developments. As technology produced surer methods of birth control, smaller families and planned pregnancies became more common. Improved contraception and increased life expectancy gave married women more pre- and post-nurturing years in which to enter the workforce. Economic necessity also sent many women searching for paying jobs. The inflation of the 1950s resulted in the need for more than one income among married couples, and the higher divorce rate reduced formerly married women's incomes.[30] In addition, the draft laws were changed during the Vietnam War to eliminate deferments for postcollege education, leaving law school seats that might have been claimed by men empty, and leading the law schools to welcome and even recruit women students. (Harvard president Nathan Pusey lamented that the university would be left with the blind, the lame, and the women.)[31]

There was, in short, a growing number of women in law schools and law firms, in a few other professions, and in numerous areas of paid work. Nothing less than a cultural revolution was taking place, leading women to ask, for example, why occupations traditionally considered male were not open to women. It was, in fact, the EEOC's promulgation of a rule permitting newspapers to continue publishing separate "help wanted male" and "help wanted female" advertisements that contributed to a decision by women such as Betty Friedan and ACLU National Board member Pauli Murray to organize

NOW.[32] As the movement grew, so did opposition to it, and the culture wars that had been forecast by the civil rights movement would become hotter for the remainder of the twentieth century.[33] One battleground would be affirmative action. Ginsburg was convinced that both her job at Rutgers and her subsequent one at Columbia Law School were obtained in large part thanks to affirmative action.[34]

The most volatile moments of the culture wars were still ahead in the mid-1960s, however, when Ginsburg's students began asking for a course about women and the law. In her typically methodical fashion, she prepared for it by reading every case and law review article ever written about women's status under the law. "That," she commented dryly, "was not a very taxing undertaking. There were not many decisions, and commentary was slim."[35] She was particularly impressed by the Grimke sisters, who had advocated feminism and abolition in South Carolina in the mid-1800s, and by an article entitled "Jane Crow and the Law" by Pauli Murray and Mary O. Eastwood. "That manifestations of racial prejudice have been more brutal than the more subtle manifestations of prejudice by reason of sex," the article stated, "in no way diminishes the force of the equally obvious fact that the rights of women and the rights of Negroes are only different phases of the fundamental and indivisible issue of human rights."[36]

Ginsburg's association with the ACLU would literally change legal and social history. The organization had been interested in women's equality since at least the 1940s, when it established a Committee on Discrimination Against Women in Employment that sought equal pay for equal work and the abolition of laws prohibiting the distribution of birth control information and the use of contraceptives. In 1965 the ACLU became the first national organization to call for the right to abortion, and in 1970 it came out for the proposed Equal Rights Amendment to the Constitution and against protective labor laws—statutes that "protected" women by keeping them out of jobs that a legislature considered dangerous or inappropriate.[37]

When Ginsburg was at Rutgers, Marvin Karpatkin was one of the national ACLU's three general counsels, a voluntary group that helped the staff decide which cases to take, and a member of the organization's Committee on Equality. In 1970 Karpatkin noticed a report in the legal newspaper *Law Week* about a decision by the supreme court of Idaho in a case called *Reed v. Reed*. It involved a couple, Sally and Cecil Reed, who had separated years before. The courts had given Sally Reed custody of their young son Richard but increased Cecil Reed's visitation rights when Richard got older. The young man had a troubled adolescence and eventually committed suicide with his father's gun. His mother, wanting her son's belongings, applied to be named administrator of his estate; Cecil Reed filed a competing application a few days later. The probate court followed Idaho law in naming the father as administrator without holding a hearing: "males must be preferred to females," said the relevant statute. Sally Reed appealed, and the state supreme court upheld the ruling.[38]

Karpatkin thought that the case could be a turning point in gender equality law. The ACLU offered its services to Sally Reed's lawyer in Idaho, and Ginsburg asked Mel Wulf, the organization's legal director, if she could write the brief when *Reed v. Reed* reached the U.S. Supreme Court. Wulf decided that they would write it together. ACLU lawyers would have been glad to argue the case before the Court, but the Idaho attorney wanted to do it himself—and he made Ginsburg wince early in his presentation when he asked the Court in 1971 to do for women what it had done for "colored people" in 1954.[39]

Ginsburg and Wulf were aided on the brief by female law students recruited from Rutgers, Yale, and New York University to compile the copious amount of material on women's history and the discriminatory use of law that would appear in it.[40] Their argument would rest on the Constitution's equal protection clause.

The meaning of "No state shall . . . deny to any person within its jurisdiction the equal protection of the laws" was unclear. The Supreme Court of 1896 had held that it permitted states to provide "separate but equal" public services for white and black citizens.[41] The Court in 1954, in *Brown v. Board of Education,* said that the earlier justices had gotten it wrong and that the clause forbade the states to treat the races differently.[42] In litigation that followed *Brown,* the Court held that any statute or governmental action that differentiated among people on the basis of their race was presumptively unconstitutional and would be subjected to "strict scrutiny" by the nation's courts. Race was declared a "suspect classification," so that the burden of proof, which usually rests on anyone challenging the constitutionality of a law, was shifted to the state. Normally, a law is presumed to be legitimate unless someone proves otherwise. A race-based statute, however, would be presumed to be illegal unless the state could prove that it was not.[43]

The rule of thumb under the equal protection clause for laws that differentiated between people on a basis other than race was called the "rational relation" test. If a state could demonstrate that a statute had been enacted

in an area over which the legislature had power—education, for example—
and that it embodied a rational approach to whatever problem the legislature
meant to address, the courts would hold that the law did not violate the equal
protection clause. "Rational" did not mean that the state's solution had to
be the best one or one with which the justices agreed, because it was not the
judges' function to decide what constituted the best policies; rather, it was
their function to acknowledge the leeway permitted to states under the Constitution and to take them to task if they went beyond it.

Ginsburg and Wulf believed that the Idaho law could be struck down
under the rational relation test; that is, there was no rational reason to give
men automatic priority when it came to administering an estate. But they decided to use the case as a way to move the Court toward holding that laws
that differentiated among people on the basis of gender were subject to the
same strict scrutiny given to those relying on racial categories. Their brief
made the analogy between race and sex: "Both classifications create large,
natural classes, membership in which is beyond the individual's control; both
are highly visible characteristics on which legislators have found it easy to
draw gross stereotypical distinctions."[44]

Stereotypes about the sexes were as unacceptable a justification for governmental action as were those about race, the brief said. Although govern-
ment-sanctioned discrimination against women had been part of the problem in the past, the Congress and the president of the mid-1960s had moved
away from stereotyping. As evidence of this, the brief cited the Equal Pay Act
and the 1964 Civil Rights Act, thereby tacitly inviting the Court to catch up.
The new laws, however, did not take care of most discrimination, "as in the
case at bar for example, where women are relegated to second class status."[45]

The brief established a pattern that Ginsburg would use in all her subsequent litigation before the Court and, for the most part, in her opinion in
United States v. Virginia. First, gender-based laws had to be viewed in light
of the entire history of the country's treatment of women rather than as isolated enactments that might otherwise be viewed as "rational." "American
women have been stigmatized historically as an inferior class and are today
subject to pervasive discrimination," the brief declared. It backed that statement up with a survey of attitudes and laws about women dating back to the
days of Thomas Jefferson. It went on to review the situation of women in
1971, emphasizing the extent of their education and their participation in
the workforce.[46] There was nothing "rational" about assuming that any man
was better prepared than any woman to serve as administrator of an estate.

The brief's emphasis on facts and the relationship between real lives and the law would become one of Ginsburg's hallmarks.[47] So would the insistence that gender was as much of a "suspect classification" as race was—carefully hedged with the argument that the case could be decided her way even under a less stringent standard.

> It is appellant's principal position that the sex line drawn by Sec. 15-314 of the Idaho Code, mandating subordination of women to men without regard to individual capacity, creates a "suspect classification." . . . It is appellant's alternate position that . . . the line drawn by the Idaho legislature, arbitrarily ranking the woman as inferior to the man . . . lacks the constitutionally required fair and reasonable relation to any legitimate state interest.[48]

Finally, *Reed v. Reed* forecast Ginsburg's constant homage to other women who had paved the way for the work she was doing. As she wrote later:

> In preparing Sally Reed's appeal to the Supreme Court, I placed on the brief the names of two women, one was Dorothy Kenyon, who had represented Gwendolyn Hoyt, the other was Pauli Murray . . . who had long fought for racial and gender justice. Both were then too old to be part of the fray, but people of my generation owed them a great debt, for they bravely pressed arguments for equal justice in days when few would give ear to what they were saying.[49]

Kenyon and Murray were two of "the people who were making these arguments when nobody was listening." "They would have been writing the Reed brief if they were younger and physically able."[50] Among the other women Ginsburg considered to be leaders in the drive for equality were ACLU volunteer attorney Faith Seidenberg; Burnita Shelton Matthews, counsel to the National Women's Party, which had introduced the Equal Rights Amendment, and the first woman to sit on a federal district court; and three from the past: Virginia Minor, who had petitioned the Supreme Court unsuccessfully in 1874 to recognize women as citizens with a right to vote, and suffragists Susan B. Anthony and Elizabeth Cady Stanton.[51]

Kenyon and Murray must have been pleased at the outcome of the case. Chief Justice Warren Burger, holding for a unanimous Court that the gender classification for administrators was irrational, repeated Ginsburg and Wulf's quote from a 1920 decision involving the state of Virginia: "a classification 'must be reasonable, not arbitrary, and must rest upon some ground of difference having a fair and substantial relation to the object of the legislation, so that all persons similarly circumstanced shall be treated alike.'"[52] "For me," Ginsburg said, the decision was "just right. The Court was unanimous; the opinion was written by the Chief Justice. The Court accepted the position that equal protection was a check on arbitrary discrimination against women."[53] It was a momentous step in the quest for gender equality.

It was, however, only one step. Ginsburg spoke about the case at a late 1971 meeting of the ACLU National Board, which voted to create the Women's Rights Project (WRP). The organization allocated $50,000 for it, the Rockefeller Family Foundation contributed some start-up money, and the Ford Foundation later weighed in with the bulk of the project's funds.[54]

Ginsburg was asked to direct the new project. She was about to move from Rutgers to Columbia Law School, where she would become the first woman ever tenured. But to underscore the importance of gender equality litigation, and "to indicate that good lawyers should be interested in doing this kind of thing," she worked out an arrangement that permitted her to work half time at Columbia her first year there and half time for WRP.[55]

She had an agenda.

> One of the students who worked on Sally Reed's brief helped me put together an appendix of statutes that treated women specially, a true sign of the time, a sampling of laws of the kind that then riddled the statute books of the U.S. and all 50 states. . . .
>
> After that 1971 decision and until 1980, the year I became a U.S. Court of Appeals judge, the business of ridding the statute books of laws of the kind collected in the appendix to Sally Reed's brief consumed most of my days.[56]

As she had signaled in her *Reed v. Reed* brief, Ginsburg wanted to establish strict scrutiny as the judicial standard, and she was determined to overturn three Supreme Court cases: *Muller v. Oregon, Goesaert v. Cleary,* and *Hoyt v. Florida.* The Court had declared in *Muller* that protective legislation for women was constitutional. *Hoyt* had upheld the legitimacy of all-male jury pools. In *Goesaert v. Cleary* the Court had sustained a law denying bartending licenses to women generally (a piece of protective legislation) but excepting the wives and daughters of male bar owners.[57] Ginsburg would tell an interviewer that she opposed protective legislation because she "came from a world where women were protected out of being lawyers, out of being engineers, and out of being bartenders."[58] The effect of protective legislation, she knew, was that "men's jobs [were protected from] women's competition."[59]

> For example, women couldn't work more than so many hours, and night work was off limits to them. Consider the impact on serving tables. The best tips are at night, not in the day. A worker got time-and-a-half for overtime. Women were protected against overtime work. They were protected against working in certain occupations like truck-driving, bartending, mining, jobs that paid more than the clerical jobs that women could get.[60]

It was not unlike the way Virginia would later claim to be protecting women by keeping them out of VMI. In a case she argued three years after *Reed,* one of the justices asked if she was opposed to classification on the basis of sex even when that classification helped.

> MRS. GINSBERG: My question is if it ever does help.
> QUESTION: Ever does.
> MRS. GINSBURG: Yes.
> QUESTION: But, even if it does, you would assume, on that assumption that—
> MRS. GINSBURG: But I have not yet found any such classification in the law that genuinely helps. From a very shortsighted viewpoint, perhaps, such as this one, yes. But long run—no, I think that what women need is, first of all, a removal of exclusions and restrictive quotas. They are the only population group that today still faces outright exclusions and restrictive quotas. . . . But the notion that they need special favored treatment, because they are women, I think has been what has helped to keep women in a special place, and has kept them away from equal opportunity for so long.[61]

Ginsburg's goal was to "build eventually to the point where the Court would say: 'None of these sex lines in the law are rational.'"[62] She thought that it would take a number of cases to bring the justices to that point, as the Court was "an audience with barely a kindergarten education" about gender discrimination; she had to "start with A, B, C's, not with a post-graduate course."[63] Her approach would be a gradual one, centered around

> an appreciation first of how I could reach male decision makers psychologically. People came to this notion of sex discrimination with a certain bias; that is, they [believed that they] were very good fellows. They treated their wives well; they treated their daughters well. How could they be accused of gender discrimination? For them to see the gender bias in the law as limiting human capacity, both male and female, so they wouldn't treat this as a bunch of rabble-rousing women's lib-bers—they could understand the confining factor of putting people in pigeonholes, whether male or female. By showing them the disadvantage to males of being pi-geonholed, I think that got their eye and made them more receptive to the argu-ments we were making about holding women down than they would have been if they hadn't seen it.[64]

The way to convince the Court was to show the justices that gender dis-crimination hurt men as well as women. The first WRP case Ginsburg took to the Supreme Court was *Frontiero v. Richardson,* brought on behalf of twenty-three-year-old air force first lieutenant Sharron Frontiero.[65] Fron-tiero's husband was going through college on the GI Bill, receiving a stipend of only $205 a month. The air force, however, refused to recognize him as her dependent. This meant that the young couple had no right to either married quarters on base or the supplemental housing allowance available to married men, and Joseph Frontiero was not entitled to use medical facilities available to female spouses.

Ginsburg's seventy-page brief tracked the one in *Reed*. It contained an extensive summary of the treatment of women throughout American history and of the law's participation in legitimizing discrimination; again, *Muller*, *Goesaert*, and *Hoyt* were targeted for criticism. The Defense Department claimed that requiring proof of spousal dependency from servicemen would be an administrative burden; it was more cost-effective to assume that all wives were dependent and all husbands were not. Ginsburg pointed to current employment statistics—almost 60 percent of all married women living with their husbands were employed outside the home—and noted that many of them undoubtedly met the standard of independence, which was the provision of more than half their own living expenses. The armed services might actually save money by eliminating its assumption of female dependence.[66] In any event, after *Reed*, administrative convenience was not an acceptable excuse.

Because she was denied benefits that male military personnel received, Frontiero was effectively receiving less pay than similarly situated male officers. She was being discriminated against as a breadwinner, while her husband was being discriminated against as a family member. It was double-edged discrimination, and the brief urged the Court to adopt the strict scrutiny standard in striking it down. But again, the introduction of the standard was a tactic designed to familiarize the justices with the idea; the brief indicated that the discrimination also violated the less stringent standard. The opposing brief submitted by Erwin Griswold, Ginsburg's former dean at Harvard and by then solicitor general, argued against adoption of the strict scrutiny criterion.

Frontiero had been represented by the Southern Poverty Law Center in the case's early stages. Because the Center had had no time to write the early Supreme Court papers in the case, it had brought in the WRP, but it later insisted on remaining Frontiero's representative. After extensive negotiations, the Center agreed to let Ginsburg, technically representing the ACLU rather than Frontiero, share oral argument. She knew exactly how she would use her time: "I was going to argue strict scrutiny and nothing else in my twelve minutes."[67]

It was Ginsburg's first oral argument before the Court. The technique she developed was to prepare "a good first sentence and last sentence" and be flexible about what went in between, because the justices tended to jump in with questions whenever they liked. "If you're wedded to a script and believe you must say this before that, then you're not going to do very well. Oral argument should be a conversation between the Court and the lawyers."[68] She was understandably nervous about the *Frontiero* argument and found it hard to get the first sentence out. Then, however, "I looked at these people and said to myself: 'They are a captive audience, they have no place to go. The nine most important judges in the country have to listen to me for the remainder of this argument.'"[69]

That might have been daunting to many, but what Ginsburg found more puzzling was the total silence from the bench during her entire twelve minutes. The justices asked not a single question, and she was certain that they were simply uninterested in what she had to say.[70] She plowed on nonetheless, reminding the all-male Court that the framers of the Fourteenth Amendment viewed racial discrimination as "odious" because "a person's skin color bears no necessary relationship to ability," just as sex and ability bore no such relationship. But women were still classified differently, and she pointed to *Muller, Goesaert,* and *Hoyt* as similar in their effect: "They help keep woman in her place, a place inferior to that occupied by men in our society." Ginsburg concluded by telling the Court about Sarah Grimke: "She spoke, not elegantly, but with unmistakable clarity. She said, 'I ask no favor for my sex. All I ask of our brethren is that they take their feet off our necks.'"[71]

Ginsburg was wrong about one thing: the justices were not uninterested. Their silence was an extraordinary indication that, just as she intended, the Columbia Law School professor was educating successfully. Justice William Brennan's opinion for himself and three other justices concluded that "classifications based upon sex, like classifications based upon race, alienage, or national origin, are inherently suspect, and must therefore be subjected to strict judicial scrutiny."[72] Brennan then "paid us the greatest compliment" by repeating whole passages of Ginsburg's brief and citing the cases, history, and articles that she had brought to the Court's attention. "That doesn't happen very often," she commented later.[73]

The sole dissenter in the case was Justice William Rehnquist, the future chief justice with whom Ginsburg would serve on the Court, who believed that the statute should have been upheld.[74]

But the seemingly happy ending was not a total victory. Justice Potter Stewart concurred with the finding that the law violated equal protection,[75] but he said nothing about the strict scrutiny standard. Justice Lewis F. Powell and two others rejected the standard, although they also agreed that the statute at issue was unconstitutional. The Equal Rights Amendment ("Equality of Rights under the law shall not be denied or abridged by the United States or any state on account of sex"), which would have had the same effect as the strict scrutiny test, had been sent to the states for ratification. Powell thought that the Court would be preempting the democratic process if it acted before the states had spoken, and said so in his concurrence.[76] Thus, it was only a plurality of four justices rather than a majority of five who decided on the basis of the tighter standard, which meant that sex had not yet been declared a suspect classification and that courts below were free to uphold gender-based classifications they considered to be rational.

Then, in 1982, the time for ratification of the Equal Rights Amendment expired without a sufficient number of states having voted to adopt it, and the question of whether gender discrimination cases should be decided on the basis of strict scrutiny was bounced back to the Supreme Court. It remained an open issue right up to the time of the VMI litigation.

Ginsburg was amazed that the four justices had gone as far as they did in *Frontiero*. She had calculated that it would take about five cases before the justices adopted the strict scrutiny standard.[77] She considered the judgment "a notable way-paver" that "set the stage for its subsequent disallowance of the stereotype in a setting . . . where the price tag for upward equalization could run many hundreds of millions of dollars."[78] That setting, unlikely as it seemed, was the Social Security system.

5

Women Making Law for Women— and Men

History provides numerous examples of legislative attempts to exclude women from particular areas simply because legislators believed women were less able than men to perform a particular function.

—Sandra Day O'Connor, *Mississippi University for Women v. Hogan*

In 1972 Paula Wiesenfeld, a New Jersey schoolteacher, died in childbirth. Her husband, Stephen, wanted to raise their son himself, but money was a problem. Paula's salary had been substantially larger than his. If he were a widow, he would have been eligible for a Social Security benefit based on his wife's earnings. The survivors' benefit, however, was contained in a section of the Social Security law entitled "Mother's insurance benefits," and Wiesenfeld was told by his local Social Security office that he obviously did not qualify. There was no similar benefit for a widower.[1] The letter he sent to a local newspaper about his situation was read by a Rutgers faculty member, who told Ginsburg about it. She commented that it sounded like a denial of equal protection and that Wiesenfeld ought to get in touch with the ACLU.[2] He did, and Ginsburg took on the case that she later described as "very dear to my heart"[3] and "a gem of a case."[4] It was the first case she handled from inception through Supreme Court appeal.

The law served no legitimate governmental interest, Ginsburg argued.

It had been written when "legislators were accustomed to coupling widows and orphans, mothers and children; they did not conceive of men in a child-care role."[5] But, Ginsburg reminded the courts (as she had in *Frontiero*), the majority of working women were married, and 3.2 million of them earned more than their husbands.[6] What could be the governmental interest in depriving their survivors of "social security"?

The government's answer was that far from being discriminatory, the statute was intended to compensate women for their lower economic status and the discrimination they still faced in the marketplace. Not true, Ginsburg replied. That clearly had not been in the legislators' minds when the law was enacted in 1939, because it was specifically intended to provide for a "child in care" after the death of a family's wage earner. Legislators back then were not concerned about gender discrimination.[7]

When the case reached the Supreme Court, Ginsburg's oral argument emphasized its human side. She believed that the most successful litigation was in "flesh-and-blood cases" involving "a live challenger, a person tangibly hurt by discrimination,"[8] and all her Court presentations concentrated on that person. Instead of beginning her presentation with the fairly common approach, along the lines of "This case involves the Constitution's due process clause," her first sentence was, "Stephen Wiesenfeld's case concerns the entitlement of a female wage earner's family to social insurance of the same quality as that accorded a family of a male wage earner."[9] She told the Court that all three family members had been denied the equal protection of the laws:

> Paula Wiesenfeld, in fact the principal wage earner, is treated as though her years of work were of only secondary value to her family. Stephen Wiesenfeld, in fact the nurturing parent, is treated as though he did not perform that function. And Jason Paul, a motherless infant with a father able and willing to provide care for him personally, is treated as an infant not entitled to the personal care of his sole surviving parent.[10]

The justices agreed, unanimously. In an opinion for four of them that drew on Ginsburg's brief and the *Frontiero* decision,[11] Justice William Brennan explained to the country that reliance on outmoded stereotypes hurt men as well as women.

> The classification discriminates among surviving children solely on the basis of the sex of the surviving parent. Even in the typical family hypothesized by the Act, in which the husband is supporting the family and the mother is caring for the children, this result makes no sense. The fact that a man is working while there is a wife at home does not mean that he would, or should be required to, continue to

work if his wife dies. It is no less important for a child to be cared for by its sole surviving parent when that parent is male rather than female. And a father, no less than a mother, has a constitutionally protected right to the "companionship, care, custody, and management" of "the children he has sired and raised, [which] undeniably warrants deference and, absent a powerful countervailing interest, protection."[12]

Paula Wiesenfeld had been treated unfairly, Brennan wrote, as "she not only failed to receive for her family the same protection which a similarly situated male worker would have received, but she also was deprived of a portion of her own earnings in order to contribute to the fund out of which benefits would be paid to others."[13]

Ginsburg's decision to present the case as a human story clearly worked. The justices interrupted with relatively few questions during her oral argument, and not at all when she was speaking of the individuals involved rather than the legalities. Even Justice William Rehnquist, who voted against Ginsburg in every other case she argued, wrote a concurrence declaring that the law was irrational.[14] "I think maybe the oral argument had some effect on Rehnquist in the Wiesenfeld case," she ruminated. "That vote was totally out of character. . . . I think the image of the baby did it. Here was a child with only one parent who didn't have the opportunity for the personal care of that parent. . . . Maybe that made a difference to him."[15] Years later, Rehnquist would ask Ginsburg, "Tell me this: did he really take care of the baby?"[16] (He did.)

Ginsburg and the WRP then brought a number of cases in lower courts challenging other aspects of the Social Security system.[17] *Califano v. Goldfarb,* the one that reached the Supreme Court first, involved a widower who had been denied survivors' benefits because he had not depended on his wife for more than half his support. Widows were granted the benefit without proving such dependency. Ginsburg argued once more that both sexes were being unfairly treated and that the reason lay in outmoded thinking and stereotypes.[18] (It is worth noting that one of the justices, perhaps having difficulty with the concept of women keeping their own names while taking those of their husbands, referred to her during oral argument as "Mrs. Bader." She corrected him.)[19]

Reading the gender equality cases, one gets a sense of Ginsburg and Brennan in a balletic pas de deux. Ginsburg presented a case, Brennan relied on the points she had made in deciding for her client, she cited his opinions in her next case, and so on. In *Goldfarb,* Brennan, again writing a plurality opinion for four justices, now had two Ginsburg-argued precedents to draw on.

He relied on *Frontiero* and *Wiesenfeld* in finding that the classification violated the equal protection rights of both men and women, for the reasons he had laid out in those cases. The Court rejected the government's argument that "Congress may reasonably have presumed that nondependent widows, who receive benefits, are needier than nondependent widowers, who do not, because of job discrimination against women (particularly older women)," since "the general purpose of the [law] was 'to afford more adequate protection to the family as a unit.'"[20] Justice John Paul Stevens's concurrence noted that "habit, rather than analysis or actual reflection," had led Congress "to equate the term 'widow' and 'dependent surviving spouse.'"[21]

Justice Rehnquist wrote a dissent for himself and three other justices, and Ginsburg speculated that the high cost of giving benefits to widowers as well as widows might have led to the dissenting votes of one or more of the justices on whom she otherwise could have counted.[22] "*Califano v. Goldfarb,*" she commented, "might be described as *Frontiero* revisited with a hefty price tag . . . or *Wiesenfeld* without the baby."[23] Rehnquist utilized the rational relation test in declaring that because more widows than widowers had been dependent on their spouses, Congress could rationally decide that the value of providing survivors' benefits to needy widows outweighed the demands of equal protection.[24] Justice Brennan implicitly used a higher standard when he wrote that *Frontiero* and *Wiesenfeld* "plainly require" that the law be struck down.[25]

The relevant legal standard, which would become a major issue in *United States v. Virginia,* was refined by the Court when it decided a case argued the same day as *Goldfarb. Craig v. Boren* challenged an Oklahoma law that allowed women but not men to buy 3.2 percent beer at age eighteen. Oklahoma relied on arrest statistics to show that the classification was rational because men aged eighteen to twenty-one were more likely to drive while drunk than were women of that age. In rejecting the idea that "maleness is to serve as a proxy for drinking and driving," Justice Brennan suggested that even arrest records could be affected by old attitudes:

> The very social stereotypes that find reflection in age-differential laws are likely substantially to distort the accuracy of these comparative statistics. Hence "reckless" young men who drink and drive are transformed into arrest statistics, whereas their female counterparts are chivalrously escorted home.[26]

In the process of striking down the statute, Brennan articulated a new standard. He referred to it as already established, but in fact it was his formulation in *Craig v. Boren* that would be used in the future.

To withstand constitutional challenge, previous cases establish that classifications by gender must serve important governmental objectives and must be substantially related to achievement of those objectives.[27]

Essentially, the test fell somewhere between the more easily met rational relation criterion and the tighter strict scrutiny standard. Gender classifications that were "substantially related" to "important governmental objectives" were legitimate. Ginsburg did not handle the case for Craig but submitted an amicus brief for WRP. Amicus briefs are filed by people or organizations that are not parties in a case but have an interest in its outcome. Ginsburg recognized that the Court had adopted a kind of "heightened scrutiny" in gender cases such as *Reed, Frontiero,* and *Wiesenfeld.*[28] She understood that a majority of the Court was not ready to extend strict scrutiny to gender discrimination cases and therefore argued successfully for heightened scrutiny. Brennan again drew on her brief in writing his opinion.[29]

The result was that strict scrutiny would continue to be used in judging equal protection claims in race and national origin discrimination cases, meaning that the law at issue would almost always be found unconstitutional. Rational relation, used for other categories, almost inevitably resulted in a decision that the law was legitimate. Gender cases were relegated to the constitutional twilight zone of intermediate or heightened scrutiny. They could go either way, which was why both sides could predict victory in *United States v. Virginia.*

THIS IS NOT THE PLACE FOR a thorough exploration of Ginsburg's life as a litigator, the cases she handled, or her litigation tactics.[30] Similarly, it is unnecessary to go into greater detail here about the development of gender equality law, with all its twists and turns. Before returning to the VMI case, however, it is necessary to touch on two other sets of gender equality cases that were directly relevant to it. The first has to do with women and juries, one of the areas that helped define the new role of women as citizens; the second involves single-sex education, which was directly affected by the nation's first female Supreme Court justice.

In 1975 Ginsburg argued the Supreme Court case of *Edwards v. Healy,* challenging a Louisiana constitutional provision and statute that required women but not men to file written declarations of their desire to serve on juries. Louisiana mooted the case by changing its laws after oral argument.[31] The appellant in *Taylor v. Louisiana* had already been convicted by an all-male jury under the old law, however, so his case, argued by another lawyer, continued. The Court (with Justice Rehnquist in his usual posture of dissent) held that a person accused of a crime had a right to a jury drawn from a cross section of the community—women as well as men. It rejected what it considered the outmoded conclusion of *Hoyt v. Florida* that "women as a class serve a distinctive role in society and that jury service would so substantially interfere with that function that the State has ample justification for excluding women from service unless they volunteer, even though the result is that almost all jurors are men."[32]

The Louisiana law had required any woman who was willing to serve on a jury to "opt in." The state of Missouri reached the same result of excluding women from juries by permitting women, but not men, to opt out of jury duty simply by saying without explanation that they did not wish to serve. Ginsburg went back to the Supreme Court with *Duren v. Missouri,* the last case she argued there. Duren had been convicted of murder and robbery by an all-male jury, in spite of his assertion that he had a right to be tried by a jury chosen from a fair cross section of the community. While Ginsburg maintained that Duren's right to a trial by a jury of his peers was the major issue, and although defendants' rights were the basis for the Supreme Court's decisions in both *Taylor* and *Duren,* she wanted the Court to understand "the historic roots and contemporary impact of the vaunted 'women's privilege' . . . only a court wearing blinders could shut from sight the reality that 'statutes exempting women from jury service . . . reflect the historical male prejudice against female participation in activities outside the family circle.'"[33] The Missouri statute "reinforces the stereotype that government is not a woman's business."[34]

The Court struck the law down, with Rehnquist dissenting. His vote could have been predicted when he asked at the end of Ginsburg's argument in *Duren,* in which she was arguing against gender stereotyping, "So you won't settle for Susan B. Anthony's face on the new dollar?" Ginsburg thought of a rejoinder only afterward, when she was on her way home: "No, Mr. Justice. Tokens are not enough."[35]

As chapter 8 shows, any group of citizens excused from fulfilling the responsibilities of full citizenship, including voting and serving on juries and in the military, is in effect precluded from full citizenship itself. That was Ginsburg's concern. Rights and responsibilities are two sides of the same coin. In a sense, women were fighting for the right to be recognized as equally capable of fulfilling the responsibilities of citizenship. "Jury service is an obligation as well as a right," she believed, "and if women are full citizens, they have to be called for jury duty just like men."[36] Her strategy of leading the Supreme Court from case to case—not dragging it faster than it was prepared to go, but always pushing for a little bit more—was designed to reach the goal of equal citizenship.

Ginsburg did not control all the gender discrimination cases being appealed to the Court, however, and other attorneys brought pleas for which the Court was not ready.[37] Among those that Ginsburg would have postponed were cases dealing with single-sex education.

A few months before *Reed v. Reed* was handed down, the Supreme Court decided *Williams v. McNair,* in which male plaintiffs challenged the admissions policies of a publicly funded women's college in South Carolina. The lone all-male state college was The Citadel, which offered only a military-style education, and a number of young men living near all-female Winthrop College wanted a liberal arts education in a civilian environment. (There were six public coed institutions elsewhere in the state.) The federal district court in South Carolina upheld all-female admissions at Winthrop because the school, "designed as a school for young ladies . . . gave special attention to many courses thought to be specially helpful to female students." These included education, stenography, typewriting, telegraphy, bookkeeping, drawing, sewing, dressmaking, millinery, art, needlework, cooking, housekeeping, "and such other industrial arts as may be suitable to their sex and conducive to their support and usefulness."[38] The Supreme Court affirmed the ruling without a written opinion.[39]

Five years later, in 1976, the case of *Vorchheimer v. School District* was brought to the Court. Philadelphia's flagship Central High admitted only academically gifted boys, in contrast to the newer and less prestigious Girls High. (Surprisingly, the trial lawyers had put almost nothing in the record about the equally important fact that Girls High also had fewer resources.) An appeals court upheld the system, believing that otherwise, "all public single-sex schools would have to be abolished . . . [and] those students and parents who prefer an education in a public, single-sex school would be denied their freedom of choice."[40] The Supreme Court was divided four to four (Justice Rehnquist was away and did not hear the case) leaving the lower court's decision in effect.[41]

Ginsburg was involved in *Vorchheimer* only in the early stages of the appeal to the Supreme Court. Vorchheimer's lawyer first accepted her and the WRP's assistance and then rejected her suggestions, in spite of Ginsburg's having "struggled to accommodate" the other attorney. The result was what

Ginsburg considered a "rather poor" presentation, and although the Court listed both Ginsburg and Melvin Wulf as attorneys in the case, neither participated in writing the important reply brief that Vorchheimer's lawyer submitted.[42] Though disturbed by the outcome of the case, Ginsburg believed that it had been brought too soon: the Supreme Court was not yet at a point where it could understand that reserving institutions for men carried a tacit message of female inferiority.[43] "I knew, I knew that case was going to be a cliff-hanger."[44]

The Court had traveled a substantial distance by the time the next single-sex education case reached it in 1982. It also had its first woman justice.

SANDRA DAY O'CONNOR GRADUATED THIRD in her class from Stanford Law School, two places behind future chief justice William Rehnquist. She became active in Republican politics in Arizona, serving the state as an assistant attorney general, legislator, and appellate court judge. When President Ronald Reagan decided in 1981 to take the revolutionary step of appointing the nation's first female Supreme Court justice, she was a natural choice.

Although much of the Republican rhetoric in the 1980 presidential campaign was antifeminist—the party promised, for example, to undo *Roe v. Wade*'s declaration that women had a constitutional right to abortion—and Reagan's election itself was a reflection of that side's power in the culture wars, the drive for gender equality had made solid and probably irreversible gains. The cases Ginsburg won in the Supreme Court were both an indication of and an element in that development. As she was aware, "Judges do read the newspapers and are affected . . . by the climate of the era."[45]

That applies to politicians as well. A 1962 Gallup poll had found that most American women did not believe that women were discriminated against; in 1974 women who believed that gender inequality needed to be addressed outnumbered those who did not, by a ratio of two to one.[46] Women of child-bearing age accounted for the greatest increase in new employees, and female employment had become the rule rather than the exception. By the 1980s, women judges and lawyers, a politically active segment of the population, constituted 14 percent of those professions, compared with the 1971 figure of 4 percent. Women were earning almost a third of the nation's Ph.D.s and were being elected to legislative office.[47] It was the political moment to put a woman on the Supreme Court.

That did not prevent some of the media from concentrating less on O'-Connor's accomplishments and more on such burning questions as what she would wear as a Supreme Court justice. Would her judicial robes cover her ankles? When she was sworn in, Chief Justice Warren Burger's comment to photographers was, "You've never seen me with a better-looking Justice, have you?" The media said little about the content of the questions she asked during her first few oral arguments but made much of the fact that she looked "small but undaunted" in the courtroom and that she wore glasses. The Court got questions about where she exercised. The use of the traditional "brethren" to describe the justices led a speaker who introduced the new justice at the Washington Press Club to speculate that it should be altered to "eight brethren and a cistern."[48]

It was not particularly comfortable for O'Connor to be the first and only woman on the Court, which is one reason she would take care to smooth the path when Ginsburg joined her there.[49] It took others time to get used to her as well. Shortly after O'Connor took her seat, attorney Harry McCall was arguing before the Court. "I would like to remind you gentlemen" of a legal point, he said, leading O'Connor to ask, "Would you like to remind me, too?" A few moments later McCall addressed the Court as "Justice O'Connor and gentlemen." Justice Byron White interrupted, "Just Justices would be fine."[50]

The following year the justices decided *Mississippi University for Women v. Hogan,* with O'Connor writing the Court's opinion.[51] The decision was handed down one day after the extended deadline for ratification of the Equal Rights Amendment had expired, and it gave feminists some cause for celebration at that otherwise gloomy moment. Ginsburg would later comment that O'Connor's opinion, written at the end of her first term on the Court, "paved the way" for *United States v. Virginia.*[52] Both sides in the VMI litigation agreed that *Hogan* was controlling.

The Mississippi University for Women's School of Nursing denied admission to Joe Hogan because the university was reserved for women. The only other program available to Hogan was a considerable distance away. Mississippi argued that its motivation for keeping the nursing school single sex was to compensate women for past discrimination.[53]

That was hard to believe, O'Connor wrote. Far from being deprived of nursing opportunities, women dominated the field. The school's admissions policy only "perpetuate[d] the stereotyped view of nursing as an exclusively woman's job."[54] Mississippi also asserted that the presence of men would have a negative effect on the women students, which was precisely the claim VMI would make, in reverse. That argument was negated for O'Connor and the Court in *Hogan* by the fact that the nursing school permitted men to audit classes without receiving credit and allowed men and women to take continuing education classes together.[55] The admission of women to VMI's summer and evening courses would therefore be emphasized by the Justice Department in *United States v. Virginia.*

The most important part of *Hogan* for the VMI case was O'Connor's restatement of the standard to be used by the Court in deciding gender discrimination cases. "Our decisions also establish that the party seeking to uphold a statute that classifies individuals on the basis of their gender must carry the burden of showing an 'exceedingly persuasive justification' for the classification," she declared; thus, "exceedingly persuasive justification" would be the criterion in the VMI case. "The burden is met only by showing at least that the classification serves 'important governmental objectives and that the discriminatory means employed' are 'substantially related to the achievement of those objectives.'" O'Connor added another element to the criterion:

> The test for determining the validity of a gender-based classification . . . must be applied free of fixed notions concerning the roles and abilities of males and females. Care must be taken in ascertaining whether the statutory objective itself reflects archaic and stereotypic notions. Thus, if the statutory objective is to exclude or "protect" members of one gender because they are presumed to suffer from an inherent handicap or to be innately inferior, the objective itself is illegitimate.[56]

The standard articulated in *Hogan* was not new, drawing as it did on earlier Court decisions.[57] In fact, Ginsburg described the opinion as "vigorously recapitulating the main themes of the 1970s."[58] It was particularly important to *United States v. Virginia,* however, because it emphasized the illegitimacy of reliance on outmoded stereotypes in the context of single-sex education. Lower courts would have to ask whether a state's goal was important, whether the means chosen to reach it were directly related to the goal, and whether either the goal or the means reflected dated and constitutionally impermissible ideas about gender roles. The *Hogan* Court concluded that the nursing school's admissions policies were "not substantially related to an important objective" and that the justices therefore did not have to consider "whether classifications based upon gender are inherently suspect."[59]

In other words, the Court decided *Hogan* under the intermediate, or heightened, standard without reaching the question of whether strict scrutiny should be applied in gender equality cases. Ginsburg commented that the *Hogan* decision "indicated that designating sex a 'suspect' category remains an open question. If the Court continues to review categorization by gender as rigorously and incisively as it did in *Mississippi University for Women,* the 'suspect' seal may be placed on accumulated precedent in the 1980s."[60] By the time of the VMI case, however, the question of which standard to use was still alive.

There was one remaining issue in *Hogan.* When Congress passed the 1972 Education Amendments to the 1964 Civil Rights Act, prohibiting colleges from discriminating on the basis of sex, it specifically exempted "any public institution of undergraduate higher education which is an institution that traditionally and continually from its establishment has had a policy of admitting only students of one sex."[61] That was the case with the Mississippi University for Women and with VMI. The Court held that since Congress had no power to deny constitutional rights through legislation, the Education Amendments could not have been meant to permit gender discrimination.[62] The implication was that gender *separation* rather than discrimination must have been in the legislators' minds—although whether that was legitimate remained an undecided matter.

Chief Justice Burger and Justices Blackmun, Powell, and Rehnquist dissented. Powell, writing for himself and Rehnquist, chastised the Court for what he saw as its elimination of single-sex education, "an element of diversity that has characterized much of American education and enriched much of American life."[63] VMI would rely on his statement that diversity was a legitimate state goal and was in fact "the essence of our democratic system."[64] It would also pick up on his citation of Alexander Astin's *Four Critical Years,* which studied elite men's colleges in the 1970s and concluded that single-sex colleges had "a positive effect on intellectual self-esteem" and on student involvement in academics and interaction with faculty.[65] Exactly what that meant for VMI would become a matter of dispute.

BY THE END OF 1979, Ginsburg had participated in writing the main briefs for nine cases decided by the Supreme Court, argued six of those, participated in amicus briefs in another fifteen Supreme Court cases, worked on eleven major cases the Court chose not to take, and helped draft other memoranda and petitions. "Think of any Supreme Court decision on women's rights in the 1970s," Kenneth Karst has written, "and you can be sure that Ruth Bader Ginsburg was there."[66] Then, in December, she was invited to give up her career as an advocate.

In December 1979 President Jimmy Carter nominated Ginsburg for a seat on the federal Court of Appeals for the District of Columbia Circuit. She was certain that the nomination was an affirmative action one, reflecting Carter's interest in appointing officials who represented the full range of the nation's population.[67] "Affirmative action," of course, does not mean "unqualified." The American Bar Association gave Ginsburg its highest rating of "exceptionally well qualified," and she took the oath of office in June 1980. The solid reputation she earned on the D.C. Circuit as a "judge's judge" was illustrated by a vignette from 1993. When President Bill Clinton nominated her for the Supreme Court (Stephen Wiesenfeld was one of the people who testified at her confirmation hearings), conservative Senator Strom Thurmond, who had voted against her in 1980, beamingly presented her with his pocket Constitution.[68] In accepting the nomination, Ginsburg thanked "a revived women's movement in the 1970s that opened doors for people like me," as well as various family members. She particularly hoped, she said, referring to her mother, "that I may be all that she would have been had she lived in an age when women could aspire and achieve and daughters are cherished as much as sons."[69]

Ginsburg was confirmed by a vote of ninety-seven to three. An immediate order went out for installation of a women's bathroom to complement the one for men in the justices' robing room.[70] No such order had followed Sandra Day O'Connor's appointment to the Court. Either there were some who were unsure that women were on the Court to stay, or it took Ginsburg's presence to raise a degree of judicial consciousness.

O'Connor had been on the Court for twelve years when Ginsburg joined her in 1993, and O'Connor "welcomed me with joy because she had longed not to be the only woman" on the Court.[71] The first female justice, whom Ginsburg once referred to as "my savvy, sympatique colleague and counselor,"[72] "tipped me off to the ways of the brethren. . . . She told me a few things, not too many, so I wouldn't be confused, but just a few things she thought were important. She said when she came on this Court nobody told her anything." The result for Ginsburg was, "I feel like I have a big sister"[73]— something she had wanted since childhood, as her older sister had died tragically young.[74]

When the Supreme Court decides a case and the chief justice is in the majority, he chooses the justice who will write the opinion for the Court. Traditionally, the first time the chief justice assigns a majority opinion to a junior justice, it is an "easy" case—one in which both the relevant law and the application of it are relatively straightforward. Rehnquist did not extend that courtesy to Ginsburg; instead, he gave her *Hancock Mutual Life Insurance Co. v. Harris Trust & Savings Bank,*[75] a complicated pension and retirement fund dispute. "I was devastated. I was told that a new judge gets an easy case, one in which the Court was unanimous. This one wasn't easy and it wasn't unanimous. And I went to Sandra and I asked, 'What should I do?'"[76]

Ginsburg knew that O'Connor and Rehnquist had been friends from their days together at Stanford Law School. She thought that O'Connor "might go to him and say 'You shouldn't have given this to her' and ask him to let me switch with somebody else, to give me an easier case." Instead, O'Connor told her, "'Ruth, you just do it, you can do it, and you get out your opinion before he makes the next set of assignments because if you do that, he won't give you the worst one next time around.'"[77] Ginsburg, of course, just did it.

She was all the more grateful because she and O'Connor were not on the same side in that case; O'Connor was one of three dissenters. After Ginsburg announced the decision in the courtroom, however, O'Connor passed her a note complimenting her on the opinion.[78] "On very important questions we sometimes divide so sharply, and yet I feel that [in] anything that has to do with human relations on the Court," O'Connor would be helpful.[79]

One area of disagreement concerned affirmative action. Ginsburg believed that affirmative action, although occasionally misused, "has helped to realize the American dream—an ever widening concept of 'We, the People' . . . the idea of including people who were once left out is vital."[80] O'Connor had written the Court's 1989 opinion in *Richmond v. Croson,* using the strict scrutiny test to strike down the city of Richmond's race-conscious affirmative action plan and setting a high bar for all such plans in the future.[81] Just one year before *United States v. Virginia* reached the Supreme Court, O'Connor wrote again for the Court when it struck down a federal affirmative action plan. Ginsburg joined a dissent by Justice David Souter and added another of her own to emphasize that the government could take race and sex into account when it was "legitimate" to do so; that is, when a program had been adopted to remedy the effects of past invidious discrimination.[82]

Although adoption of the strict scrutiny standard for gender discrimination cases had been one of Ginsburg's goals as a litigator, O'Connor's opinions in the two racial affirmative action cases indicated that the standard could create difficulties for programs designed to compensate women for past discrimination. This would become an issue for women's groups and for Ginsburg in the VMI case. For the moment, however, Ginsburg continued to consider the standard desirable. When O'Connor wrote for a unanimous Court in a 1993 sexual harassment case (*Harris v. Forklift*), Ginsburg added a short concurrence emphasizing that "it remains an open question whether 'classifications based upon gender are inherently suspect.'"[83]

The following year Justice Harry Blackmun spoke for the Court when it decided *J.E.B. v. Alabama,* a jury selection case that would be cited in the VMI litigation.

> Today we reaffirm what, by now, should be axiomatic: Intentional discrimination on the basis of gender by state actors violates the Equal Protection Clause, particularly where, as here, the discrimination serves to ratify and perpetuate invidious, archaic, and overbroad stereotypes about the relative abilities of men and women.[84]

Blackmun declared that the standard since *Reed v. Reed* had been "heightened scrutiny" and "exceedingly persuasive justification," and although he referred to Ginsburg's comment in *Harris v. Forklift,* he said that there was no need to decide whether gender classifications merited strict scrutiny.[85] O'Connor's formulation in *Hogan* remained the rule.

Ginsburg would have liked to have written the opinion in the case,[86] and if she had, perhaps the standard used would have been different. But she was beginning to wonder whether the wording of the test mattered as much as it once had. "Do you think that the strict scrutiny issue is dead forever?" an interviewer asked her in 1995, before *United States v. Virginia* reached the Court.

> RBG: No. I think it's waiting for the right time and case.
> SW: Do you predict that it will be raised in a certain area?
> RBG: Education is a possibility. But "strict scrutiny" is no longer "fatal in fact" [i.e., the Court would allow some classifications to stand even after submitting them to strict scrutiny], and the intermediate standard has real bite. So the practical difference the label makes may not be large.[87]

GINSBURG WAS ENTIRELY AT ONE with O'Connor in wanting to make the Supreme Court more friendly to women, but that definitely did not imply that the women on the bench would decide one way and the men another; the different voting patterns of O'Connor and Ginsburg made that obvious. Between the time Ginsburg joined the Court and the beginning of 1996, when *United States v. Virginia* was argued, they had been on opposite sides in more than fifty cases.[88] "I don't think I vote one way rather than another because I'm a woman," Ginsburg ruminated, saying that she and

O'Connor agreed about that. Her litigating career, after all, had revolved around the elimination of discrimination based on stereotypes.

> What is a stereotype? It's an average. It is true for a large portion of the class you're describing . . . yes, differences [between the sexes] exist on average, but most of those difference should not determine what people do with their lives. . . . Do I think there's a difference? Yes. Do I think it matters for most occupations in life? No.[89]

She nonetheless thought that the presence of two women on the bench, in addition to the women lawyers who argued before the Court, was crucial. "I think it's very important that my colleagues are getting accustomed to hearing a woman's voice and listening to it," she commented.

> You know, one of the biggest problems that we all had—I'm sure you've had this—when you were at a meeting and you said something and then maybe half an hour later somebody [male] said the same thing you were saying and they all said, "Oh that's a good idea" and they all engage it, but you said it earlier. There's an automatic tuning out when a woman is speaking—they're really not listening because they're not expecting anything that would be worth listening to. I certainly have seen that change on this Court. When women are there on the bench, they [the male justices] are listening to women's voices in a way that they didn't before, and it extends to women advocates as well. Listening to women's voices I think is a major contribution.[90]

Both Ginsburg and O'Connor are "sensitive to barriers women encounter,"[91] and having women on the Court "certainly affects the atmosphere in large things and small. If you notice downstairs, you will no longer see a sign labeling the 'ladies' dining room,'" as it was still called when Ginsburg reached the Court. In 1995, a male visitor to the Court wanted to use the first-floor men's room before the morning session began and was shown to it by a guard. When his wife asked the way to the women's room, the guard told her that it was locked until nine o'clock. Disgruntled, the wife sent a letter about the incident to Ann Landers, who forwarded it to Ginsburg and O'-Connor. The women's room is now open at the same hours as the men's room.[92]

It took some people quite a while to adjust to the presence of two women justices. The Reverend Jesse Jackson mentioned Ginsburg's opinion in *Shaw v. Reno* in one of his syndicated columns, but the case had been decided in April 1993, before Ginsburg joined the Court; the opinion had actually been written by O'Connor. Jackson later sent Ginsburg an apology.[93] Others were equally confused.

I was reminded just last Term when our Acting Solicitor General three times called me Justice O'Connor, and the same slip was made by a distinguished advocate, Harvard Law School Professor Laurence Tribe. The National Association of Women Judges, anticipating that such confusion might occur, presented Justice O'Connor and me with T-shirts the month after my appointment. Hers reads: "I'm Sandra, not Ruth"; mine, "I'm Ruth, not Sandra."[94]

The cases Ginsburg had won in her ACLU days had changed American law dramatically.[95] As with any set of cases that engender and reflect major social change, however, the decisions left quite a lot undone. Ginsburg believed that the function of the Court was to carry on a dialogue with the other branches of government,[96] and that was what the Court had done since 1971. Its decisions had neither eliminated all gender discrimination from the law nor dislodged long-entrenched attitudes and stereotypes. The VMI case would make that very clear.

6

Birth of a Lawsuit

> If the student in question meets all other requirements for
>
> admission to VMI, I see no justification for the Institute to
>
> preclude her attendance simply because she is a woman.
>
> —Governor Gerald L. Baliles

The 1986 *Washington Post* article about VMI's decision to continue excluding women made Judith Keith angry. And, as a lawyer for the Justice Department's Civil Rights Division (CRD), she was in a position to do
something about it.

Keith had earned her bachelor's degree at Florida State University, worked
for seven years, and then returned to study law. Her first job as an attorney,
at the Environmental Protection Agency, led to her being invited to clerk for
federal judge Lawrence Margolis. She did so during Margolis's last year on
the District Court for the District of Columbia and then followed him to the
Court of Claims for another year of clerking. In 1983 Keith moved from the
judicial branch of the federal government to the CRD—and a job that would
bring her into a consuming conflict with VMI.

Her work at the Justice Department consisted primarily of race discrimination cases, which constituted the bulk of the CRD's work. One of her first
cases, however, involved gender discrimination and would affect her handling
of the VMI case. *United States v. Massachusetts Maritime Academy* involved
a state-funded quasi-military academy (like VMI) that was insistent on keeping women out.[1] *Massachusetts Maritime* even began the same way the VMI
case would: in 1974, a high school senior who wished to apply to the acad-

emy was told by its admissions director that women were not eligible, and she complained to the Department of Justice.

The Civil Rights Act of 1964 authorizes the Justice Department to bring suit on behalf of an individual alleging discrimination on the basis of race, religion, or sex if the individual is unable to bring the case alone and if the attorney general certifies the matter as one that is important to public policy.[2] The first step in the process is for a complainant to lodge a written protest with the Justice Department. The complaint goes to one of the CRD attorneys, who if he or she believes that the Justice Department ought to take the case, writes a justification memorandum explaining why.

If the justification memorandum is accepted by the assistant attorney general for the CRD, he or she issues the relevant certification and files a formal complaint. The Department then sends a letter to the person or organization accused of illegal discrimination, requesting information. If the Department finds the response unsatisfactory, it asks for remedial action. Finally, in the absence of acceptable remediation, the Department brings suit.

That is what happened in *Massachusetts Maritime*, as it would happen in the VMI case. Faced with a lawsuit, the academy's Board of Trustees voted in 1976 to admit women, but that did not mean that women were welcome. Federal courts found that even after the formal vote to admit women, the academy's recruitment materials continued to picture the school as all male. Its catalog still said that applicants had to be "male U.S. citizens." Physical examinations for male applicants were scheduled for weekends and holidays, but examinations for women were held only on workdays. Some men who did not fulfill the academy's math and science requirements or did not show up for the physical exam were accepted, but no women were treated that way. Not surprisingly, few women applied or enrolled. The Justice Department took the academy's post-1976 treatment of women to court.

When the case was argued, the academy claimed that its single-sex admissions policy furthered an important governmental interest, because its mission was to prepare students for combat in times of war or national emergency, and women were not permitted to serve in combat. VMI, too, would argue that excluding women furthered an important governmental interest. The district court that heard the case rejected the academy's position. Understandably skeptical of the school's good faith, the court ordered it to file extensive material with both the court and the Justice Department for the next three years. This included back application files and proposed new application materials, as well as statistics on the College Board scores of applicants, the timing and results of physical evaluations, recruitment efforts, and comparative admission and rejection rates.

The impact of *Massachusetts Maritime* on Keith, the CRD in general, and the community of women's organizations would be felt during and after the VMI case. The academy, adamantly opposed to gender integration, had brazenly flouted the law even after women had been formally admitted. The assumption of Keith and others was that VMI—equally opposed to gender integration—would do the same. That belief would drive the CRD's actions and help create an enormous chasm between the two sides before *United States v. Virginia* even reached the Supreme Court, and for some years thereafter.

Keith was fresh from *Massachusetts Maritime* in 1986 when she read the *Washington Post* article. She considered the VMI board's action to be a flagrant example of illegal gender discrimination. Eager to bring a case against the Institute, she asked civil liberties organizations whether they knew of any women who wanted to go to VMI and would be willing to file complaints with the Justice Department. They did not. Finally, in early 1989, exactly that kind of letter arrived on her desk.[3] The northern Virginia high school student who wrote it—her identity is still carefully guarded by the Justice Department[4]—had tried to apply to VMI and been told that the Institute did not accept applications from women.

On March 21, 1989, again acting under the 1964 Civil Rights Act, the Justice Department sent a letter of inquiry to VMI's acting superintendent, Major General John Williams Knapp (class of 1954). The inquiry went out over the name of James P. Turner, Acting Assistant Attorney General, Civil Rights Division, and was signed by D. Judith Keith, Trial Attorney, Educational Opportunities Litigation Section.[5]

> The United States Department of Justice has received a written complaint of discrimination from a female high school student who is interested in attending the Virginia Military Institute (VMI), but is unable to do so because VMI allegedly admits only males to its undergraduate four year degree program. Such a policy restricting admission to males only may constitute unlawful discrimination on the basis of sex in violation of Title IV of the Civil Rights Act of 1964 . . . as well as the Equal Protection Clause of [the] Fourteenth Amendment to the United States Constitution. ["No state shall . . . deny to any person within its jurisdiction the equal protection of the laws."]
>
> Pursuant to our statutory authority and responsibility under Title IV of the Civil Rights Act of 1964, we are conducting an investigation to determine whether VMI's policies and practices unlawfully deny admission on the basis of sex.

The letter asked VMI to inform the Department, within twenty days, whether the Institute's policy was to restrict admission to men and, if so, to give the justification for the policy. The Institute was also asked to forward a copy of the 1986 Mission Study report and to indicate whether it had received any applications from women.

The letter hit VMI, its Board of Visitors, and Virginia officials like a bombshell. Governor Gerald L. Baliles responded by holding a meeting with the Board of Visitors. What happened at it can be inferred from the letter he subsequently sent to the board. "Our meeting was cordial, but your comments left me with the impression that the members of the VMI Board and I do not share the same perspective," Baliles wrote.[6]

Their perspectives certainly differed, and Baliles's letter made his clear. "Virginia Military Institute has a proud and distinctive history," he acknowledged, but "history does not negate your responsibility to the present. The historic fact that VMI has never admitted a woman student, by itself, does not justify the continuance of that policy today. If the policy is to be maintained, other, more pertinent rationales must be deployed in the policy's defense." He had sought for such a "moral, legal, or educational rationale," Baliles said. "My search was unavailing."[7]

Baliles, a former state attorney general, cited not only the Constitution's equal protection clause but also the Virginia Constitution, which states that the "right to be free from any governmental discrimination upon the basis of religious conviction, race, color, sex or national origin shall not be abridged."[8] "If the student in question meets all other requirements for admission to VMI, I see no justification for the Institute to preclude her attendance simply because she is a woman," Baliles stated. He reminded the board that he was charged with appointing its members, implicitly threatening to make changes if the board remained recalcitrant.[9]

The board was unfazed. The VMI Foundation sought an opinion from former U.S. attorney general Griffin B. Bell, who thought the Institute could withstand a court challenge. It also turned to Virginia attorney general Mary Sue Terry, who promised to look into the legalities of the situation.[10]

Superintendent Knapp, who had been in his position for only four months, replied to Turner on April 28, 1989. Women had never been admitted to VMI, he noted, and he claimed that the Institute had received only two applications from women during the past twenty years and none in the past eleven. Although women were permitted in the summer school and evening college, neither was conducted as part of a military education.[11]

While the Justice Department digested Knapp's letter, the matter was roiling Virginia state politics. State senator Elmon T. Gray, chairman of the legislature's education committee, had been Terry's campaign treasurer since 1985. He was also a VMI alumnus and past president of the Board of Visitors and had helped lead a $150 million fund-raising drive for the Institute.[12] Baliles, Gray, Secretary of Education Donald Finley, and Joseph Spivey—a VMI alumnus who had served on the 1986 Mission Study Committee and was now president of the Board of Visitors—conferred at the state capitol in early May. When the men emerged, Spivey told the press that Baliles and Terry should concentrate on fulfilling their "obligation" to defend VMI rather than "pressuring the Institute to abandon its traditions under federal duress." He released a letter to Baliles saying that Terry's office was prepared to defend the school and that it would consult with the VMI board if the Justice Department decided that the admissions policy was unconstitutional.[13]

The state legislature also weighed in—or, at least, one of its members did. Emilie F. Miller had been elected to the senate in 1987 as a representative from Fairfax. During her campaign, a number of women had pointed out to her that VMI was closed to women and that there was no equivalent tax-supported institution for women in the state. She did some research in 1988 and discovered that while a section of the Virginia Constitution forbids invidious discrimination, the Virginia Code used the word "men" when referring to the fifty "state cadets" whose education at VMI would be subsidized by the state. Miller asked Terry's office for a formal opinion about whether the provision constituted illegal sex discrimination. A staffer, knowing that the attorney general would be running for office again, replied by asking Miller, "Do you want to see Mary Sue Terry defeated?" She did not, and Terry's office took the matter no further. Miller then asked the chair of the senate's finance committee if the senate could eliminate the gender disparity by creating fifty scholarships for women at a state-supported college. That effort went nowhere. Finally, she raised the issue with Baliles, who said that he would see what he could do, and Miller assumed that she could leave it in his hands.[14]

Once General Knapp had replied to the Justice Department and Miller realized that the commonwealth was about to leap to VMI's defense, she sat down and wrote a speech to the senate, saying in part, "Privately I have spoken to some of you. Some of you have said it's a woman's issue and I would be cast as a feminist if I speak out. Well—I am a woman and I care about what affects us. . . . So, before the U.S. Department of Justice speaks out and tells Virginia what to do, I would like to." She suggested that the state either stop funding VMI or require it to admit women. If the Justice Department or the courts had not settled the matter by January 1990, she promised, "I will be back with legislation." Aware of VMI's political power, she kept the speech as quiet as possible until she delivered it on August 27. It seems to have persuaded no one and certainly contributed to the demise of her legislative career.[15]

By the fall of 1989, it was clear that one of the candidates for governor would be Republican former state attorney general Marshall Coleman, who called VMI "a special institution" and criticized Baliles's position.[16] The VMI controversy had become a political hot potato.

All this was observed with bemusement by Gordon Davies, head of the Council of Higher Education, which coordinated the activities of Virginia's largely autonomous institutions. He had worked for the council since 1973 and become its director in 1977, and he considered it the best such council in the United States.[17]

He did not, however, consider VMI the best of institutions. As far as he was concerned, the adversative system merely created bellicosity and a tendency toward social violence. Once it became clear that the VMI situation was going to result in expensive litigation, he hoped that Virginia would just give up its single-sex policy at VMI and devote its limited resources to improving education for the almost 300,000 other students in the state's colleges and universities.[18]

But he knew that that was not going to happen—for two reasons. One was the story of the VMI cadets at New Market, which Davies knew held a place in the Virginia mind that was incomprehensible to many outsiders. The second was the enormous power of VMI alumni in both the corporate and the legal life of the commonwealth.[19]

The *Washington Post* noted that the 6,000 VMI alumni in Virginia held a "disproportionately large number of influential positions" in the state, including two congressmen, two state senators, the former speaker of the House of Delegates, the managing partners of the state's two biggest law firms, and numerous industrialists and investors. They were, a University of Virginia political scientist noted, "influential, fiercely loyal to their institution," and able to write large checks in political campaigns.[20] They were equally opposed to change at VMI. As one alumnus commented, "Most of us didn't like it while we were there. But most of us don't want it altered."[21] The former VMI cadets had paid painfully for their initiation into manhood. Many would continue to resist any alteration in the process, as change would imply a questioning of the program's legitimacy or necessity. A member of the class of 1970 told a journalist that the VMI ethos was "heavily ingrained in male bonding and all the things the feminists of our society are against."[22]

The alumni demonstrated their clout when the Survey Research Laboratory of Virginia Commonwealth University (VCU) released the results of a poll showing that Virginians believed, by a 57 to 34 percent majority, that VMI should admit women.[23] Professor Scott Keeter, a widely respected political scientist known nationally for his survey analyses, was the laboratory's director. The Richmond law firm that represented the VMI Foundation (and that was headed by a VMI alumnus) spearheaded an attack on the survey by getting two other political scientists—one at the University of Virginia and one at the University of Richmond—to state that the poll was biased.[24] The *Richmond Times-Dispatch* quoted them at length in an editorial urging VMI to "strike back." It should do so, the newspaper said, first by "demand[ing] parity with VCU in taxpayer support for a biased public opinion polling operation" and then by conducting its own survey designed to elicit criticism of VCU's expansion into local neighborhoods.[25]

Apparently overwhelmed by the alumni's political clout, Baliles backed off and reappointed the Board of Visitors members whose terms were expiring. But the unhappiest reaction to alumni power and VMI's hold on the emotions of many Virginians came from the Democratic gubernatorial nominee, Lieutenant Governor L. Douglas Wilder. Wilder had been kept out of Virginia's law schools in the 1950s because he was black. For the moment, however, he declined all comment other than that the courts would have to decide. Wilder, who reportedly had dreams of running for national office after his hoped-for governorship, found himself in the midst of an electoral nightmare. He could not afford to fight the political power of VMI, but at the same time, he could not risk alienating the women voters whom he considered his natural allies. He would vacillate wildly in the next months.[26]

Some Virginia political activists wondered whether Wilder's aspirations were not partially responsible for the case. The administration of President George Bush, in office when the VMI case began, was so little known for its concern about gender equality that Bush's 1992 reelection effort would founder in part on the gender gap. One question raised by the VMI case was why the Bush administration permitted it to be brought at all, given the power of VMI alumni in Virginia politics and Bush's need for Virginia's electoral votes in 1992. Richard Thornburgh, Bush's attorney general, later said that the president had not been consulted and that there had been no politics involved in the decision to take the case.[27]

Even if the president had not been consulted, that did not necessarily mean that no member of his immediate staff had been consulted. There was also speculation in Virginia about the impact of a well-known and particularly bitter feud between Wilder and Senator Charles Robb, who was close to the administration. A case that required Wilder to take either a pro-VMI (and therefore anti–gender equality) stance or an anti-VMI stance that would alienate VMI alumni might prove highly detrimental to his career—as indeed proved to be the case.

Wilder's was not the only politically motivated stance. Mary Sue Terry had been one of the few women in her class at the University of Virginia Law School. After serving in the state legislature, she ran successfully for attorney general, becoming the first woman elected to statewide office in Virginia. In 1989 Terry, one of only two female state attorney generals in the nation, was up for reelection and was well aware of the influence of VMI alumni. After all, she depended on one of them for her campaign chest.[28] As columnist James Kilpatrick noted, "Terry's problem is to respond to the suit, mollify the women's vote, pacify the alumni and uphold the Constitution without actually appearing to do so. And she must do all these things at the same time."[29]

And Terry was not aiming merely at reelection. Both she and Wilder had wanted to run for governor in 1989. She had spared the Democratic Party a nasty primary by deferring to him. As the Virginia governor is limited to one term, she could expect the party to repay its debt to her by nominating her for governor in 1993. The support of both women and the VMI alumni would be important then.

In November Wilder was elected governor by a margin of 0.38 percent of the vote—the smallest margin in the history of the state. Terry was returned to the attorney general's office.

Emilie Miller sent Terry a letter asking once again for a formal opinion about admitting women to VMI, this time citing a 1973 Virginia court decision holding that the state constitution's antidiscrimination clause prohibited invidious, arbitrary discrimination on the basis of sex.[30] A reply from Terry's office in January 1990 said that it was the policy of the attorney general's office not to render opinions on matters in litigation, and the Justice Department currently had this one under "administrative investigation."[31] Miller next spoke with Nathaniel Douglas, Judith Keith's boss at the Justice Department's Educational Opportunities Section. Distressed at what she considered his lack of enthusiasm, Miller sent him a formal request for information about the status of the complaint.[32]

Then she dropped a bombshell of her own. On January 23, five minutes before the deadline for filing bills in the 1990 session of the General Assembly, Miller introduced SB 477, which would have amended the Virginia Code to say, "All public institutions of higher education shall admit qualified students without regard to race, sex, religion, national origin, or political affiliation." Superintendent Knapp was in her office early the next morning declaring that VMI would "fight to the death" against admitting women.[33]

On January 31 Governor Wilder and VMI received another letter from the Justice Department. The letter, again signed by Turner, went to Wilder as governor of the state and to Spivey as president of the Board of Visitors.

> I am writing to inform you that we have determined that the policy of limiting admission to the four year undergraduate program at VMI to males only, and of refusing to consider qualified females for admission to this program violates Title IV of the Civil Rights Act of 1964 . . . and the Fourteenth Amendment to the Constitution of the United States. . . . We, of course, would like to resolve this important matter amicably.

It therefore requested that the Department be notified by February 20 of the commonwealth's willingness to change the policy and to adopt a remedial program that would include "appropriate recruitment activities." In the absence of an appropriate response, the Department would bring suit in federal court.[34]

VMI did not wait for February 20. On February 5 the Board of Visitors held a closed meeting in Richmond, and less than an hour later, Mary Sue Terry and the VMI Foundation each filed suit in federal district court in Roanoke "to prevent federal encroachment seeking to enforce unnecessary conformity in the state supported system of higher education in Virginia" and asking that VMI's admissions policy be declared constitutional.[35] The Institute had decided that it, rather than the Justice Department, would choose the battleground and fire the first salvo of the litigation war.

Countersuit

Forces are at work to misconstrue the rationale of our

current policy and to confuse the public by labeling VMI as

an "anachronism."

—VMI Superintendent John W. Knapp

While Sandra Day O'Connor and Ruth Bader Ginsburg were working in Washington to make the Supreme Court a bit more woman-friendly, some members of the next generation of women lawyers were battling in Virginia to keep their professional careers alive.

When she filed suit against the Justice Department, Mary Sue Terry said that she did so "at the behest of" the Board of Visitors, a governmental entity that she, as attorney general, had the responsibility to represent. The statement made it seem as if she had no choice in the matter. Local media, however, focused on her reported concern about the alumni's electoral power, and the timing and location of her suit seemed to bear that out.[1]

Federal law would have permitted the Justice Department's attorneys to sue in any federal court in Virginia. They were planning to do so in the state capital of Richmond, where they thought the case might be assigned to a sympathetic or at least a neutral judge. But VMI's lawyers assumed that the suit would be brought in Alexandria, right across the river from Washington. Based on the records of the judges there, VMI's attorneys thought that they would have a better chance in Roanoke, which was just down the highway from Lexington.[2]

Both the Department and the VMI attorneys were correct in thinking that geography might affect substance. Federal district court judges are appointed to courts in the areas where they live, and they frequently mirror the attitudes of the other residents. Bringing suit in Roanoke was a preemptive strike worthy of the military training VMI gave its students—and indeed, a VMI alumnus would head its legal team. The Institute's lawyers must have smiled as they faxed word of their action to the Justice Department, which was taken completely by surprise.

The two suits, which named the Justice Department and Attorney General Thornburgh as defendants, stated that VMI was part of a "richly diverse" system of higher education. The suits dismissed the charge of gender discrimination by claiming that sex segregation had been eliminated from Virginia's system of higher education as a whole, thereby rendering gender integration at a specific institution such as VMI unnecessary. Under the coordinating aegis of the Council of Higher Education, the state's public and private schools provided "a balance of educational choices." Among them were "high-quality, single-gender educational programs" at other institutions of higher education, including the ROTC program and military lifestyle offered at Virginia Polytechnic Institute and State University.[3]

The VMI Foundation had already raised more than $100,000 for its legal effort, and it would spend an estimated $6 million before the case ended. It added Griffin Bell to its legal team, but VMI chose Robert H. Patterson, Jr., as the lawyer who would carry the case. Patterson, VMI class of 1949, was a senior partner at Richmond-based McGuire, Woods, Battle & Boothe, one of the state's most powerful law firms.

Like fellow alumnus Elmon Gray, Patterson—a tall, white-maned, distinguished-looking man in his seventies—was one of VMI's most successful fund-raisers. He was described by the *Washington Post* as a "barrel-chested, vodka-drinking, chain-smoking big-game hunter, with an expletive-spiked vocabulary."[4] The walls of his opulent office were lined with pictures of his hunting exploits and of Patterson with political figures such as President Ronald Reagan. He had grown up in a working-class Richmond household and frequently spoke gratefully of VMI as a place where wealth was unimportant. Patterson and VMI did not bond immediately when he was a student there, however; in fact, he was thrown out of the Institute for being a troublemaker. (One of the few things Patterson and the aristocratic Bunting seemed to have in common was their rather rambunctious adolescent histories.) The school took him back after he had served with the navy in World War II and appealed directly to the governor for readmission. He validated its decision by going on to law school at the University of Virginia and doing so well there that he be-

came editor of the *Law Review* and, later, president of the Virginia bar for
one term.

Patterson's service as president first of the VMI Alumni Association and
then of its Board of Visitors was perhaps more important to him than his pres-
idency of the state bar association. He was passionately attached to the school
that he credited with turning him into a man and starting him on the road
to social status. "I feel very strongly about this case," he would say in one of
his rare understatements.[5] He believed that VMI was unlike any other institution in the world, and for him, keeping VMI as it had always been became
a crusade. His emphasis on VMI's uniqueness, however, put him on a colli-
sion course with Mary Sue Terry.

Terry's argument would rest on the assertion that VMI was only one element in a system of diverse educational institutions and that nothing about
it was so unique that Virginia women were being deprived of an equal educational opportunity. Supreme Court decisions had held that treating women
differently was justifiable if doing so served an important governmental interest. Terry's formulation was that "VMI's academic mission contributes to
the diversity and balance of Virginia higher education, thereby serving the important governmental interest of the Commonwealth in offering its citizens
a wide diversity of educational choices."[6] Patterson, however, speaking for the
VMI Foundation, was insistent that VMI *was* unique and that the mainte-
nance of its uniqueness was entirely legal. Terry viewed his argument as destructive of hers and "fundamentally incompatible" with it. Although she was
correct as a matter of legal logic, the *Richmond Times-Dispatch* wondered
whether her public complaints might not be a prelude to her withdrawing
from a stance that would inevitably alienate black and female voters.[7]

Another female political figure was faring no better. On February 8, the
last day that the Virginia senate's Education and Health Committee would
meet in that legislative session, Emilie Miller summoned reporters to sit in
as she asked chairman Elmon Gray to have the committee consider her bill.
Gray promptly ruled Miller's request out of order on the grounds of pending
litigation, and a majority of the committee voted to sustain his ruling. That,
in turn, generated calls to Miller's office from *ABC Evening News, Nightline,
Inside Edition,* and what she described as "every major newspaper in the
United States."[8]

Miller's stance was supported in a letter that the Virginia Women Attorneys Association sent to members of the legislature—a letter that picked up
on the lawyers' different approaches. "The Institute coalition in favor of VMI's

all-male policy argues that VMI adds to the Commonwealth's educational diversity by providing a college education and a distinctive military discipline in an all-male environment and that this is unique in the state," the letter noted. "Yet it also argues that this 'unique' educational opportunity is available to women at other schools in the Commonwealth. Such circular reasoning belies its own inherent inconsistency—as VMI is the only all-military institute in the Commonwealth, it is the only place where a student, male or female, may receive an all-military education."[9]

By this time, the Virginia newspapers were headlining the VMI case every day, and it had become a common topic of heated conversation across the state. It had also become a national concern, as exemplified by the New York–based media's beating a path to Miller's door. She appeared on the CBS Morning News. The Virginia Federation of Business and Professional Women passed a resolution of support for her,[10] and the Equal Rights Amendment Ratification Council held a silent vigil outside the senate chamber, carrying signs such as "VMI is a dinosaur" and "Virginia has many long traditions, including sex discrimination." Lieutenant Governor Donald S. Beyer, Jr., who was expected to oppose Mary Sue Terry for the 1993 Democratic gubernatorial nomination, attended the council's news conference.[11] The Wall Street Journal quoted Kathryn Gravatt, president of the Virginia Division of the American Association of University Women, as saying, "We don't want tax dollars spent to defend a non-winnable case on behalf of a discriminatory institution."[12] Judith Lichtman of the Washington-based Women's Legal Defense Fund addressed the question of whether male bonding would be irretrievably destroyed if VMI had to give up its stall-less bathrooms: "In your own home, you are one family," she told the press, "but you close the door when you go into the bathroom."[13]

Sylvia Clute was among the attorneys active in the fray. One of two partners in a small Richmond law firm, Clute was also the mother of a young woman who was a medic in an army reserve unit. Within a few months, Clute's daughter would be shipped to Saudi Arabia to participate in Operation Desert Storm.[14] Now, in February 1990, Clute and several dozen women who called themselves Concerned Women of Virginia rallied on the capitol grounds and released copies of a letter to Governor Wilder that referred to "the indignity which we suffer from the statement of women's inequality which VMI makes to the world." It noted pointedly, "It is no different than the indignity you felt when the University of Virginia denied you admission because you were black."[15]

Defenders of VMI held rallies of their own, and theirs were bigger. Phyllis Schlafly, president of the Eagle Forum and right-wing gadfly, wrote a column entitled "Leave the Military Colleges Alone" for *USA Today*.[16] The *St. Louis Post-Dispatch* interviewed some of the sixty VMI alumni from Missouri. It also talked with Josiah Bunting at Lawrenceville, eliciting the comment, "The worst thing that could happen would be if the institute would be ordered to become co-ed, made a bona fide effort to recruit and wound up with only 50 young women. . . . This Barracks, this communitarian life, this intellectual Spartan life would be changed into we don't know what."[17]

VMI quickly demonstrated that it knew how to deploy its forces in the media as well as in the courtroom. It opened its gates to reporters and had them escorted around the post by cadets. At least one of the journalists got a taste of how the students felt about the case. A woman reporter, given rare permission to accompany men into the Barracks, was hooted by cadets, one of whom deliberately strolled around naked to the cheers of his fellow students. The editor of the VMI student newspaper told media representatives that the cadets were almost unanimously opposed to the admission of women and found himself being quoted around the country. CBS News was there for the tour, as were NBC News, the *Wall Street Journal*, and the *Washington Post*. The list went on and even included the Winnipeg, Canada, *Free Press*.[18]

Back on the legal front, Terry named deputy attorney general R. Claire Guthrie to lead Virginia's defense of VMI. Guthrie, the daughter of a four-star general who had attended West Point, had been a founding member of Virginia Law Women while a student at the University of Virginia Law School and had worked briefly for the Civil Rights Division of the U.S. Department of Health, Education, and Welfare.[19] She did not indicate whether she personally favored keeping women out of VMI or whether she was simply doing her job. Anne Marie Whittemore was more forthcoming.

Whittemore had gone first to an all-girls high school, then to Vassar when it was still a women's college (she graduated summa cum laude), and finally to Yale Law School, where she was class of 1970. By the time *United States v. Virginia*[20] began, Vassar had become coed, and Whittemore considered that a mistake. It was, she believed, a move dictated by the marketplace rather than sound pedagogy. She thought that Vassar had deteriorated into mediocrity because it no longer acknowledged that women learn differently from men. To Whittemore, that was a simple statement of reality, not an insult. "The cutting edge of feminist theory recognizes that," the coolly elegant blonde told a reporter. Women mature faster; women prefer to work as teams. She had seen the difference in learning styles at single-sex Vassar and at coed Yale Law School. The emphasis of educators had to be "not on equal treatment but on equitable treatment."[21]

After Yale, Whittemore clerked for Judge Albert Bryan, Sr., at the federal court of appeals in Richmond and then applied for a job at Robert Patterson's law firm. Patterson, the firm's managing partner, was adamantly opposed. A woman was likely to get pregnant during a big case, he told his partners, but he was overruled.[22] By 1990, Whittemore was a partner herself and on the board of the Federal Reserve Bank of Richmond. She had served the American Bar Association and the Virginia State Bar Association and Law Foundation in a number of capacities and had been mentioned as a possible candidate for a federal judgeship. And, as befitted someone named to Patterson's VMI legal team, she was a fervent defender of VMI.

Whittemore was afraid of the effects of coeducation on the men at VMI, who now benefited from its rigidly disciplined, all-male environment. VMI, she thought, was particularly valuable "for late adolescent males trying to work out an inherent sense of aggression." One example of its success was the high graduation rate of African American men who attended the Institute. The twenty-four-hour adversative method that worked so well for them and other cadets, she feared, would be a victim of coeducation, and she was determined to prevent that.[23]

The Justice Department's Civil Rights Division was equally determined to bring coeducation to VMI. On March 1, 1990, it filed its own suit in Roanoke. In it, the Department accused the commonwealth of Virginia; the governor of Virginia; VMI, its superintendent, and Board of Visitors; and the State Council of Higher Education, its members, and director of violating Title IV of the Civil Rights Act of 1964 and the equal protection clause of the Fourteenth Amendment. It asked the court to issue a permanent injunction prohibiting the defendants from discriminating on the basis of gender in the operation of VMI. The cases were assigned to Judge Jackson L. Kiser, appointed to the federal bench by President Ronald Reagan in 1982. Kiser had held against a sex discrimination complaint brought by a Virginia woman in 1983, but the Fourth Circuit Court of Appeals had overturned Kiser's ruling and sent it back to him on remand. The appeals court would do so two more times as the judge insistently refused to follow gender discrimination law.[24] It was also Kiser who would later strike down a major provision of the federal Violence Against Women Act.[25]

By the time the VMI case went to trial, the Council of Higher Education, its members, and executive director Gordon K. Davies would be dismissed as defendants by the court. Ironically, as indicated in chapter 6, Davies believed that women should be admitted to VMI, and he was prepared to express that opinion if VMI subpoenaed his testimony. He was, in fact, rather surprised that the Justice Department did not call him as a witness for its side, as the council was empowered with the task of articulating goals for the state's system of higher education. Whether "diversity" was one of those goals became a major bone of contention at trial. Apparently, the Justice Department was unaware of Davies's views.[26]

Governor Wilder, still carefully keeping his feelings about VMI to himself, was understandably less than delighted at being named a defendant in the case. He quickly filed a petition asking to be excused from it, claiming that he had no control over the VMI Board of Visitors.

Wilder had been asked to speak at VMI's 1990 graduation ceremony long before the Justice Department sued. In the remarks he delivered there on May 19, he declined to take a stand. "Let me put it simply," he said instead. "VMI has been too good for too long for me to intervene now. I am prepared to have the Department of Justice make its case, for VMI to defend its position . . . and for the courts to rule."[27] Two days later, he retained former U.S. attorney general Benjamin R. Civiletti to represent him; Civiletti had volunteered his services. The Justice Department, replying to Wilder's claim that he did not control VMI policy, retorted that one of his jobs was to appoint VMI's governing body; certainly, that made him partially responsible for the policies it adopted. Further, he had just reappointed four members who were opposed to gender integration. In addition, he had the power to veto any appropriations bill that included the state's share of VMI's budget.[28]

While the matter of Wilder's participation in the suit was before Judge Kiser, General Knapp, who had been serving as VMI's acting superintendent, was installed as the Institute's twelfth superintendent. VMI's preference for administrators and faculty who are VMI graduates is among the many indications of the Institute's belief that those who make it through the rat line are an elite group. There were non-VMI graduates at Knapp's installation ceremony, of course. One of them was state senator Emilie Miller. She went on the tour of the post offered to the other guests but, as a woman, was not permitted inside the Barracks.[29]

Earlier, Knapp had sent a letter to VMI's 11,000 alumni, laying out the Institute's strategy and emphasizing its intention to fight to the end:

> The Department of Justice's lawsuit is not merely an attack on VMI. It is a federal attack on Virginia's system of higher education . . . even if our admissions policy is determined by the courts to be legal and constitutional, that does not mean that it is understood by everyone and that victory in the judicial forum will end efforts in Congress, in the Defense Department, or in the General Assembly to force VMI to change. Forces are at work to misconstrue the rationale of our current policy and to confuse the public by labeling VMI as an "anachronism."

The letter counseled alumni to leave the public relations war to the professionals: they should refrain from "speak[ing] out," although "of course, you cannot be mindlessly silent with your friends, neighbors and colleagues."[30]

As is the usual procedure in such cases, the Justice Department filed a motion with Judge Kiser for summary judgment, meaning that it asked for a decision in its favor without a trial. "The aim of 'diversity' claimed by Defendants is not an 'important state interest' sufficient to pass constitutional muster," its papers said. "It is quite clear that Defendants are offering educational diversity, not to *all* the citizens of the Commonwealth, but to males only."[31] For its part, VMI claimed that its admissions policy was permitted under Title IX of the 1972 Education Amendments to the Civil Rights Act. That law amended the act's prohibition of gender discrimination by permitting institutions of higher education that "traditionally and continually from . . . establishment . . . had a policy of admitting only students of one sex" to continue their policy.[32] The Justice Department replied that a congressional statute could not undo the guarantees of the equal protection clause.

The two claims delineated the great difference in the two sides' perceptions of the issue. To the Justice Department, the case was a simple one about unequal treatment of men and women. Virginia used taxpayers' money to offer a military education in an adversarial system to its male citizens; it gave its women citizens no such opportunity. To Judith Keith, the point of the case was to "insure that women had the same right of access to what VMI offers as men." It was all about not spending public money to discriminate in education and in access to a vast and influential alumni network.[33]

VMI did not consider that the issue at all. In its view, the case was about the legitimacy of single-sex education. Robert Patterson and Anne Marie Whittemore saw it as asking "whether or not you can have single-sex education—public education—and we knew if we could not prevail with VMI that no school could prevail."[34] VMI's commandant of cadets Colonel Norman Bissell agreed; the case concerned "single-sex education: is there a value to it, when considered against the trade-off?"[35] If the equal protection clause was used to strike down VMI's admissions policy, no single-sex educational institution in the country would be safe.

The Institute would maintain throughout the case that single-sex education is beneficial for some students, particularly adolescents. As Bunting acknowledged, there had been little research about all-male schools. One of the few studies was Alexander Astin's 1978 examination of all-male colleges,[36] and VMI would rely heavily on it, as subsequent chapters show. The Institute would also cite research indicating that young women in single-sex schools did particularly well academically, had higher self-esteem than their peers in coeducational classes, and showed greater willingness to enter traditionally male professions.[37] Critics of these studies claimed that the results were skewed by the fact that the institutions under examination drew their students from elite sectors of the population or had smaller classes and greater resources than most schools, or both.[38] A widely quoted American Association of University Women (AAUW) report charged that coeducational public schools were shortchanging girls, particularly in math and science.[39] (Another AAUW report, published two years after the litigation ended, declared that single-sex schooling was not the answer.)[40] In fact, the evidence about the effects of single-sex education was mixed—which was the conclusion of a two-volume report prepared for the U.S. Department of Education that was published during the litigation.[41] In any event, that was never the real issue for the government, given its focus on the inequality it saw in Virginia's providing a single-sex military education for men but not for women.

VMI had always been all male, and VMI believed that it had to stay that way. When the Institute invoked single-sex education, it was thinking specifically of itself rather than about single-sex education in the abstract; that is, it assumed that single-sex education for young men worked well, based on the fact that there were only men at VMI and VMI was successful at what it did. And the Institute had indeed worked extraordinarily well for generations. It had taken relatively mediocre young male students—including, in its earlier days, students who were extremely troublesome—and turned them into citizens who were at least responsible and in many cases prominent. To many Virginians, as to VMI alumni, the Institute was a 150-year-old success story, and they cared about it deeply.

VMI eventually acknowledged, grudgingly, that there were some women who could make it at VMI. Its argument paralleled Bunting's view that because not many women would be interested in doing so, women would become a permanent tiny minority that could not be fully integrated into the study body. The Institute and its allies rejected the analogy of race. Bunting, for example, would say that there had never been a justification for separating the races in schools, because the presence of African Americans would not interfere with the education of whites, or vice versa. For some young men, however, having to deal with both adolescent hormones and the learning process was too much. They learned better away from women.[42]

The question, of course, was *what* they learned better. Might they be mastering physics and engineering but sacrificing knowledge of and familiarity with members of their society that would be vital in a coeducational professional world? Might VMI's supposition that the presence of women would end cohesiveness be based on the assumption that men and women could not form real communities together? Nothing had been more central to the South than racism, expressed first in slavery and then in segregation. But when VMI was forced to admit African American students, it integrated them well—not without stumbling along the way, but with the kind of eventual success that resulted in the ability of white VMI cadets to understand why African American cadets should not be required to salute the Confederate flag or sing "Dixie." There was no question, when *United States v. Virginia* was litigated, that African Americans would constitute a small minority of cadets for the foreseeable future—just as women would, if VMI opened its doors to them. Yet VMI could not imagine that it might assimilate women as well.

The Justice Department, with a history of litigating against racial segregation, viewed the matter as a similar one of simple fairness in the allocation of public resources. Virginia provided a military education for men but not for women; women could not be deprived of a public benefit for no better reason than that they were women. VMI's defenders, certain that VMI had worked as well for others as for themselves, did not concede that perhaps there was some merit in *that* claim. And, as with racism, the Department considered the Institute's objections to be, at best, a legally unacceptable form of ignorance or, at worst, a poor excuse for animus against women. As the presidents of many women's colleges would demonstrate by refusing to take VMI's side in the case, the possible benefit of single-sex education was not the issue—but it was the heart of the matter as VMI saw it.

One of the few people to look beyond his own position was Michael Maurer, a young lawyer from New Jersey who became Judith Keith's colleague not long before *United States v. Virginia* went to trial. Formally, Maurer said, the case was about Virginia excluding women from a public benefit, thereby violating the Fourteenth Amendment's equal protection clause, as well as basic fairness. But what really lay underneath VMI's passionate opposition to admitting women, he believed, was something else. A way of life and an entire value system were at stake. "VMI is very much a bastion of old Virginia tradition. I don't think people like me fully appreciated what it means to wear a VMI ring." The case was about male bonding over the generations; about the family tradition of going to VMI and enduring the rat line. "They take it as a given that that's the way it's supposed to be. They have the notion that you cannot change tradition, and people stop asking why. The more I got involved in it, the more I got to understand."[43]

THE FIRST HEARING IN THE CASE took place on June 4, 1990. For an hour and twenty minutes, the lawyers battled over who would and would not be parties to it. VMI wanted Wilder removed as a defendant and argued that there was not even a real case because there was no bona fide complaint from a real person. The Justice Department insisted that, as independent entities, the well-financed VMI Foundation and VMI Alumni Association had no standing in the case and therefore should not be permitted to join it as defendants. In a sixteen-page opinion issued on November 2, Judge Kiser dismissed VMI's lawsuit against the Justice Department but allowed the VMI Foundation and VMI Alumni Association to participate in defending against the Justice Department's action. He went on to rule that Wilder clearly had the power over VMI policy attributed to him by the Justice Department and therefore would play a key role if any remedial plan had to be implemented. The governor was not going to be permitted to wiggle off the political hook quite so easily.[44]

Wilder filed his answer to the suit on November 16 and, four days later, finally spoke out in a manner designed to maximize political gain and minimize legal liability. Saying that Kiser's decision to keep him in the case impelled him to take a stand on the matter, Wilder called a press conference to announce, "I believe that no person should be denied admittance to a school supported by state funds solely because of his or her race or gender."[45] Lieutenant Governor Beyer added that he, too, favored gender integration at VMI and had not said so earlier "out of courtesy for the governor."[46]

The officials' announcements were wise political maneuvers, but they cut no ice at VMI. Regimental commander Fredrich Lehman clearly spoke for the overwhelming majority of his fellow cadets when he planted himself in front of the Jackson Arch and announced to reporters, "We feel that women are not equals. We espouse the attributes of being a gentleman. When the governor comes forth and states politically that women should be allowed into VMI, we take the other side."[47] Engaging in a bit of political correctness himself, he hastily added, "We're not being discriminatory by saying women are not equal. We're saying VMI is a different kind of school, a special kind of school. Women would change that."[48]

Back in Richmond, a triumphant Emilie Miller announced that she would reintroduce the bill that the Education Committee had refused to consider the previous year and ask the attorney general to block the state from spending any further funds to defend VMI.[49] That left Mary Sue Terry standing alone as a governmental defender of the Institute.

Terry immediately declared that she, too, wanted out. "As soon as the governor announced his position, it pretty much eviscerated our legal argument," she told the media on November 27. "I'm not going to second-guess the governor." Wilder had followed his declaration of support for the admission of women by announcing that he was prepared to testify against the VMI policy and that he would, if necessary, withhold funds from the Institute in order to get the policy changed. An angry Patterson commented that Terry's proposed withdrawal should not be permitted to cloud the validity of VMI's position and stated, "this isn't a political issue, although it's going to be made into one apparently . . . it's not even a civil rights issue. It doesn't have anything to do with being anti-female. Our position is nothing more than plain common sense. Maybe there is no room left in the American world for common sense and practicality."[50]

Conservative columnist Patrick Buchanan nominated Wilder and Terry for "The Southern Partisan's Scalawag Award."[51] Civil rights activist Roger Wilkins, then a visiting professor at George Mason University in northern Virginia, had nothing but praise for the two; professor Ronald Walters of Howard University's Government Department denounced them as opportunistic.[52] A spokesman for Jesse Jackson, noting that Wilder had refused to take a stand on VMI but had criticized President George Bush for vetoing the Civil Rights Act of 1990, commented caustically, "That may have caught up with him. You can't deal with a national piece of legislation like the civil rights act and remain silent on VMI."[53]

Terry filed papers with Kiser claiming that since there was no statute detailing the commonwealth's position on the admissions issue, Wilder's declaration represented state policy: Virginia now officially believed that VMI had to admit women. She added that she could not continue to represent Virginia in its new position because she had been given confidential information in the course of representing VMI. Kiser replied that she could withdraw only if that did not leave VMI without counsel. Wilder, in turn, refused to replace her with state-paid lawyers. She turned to Benjamin Civiletti, who was already representing Wilder, but Wilder objected that Civiletti would have a conflict of interest. Patterson, the attorney for the VMI Foundation and VMI Alumni Association, agreed to take on VMI as an additional client without a fee—technically, he would now be representing the state of Virginia—and Terry was finally able to bow out of the politically costly drama.[54]

THE CAST OF CHARACTERS changed somewhat with Terry's departure from the case, but the excitement continued. Emilie Miller had reintroduced her bill, as promised. A new Richmond-based group called Virginia Women for VMI, made up of about thirty women whose husbands and sons had attended VMI, promised to lobby against the bill.[55] The Virginia Women Attorneys Association sent a letter of support for the bill to the General Assembly, but Elmon Gray again ruled the bill out of order because of pending litigation, and the committee again sustained his ruling.

A group of 450 alumni, spouses, parents, and friends, including Patterson's wife and one of his daughters, demonstrated outside the capitol. So did nine women calling themselves Friends of VMI for Equality and holding a sign proclaiming, "Don't Teach Male Bonding with My Taxes."[56] An informal poll of VMI faculty showed that most of them had long expected a legal challenge to the admissions policy and were in favor of changing it, and surveys demonstrated that most Virginians also thought that it was time for a change.[57] Although *change* was a six-letter word to most people, to the harder-nosed members of the VMI "family," it packed all the emotion of a four-letter epithet. And they were the ones who got most of the media attention; they were the ones who made sure that the case would end up in court.

Judith Keith, who would argue the case for the other side, was having a hard time keeping her head above water. The Justice Department had signed off on the case, but there was not much enthusiasm for it outside the Civil Rights Division. Major civil rights cases routinely involve teams of attorneys. As the then-head of the ACLU's Women's Rights Project commented, a case can be killed without being formally jettisoned, simply through understaffing. "The lawyers can be tremendously hard-working and enthusiastic and right thinking about it but if they don't have the resources to litigate, the litigation turns out badly." When the parallel case involving Shannon Faulkner and The Citadel was brought in 1993, for example, the WRP had three lawyers and two secretaries spending most of their time on it. That was not enough, so the project persuaded the huge New York law firm of Sherman and Sterling to come in. The firm assigned two partners, a senior associate, mid- and junior-level associates, and paralegals to the effort.[58] (The Citadel case is summarized briefly in chapter 15.)

But Judith Keith was fighting almost entirely by herself. The lack of assistance was glaring, and it cannot be explained by lack of personnel. The Justice Department is always shorthanded but manages to bring in enough troops when the battle is considered sufficiently important. Perhaps the Bush administration had second thoughts about putting resources into a gender equality case; perhaps Keith's lack of popularity within the CRD was responsible. The very junior Michael Maurer was brought in only when the trial date was near, and Keith and Maurer had to rush up to West Point to comb through the archives for evidence in their favor. They got through 40,000 documents in two weeks.[59]

Whatever the difference in the number of troops on the two sides, the lawyers filed their preliminary motions and took depositions from expected witnesses. Judge Kiser declined to award summary judgment and ruled that the trial would take place in two stages, with the question of the legitimacy of the admissions policy being heard first. A second trial on a possible remedy would be held only if he found VMI to be in violation of the Constitution. The stage for the courtroom drama was set.

GI Joe and GI Jane

Men must provide the first line of defense while women keep

the home fires burning.

—*Chandler v. Callaway* (N.D. Cal. 1974)

Rhonda Cornum did not see the Iraqi missile that slammed into her Blackhawk helicopter. When she regained consciousness she was lying on the ground with both arms broken, a bullet in her back, a badly injured knee, and five armed Iraqi soldiers standing over her. Five of the other seven soldiers in the plane were dead. Cornum, an army flight surgeon, had been on a mission into Iraq, determined to rescue a wounded F-16 pilot who had been shot down earlier. It was 1991, Operation Desert Storm, and Cornum was about to spend a week in Iraq as a prisoner of war.[1]

GI JOE, OR HIS PRE–WORLD WAR I EQUIVALENT, has long been familiar to Americans. There is a series of mental images: Washington crossing the Delaware. The Minuteman statue in Lexington, Massachusetts. Bunker Hill. Teddy Roosevelt charging up San Juan Hill. Planting the flag at Iwo Jima. The wounded soldiers in *M*A*S*H*.

GI Jane, in contrast, is a very recent addition to American popular culture. There have been war movies since the early days of the film industry, but actress Meg Ryan's portrayal of a killed-in-action pilot nominated as the first female recipient of the Medal of Honor (*Courage Under Fire*) arrived in movie theaters only in 1996. *GI Jane,* the movie starring Demi Moore as a shaven-head Navy SEAL, would not premiere until the following year. As long as the nation believed that biology was destiny and that the most natural uniform for women was maternity clothes, there was no interest in seeing them in fatigues.

The VMI case was not really about women in the military. Less than 20 percent of VMI graduates chose a military career, and by the time the case began, women were already a part of the armed forces. But the self-proclaimed essence of VMI was and is an exaggerated form of training for combat, and until the idea that women could fight for their country gained popular credence, there was no lawsuit to get them admitted to the Institute. The questions, then, are why the notion of women warriors was anathema for so many generations, and what effect its absence had on the culture VMI was seeking to protect and on the judges who handed down decisions in the case.

CITIZENS ARE MEMBERS OF A SOCIETY who are prepared to fight to protect it. There have long been "corollary" citizens who do not fight, such as women attached to citizen-soldiers, or their children, but full citizenship and all the respect implicit in the word have historically been reserved for the citizen-soldiers themselves.

That has been the norm in Western civilization since the days of Cincinnatus in ancient Rome and the Greek city-states.[2] (It may be remembered that one of the statues at VMI depicts the citizen-soldier Cincinnatus.) The American and French Revolutions both emphasized the right as well as the responsibility of the citizen to be prepared to bear arms. Those wars were revolutionary not only in sweeping out the people in power but also in establishing the idea that political rights belong to those who fight for the nation.[3] Throughout American history, male foreigners who arrived in the United States and then served in its armed forces were entitled to citizenship—a route denied to women until recently. The production of children is obviously as important to the continuation of society as is its military defense, but childbearing is not considered the kind of service to society that merits full citizenship. It is merely what women do.

Perhaps the traditional link between military service and citizenship is best demonstrated by the way African Americans were systematically kept out of the military throughout much of American history. When the Supreme Court heard the 1857 case that asked whether African Americans could ever be full citizens, and answered that they could not, Chief Justice Roger Taney pointed to the 1792 act of Congress that specifically excluded black men from state militias. Anyone ineligible for combat, he reasoned, was not a citizen.[4]

The gradual acknowledgment of African Americans as full members of the body politic can be measured by their slow acceptance in the military. They were permitted into combat positions in substantial numbers only after World War II.

Soldiers are presumed to be aggressive. Aggressiveness by American blacks, however, was something that American whites feared throughout most of the nation's history, so they could not be soldiers. Aggressiveness by women of all races was unacceptable, so they could not be soldiers either. And neither group could be taken seriously as citizens. A woman could no more be a soldier than she could be president of the United States.

Aggression is defined as a male trait; so is power. But paradoxically, whereas anyone who served in the military was presumed to be powerful, physical power was not a prerequisite for service. Short, weak men were welcome in the military, even if they were among the 30 percent of men below the median male height and weight. Women, even if they were tall and strong and among the 30 percent of women above the median, were not welcome. It seems reasonable to assume that something other than a search for the fittest soldiers was at work in the exclusion of women.

That becomes even clearer when one remembers that the institutions historically closed to women but thought of as open to "citizens" were the voting booth, the jury room, the halls of government, and the military. Only the last required particular physical strength, but many Americans mentally connected eligibility for military service with the ability to participate in the political sphere. Military heroes—Washington, Jackson, Grant, Marshall, Eisenhower, Kennedy—were regarded as desirable candidates for political office. Even today, those who have not served in the military are considered more skeptically and find themselves having to parry doubts about both their patriotism and their manhood, as Bill Clinton did in his 1992 presidential campaign.

It is the perceived tie between masculinity and power that has kept women out of the military and out of the government, but it has also helped define "malehood." If aggression and power are male traits, then one can prove one's masculinity by being aggressive and powerful. Similarly, if women exercise a "masculine" function by serving in the military, then such service is no longer an automatic proof of masculinity. If one element of masculinity is the ability to protect women, what happens to the definition of masculinity when women demonstrate their ability to protect not only themselves but men as well? The analog to the military, in the VMI situation, was the rat line and its symbolic creation of men: if women could perform well on it, how could it continue to function as evidence of manhood?

It is hard to find an explanation more telling than this psychological one for the historical inclusion in the military of unfit men but not physically qualified women—or for the exclusion of women from VMI. One way to keep women out of the military was to raise questions about both the femininity of the women who sought to serve and the safety of the men who would fight alongside them. A West Point educator has remarked on "the supposed hypersexuality of women soldiers, who somehow manage the feat of being prostitutes and lesbians simultaneously [and] are responsible for poor morale and unit unreadiness."[5] Recognizing the depth of the prejudice, Ruth Bader Ginsburg deliberately decided in the 1970s against bringing cases involving combat occupational specialties. This even extended to potential plaintiffs such as Grace King, who had been the star of her tank training course but was refused assignment to an armored car troop unit.[6]

But perhaps the greatest barrier to women's participation in the armed forces, and to women's enrollment at VMI, was the argument based on supposed truths about female psychology. Women could not hack it. The testimony of VMI administrators at trial would reflect the belief that women could not stand stress. Women would crumble under pressure. They lacked the aggressiveness necessary to a fighting force. And, if they were *real* women, they would not *want* to be sufficiently aggressive.

That belief would be serious enough if its sole effect had been to deprive women of the opportunity to express their patriotism and to use it as a means of economic advancement—or, in the VMI case, to be acknowledged as citizen-soldiers. But as Justice Louis Brandeis once remarked, the government is an "omnipresent teacher"; what it does is considered to be right, and the values implicit in its actions are taken as a model for others to follow.[7] Law is an equally influential instructor, even when it teaches the lessons of subordination and exclusion. That is why the fact that women could not *legally* participate in the military or the jury room or the voting booth was so important. A view of women as inferior, as subordinate to men, was reflected in and validated by the legal exclusion of women. By the time of the VMI case, women had been recognized by law as voters and jurors, but they had gained only partial acceptance in the military. They were still not eligible to serve in combat, and their military service had not yet been validated by the culture at large. There might be women in the military, but they were not *real* soldiers—at least not in the popular mind.

It was therefore important to the public relations war that VMI make the same argument that was accepted about women in the military. Women were

unfit and dangerous. The sweat, the dirt, the toil, the stress of the adversative system (the overtones of war were not accidental)—none of it could be
handled by women, and their very presence would destroy it. *Destroy* was a
key word in VMI's battle. Women were not only incapable of making it
through the adversative system. In some almost existential way, their very
presence would contaminate and destroy it. The enormously powerful psychological mechanism at work in VMI's resistance was an offshoot of national
beliefs about women in the military

IN FACT, A FEW WOMEN HAD FOUGHT for the United States
since the days of the Revolution, but they were just that: few, and largely un-
acknowledged.[8] The breakthrough for women in the military came during
World War I, when more than 21,000 served in the Army and Navy Nurse
Corps.[9] Secretary of the Navy Josephus Daniels sent out the first official call
for female military volunteers other than nurses in 1917, eventually recruiting nearly 12,000 for shore jobs.[10] For the most part, the women working in
the navy, marines, and coast guard filled clerical positions; they were perceived by the larger society as helpers rather than fighters, so they were no
threat to stereotypes.[11]

All the conflicting feelings that most men and women had about women
fighting in defense of the nation—a desire to protect women, a strong impulse
to safeguard the military as a "boys'" club, a threat to clearly defined roles if
women could protect not only themselves but men as well—would be jolted
from the realm of unarticulated emotion into the world of necessity by American participation in World War II.

VMI's most celebrated alumnus, George C. Marshall, became army chief
of staff in 1939. The hostilities in Europe that began escalating in the late
1930s led him and other American military planners to assess the nation's
manpower reserves. Ironically, given the resistance of his alma mater to gender integration, Marshall was eager to employ women in the war effort. After
the trauma of the Japanese attack on Pearl Harbor in late 1941, Congress was
ready to respond to his plea that women be enrolled as army auxiliaries. In
the summer of 1942 Congress established the Women's Army Auxiliary Corps
(WAAC). It was joined by the Women's Reserves of the Navy (WAVES), Coast
Guard (SPARS), and Marine Corps, and was reorganized in 1943 as the
Women's Army Corps (WAC).[12]

Marshall would have gone further. In 1942–1943 he sponsored an experiment that used women in mixed battery antiaircraft artillery units. According to military historian D'Ann Campbell, senior officers were amazed to find that "units mixed with men and women in equal proportion performed better than all-male units, and had high unit cohesion or bonding."[13] It might have been wise for VMI to remember this fact when it insisted that women would destroy the morale of Institute cadets. Marshall's experiment, however, was before its time and had no impact on the use of women in the military during World War II.

Initially there were only 440 women in the WAAC, but when the supply of able-bodied men proved insufficient, the number of women in uniform soared to 120,000.[14] Necessity did not end all psychological resistance, however. The secretary of war had to beat back a demand that, rather than employ more women, the armed forces recruit men classified as 4-F, or "physically unqualified."[15] This willingness to rely on unfit men rather than on qualified women to help defend the country in the most threatening war it had ever known was a dramatic illustration of the intensity of the resistance to women in the military.

Qualifications for women were set higher than those for men; that is, women who were permitted to enlist were already better trained than the average male recruit.[16] They went into virtually every occupation that did not involve direct combat: control tower and radio operators, radio repairers, engine mechanics, naval air navigators, parachute riggers, gunner instructors, stenographers, typists, clerks, telephone operators.[17] They served overseas as well as at home. The fact that women were crucial to the war effort, however, did not make military men comfortable with their presence or with the unspoken questions it raised about gender roles. In 1942 the army classified all military occupational specialties as suitable or unsuitable for women, finding that almost 4 million jobs were suitable. Among them were jobs that would involve women supervising men. Discomfort with that idea led the army to reclassify the jobs, and the number of slots available to women dropped to 1.3 million, minimizing the possibility of female supervision.[18]

There were nonetheless over a quarter of a million women on active duty by mid-1945: almost 100,000 WACs, 86,000 WAVES, 18,000 marines, 11,000 SPARS, and 68,000 army and navy nurses, out of a fighting force of 12 million.[19] They served everywhere there was an American military presence: Europe, China, Southeast Asia, North Africa, the Southwest Pacific.[20] They were not, however, given full military status or the same pay and benefits as their male counterparts. It was fully expected that when the war ended they would all disappear. They did not.

Dwight D. Eisenhower, who by the war's end had replaced Marshall as army chief of staff, wanted to keep women in the army.[21] Congress did not, but it relented to military demands and in June 1948 grudgingly passed the Women's Armed Services Integration Act.[22] The legislators feared, however, that women would not understand that the emergency was over and that they were expected to reembrace domesticity. To prevent large numbers of them from forsaking hearth and home for military careers, Congress strewed the path of military women with boulders of impressive proportions. The act set a 2 percent ceiling on the proportion of women in the military and a 20 percent ceiling on the number of women officers. Assuming that young women could not make intelligent decisions for themselves, Congress decided that men could enlist at age seventeen, but women had to wait until they were eighteen; women, unlike men, required parental permission to enlist if they were younger than twenty-one. They were specifically excluded from combat and forbidden to be assigned to duty "in aircraft that are engaged in combat missions" or "on vessels of the Navy other than hospital ships and transports."[23]

These exclusions created institutional segregation and a double standard. In effect, Congress not only approved gender discrimination but ordered it. Women could not attain a rank higher than colonel, which they could hold only temporarily. Their husbands and children would not be considered dependents unless the women could show that they were their families' "chief support." It was all in keeping with the country's postwar reversion to the kind of stereotypical thinking about roles that Betty Friedan would later label "the feminine mystique."[24] Freed of wartime exigencies, the services now provided makeup lessons for female members and encouraged them to wear high heels, hats, and gloves whenever possible. Women had no fatigue uniforms or boots. Their basic training was separate from that of the men and did not include instruction in the use of weapons. In the late 1960s, the Marine Corps published a photograph of a model women's barracks. Each bed in the picture bore a cozy stuffed animal.[25] It was no wonder that most Americans inside and outside the military did not take women's participation seriously.

There seemed to be no pragmatic reason, during the 1950s and 1960s, to do otherwise. The entire history of women in the military is of their being thrown into the breach when society considered it necessary, almost always with too little thought or planning, and pushed into leaving when the emergency ended. With the restoration of "normalcy," the discovery that women could do "men's" jobs invariably was dismissed as irrelevant. There was a surplus of young men for the armed forces in the 1950s. This was particularly true early in the decade, given the Eisenhower administration's policy of focusing on massive retaliation and nuclear war rather than large numbers of ground forces; it remained true as military planning changed somewhat because of the Korean War and the debacle at the Bay of Pigs, neither of which involved massive numbers of troops. As of 1969, women constituted less than 1 percent of the armed forces.[26]

Women enrolled in the armed services for the same reasons as men. The military offered opportunities for college and postgraduate education, including the acquisition of skills that could be used for upward mobility back in civilian life, and provided them with full pay. Its economic benefits included not only salaries but also medical care, housing, dependency allowances, and retirement annuities. And, of course, women as well as men wanted to serve their country. Few if any of the women enlisted to make a point. Most, as Judith Stiehm discovered, were "personally conservative" and "politically conservative"; few were feminists.[27]

The women's movement of the 1960s and 1970s nonetheless inevitably affected the military, as it affected every other institution in society. The effect was very slow in coming, however, and it might well be argued that the movement and the efforts by determined career military women to open up opportunities for other women were less significant than the antiwar feelings generated by the Vietnam War and the consequent shortage of men willing to serve.

Two phenomena of the late 1960s proved to be of great importance to the future of women in the military. One of the vagaries of the 1948 Women's Armed Services Integration Act was that the definition of "combat" was left to each of the armed services, with the result that its meaning was both arbitrary and unclear. The efforts of a small but dedicated band of professional military women and their allies bore fruit in 1967 with the passage of Public Law 90-130, which required the Defense Department to submit a definition of combat to Congress. It also ended the 2 percent ceiling on women in the military and removed the restriction on the percentage of officers who could be women. Then, at the end of the decade, the President's Commission on an All-Volunteer Force was established to examine the possibility of ending the peacetime draft.

Increased opposition to the draft was, of course, another result of the Vietnam War. The Commission on an All-Volunteer Force recommended in February 1970 that the draft be ended; it was, early in 1973. The commission report did not discuss women in the military but noted, tellingly, that only some 20 to 30 percent of military personnel were in ground combat forces. With World War II setting an important precedent for women serving in noncombat positions, and resistance to the draft at its height, the Defense Department's Central All-Volunteer Task Force was ordered early in 1971 to consider possible ways of using women to offset shortages of men. Various studies by the individual services, think tanks, and Congress all discussed the potential utilization of women.[28]

The fact that most people serving in the military were not in combat units and the existence of a number of thoughtful reports about the possible efficient use of women made no difference to many policy makers. In 1970 the House of Representatives held hearings on the proposed Equal Rights Amendment (ERA). Both politicians and the electorate believed that under the ERA, women would be drafted to serve in combat, and that became a major argument against it.[29] Nonetheless, by lopsided votes of 354 to 23 in the House of Representatives and 84 to 8 in the Senate, Congress rejected Senator Sam Ervin's proposal that the ERA be amended to exempt women from the draft and from combat. The ERA was adopted without the amendment and sent to the states for ratification.

The 1970s brought major advances for women in the military. In 1970 the first women were named as army brigadier generals: Anna Hays (Army Nurse Corps) and Elizabeth Hoisington (WAC). (Hoisington was later the first woman on VMI's Board of Visitors.)[30] In 1975 the army made individual weapons training mandatory for women, and the Defense Department, reacting in part to litigation brought by Ruth Bader Ginsburg, ended the practice of issuing involuntary discharges to military women who became pregnant.[31] The services were gradually replacing the low-privacy barracks of World War II with dormitories that had semiprivate rooms and bath facilities; as they did so, they also eliminated separate housing for enlisted women. By the end of the 1970s, basic training was gender integrated, and women were wearing fatigues rather than high heels.[32]

Despite the progress, there was still a strong sense in the military that although women *could* serve, if they did so, they were not quite women. It was in 1970 that Sharron Frontiero was told that she and her husband could not move into Maxwell Air Force Base's family housing because her husband did not qualify as a dependent. The idea that women could be both members of the armed forces and wives remained difficult for some, and the notion that mothers could serve in the armed forces was even more so. Captain Tommie Sue Smith, a judge advocate at Andrews Air Force Base, filed suit in 1970 to block enforcement of the regulation that mothers could not serve. Captain Smith was a divorced mother who gave up legal custody of her son, as ordered, but kept personal custody of him until the air force ruled that she could not have a child in her home for more than thirty days a year. She then enrolled him in a nearby military school so that she could see him on weekends. When she was assigned to the Philippines, she was told that her child could not go, and she brought suit. A reporter quoted her as saying, "We have a general right here on base with eight kids and his wife isn't with him." One day later, the air force changed its policy.[33]

The next frontier would be the federal military academies, where the arguments on both sides of the issue of admitting women would foreshadow those made about VMI.

POTENTIAL CADETS IN THE FEDERAL SERVICE academies are nominated by members of Congress. In 1972 Senator Jacob Javits of New York nominated a woman to the U.S. Naval Academy at Annapolis. It refused to consider her, and Javits took the fight to the public arena. He and Representative Jack H. McDonald introduced a concurrent resolution prohibiting gender discrimination in the service academies' admissions procedures. The resolution passed the Senate but was killed by the much more conservative House Armed Services Committee.[34] Women and their male supporters turned to the federal courts.

In September 1973 four members of the House of Representatives sued Secretary of Defense James Schlesinger. Along with two women who wanted to attend Annapolis and the Air Force Academy, respectively, they filed suit in the federal district court of the District of Columbia, charging that legislators' discretion in nominating citizens to the academies was unconstitutionally hampered by the men-only admissions policies.[35] The following month, Representative Pierre du Pont introduced a bill to admit women to the service academies.[36] The House of Representatives refused to take action on the bill but agreed to hold hearings about the matter. In December 1973 the Senate passed the Armed Forces Enlisted Personnel Bonus Revision Act, which included a provision to admit women to the academies, but the provision was later deleted by the conference committee of the Senate and House. Suddenly, however, the issue was being debated in both the legislative and the judicial branches of the federal government, and the military thought that it was time to send in the big guns.

In the two cases involving female plaintiffs' right to attend the service academies (*Waldie v. Schlesinger* and *Edwards v. Schlesinger*), the federal government relied heavily on affidavits from the superintendents of the three service academies and W. P. Clement, the deputy secretary of defense.[37] Clement summarized his position in a letter to F. Edward Hebert, chairman of the House Armed Services Committee. The academies' mission, Clement wrote, was "to produce male officers to fill combat billets"; because women could not serve in combat, accepting them at the academies would necessarily reduce the number of men being prepared for combat, causing "serious harm to fleet and combat units." As for the claim of the two women that they were being deprived of federally subsidized educational opportunities available to men, he said that there were "alternative procurement sources for female officers that offer excellent education opportunities," such as the ROTC scholarship program, which had recently been opened to women.[38]

Formal congressional hearings on the question began in May before the Military Personnel Subcommittee of the House Committee on Armed Services. On June 5, Defense Department general counsel Martin R. Hoffmann and Secretary of the Navy J. William Middendore II testified in agreement with Clement. Middendore also cited *An Appraisal of the Impact of Integrating Women into the U.S. Naval Academy and Aboard Ship,* a navy document prepared for the hearings, which said that women had no place on board ships because the men would not like it:

> The role of women aboard ship poses . . . problems in terms of sociological, psychological and readiness implications. Most professional officers and, particularly, USNA alumni are adamant in their disbelief that such a change is either feasible or desirable.
>
> The present male-dominated, sea-going facet of Navy life, is one that is understood and accepted by the country and the men in the Navy. Men join the Navy for many different reasons; however, a certain portion join and remain in the Navy because they enjoy being in a job which has been historically associated with fellowship among men in a difficult and dangerous endeavor. Changing the fabric of the Navy by integration [sic] women into all combat roles might well reduce the attractions of the Navy to this segment of mankind.[39]

Women had to be kept out of the navy because their presence might interfere with male bonding. The navy warned that "the prospect of long deployments with mixed crews could be viewed with some degree of uneasiness by spouses of crew members. If this occurred, morale and readiness would certainly be affected."[40] The navy was prepared to give not only male sailors a veto over possible female colleagues; their wives got a vote as well.

The military academy superintendents testified against gender integration, as did the secretaries of the army, navy, and air force and the deputy assistant secretary of defense for military personnel. So did renowned pilot Jacqueline Cochran, who had directed training of the Women Airforce Service Pilots (WASP) during World War II. In spite of having logged more than 15,000 hours in the air and flown experimental planes in test runs, she told the committee that female pilots had to be "women first and pilots second." Her testimony demonstrated the insistent emphasis on traditional roles that was maintained even by some "liberated" women. "A woman's primary function in life is to get married, maintain a home and raise a family," Cochran stated. Women therefore ought to leave the military when they marry, which made it pointless to give them expensive training. If women wanted to be at the academies and in the professional armed services permanently, "they should be restrained." After all, Cochran said, all women were "future mothers."[41]

Her sentiments were echoed by Lieutenant General Albert P. Clark, superintendent of the Air Force Academy. He predicted damage to the appropriate roles for both genders if women were admitted:

> For this Nation to open combat roles to our women, short of a dire emergency, in my view, offends the dignity of womanhood and ignores the harsh realities of war. . . . The environment of the Air Force Academy is designed around these stark realities [of combat]. The cadet's day is filled with constant pressure. His life is filled with competition, combative and contact sports, rugged field training, use of weapons, flying and parachuting, strict discipline and demands to perform to the limit of endurance mentally, physically, and emotionally.
>
> It is this type of training that brings victory in battle.
>
> It is my considered judgment that the introduction of female cadets will inevitably erode this vital atmosphere . . . the Academy will inevitably find it necessary to create a modified program to accommodate the female cadet or, God forbid, be required to water down the entire program.

In addition, the nation's enemies were defended by "implacable, well-trained, ruthless, all-male military forces," and it "would not look well in the history books" for the United States to impair its ability to fight against them by allowing women into its academies.[42]

The testimony that most prefigured that of VMI officials, however, came from Secretary of the Army Howard H. Callaway. His primary points were that women would make men uncomfortable and that the soft, feminine influence of women would destroy military preparedness.

> Admitting women to West Point will irrevocably change the Academy. The Spartan atmosphere—which is so important to producing the final product [combat leaders]—would surely be diluted, and would in all probability disappear before long. To modify the curriculum and alter the training so as to permit women to attend would weaken or destroy that intangible but indelible spirit which is the unmistakable hallmark of West Point graduates. . . .
>
> [There would be] a very different West Point, one like ROTC with high academic standards, but not with the rigorousness, the Spartanness, the training of duty-honor-country, the spirit of being the hardcore that has made up the kind of leadership that inspires the ROTC and OCS graduates to all become equal officers in the Army as you go forward.[43]

The assertion that academics would not be changed but that an indefinable "something" would suffer would also feature prominently in *United States v. Virginia*. So would the claim that men could not possibly think of women as equals, as Callaway articulated it:

> In the confusion of the ground combat environment, the need for having the physical and mental qualities under stress and the need for the belief by everyone there in the leadership that's there is total. Without belief in the lieutenants and captains and colonels who are there, it all falls apart, and we've seen that in every war.
>
> Now at the present time it's my personal judgment that the attitude of the American soldier is not such that he sees the female role as one of a platoon leader in combat, of a company commander in combat, or doing the kinds of things, with the kinds of leadership skills, that platoon leaders and company commanders in combat do. I personally don't think that many soldiers see a woman in that role. I think that the attitude of most soldiers in combat would be that they would be very uncomfortable in that role. They would see the woman as someone who needs to be protected rather than their leader whose judgment they must have enormous respect for. . . .
>
> To the extent that one soldier feels that way, he's being deprived of the leadership that is absolutely vital to him.[44]

"If you've got something . . . that's working—and West Point is working, it has never failed this country"—you should not fool with it, Callaway said, using almost the precise words that would be spoken by VMI's supporters in 1991. "I think it's a little dangerous to make such a fundamental change in something that has been that good for the country."[45]

Women got pregnant, Callaway also reminded the legislators; the result would be a high dropout rate. Lieutenant Colonel Grace M. King, U.S. Army Reserve, took on that argument:

Since women are denied the opportunity of attending the Academies we may only speculate on their retention rate. On the other hand, the Secretary of the Army himself presents a factual male example. Graduating from West Point in 1949, Lieutenant Callaway served briefly in Korea, returning home after a few months to be with his wife who was expecting a difficult delivery. Fortunately, all went well but Lieutenant Callaway did not return to Korea. He served out his time at Fort Benning as an instructor . . . I see no reason why any female officer who becomes pregnant could not follow this same pattern with no more nor less impact upon the combat mission nor any difference in the cost effectiveness involved.[46]

Seven members of the House testified in favor of gender integration. One of the points repeatedly made by the services was that the academies' mission was to produce people for war, and war meant direct involvement in combat. As Congress had forbidden women to participate in combat, the admission of women to the academies would be counterproductive; women would only take up precious space that could be used for combat training. Representative Patricia Schroeder pointed out that, in fact, "85 percent of the Army officer positions are noncombat oriented"; she then went on to challenge the combat exclusion.[47] Replying to the assertion that men would not take orders from women, Representative Charles H. Wilson commented, "I think it wasn't too long ago that we questioned whether white soldiers would take orders from black officers and I think it has proven that they will and they have. I think the same thing would be true if women were given the opportunity to lead."[48]

Representative Samuel S. Stratton, a former navy officer and captain in the naval reserve who had been awarded a Bronze Star during World War II, was known for his hawkish views.[49] But he did not agree that women would hurt military readiness. It was clear, he told the committee, "that the overwhelming bulk of the opposition to women in the service academies . . . is based on nothing more than inertia to change." Stratton called the male bonding rituals that allegedly would be affected by the presence of women—similar to the rituals at VMI—"sophomoric, neanderthal traditional practices . . . designed to inflict physical and psychological punishment. Actually," he went on, "there is no excuse for these practices in the military academies anyway. . . . They ought to be abolished altogether, and if the admission of women is needed to do it we ought to admit women to the Academies for that purpose alone."[50]

Various women's groups testified that women were working well in dangerous situations, such as the ones they frequently faced as police officers, and that it was unjust to keep the academies closed to women but not to male foreigners who would not go on to fight with American troops. A speaker for the Women's Lobby noted, "Women are now 44 percent of the work force. Their median income is $5,593. This means that women taxpayers are paying almost half of the cost of the academies that they are unable to attend."[51] Virginia M. Dondy of the Center for Women's Policy Studies emphasized that women "are not asking for any changes in curriculum or training."[52] "Do you include in that statement the physical training that is required at the academy?" one committee member asked.

> MS. DONDY: That is correct.
> MR. NEDZI: The same rigorous physical standards are to be maintained, as far as you are concerned?
> MS. DONDY: That is correct . . . it is my impression that [in] most physical aptitude examinations, women can meet the same standards as men if they are trained to the same level.
> MR. NEDZI: On the average?
> MS. DONDY: We are not talking about average people. We are talking about very physically fit people.[53]

Senior female officers were not heard from. Neither the armed services nor the legislators invited them to testify.[54] The Defense Advisory Committee on Women in the Military sent a statement supporting women's admission: "Let us be clear that patriotism is not a sex-linked characteristic."[55]

The subcommittee ended the hearings without taking action.

On June 19, 1974, the district court of the District of Columbia granted the United States summary judgment in *Edwards* and *Waldie,* saying that the government had shown that there was a rational relationship between the combat-oriented goal of the military academies and their exclusion of women. On November 20, the court of appeals for the District of Columbia overturned the district court's decision and sent the case back for a full trial on the merits. The trial court had erred, the new decision said, in accepting the Defense Department's affidavits as proof that women could not be trained for combat support positions or that doing so would interfere with the mission of the academies. Noting that the affidavits came from "the very persons charged with unconstitutional discrimination," the appeals court also held that the Supreme Court had long since rejected the rational relation test as the standard in gender discrimination cases.[56] Whether the service academies and the Defense Department would prevail under a more stringent standard was unclear.

IN JANUARY 1975 THE ISSUE moved from the courts to the full House Armed Services Committee, which failed to act. An exasperated Representative Stratton, apparently more in tune with the rest of Congress than the committee was, leapfrogged the committee by adding an amendment to a military appropriations bill that would grant women access to the academies. It passed the whole House by a vote of 303 to 96. Eighteen senators cosponsored a similar amendment in the Senate, which adopted it by a voice vote in June. After intense negotiations, a House-Senate conference report was finally accepted by both houses, and on October 7, President Gerald Ford signed Public Law 94-106, requiring the service academies to admit women beginning in 1976. The law stipulated that the admission of women was to be "consistent with the needs of the services," which were to be determined by them. That proved to be no problem, as the service academies were already having difficulty getting enough qualified students to apply.57

A country that had kept women out of the military for over 150 years was now prepared to see women cadets slogging their way through the intensive, physically demanding training at West Point. What had brought the nation to that point?

Women were ready, academically, for the service academies. They were receiving 45 percent of the country's bachelor's degrees, 45 percent of its master's degrees, and 21 percent of its Ph.D.s and professional degrees.58 The classrooms of the nation's elite universities were coeducational; many of them had been that way for years. And now, more and more women were ready physically as well.

Athletics was one of the areas of life emphasized by the women's movement. The 1972 Education Amendments to the 1964 Civil Rights Act, enacted at the urging of the women's movement, mandated equal athletic opportunities for boys and girls and men and women in educational institutions receiving federal assistance.59 Both in and out of school, girls were beginning to seek inclusion in Little League, on basketball teams, and on interscholastic sports teams. Their mothers and older sisters, delighted to realize that one could *be* fit as well as *look* fit, were participating in a nationwide movement toward regular exercise as a normal part of life. Women were boxing, wrestling, and weight lifting. The differential in physical conditioning for men and women was starting to be reduced accordingly.

When the House hearings began, women were serving in police and fire departments in an increasing number of localities. It had taken lawsuits to get them hired, and in fact very few had made it, but as the subcommittee heard, those who had were functioning well.[60] In doing so, they gave the lie to the contentions that women could not perform under stress and that all women lacked the requisite physical strength. It was true that most women had less upper body strength than most men. It was untrue that *all* women had less body strength than the *average* man—or that all women would be attracted by the prospect of serving in their local police or fire department or in the military. If desire to serve was a factor in successful performance, however, it was worth noting the extraordinarily high motivation possessed by the young women seeking admission to fields that traditionally had been and still were hostile to them.

Thus, many women were well prepared for the nation's military academies both academically and physically, and the relevant question is why the service academies were behind the times. The corollary question, of course, is why VMI was equally opposed twenty years later.

As we have seen, a number of reasons were advanced for keeping women out of meaningful participation in the military and out of the military academies entirely. The first argument was that the nation's military capability would be jeopardized. This was in part because women could not—and, many felt, should not—participate in combat. They did not have the necessary physical strength, and their presence would destroy group cohesion and morale. The second was that it would simply be unladylike. These concepts deserve exploration in some detail in the next chapter, because they would be the same assertions made by VMI.

9

The Lady and the Soldier

I want my name on record as having stood up to oppose women
being trained or assigned to combat units . . . such as riflemen,
driving a tank, firing an artillery piece, piloting a fighter plane
or serving aboard a naval ship. . . . My male colleagues tell me—
and I believe it—war is hell . . . it is bad enough that our young
men have to endure this. But do we want our women to suffer
it too?

—General Anna Hoisington (Retired), VMI Board of Visitors

The idea of women in the military ran smack into the popular
idea of what might be called woman-as-lady. Some people thought it bad
enough, in the second half of the twentieth century, that women were demanding acceptance in the workplace; surely *some* place should be left as
an all-male preserve. When the question arises of why, given the integration
of women into other walks of life, there was particular resistance against their
presence in military academies and the armed forces, much of the answer
can be found in the concept of woman-as-lady.

It is an image that is hard to reconcile with the role of the aggressive, protecting soldier. Ladies are passive. Ladies, or "real women," do not *do;* ladies
are done to. They depend on gentlemen, sometimes referred to as "real men,"
to order their world, protect them from unspeakable horrors that would otherwise be their lot, and mount the ramparts when they are not otherwise engaged in dragging home the carcasses of newly slaughtered animals. Biology

differentiates "women" from "men," but "ladies" and "gentlemen" are separated by a societal construct.

The definition of a gentleman is tied to that of a lady. Men are those who protect and provide. In order to function as men, they must be responsible for ladies, who are incapable of protecting and providing for themselves. But if women actually can care for themselves, they do not need male champions. If they can defend themselves, what, other than the act of impregnation, becomes the peculiarly male role?

American notions about ladies and gentlemen had their genesis in Europe and were accepted throughout the new nation, but nowhere were those ideas as commanding as they were in the South. The construct of woman-as-lady was refined there in the very tradition that gave birth to VMI.

SOUTHERN HISTORIAN DOUGLAS SOUTHALL FREEMAN commented in the 1940s that Virginians could best understand themselves and their values by paying attention to the history of women. What that history showed, as Anne Firor Scott has noted, was that "the social role of women was unusually confining . . . and the sanctions used to enforce obedience peculiarly effective."[1]

Before the Civil War, Southern women were taught that the role of the submissive, modest, weak, but pious wife was ordained not only by man but also by God. There was a close connection between the concept of woman and the institution of slavery. "Southern women have been shaped by their relationship to chattel slavery and its aftermath," two scholars have observed.[2] The idea of the "weak, dependent, illogical and pure" Southern lady was used "to keep the ruling gender/class/race ruling," so as to continue "the domination of both Southern ladies and slaves by elite white men."[3] "Any tendency on the part of any of the members of the [patriarchal] system to assert themselves against the master threatened the whole, and therefore slavery itself."[4]

Theorists of slavery such as George Fitzhugh, Thomas Dew, and William Harper argued that white women were such delicate creatures that they had to be freed from the more mundane chores of life, and the only people available to pick up their burden were slaves. "The institution of slavery is . . . calculated to relieve the sufferings and wrongs of injured woman, and elevate her in the scale of existence," Dew wrote. "The labor of the slave thus becomes a substitute for that of the [white] woman."[5] Her delicacy was her only protection; or, as Fitzhugh said, "her weakness is her strength," because in its presence, men would take care of her by commanding others to do her work. "Let her exhibit strength and hardihood, and man, her master, will make her a beast of burden. So long as she is nervous, fickle, capricious, delicate, diffident, and dependent, man will worship and adore her."[6] Any rebelliousness on the part of a wife—and all real women aspired to wifehood and motherhood as the highest possible callings—would be seen as "masculine," and she would lose her husband's love.[7]

The white man considered himself the bearer of a terrible burden: it was his lot in life to assume responsibility and provide for children, slaves, and women, all of whom thrived because of his beneficence. Even the South's many non-slave-owning white men trumpeted the mythology, "so grateful were they to enjoy the privileges that came with a white skin, and so hopeful were they of joining the planter class themselves one day."[8]

The myth of womanly helplessness was so powerful, so important to the justification of slavery, that it survived even in the face of the extensive duties performed by slaveholders' wives and daughters. They ran the household, the dairy, the smokehouse, the poultry yard, and the garden; tended the sick, both family and slave; produced or procured food for all; and saw to the slaves' clothing. In fact, they worked alongside female slaves everywhere but in the field.[9] The difficulty of their lives was, of course, minimal compared with that of slave women, but the point is that if one looked closely, the lives of Southern women clearly belied the notion of the helpless lady. The tenaciousness of the myth is testimony to its place at the center of the Southern economy and ideology.

The myth also survived the beginnings of educational options for white women. Public speakers in the South of the 1830s—the decade VMI was born—frequently referred to the need for women to be educated so that they could be more interesting wives and better-informed guardians of their fledgling slave-owning sons. The need was perceived in the North as well. Daniel Webster, speaking of the generations of good Christian men whose minds would be formed by their gentle mothers, said that they would hold as a tenet of their faith that "all that I am I owe to my angel mother."[10] The dominant belief in all sections of the country was that women had to be kept in their place by the home fire. If the hand that rocked the cradle was busy elsewhere, what would become of civilization? But the hand ought to belong to a woman who could bring a modicum of educated sensibility to her rocking. By the 1850s, the South was dotted with schools for girls and young women.[11]

The Civil War resulted in both the abolition of slavery and the destruction of a way of life. Economic necessity forced women to cope by moving into paid jobs such as teaching. As mentioned in chapter 2, teaching gradually became a woman's preserve, and women's normal schools proliferated throughout the South.[12] Newly urbanized women also became dressmakers, milliners, seamstresses, and mill workers. White upper-class women began to organize women's clubs in civil society that helped provide basic services. They created garbage collection systems, built hospitals and schools, opened settlement houses, and began to agitate against child labor, alcohol, and the worst abuses of the penal system.[13] Black women, shut out of the white women's activities, organized an extensive service club network of their own.[14]

Not surprisingly, all this post–Civil War activism led to women's demands for recognition and for the rights that logically accompanied the assumption of responsibilities. According to Edward Ayers:

> Many young Southern white women belied the stereotype of passivity. The clubs they formed, the kindergartens and philanthropic groups they founded, the work they performed, the education they won all marked them as new women. Some went farther, demanding political and legal rights, demanding access to careers of the highest prestige. But the New South left little room for their ambitions. Politicians sneered. Husbands balked. Colleges turned their backs.[15]

Women's social welfare clubs did nothing to alter the mythology of the lady; indeed, the segregated society of the late-nineteenth-century South was justified in large part by the joint myths of black inferiority and the need for white men to protect white women from black men. Southern trains not only had separate cars for whites and blacks; they also had "smoking" cars for men and "ladies'" cars for women and families.[16] Women who had to sully themselves by going into the paid workforce were pitied by respectable members of society.

Upper-class women's involvement in public life through their women's clubs was acceptable because it was "women's work."[17] As Jean E. Friedman wrote, the "conservative nature of southern women's reform" was reflected in its support for racial segregation and, later, its reticence toward the idea of women's suffrage. The "most successful southern women's reform movement," she noted, was the Women's Christian Temperance Union, which was "a movement dedicated to the preservation of home and family."[18] The autonomous women's culture that developed in the North and West was barely reflected in the South, where a "rural, kin-oriented church-related society" still defined women's lives.[19] Virginia was in fact the last state in the Union to grant married women the right to own property in their own names.[20]

Small groups of Virginia women campaigned for suffrage in the last decades of the nineteenth century and the first decades of the twentieth.[21] The suffragists' effort was greeted with even greater condemnation in the South than elsewhere in the country, and their numbers were so few that some historians question the existence of anything resembling a women's "movement" there.[22] Whether or not the effort deserves to be called a movement, it was one that wore white gloves and deliberately belittled itself in order to maintain the appearance of respectability. Virginia suffragists reminded one another constantly that they had to act like ladies if they were to reach Virginia audiences. One of them, Orie Lathan Hatcher, wrote in the *Nation*, "the wise suffrage leaders here have realised . . . that success depends upon showing their cause to be compatible with the essentials of the Virginia tradition of womanliness."[23] In 1913 Mary Johnston, a best-selling author of romantic fiction and one of the leaders of the Virginia suffrage effort, tried to assuage a Richmond audience's fears that women voters would attempt to strip men of their rightful and dominant place. "Men have their minds too much fixed on the large political issues," she said reassuringly, "and there are a multitude of details that slip through their fingers, so to speak, and which women can better attend to." The "details," she suggested, might include education and the welfare of children—extensions of the nurturing function.[24]

As Virginia's suffragists moved into the early twentieth century, their Equal Suffrage League was countered by the Virginia Association Opposed to Woman Suffrage, which blanketed the state with literature warning that female suffrage would apply not only to white women but to black women as well. Richmond newspapers cautioned that in some counties the black population would have a majority of the votes—as if black Southerners had much hope of being allowed to cast their ballots, no matter what their sex.[25] Virginia was one of five Southern states that wrote to Congress while the proposed Nineteenth Amendment was awaiting ratification, asking the legislators to pass a "Proclamation of Defeat" declaring the amendment dead.[26]

The race-gender nexus in the reaction to the suffrage effort was striking. Just a few years earlier, in 1907, 200,000 people had turned out for the unveiling of a statue of Jefferson Davis on Richmond's most impressive boulevard; 12,000 Confederate veterans paraded past.[27] When Carrie Chapman Catt appeared before Virginia's House of Delegates to urge ratification of the amendment, a flyer appeared on every legislator's desk with the information that Catt advocated not only free love but also interracial marriage.[28]

The Virginia effort was doomed to failure. Nine of the eleven states that voted against the Nineteenth Amendment were from the South, Virginia prominently among them. Virginia, in fact, did not ratify the amendment until 1952. Most white Southerners viewed the Nineteenth Amendment as another battle in the War Between the States—another "unfortunate product of an inferior Northern culture," like the abolitionist movement and the Fourteenth and Fifteenth Amendments.[29] The question raised by the drive for suffrage, as two scholars put it, was "whether or not women would be defined or classified essentially by traditional views of behavior thought to derive from their sex." The answer was a resounding yes.[30]

There was, of course, opposition to the Nineteenth Amendment all over the country. One of the things that made the South in general and Virginia in particular different was that women's suffrage—the idea of women playing a public role—was seen as part of an outside attack on the South. Surely Southern women would never come up with such ideas by themselves. Maintaining the mythology of Southern womanhood was an important element in the South's effort to beat back the barbarian culture of the North.[31]

This remained true after the Nineteenth Amendment was ratified. Just as Virginia women had created an impressive number of civic-minded women's clubs long before ratification, so some of them undertook to inform themselves about the political process in the 1920s and bring pressure to bear on it. They attempted to improve election laws and the administration of tax laws, sought without success to create a civil service, and tried to better the state's educational structure. "Through it all [the reform efforts], the outward aspect of the southern lady continued to be maintained as the necessary precondition for securing a hearing."[32] Although going out to work became an accepted and indeed patriotic activity during World War II, Virginia women returned to their homes and the image of the "true woman" as soon as the war ended.[33]

The South kept the myth of the lady intact in spite of the changes wrought by the Second World War. The war not only altered the role of women in the military and in the civilian paid workforce; it also transformed the South from an overwhelmingly rural region. The combination of a large number of Southern senior congressmen, a moderate climate, and an abundance of free space led to the South's becoming the home of what historian Dewey W. Grantham described as "a disproportionate number of the nation's military bases and training centers." More than 60 of the army's 100 new camps were built there, two-fifths of the country's expenditures on wartime military and naval installations went to Southern states, and massive shipyards at such places as Newport News and Norfolk, Virginia, became important elements of the southern economy.[34] The Southern militarism implicit in the existence of VMI and The Citadel began to be reinforced by Northern-generated funds.[35] But the women on military bases would be wives, not warriors.

Militarization of the Southern culture increased in the decades after the war, as federal military money continued to flow in. By the 1970s, there were more major military installations per capita in the South—more than half of all the installations in the United States—than in any other region of the country. In 1980 almost 40 percent of the Defense Department's budget was spent in the South, and 48 percent of the nation's military personnel were stationed there and in Washington; almost every member of the armed forces was assigned to the South at some point in his (or her) career. Many of them felt at home in the South, because that is where they had come from; both officers and enlistees were disproportionately from Southern families. While Northern students were chasing the ROTC off their campuses during the Vietnam War, ROTC programs in the South were thriving.[36] To a large extent, the South remained a place where soldiers were men and women were ladies.

The idealized image of women was still in place for many Southerners at the time of the VMI case, more so than elsewhere in the nation. "In the twentieth century, as in the nineteenth," according to Grantham, "the South has been the region most sharply at odds with the rest of the nation."[37] A major element in the South's divergence from the larger national culture lay in its peculiarly conservative attitude toward women and their proper place.[38] Scholars reported that the myth of the Southern lady was alive and well among Southern men and women of all classes.[39] This was true in spite of the facts that the national women's movement of the 1970s had led some Southerners to begin rethinking women's roles and that, by 1970, economic necessity had 42 percent of Virginia's women working outside the home. Forty-two percent of those workers were married, and even more, 58 percent, were mothers of minor children.[40]

If many of the South's young men were joining the military, many of its young women were going to college. That was a major change for the region, and particularly for Virginia. The Southern Regional Educational Board reported in 1978 that for the first time, women made up a majority—50.1 percent—of the students in the South's colleges and universities.[41] And women in Virginia, as elsewhere in the South, were not only voting but were voting for themselves. Mary Sue Terry, after all, had been elected attorney general. Between 1980 and 1983, sixteen women served in the General Assembly, and the first woman was elected to the state senate.[42] By 1987, the state legislature, which chose the commonwealth's judges, had named eight women to the bench; in 1989 Virginia's first female supreme court justice was selected.[43] Women were voting in presidential elections in higher proportions than men.[44] They were teaching in the state's universities, running businesses, practicing law, practicing medicine; in short, they were carrying out the jobs performed by American women throughout the country.

Even though the facts on the ground challenged the idea of the passive lady, the stereotype remained alive and well. "What is striking about the South is the tenacity and consistency of the patterned constellation of sex-stereotypic images and ideas," Susan Middleton-Keirn reported. "Without the gender role ideology . . . the south would not be the South."[45] Surveys showed that the South remained less in favor of expanded roles for women than the rest of the nation. In an analysis of data from 1975 to 1989, two political scientists found Southerners highly traditional in the area of gender and politics; a 1987 Gallup poll reported that fewer Southerners than Americans elsewhere would be willing to vote for a woman for president.[46] The culture of the South in the second half of the twentieth century was heavily militaristic and chauvinistic—much like its culture at the time VMI came into existence. By 1989, when most of the nation's single-sex institutions of higher education had become coeducational, five of the country's women's colleges were in Virginia, although none was funded by the state. The only state-supported men's colleges in the nation were VMI and South Carolina's The Citadel.

So it was not entirely surprising that throughout *United States v. Virginia,* there would be those who saw the attempt to admit women to VMI as yet another misguided attack on Southern culture. Partisans of an all-male VMI considered the idea of a gender-integrated military institute to be the reflection of laughable notions about women's equality. Responding to the argument that VMI would be much the same institution if women were admitted, VMI's chief lawyer would scoff, "You can take anything in the world, you can take the place where these people [the Justice Department] are located up here in Washington and turn it into a day care center."[47] Few things were as foolish as a place where women could abandon their children while they attempted to do men's jobs. Not all VMI supporters shared that view, but the more vociferous ones, those who were most active in donning metaphoric battle dress and providing funds for the litigation, clearly did.

Virginian women might have become a permanent part of the state's college-going population in both single-sex and coeducational schools, but they were not going to the state's only military academy, which in some ways constituted the last frontier. The disconnect between the reality of Virginian women and the myth of the Southern lady was about to be confronted.

THE VMI LITIGATION BECAME A SHOWCASE for what was perhaps one of the last gasps of the myth of woman-as-lady. The Virginia educational system had long incorporated the idea that women should not be subjected to too much education, not only because it would be bad for them but also because the female presence in a classroom could endanger men.

Richmond-born novelist Ellen Glasgow, traveling through the South in the 1880s, described a typical student in Virginia's "female academies": "She was taught that a natural curiosity about the universe was the beginning of infidelity."[48] Virginia suffragist Mary Johnston said at the turn of the twentieth century that Virginia's educational policy, which made it one of the nation's five states "without any provision for the higher education of women," was "a disgrace to the state of Jefferson, Marshall, and Madison."[49] None of the commonwealth's normal schools for girls was accredited. Six Southern universities admitted women to many of their programs, but all of Virginia's state-supported colleges—William and Mary, Washington and Lee, the University of Virginia, and, of course, VMI—excluded them.[50] The 1912 convention of the Equal Suffrage League of Virginia included in its platform a call for equal educational opportunities for girls and women from kindergarten through university.[51] It, along with the rest of the platform, was happily ignored by the rest of the state.

The first major challenge to Virginia's failure to offer its young women an equal college education came early in the twentieth century. Led by a member of an aristocratic Virginia family, it presaged in almost eerie fashion the debate over VMI.

Mary-Cooke Branch Munford became president of the Richmond Educational Association in 1904, at a time when many genteel Southern women were involving themselves in matters of education and health.[52] "Education has been my deepest interest from my girlhood," she wrote to a friend, "beginning with an almost passionate desire for the best education for myself, which was denied because it was not the custom for girls in my class to receive a college education at that time."[53] In 1910—aware that colleges and universities such as Wisconsin, Cornell, Michigan, Oberlin, and Antioch were coeducational and others such as Harvard, Columbia, and Tulane had created coordinate colleges for women—Munford organized the Women's Committee for a Co-ordinate College at Charlottesville Affiliated with the University of Virginia (UVA), the state's flagship university. Her plan was scarcely radical. The coordinate women's college was to have its own dormitories and classrooms and would share only libraries and laboratories with the men's school, following the pattern at women's colleges such as Radcliffe, Barnard, and Sophie Newcomb (the women's college of Tulane University).[54]

By 1910, Edwin A. Alderman, who had been the president of Tulane, was the president of UVA. He supported Munford's proposal, as, eventually, did luminaries such as Woodrow Wilson, who had gone to UVA; A. Lawrence Lowell, Harvard's president; Charles W. Eliot, Harvard's president emeritus; Virginia's superintendent of public instruction; the rector of UVA; and most of the state's newspapers.[55] None of that mattered, however. As would be the case with VMI more than half a century later, UVA alumni just said no.

One of their claims was that UVA's honor system would be ruined—a cry to be repeated at VMI. President Alderman came under heavy alumni pressure. The UVA *Alumni News* reported that students feared women would end up "injuring its traditions and destroying its virility."[56] Opponents claimed that women students "would encroach on the rights of men; there would be new problems of government, perhaps scandals; the old honor system would have to be changed; standards would be lowered to those of other coeducational schools; and the glorious reputation of the university, as a school for men, would be trailed in the dust." The author of the leading treatise on women's education would comment that "no struggle for the admission of women to a state university was longer drawn out, or developed more bitterness, than that at the University of Virginia."[57] As would be the case at VMI, a majority of the faculty supported the plan, and a majority of students opposed it.

The creation of a women's coordinate college would have to be ordered by the state legislature. In 1912, and again in 1914 and 1916, the new Coordinate College League took the proposal to the General Assembly. In each year it failed. It came closest to success in 1916, when the vote was forty-six to forty-eight. The majority of legislators became so fearful that the effort might succeed that they staved off further efforts by passing a bill admitting women to William and Mary.[58]

World War I drew attention away from the effort. Munford continued to push the UVA board nonetheless. She and Alderman agreed on an interim plan to have women admitted to UVA's graduate programs, which was accepted by the board in 1920.[59] The fight for coeducation on the undergraduate level was given up. UVA put Munford on its board and named its first dormitory for graduate women, built in 1952, Mary Munford Hall.[60]

There was no need for an undergraduate women's dormitory. Throughout the years of World War II, the civil rights movement, and Lyndon Johnson's Great Society, UVA kept women out. Then, as the 1960s drew to a close, four female students and the U.S. National Student Association sued the university. At the first hearing of the case in 1969, a federal district court found that the days of excluding women had ended but expressed its "reluctance to interfere with the internal operation of any Virginia college or university, and particularly that of the University of Virginia at Charlottesville." Instead, it urged the parties to negotiate before the next hearing.[61]

The university, seeing the handwriting on the wall, drew up a plan to admit women gradually and actually enrolled a few staff members' daughters and students' wives who had completed two years of college.[62] When the parties returned to court, the three-judge panel found, in language similar to that of the Supreme Court in its 1996 VMI decision, that the education offered at UVA was different from that offered at other schools in the state. "The facilities at Charlottesville do offer courses of instruction that are not available elsewhere," the court stated. "Furthermore, as we have noted, there exists at Charlottesville a 'prestige' factor that is not available at other Virginia educational institutions." Two of the plaintiffs were married to UVA graduate students, and the court declared, "A pattern of continued sex restriction would present these plaintiffs with the dilemma of choosing between the marriage relationship and further education." It concluded, "We think the state may not constitutionally impose upon a qualified young woman applicant the necessity of making such a choice."[63]

The plaintiffs also asked for an injunction forbidding the state to fund any single-sex educational institution. That was too much for the court, which referred to VMI in declining to grant it: "Obvious problems beyond our capacity to decide on this record readily occur. One of Virginia's educational institutions is military in character. Are women to be admitted on an equal basis, and, if so, are they to wear uniforms and be taught to bear arms?"[64]

In fact, increasing numbers of women outside Virginia were wearing uniforms and bearing arms, and doing so in actual combat.

THE TWO DECADES BETWEEN the admission of women to the service academies and the Supreme Court's order to admit women to VMI were extraordinarily important to the future of women in the military. Attitudes changed slowly, and with a great deal of backing and filling, but change they did, and so did the law.

In 1977 Secretary of Defense Harold Brown ordered the services to find ways to increase the utilization of women. The army responded by integrating basic training. The following year, a federal court held that the navy had to give up its blanket policy of excluding women from combat ships and take "measured steps" to include them, based on the capabilities of each woman.[65] A new statute permitted women to serve for no more than 180 days on combat ships not expected to have combat missions and on noncombat ships.[66]

That did not imply that women were about to gain full acceptance in the military. In 1979 the House Armed Services Committee's Military Personnel Subcommittee held four days of hearings on the subject of women in combat. General Hoisington, by then retired from the army but not from VMI's Board of Visitors, told the subcommittee, "I want my name on record as having stood up to oppose women being trained or assigned to combat units . . . such as riflemen, driving a tank, firing an artillery piece, piloting a fighter plane or serving aboard a naval ship. . . . My male colleagues tell me—and I believe it—war is hell . . . it is bad enough that our young men have to endure this. But do we want our women to suffer it too?" Women would be "weak links in our armor [in protracted engagement against an enemy]. We cannot build a winning army if the soldiers in it have no confidence in the long-term mental and physical stamina of their comrades." She was concerned that mixed-gender relationships would be "costly distractions" in combat. "In my whole lifetime, I have never known ten women whom I thought could endure three months under actual combat conditions."[67]

President Jimmy Carter asked Congress in February 1980 for authority to register women as well as men for the draft. Bernard D. Rostker, director of the Selective Service System, had testified that year, "It is our determination that excluding a majority of the population that could serve, for reasons that were apparently not sufficient, given the substantial contribution that women make in the defense effort of this country today, is not consistent with the equity that we hope to strive for in the Selective Service System." Congress did not debate Carter's proposal; instead, it registered its contempt by deciding without discussion to authorize funds for the registration of men only.[68] In 1981 the Supreme Court declared that all-male registration did not violate men's right to equal protection.[69]

The impact of the culture wars on the military continued. Carter was defeated in the presidential election later that year. In 1981 the new Reagan administration endorsed the army's "womanpause," which put on hold a plan to increase the number of women in the military. Instead, as the civilian economy faltered, the military raised salaries, and both enlistment and retention rates of men increased. Although women in the active forces had gone from 40,000 (1 percent) in 1971 to 184,000 (8.5 percent) in 1981, they had become expendable. Army basic training was resegregated by gender in 1982. The army and air force cut down on their female recruitment goals.[70]

That did not prevent women from serving their country in the military in succeeding years, although the nation saw no large-scale combat and paid little attention to the question of women in the armed forces. There were 110 women in the 1983 invasion of Grenada, and 600 in the 1989 attack on Panama.[71] One of the women who served in Panama was army captain Linda Bray. She came under fire when the unit of military police she commanded engaged in combat. Men who encountered similar situations were awarded combat infantry badges; neither Bray nor the other women who served under fire received them.[72] Representative Patricia Schroeder called once again, unsuccessfully, for combat positions to be formally opened to women.[73]

So the picture was decidedly mixed when, in 1991, Iraqi leader Saddam Hussein's armies invaded Kuwait and the United States began to prepare for what would become Operation Desert Storm. That engagement turned American women into a permanent part of the fighting military.

Thirteen women aged nineteen to twenty-four were killed in the Persian Gulf War, five of them in action; two, including Rhonda Cornum, were captured. Female pilots regularly flew Chinook and Huey helicopters and C-130, C-141, and C-5 planes on support missions—ferrying soldiers and supplies fifty miles into Iraq during the first assault wave, flying refueling tankers, and rescuing wounded troops. A heavily armed army sergeant, Bonnie Riddel, guarded the First Cavalry for thirteen hours a night. Lieutenant Phoebe Jeter commanded a team in Saudi Arabia charged with identifying and destroying incoming Scud missiles. Lieutenant Colonel Roslyn Goff led 800 soldiers through Iraqi minefields. Sergeant Kitty Bussell quelled a riot by Iraqi prisoners of war. It was the largest concentrated wartime deployment of American servicewomen in the history of the nation—somewhere between 30,000 and 40,000 women, constituting about 6.7 percent of the troops there.[74]

When it was all over and time for the military's performance in the Persian Gulf to be assessed, General H. Norman Schwarzkopf, the troops' commander, called the women magnificent. Members of Congress rose to state for the record that the war could not have been won without them. The print media sang their praises. Perhaps more important for American attitudes, the Gulf War—and the women who served in it—became such a staple of the electronic media that it sometimes seemed as if the war were being fought in the country's living rooms. Not only the women themselves but also their proud families appeared on television. "Women wouldn't be where they are today without the [TV] coverage of their efforts in the Gulf war," retired air force brigadier general Wilma Vaught told the press. "It showed what the women were doing."[75]

The impact on values was clear. First Lady Barbara Bush reacted to the death of army pilot Major Marie Ross in a helicopter crash by calling it "very distressing" but said that it would have been equally so—no more and no less—if Major Ross had been a man.[76] Admiral Frank B. Kelso II, chief of naval operations, had told the Senate early in 1991 that he opposed permitting women in combat; he now announced that he had changed his mind. When the House Armed Services Committee held hearings in 1993 on repeal of the exclusion of women from combat ships, all the navy witnesses supported it. The National Defense Authorization Act for Fiscal Years 1992 and 1993 repealed legal restrictions against assigning women to combat aircraft in all the services and established a Presidential Commission on the Assignment of Women in the Armed Forces to study laws and policies restricting the assignment of servicewomen.[77]

Acting for the commission, the Roper Organization undertook a telephone survey of 1,700 randomly selected Americans in July 1992. Seventy-six percent of the respondents thought that the best-qualified person should be assigned to combat without regard to gender, although the majority thought that women should have the option of volunteering for direct combat assignments. Fifty-two percent said that if conscription were reinstituted, women should be drafted even if an ample pool of men existed.[78] Similarly, in a *Newsweek* poll, 52 percent of those surveyed said that women should be permitted to serve in combat ground units.[79]

The Gulf War, with its televised images of missiles flashing in the air and pilots dropping laser-guided precision bombs from safe distances, also brought home to the nation something that advocates of women in the military had been saying for years: military prowess at the end of the twentieth century depended more on technology than on such physical characteristics as upper body strength.[80] The war had been won by American technology and the troops' ability to use it, rather than by muscle power.[81] As if to underline the emphasis on gender-neutral technology, President Bill Clinton chose a woman scientist as his secretary of the air force in 1993. She was Sheila E. Widnall, a former Massachusetts Institute of Technology professor and administrator with degrees in aeronautics and astronautics and a past chairperson of the Air Force Academy's Board of Visitors.

While the VMI case was beginning to wend its way through the courts, women became part of the military in the air, on the seas, on the ground, and in the Pentagon. Captain Carol Barkalow, one of the first female graduates of West Point and a volunteer in the Persian Gulf War, commented that the argument about the importance of "bonding" in combat units, which had been used against women, had disappeared during the war. "When the bullets started flying, that argument went away pretty fast."[82]

VMI, with its insistence that women could not do "men's work," was simply out of touch. It would march into determined battle nonetheless.

10

In Judge Kiser's Court

The issue before you, Your Honor, is a simple one. It is whether

VMI's system of education . . . is going to be permitted to

survive. And in the largest sense, one might say that single sex

education in and of itself, certainly for men, and logically also for

women, is on trial here today.

—Robert H. Patterson, for VMI

Women have the right to attend VMI, they have the right to

benefit from public funds, they have the right to choose

whatever school in this state they want to do it, and one group of

people, be it cadets, be it alumni, be it Board of Visitor members,

cannot say that they should be denied their Constitutional right

and their right under the law because they don't want them there.

—Nathaniel Douglas, for the Justice Department

Barbara Taylor checked her pencils and paper on the morning of
April 4, 1991, as she had for one trial or another ever since she had started
working at Roanoke's federal courthouse in 1959 as a court stenographer. In
1991 the fifty-one-year-old Taylor was one of the few full-time court reporters

in the United States still using shorthand rather than a stenograph machine and computer, but that limited neither her speed nor her accuracy. She maintained a steady 200 words a minute, and Judge Kiser, who had worked with her for years, depended on her. "I've never known anybody to seriously challenge the accuracy of her work," he said. "You can pretty well go to the bank with what she writes down on paper."[1]

As Taylor organized her tools, reporters walked in—so many of them that they overflowed into the jury box. There were two teams of attorneys crowding the counsel tables. Judith Keith, Nathaniel Douglas (chief of the Educational Opportunities Section), John Moore (his deputy), and Michael Maurer were there for the Justice Department. VMI and the VMI Foundation were represented by Robert Patterson, Anne Marie Whittemore, William G. Broaddus, and J. William Boland—all from Patterson's firm—and former U.S. attorney general Griffin Bell. Bell would be joined later on by his colleague William A. Clineburg, Jr.; Roanoke lawyer William B. Poff, a relative of the Virginia supreme court justice for whom the Poff Courthouse they were in was named, would also participate. They rose as Judge Kiser stepped to his seat behind the bench, and Douglas remained standing to introduce his colleagues. He then turned the floor over to John Moore, who made the opening statement for the government: "May it please the Court, distinguished counsel, while this is a very important case and in some ways a very emotional case, it is not a complicated case. . . . It is not disputed that VMI does not admit women. . . . This constitutes sex discrimination."[2]

That was the government's overarching assertion: the case was about gender discrimination. The Justice Department lawyers had decided to emphasize a few crucial arguments: VMI was a state-funded school, its admissions policy was exclusionary, there was no similar program for women available elsewhere in the commonwealth, and there was no persuasive justification for keeping women out. The last point had two prongs: women could meet the challenges at VMI, and there was a demand by women for the VMI experience.[3] When Judith Keith was asked by friends and colleagues why any young woman would want to subject herself to life at VMI as it was described at the trial—or, for that matter, why any young man would choose to do so— her answer was that VMI did not attract the average guy and would not attract the average woman. But if Virginia provided that kind of education for men, it had to make it equally available for women. The legal standard to that effect was clear, she maintained, but more important, it was a simple matter of fundamental fairness.[4]

Moore was careful to criticize the exclusion of women by VMI, not VMI it-self or its methodology. Maurer would say later, "We did not set out to attack VMI as an institution, and we did not attack VMI as an institution."[5] Some commentators wondered about that. The federal service academies had given up the adversative system back in the 1980s, with the advent of the all-vol-unteer military. As an Annapolis administrator commented, "It's not cheap to train midshipmen, so the government can't afford to throw away money training people in a way that makes them quit." An upperclassman at the U.S. Naval Academy told a journalist that shouting at plebes only shows that the shouter is "immature"; "you don't want to do anything to make them feel like they aren't a human being."[6] And no one suggested that the American mili-tary's performance had suffered because training at the academies had be-come less brutish.

That seemed to make it easy for the government to argue that any changes in the system necessitated by the admission of women were irrelevant; the adversative system itself was not a prerequisite for the production of military officers, and it clearly was not necessary to the training of civilian leaders. There was therefore speculation that VMI's political clout had led to an order by the Bush administration that VMI and its adversative method were not to be attacked by the Justice Department. Now Moore declared that the only question for the court was whether the state could show an important inter-est in keeping women out of VMI. "Frankly," he said, "we are at a loss as to what that interest could be." Was VMI arguing that "women just can't cut it as citizen soldiers"? By integrating the federal military academies, Congress had answered that "the national interest is best served by having coeducational academies," and it was, after all, the federal government that ran the mili-tary. Was VMI arguing tradition? Moore had some comments on that subject:

> We will hear a lot about tradition, and you will not hear the United States say any-thing against tradition. Nor will you hear the United States say anything against the honorable and distinguished record of VMI and its alumni. It's a fine school, but that's the point. . . . The opportunities it provides and offers should be open to everyone.

"Tradition is a critical part of our heritage," Moore told the court. "But fol-lowing the law is even more critical and more essential," and the Justice De-partment "simply is seeking to enforce the Constitution." He continued, "Where one element of VMI's tradition is inconsistent with the law, that el-ement must give way."[7]

Because the government considered it obvious that the case was a simple one about gender discrimination, its attorneys saw no need for a long opening statement. The differences between its approach and VMI's, in both style and substance, became apparent as soon as Robert Patterson rose to introduce the case for VMI.

> We had a little trouble getting used to this case, Your Honor, because when the representatives from the Civil Rights Division stand up and say the United States against VMI, it just strikes a chord in my soul, because always before it has been VMI *for* the United States. When the chips are down, VMI has never let this country down and they never will. So it troubles me and I wonder what is the motivation, which I think any lawyer would speculate on, as to why the United States Government would pick a little tiny school in a little town, 1300 students, come down with the entire forces of this government arrayed against us.[8]

Having established Virginia as a bewildered but feisty David confronted by the federal government's Goliath, Patterson argued that the dispute was entirely Washington's fault: "It is fairly apparent to me that the Justice Department, especially the Civil Rights Division, still does not understand VMI." As a result, federal bureaucrats were attacking the sovereignty of the state, asserting that "the federal government does things one way, Virginia should be forced to do it that way, too." The government said that it was merely enforcing the law, but that was not true: "The Constitution doesn't require what they ask for here."[9]

As Patterson saw it, something else was at the heart of the case, and the government was avoiding the real question. "The issue before you, Your Honor, is a simple one. It is whether VMI's system of education . . . is going to be permitted to survive. And in the largest sense, one might say that single sex education in and of itself, certainly for men, and logically also for women, is on trial here today."[10]

That was what the case was about to the VMI team: would the radicals in Washington destroy both VMI and single-sex education throughout the United States in their attempt to deny biological realities and remake the world in an unnatural image? As for the equal protection clause, well, Patterson firmly believed that it meant whatever the Supreme Court decided it meant. And he could not believe that the Court intended it to exclude single-sex colleges.[11]

Maurer and Whittemore, listening to the opening statements, each reflected that "fundamental differences" between the sides made them "ships that passed in the night"; there was no point of convergence.[12] Maurer thought that the point of the Justice Department's litigation was that women were being excluded from VMI for no better reasons than that this was the way VMI had always operated and its defenders held outmoded stereotypes of women.[13] To Patterson and Whittemore, that was not only *not* the point; it misstated the issue entirely. As Whittemore would comment, "We never said there weren't women who could do the VMI thing," but that did not negate the fact that women learn differently from men. Some women could get through the arduous VMI program, but it would serve neither sex well to think that female VMI students would be getting the education they needed or that their presence would not destroy the experience at the heart of VMI.[14]

Patterson told Kiser that to acknowledge the real developmental differences between men and women was not to make a value judgment. "It is simply a commonsense recognition that men and women have different developmental needs."[15] Virginia was seeking diversity in its educational offerings; one element of diversity was single-sex education, and the commonwealth would fight to keep that option available.

Yes, VMI's buildings could be altered to house women, Patterson continued in his folksy-with-teeth style, but that was not the relevant element in the case. And yes, the federal military academies had chosen to admit women, but that, too, was irrelevant.

> I want it to be clear to the country that VMI holds the United States Military Academy and all federal military academies in high regard and we wish them well. But the United States Military Academy is not VMI. They have got seven or eight barracks up there, they have 16,000 acres, they have a budget of $225 million . . . they got a run of a golf course, a hotel, they have everything.

Again, it was David and Goliath—a venerable Southern institution as underdog. In spite of their size, however, the academies did not have everything, and what they lacked most of all was political independence. "The change to coeducational was a political decision," Patterson said flatly. "Now, Your Honor," he continued, "let me make abundantly clear to you, sir, and clear to my colleagues from the Department of Justice, we don't want to dwell on the problems of the academies" —thereby suggesting that with political pressure on one side and the decline in quality caused by gender integration on the other, the military academies were in sorry shape.[16]

By the time the opening statements were finished and the court broke for lunch, it was apparent that both sides were fighting a holy war. If the VMI lawyers would be more aggressive in their questions during the hours and days that followed, perhaps it was because they saw the war as taking place

in their own backyard. Its outcome would affect their families, their neighbors, and, in the case of Patterson and many of VMI's witnesses, their beloved
alma mater. "VMI is using phrases like 'single-sex education' much as the
South, in the 1850s, used phrases like 'states' rights,' to justify a system that
is, while not cruel and inhuman, just plain unfair," a commentator would
write in the *Washington Post Magazine*. "Because Virginia is—and this should
not be forgotten, either—in the South."[17]

It was the torching of Richmond all over again. This time, however, Virginia would beat the Yankees back.

WHEN THE TRIAL RESUMED, Nathaniel Douglas called Gen-
eral Knapp as his first witness. Knapp was asked to describe the mission of
VMI ("To produce educated and honorable men") and to define a citizen-soldier ("It's a person who is educated for the work of civil life but prepared in
time of national peril to defend the country"), admitting that nothing in the
definition precluded the admission of women. Didn't other state institutions
produce honorable citizen-soldiers, Douglas asked? Yes, replied Knapp, but
"the method is distinctive."

> Q: Now, has the same system been in place since VMI has started?
> A: The same object has been in place. There have been natural changes.

The word *change* would be a battle front throughout the trial. VMI maintained that it would be destroyed if it was forced to change; the Justice Department sought to show that VMI had embraced and thrived under change.
Douglas pushed Knapp:

> Q: What have been the natural changes?
> A: Electricity and plumbing in the barracks.

At this point, Kiser interjected:

> THE COURT: It was tough in the old days, wasn't it?
> THE WITNESS: Yes, sir. It's still tough, but those are the kinds of changes I mean
> and I could go on with the electronic analogy. We even have computers now, but
> very few telephones.[18]

The questioning continued:

> Q: When you say change, you would have to make the change, is it your judg-
> ment that there is no other system that will work, or that you just like the one you
> have, and therefore, it should not be changed?

A: Well, it's my position that we have a successful one now that we would have to set aside, and I can't really tell you what the new one would look like.

THE COURT: Why would the females, assuming, as we have been so far, that the number of females that might demand education at VMI would be small, why would they have to participate in the rat line and the dyke system and that sort of thing? Once you say you have two classes, couldn't they function separately?

THE WITNESS: Well, yes, sir, but I think you are building another school for the females that is not VMI.

THE COURT: It would still be the same VMI for the males, wouldn't it?

THE WITNESS: I think it would become a coed educational institution. I don't think you could run a separate one. You might as well set it up in some other town.

THE COURT: Well, if you have a limited number of females and you want to continue your rat line basically in the male portion of the barracks, why can't you do it?

THE WITNESS: Well, sir, I think we could go ahead and try to run it, but our system is to have 100 percent residents in the barracks and everybody takes the same thing.

THE COURT: I understand that, but as Mr. Douglas has said, is that just a matter of preference, or is it a matter of necessity?

THE WITNESS: Your Honor, I think for us to keep VMI, it's a necessity. We don't have any other classification of students, they don't live off post, they don't go to VMI without going through the rat line and establishing their class and having the class system, and the—and we might as well be told to start that, what Mr. Patterson referred to as an all female military academy somewhere nearby but not on post.[19]

The exchange showed as much about Kiser's assumptions as it did about Knapp's: if women were admitted to VMI, it would be a "matter of necessity" either to change the rat line or to excuse women from it. Knapp listed other aspects of VMI life that he presumed would have to be altered: the lack of locks on the doors, the all-revealing windows in them, the absence of lights around the post.[20] The details were telling in their suggestion of a safe, self-contained, homogeneous institution and of the all-pervasive and ultimately cohesive atmosphere that VMI was fighting to preserve.

Judith Keith stood to call Colonel Norman M. Bissell as the government's next witness. "Mike" Bissell had graduated from VMI in 1961. After spending twenty-six years in the army and a few in industry, he had become VMI's commandant of cadets in the summer of 1990. His was one of the families that had turned VMI into a tradition: three of his five sons followed him there. He believed that whether it was a result of biology or of socialization, young men and women learned differently, and they learned better when they did so separately. The college years constituted an awkward age, he thought; learning was more efficient outside the inhibiting presence of the other sex. He knew that the men who went to VMI did so in part because of the disciplined existence they would lead there. Women might well want the same kind of leadership education, but not the kind of grueling discipline that was VMI's hallmark. He could point to his own daughters in asserting, confidently, that young women had already internalized the discipline necessary for the learning process. "Girls do it right the first time," he would say; given an assignment, they took it seriously and made themselves do it correctly. Young men lacked that kind of self-control.[21]

Keith put Bissell through a grueling series of questions about life at VMI: the rat line, the dyke system, breakout. At each stage in the testimony, she asked whether a determination had been made that women could not successfully complete the activity he described; at each stage, the answer was no. His answers to her questions and to Whittemore's during cross-examination, however, made it clear that he did not consider that to be the issue. They also provided the media with their first clear glimpse of life at VMI and so would be quoted with both bemusement and awe over the next five years. Some of Bissell's testimony appeared in chapter 3, but it is worth quoting at greater length here, not only because it helped shape media coverage but also because it provides something of the flavor of life at VMI.

> A: I like to think VMI literally dissects the young student that comes in there, kind of pulls him apart, and through the stress, everything that goes on in that environment, would teach him to know everything about himself. He truly knows how far he can go with his anger, he knows how much he can take under stress, he knows how much he can take when he is totally tired, he knows just exactly what he can do when he is physically exhausted, he fully understands himself and his limits and capabilities. . . . I think every VMI man that leaves there knows a great deal about his human capacity to do things under all kinds of duress and stress.[22]
>
> Q: At VMI is mental and physical stress critical to the leadership training?
>
> A: I would agree totally, ma'am. . . . I think our theme is to create a stressful environment and to put as much stress on a cadet as possible to see how he reacts and handles situations under that duress . . . stress is the key fundamental of what we do.
>
> Q: Is it correct, then, that stress is purposely imposed at VMI? In other words, there is stress for the purpose of inducing stress?
>
> A: Yes, ma'am.[23]

Bissell described the rigors of the rat line and then went on to the cadets' living quarters. "Basically," he said, "the rooms are very, very spartan"—a word that became synonymous with VMI during the trial—and the rat line had "far more dramatic, more pressure, more stress than boot camp or basic camp" in the military. If a rat was expelled for having violated the honor code, his disgrace was emphasized by his having to creep out of VMI in the dark hours after midnight when the other cadets were asleep.[24]

Bissell depicted breakout as symbolic of what VMI was trying to accomplish, and his description of himself—a middle-aged colonel—slithering through the muck because he "wanted to see what the rats experienced" conveyed something of the VMI spirit.[25] (He would later say that he was glad he had gone through it once but would not dream of putting himself through the experience again.)[26]

Breakout, he implicitly suggested, was not the kind of activity he would recommend for mixed groups of men and women.

> A: You are in close contact with each other, you are working with each other, in some cases hanging onto each other, as you are moving up that cliff and moving across. . . . Frequently there is a lot of exposure to bodies where clothes are ripped, as you can well imagine from pulling and tugging, there are a lot of body exposure factors that go on there.[27]

Keith asked about VMI's demanding physical education program, which Bissell said was designed both to get the cadets into "good shape" and "to bond them together."

> Q: To your knowledge, has VMI made any determination that women students could not satisfactorily participate in this military drill or any of these PE exercises?
> A: No, I don't feel that VMI or anybody has determined that probably they could or could not do it. I don't think that's the issue at all. . . . My determination is that they could come through and whack through mechanically a rat line and they could go through the motions of a rat line, but once they penetrated VMI, it would break up that totally knit value system where we are all down to the same common base, all taking showers together, all working together, all living together, without any difference whatsoever. . . . It would change it dramatically.[28]

During cross-examination, Bissell elaborated on his fear that the rat line would be changed by women:

> I have visions of standing there and watching a young lady in the rat line with five upperclassmen standing around her, and I can see one screaming at the top of his lungs, jump down and give me 20 push ups, another one standing there saying, give me the menu for lunch, the third one standing there saying, let's have the [list of] superintendents since the inception of the institute, a fourth one sending her up . . . because of a dirty belt buckle and a fifth sending her up for conduct [un]becoming a cadet. I see that young lady is going to have trouble with these people all putting full force on her.[29]

The trouble the "young lady" would have was inherent in her more sensitive nature:

> My experience in the Army has told me that women basically have not the same threshold on emotion as men do. . . . When I was a commander of a group and a battalion once . . . my battalion commanders and I had several sessions over that, how do you handle this, they break down emotionally, only because it's the culture and society.
>
> You don't treat them the same. You back off, you say come back in again when you have your composure, you have yourself back together and we will address your punishment. Inevitably you soften or reconsider the punishment over that period of time. I take that same analogy and I put a young lady in the rat line with a bunch of upperclassmen all over her, she breaks down crying, not only is it going to be terribly demeaning to her, but I wonder how the 18 to 20 year old upperclassmen are going to handle that. . . . I could see after that happened two or three times, the upperclassmen would back off, wouldn't even bother her, stop her . . . she would not be part of the rat line, be walking around the barracks and not part of the system.[30]

One of Keith's goals in questioning Bissell was to demonstrate that there were no activities at VMI that could not be done by women, and she thought she had been successful in that. She saw his testimony as a reflection of the kind of gender stereotyping the law forbade, and she believed that the VMI lawyers had reserved their cross-examination and questioned him later in the trial to give both him and themselves time to recoup. Bissell remembered Keith getting angrier and angrier as she repeatedly demanded, "'Can't women do that? Can't women do that?'" At the end of his testimony, as he recalled it, she was so irate that she crumpled up a piece of paper and threw it to the floor, announcing, "That's all I have" in a tone of disgust.[31] To her, his attempts to depict breakout as "a real rite of passage" rang hollow.[32] To Patterson, however, Bissell's description of VMI rang entirely true. That was the school as he knew it; that was the egalitarian institution about which he would say, "this is an especially good system for people like me, who come from a modest background."[33]

When Bissell stepped down, Kiser adjourned court for the day. Neither side had made any impact on the other. Bissell had perhaps unwittingly typified VMI's sense of horror at the prospect of female cadets: they would have "penetrated" VMI, the way an enemy penetrates a line of defense. The government maintained that when a public institution was involved, women had a right be on the inside along with the men. What Kiser thought was as yet unknown.

THE GOVERNMENT RESUMED ITS CASE the next morning by calling a number of witnesses to testify that military programs at other colleges, as well as at the service academies, had successfully adopted different physical requirements for men and women. VMI's attorneys, in cross-examination, countered that VMI was physically more demanding than the academies were. In the absence of a plaintiff who could take the stand, the Justice Department had to convince Kiser that there were both women who could manage the VMI regimen and women who wanted to do so. It therefore entered into the record dozens of inquiries VMI had received from female high school students. One of them, a young Virginia woman, had written in 1990, "The spartan life of the undergraduates fascinates me," and she thought she could make "a distinct contribution to your curriculum dedicated to developing young people."[34]

The United States' next witness was Joseph M. Spivey (VMI class of 1957), the current Board of Visitors president and a key figure in the board's 1986 decision not to admit women. The Justice Department doubted that the board's inquiry into the possibility of gender integration had ever been more than an empty gesture. Douglas had Spivey read into the record long sections from the minutes of the committee that had visited the federal military academies. The purpose was to demonstrate the disjuncture between the committee's positive findings and the board's decision and to ascertain whether those findings had been available to the board. Patterson responded by getting Spivey to read sections that questioned the desirability of VMI's adopting the less adversarial method it assumed would be necessary if women were admitted. "And does the Board of Visitors of VMI want to change our rat line or any of our systems?" Patterson asked Spivey rhetorically.[35]

VMI's past ability to absorb change continued to be the government's point as Michael Maurer questioned Clark King, head of VMI's physical education department and its former football coach, as well as the holder of a Ph.D. from the University of Virginia. King described the three-week "college orientation workshop" that was provided for thirty African American high school sophomores and juniors each year. The impetus, he testified, had come from a VMI graduate who wanted to attract inner-city students from New York and New Jersey. The alumnus had raised much of the money for the program, which received no state funding, and VMI supplemented it.[36] Later in the trial, the government would show that VMI ran a Cadet Retention Program aimed at helping black freshmen with English and math and that it encouraged the Promaji student club, in which African American cadets could share experiences and provide mutual support. The government saw the programs as evidence that VMI was already responding to students' differences. VMI viewed them as far more peripheral than the anticipated changes that would occur if women were admitted.

King was asked to discuss student failures of VMI's physical fitness test, which the government wanted in the record to show that VMI could adapt itself to students whose physical performance did not comport with what the Institute considered its norm. A student who failed the test "enters a physical, remedial fitness training program to help him to pass on the next test."

> Q: Do you know what percentage of VMI cadets fail the physical fitness test?
> A: It's almost 50 percent when new cadets first come in on the evaluation test. That drops dramatically. Probably something like around 10 percent of those men who will fail their test this month and it will be 4 or 5 percent for the sophomores and juniors, and jumps up a little bit, has been jumping up a little bit for the first classmen, 7 or 8 percent, guessing . . . there would be a program tailored for them, depending on their areas of weakness, most frequently upper body strength. They are put in a remedial program that is held four times a week, Monday, Wednesday, Thursday and Saturday, and the effort on that is to schedule them in, do it often enough so they realize the conditioning effect and be able to pass the test.[37]

VMI maintained that in addition to their negative impact on the bonding of male students, female cadets would not possess the upper body strength necessary for the physical fitness program. King had just admitted, however, that many VMI cadets lacked that strength when they were admitted and required VMI training to achieve it—and some of them might have graduated without ever meeting the standard.

THE TRIAL WAS, IN PART, a battle of expert witnesses who testified on both sides about the purported developmental patterns of young men and young women. The first of them was Clifton F. Conrad, a professor of higher education at the University of Arizona. Conrad was a consultant on higher education for many of the country's universities, as well as a former witness for the Justice Department in a number of desegregation cases. He had been retained by the government to undertake what was referred to as an exhaustive study of VMI and of nearby Virginia Polytechnic Institute and State University (Virginia Tech), which admitted both men and women to its military program.[38] Conrad was the government's star witness, and his testimony went on at length—too long for both Patterson and Kiser, who at times expressed their exasperation at his protracted remarks.

Conrad spoke about VMI's eight inextricably related "interlocking circles": the academic system, the military system and lifestyle, the honor system, the class system with its privileges and responsibilities, the rat system, the athletic system, barracks life, and extracurricular activities.[39] The first class was "responsible for providing overall leadership, for writing the standard operating procedures for the rat line for the following year, supervising the rat break out. . . . They are responsible for being a dyke to a first year student." Along with the first class's (seniors') responsibilities came "certain privileges," and Conrad's account of the kinds of things considered "privileges" at VMI suggested once again the highly structured nature of life there. They included "walking across the common area" and "walking around the mess hall." He also mentioned the second classmen's privilege of smoking and the second class's right to wear patent leather shoes.[40]

VMI argued that women who wanted a military education similar to VMI's could get it at nearby Virginia Tech. The boldness of the assertion is apparent in the definition of a military college as it appeared in one of the official VMI histories: "one where the students live under a system of military discipline at all times during its regular session and wear a military uniform."[41] Conrad, who had undertaken what was described as an exhaustive study of both institutions, rejected the idea that an equivalent experience was available at Tech. In contrast with VMI, only 3 percent of the students at Tech were enrolled in ROTC, so they were a small fraction of a big university with a non-military atmosphere. The university had a "philosophy of building them up from the beginning," rather than VMI's approach of "breaking them down and building them up." Individual differences were appreciated at Virginia Tech as they were not at VMI, but there was closer faculty involvement with students at VMI. "The differences outweigh the similarities," Conrad stated.[42]

Conrad had lived in Virginia from 1977 to 1981. As he studied VMI, he had asked himself, "If I still lived in this state, would my daughter be denied an opportunity if she wasn't able to go to, independent of gender, would she be denied an educational opportunity if she wasn't able to go to VMI?" The answer, he felt "very strongly," was yes.[43]

The Justice Department believed that it had shown all it had to show, because denial of opportunity to women but not to men violated the Constitution. But it knew that to VMI, and perhaps to Judge Kiser, the issue was also how VMI would have to change if women were admitted, so Moore probed those possible alterations with Conrad. The Institute, Conrad stated, would no doubt emulate the military service academies in altering its physical training and athletic systems and in providing the sexes with a modicum of privacy in the Barracks.[44] The question was, how much of a difference to VMI's basic ethos would those modifications make?

> THE COURT: I think the most pertinent question, doctor, will it [admission of women] change the mission? That is what we started off with?
>
> THE WITNESS: There is no reason why VMI cannot continue to be the basic ethos it has had for 152 years and continue to do that. That is, a mission that emphasizes or tries to develop a disciplined leadership for civilian or military life. It is not that everybody is going to choose that kind of experience, but there is no reason why they can't or must change that mission just by the fact that there is going to be women at the institute.[45]

Moore followed through on this:

> Q: Doctor, with regard to your lead premise, which has to do with the mission of VMI, producing the citizen soldier, would the presence of women defeat that purpose that mission or could that mission still be accomplished, in your view?
>
> A: The world is a heterosexual world, the military is heterosexual, the world has changed, as we all know, in many ways. We work with women. The mission of citizen soldier, as VMI has known it, and I described it in the very beginning, [is] preparing people for leadership in civilian life. That mission in no way needs to be undercut.[46]

If Virginia was to win its case, it had to knock down the government's core argument—that the only legal issue was the constitutional right of young women in Virginia to have access to the same diverse, publicly funded educational opportunities as young men—and substitute the question of whether single-sex education was constitutionally permissible. To that end, Patterson and his team had to demonstrate not only that VMI's program worked for men and would be destroyed by the presence of women but also that it was rational for the commonwealth to believe that a VMI education would be the incorrect one for women.

Both sides had to field a number of contradictory arguments. The government might have liked to argue that although some changes at VMI would be necessary, their impact—however great or small—was less important than the constitutional requirement of equality. That, however, might not convince Judge Kiser, so the government tried to show that VMI would not have to change much at all and that it had already absorbed significant changes.

The problem for the defense was arguing that VMI was unique and had to be kept intact to continue doing the job that only it could do, while at the same time convincing the court that women were not being deprived of an opportunity that they could not get elsewhere. The defense took the tack of altering the question before the court. Patterson repeatedly claimed that the real issue was the future of single-sex education. If VMI could not meet the challenge of showing why it had to be kept all male, then, he maintained, no single-sex school in the country could do so.[47] A subset of his argument, like Whittemore's, was the assertion that the tough, privacy-lacking, adversative method would be counterproductive for young women. That point, he told the court, had been made by experts in adolescent development.

The primary expert invoked by VMI to buttress its position was Carol Gilligan, a professor of psychology at Harvard University. In 1982 Gilligan had published a pathbreaking and highly regarded volume, *In a Different Voice: Psychological Theory and Women's Development*.[48] Her thesis was that psychologists who based their developmental theories solely on men necessarily missed half the picture. Psychologists had to listen to the "feminine voice" as well as its masculine counterpart; doing so was essential "for understanding in both sexes the characteristics and precursors of an adult moral conception." Gilligan wrote that "masculinity is defined through separation while femininity is defined through attachment," in effect picking up on the ideas of Chodorow, Mead, Gilmore, and Karst discussed in chapter 3. The feminine voice reflected an emphasis on nonviolence and care rather than justice and fairness as the basic components of morality. Gilligan described the feminine voice as expressing an "ethic of care" rather than an "ethic of rights."[49] Men and women were equally moral; their roads to morality, however, frequently differed.

When asked about Gilligan, Conrad questioned the relevance of her writing to the issue of gender integration at VMI, but he did a poor job of explaining what her book actually said. "What it really suggests, and these are just tendencies between men and women," he replied, "is that it really suggests that women may be less likely to enroll at VMI because it celebrates what is called a traditionally male way of knowing, than males. That's not a terribly surprising kind of thing. Overall, I think that in my judgment it's really not pertinent to the inquiry."[50] What Conrad presumably had in mind but did not mention was Gilligan's careful statement that "contrasts between male and female voices . . . [represent] a distinction between two modes of thought," rather than "a generalization about either sex."[51] The Justice Department may have suffered from its neglect of that point.

THE GOVERNMENT WAS PREPARED TO LOSE. Good lawyers must always be prepared to lose at trial, however strong they believe their case to be. So part of their strategy is to create a record that will be persuasive in appeals court. "I always knew that we would win this case—I always believed that," Judith Keith said later,[52] but at the time, she could not be certain that the case would be won at the trial level. Virginia, after all, had made its pre-emptive strike to ensure that the case would be heard in Roanoke rather than Alexandria. Judge Kiser might not be influenced by what was rumored to be his golfing friendship with Robert Patterson, but he came from the same social circle and presumably shared many of the same values. So, when the trial adjourned on Friday afternoon, Keith was determined that the week ahead would be used to make the record for appeal.

VMI in the nineteenth century. VMI Archives.

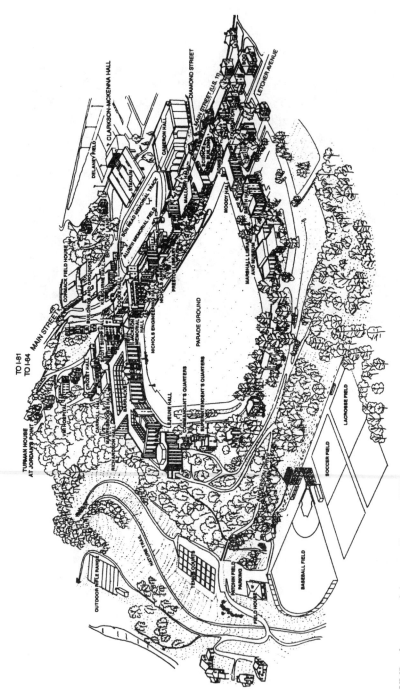

VMI today: map of the post. Courtesy VMI.

The Barracks. Nathan Beck.

Statue of Virginia Mourning
Her Dead. Nathan Beck.

Outside the Barracks and
the statue of Stonewall
Jackson. Nathan Beck.

Leaving the Barracks in traditional VMI parade dress. Andrew R. Alonso.

Rats assembled in Barracks, with upperclassmen (in uniform) looking on.
Nathan Beck.

Before 1997: male rats memorizing the *Rat Bible*. Nathan Beck.

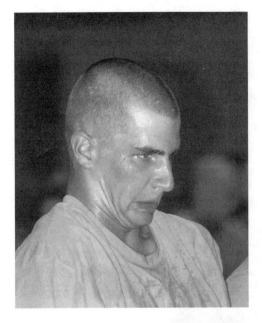

Rat trying to maintain the proper position. Nathan Beck.

Exercising the rats. Nathan Beck.

Jackson Memorial Hall, with the mural of the battle of New Market at the front. Nathan Beck.

General Josiah Bunting. Courtesy VMI.

Dressed for New Market, 1995.
Nathan Beck.

At New Market, 1995. Nathan Beck.

Justice Ruth Bader Ginsburg. Eileen Colton, Collection of the U.S. Supreme Court.

Justices of the U.S. Supreme Court, 1996. Standing (left to right): Ruth Bader Ginsburg, David H. Souter, Clarence Thomas, Stephen Breyer. Seated (left to right): Antonin Scalia, John Paul Stevens, William H. Rehnquist, Sandra Day O'Connor, Anthony M. Kennedy. Richard Strauss, Collection of the Supreme Court Historical Society.

11

If Women Were Rats

I think that if women were admitted to VMI the whole program
would collapse. . . . They can't shed their gender. They can't
shed their physical attributes.

—David Riesman

When the trial resumed at ten o'clock the following Monday
morning, Keith called James F. Brewer III to the stand in the government's
effort to get what it considered the relevant facts into the record. Brewer, an
expert in the planning, design, and operation of higher educational facilities
such as student residence halls, told the court that conversions of dormitories for coeducation at West Point and Virginia Tech had presented no difficulty. At West Point, men and women were housed in adjacent rooms, with
gang showers and toilets for each sex either on the same floor or on alter-
nating floors. Some bathrooms at Virginia Tech were used by both sexes; the
doors had chains on them, and there were signs that indicated which gender was inside. Bathrooms, Brewer said, simply were not a problem.[1]

The battle of the bathrooms continued nonetheless. Patterson elicited the
information that those at West Point and Tech were not like the ones at VMI:
bathrooms at West Point and Tech had partitions between the toilets. Attacking the idea that lack of privacy was crucial to VMI, Keith got Brewer to
mention that there were a few fifth-floor bedrooms at VMI that had solid
doors without the privacy-eliminating windows.[2] VMI would counter that the
rooms were used only until enough rats had dropped out so that all those remaining could fit into the fourth-floor rooms.

Major General Stanton R. Musser, a former air force officer, vice commandant of cadets at the Air Force Academy when it went coed in 1976, and now commandant of cadets at Virginia Tech, was next. Keith led him through a series of questions designed to show that gender integration could work in a military setting. Tech had begun admitting women to its corps in 1973; 67 of the 394 current cadets were women, and over the years, female cadets had held every leadership position in the corps. That had not impeded the military atmosphere. Cadets had to memorize the *Guidon,* which was similar to VMI's *Bullet;* they could be penalized with one-hour marching tours or calisthenics if they failed to recite it properly when told to do so by an upperclassman. Tech had a dyke system, a class system, and an honor code, and the *Guidon* stated that its mission was "to produce men and women . . . who are educated and trained for military service to their country and prepared to be effective leaders in the varied work of military and civil life."[3]

Broaddus, cross-examining, established that the number of women in the corps had declined since 1985 in spite of recruitment efforts. He had Musser testify about the many ways in which Tech differed from VMI: cadets were permitted to be married, and both married cadets and those from the surrounding area could live outside the dorms; strict discipline ended with the academic day; there was no inducement of stress for the sake of stress; and the method used was positive rather than negative motivation.[4] The implicit message was that if few women were applying to the much less strenuous Virginia Tech, they surely would avoid VMI, and the VMI ethos would have been "destroyed" for the sake of only a handful of women.

Musser was followed to the stand by Colonel Patrick A. Toffler, West Point's director of institutional research. Toffler had seen service in Korea before he went to work at the Pentagon. He might well have left the trial thinking that combat was relatively straightforward compared with litigation. The claim that West Point, the nation's leading service academy, had been successfully gender integrated was an important element of the government's case. The assertions that integration at West Point had failed and that, in any event, West Point was a holiday camp in comparison to VMI were equally crucial to Virginia's position. Toffler was caught in the middle.

Under questioning by Douglas, Toffler acknowledged that West Point administrators had been against admitting women. Women now constituted 10 percent of West Point's 4,200 cadets, however, and almost all of them went into the army as second lieutenants. There had been no alterations "in terms of policies and programs and procedures," and changes in physical requirements were minimal. In the physical aptitude exam that is part of the admissions process, "one of those events, the pull up, was changed to a flex arm hang for women. And then on admission to the Military Academy in the physical education course that takes place in the academic year, where men routinely took boxing and wrestling, women took self defense and combatives." Toffler noted that the class of 1990's brigade commander, its highest rank, was a woman.[5]

> Q: And would you tell me . . . whether or not in your judgment women have been successfully integrated into the program at West Point?
>
> A: Yes . . . they are satisfying all of the graduation requirements at [a] very high rate of completion, and they are going off to service in the Army and doing a remarkable job.[6]

Toffler described the six to seven weeks of summer field training that took place after a cadet's first year and testified that women plebes were completing it successfully. It included "hand to hand combat, bayonet training, fighting with an instrument . . . there is a considerable amount of marching and mountain climbing, patrolling, navigation . . . airborne training, survival, escape and resistance training, air assault training, northern weather warfare training . . . and women participate in all of those activities."[7]

William Clineburg rose for what would be a grueling five-hour cross-examination. His goal was to show that integration at West Point had been difficult, and he implied that Toffler's testimony would have been less positive had the colonel and other West Point personnel not been under political pressure. "And in fact, [don't] people at West Point have orders to either support that decision [to admit women] or leave?" Clineburg demanded. "And in fact, if you don't support it at West Point, your performance evaluation or your rating will be lowered? . . . No dissent on this issue is permitted at West Point. Correct?"[8]

> Q: You mentioned women were doing very well at West Point. One was selected as brigade commander?
>
> A: That's correct.
>
> Q: You explained how that worked, didn't you?
>
> A: Yes, I did.
>
> Q: I thought I heard you say based on their various academic performances and other ratings of cadets through the years, the superintendent and commandant came up with a pool of potential brigade commanders. Is that correct?
>
> A: That is a summary of the process, yes.
>
> Q: And the superintendent and commandant decided who the brigade commander would be? . . . And of course, the superintendent is responsible for assuring that West Point meets it mission?

A: That's right.

Q: And part of its application is to provide role models for women cadets? . . . So, you would agree that just because women were appointed to these various positions such as brigade commander or cadet or company commander, doesn't mean they were the best qualified. Correct?

A: No, I wouldn't agree with that.[9]

Toffler's office had done a survey in 1990 showing that 85 percent of male cadets and 40 percent of female cadets felt that they had been treated exactly the same as members of the other sex. In the years 1981 to 1990, 18 to 30 percent of men and 54 to 79 percent of women believed that they had been treated more harshly.[10] To Toffler, that meant that acceptance of gender integration took time; to Clineburg, it meant that it was failing. Then Clineburg raised the subject of whether enough women would apply to VMI to justify requiring integration and to create the kind of critical mass necessary for it to be successful.

Q: But certainly, at West Point the experience has been that you need a certain percentage of women or they are going to feel as though they are a minority? . . . I think I understand what you are saying to be that you remain concerned that women feel as though they are a minority, and that is why they have these perceptions about how they are treated. Isn't that right?

A: Women are a minority.

Q: And you think that is one of the reasons they have these perceptions about how they are treated?

A: Yes.

Q: And don't you think any institution that was considering bringing women into a formerly all male institution needs to take that into account?

A: Yes. . . .

Q: And another reason you may have difficulty attracting more women is because all of the military academies are currently competing for many of the same women. Isn't that right?

A: That's right.

Q: And in fact, you think the percentage may be as high as 50 percent of the female applicants are considering other academies as well?

A: That's reasonable.

Q: Do you also agree it would be hard for West Point, or harder for West Point to attract women if it did not provide them with essentially a free education and a job upon graduation?

A: Yes.

Q: And don't they also pay West Point cadets an allowance?

A: Yes, they do.

Q: What is that monthly allowance?

A: It comes to about $6,000, $6,500 a year.

Q: So, that's $500 or $600 a month?

A: Right.

Q: And if you took away that allowance, that might reduce the pool of applicants as well?[11]

VMI, of course, provided no such allowance, and out-of-state cadets had to pay tuition.

Next came the subject of sexual harassment at West Point. In various surveys, 24 to 60 percent of female students reported having been harassed.[12] Toffler repeatedly attempted to downplay the incidents' importance, and Clineburg became exasperated.

Q: You are an optimistic, positive person, aren't you, Colonel Toffler?

A: [No response.]

Q: Aren't you?

A: I think we should approach trying to resolve these things in a positive way, yes.[13]

WHEN COURT RECONVENED on the morning of April 9, the government rested its case, and Roanoke lawyer William Poff rose for VMI. It seemed reasonable to assume that Kiser knew Poff well and that the attorney may have been added to the VMI team with that in mind. He moved for dismissal and for a judgment in favor of the defense.

Justice O'Connor had said in *Hogan* that gender-based classifications were constitutional only if the state showed an "exceedingly persuasive justification" based on an "important governmental objective" rather than on "traditional, often inaccurate, assumptions about the proper roles of men and women."[14] The Justice Department and VMI referred repeatedly to that case during the trial, and it was clear that both they and Judge Kiser considered it controlling. Virginia therefore had to make an "exceedingly persuasive" case that maintaining a single-sex admissions policy at VMI served an "important governmental objective." To do so, Poff turned to the evidence of the government's own experts, beginning with Conrad.

> Dr. Conrad acknowledged that the VMI mission is different in a very major way from the mission of the United States military academies . . . [that] the VMI system of education provides a unique educational experience and that the admission of women to VMI would inevitably and irrevocably change the character of that experience.[15]

That point had been corroborated by Knapp, Bissell, and Musser, Poff said, for they all "agree that the admission of females to VMI would create a new class of students and that this would destroy the educational method as implemented by the rat system and the class system of treating everyone alike."[16]

Yes, admitting women to VMI would create another kind of diversity, Poff acknowledged, but the commonwealth was the proper entity to decide what kind of diversity it wanted: "the judgment as to how to achieve diversity and what kind of diversity is best is one for the State of Virginia and the VMI Board of Directors, Board of Visitors, not Dr. Conrad or the Justice Department to make." He reintroduced the themes of federalism and the perceived attempt by Washington to exceed its legitimate powers. "This Court cannot permit the United States and Dr. Conrad to substitute their judgment for that of the Commonwealth and the Board of Visitors as to what constitutes a legitimate governmental purpose effectuated by the admission policy of VMI."[17]

Douglas rose to reply for the government. He too invoked *Hogan*. "We have shown that there is no important governmental interest," he maintained. "Women have the right to attend VMI, they have the right to benefit from public funds, they have the right to choose whatever school in this state they want to do it, and one group of people, be it cadets, be it alumni, be it Board of Visitor members, cannot say that they should be denied their Constitutional right and their right under the law because they don't want them there."[18]

Kiser ruled on the motion immediately, demonstrating how aware he was that the litigation would not end in his courtroom. "There is one guiding light in this case," he declared, "and that is the decision should not be made on less than a full exposition of both sides of the problem. We need a full record on this . . . I think this Court is just the first stop for the case, and I would be remiss in my duties if I did not develop a full record in the case, so I will overrule the motion" to dismiss the suit.[19] It was time for VMI to present its case.

VMI'S FIRST WITNESS WAS Richard C. Richardson, a professor of education, leadership, and policy studies at Arizona State University. Richardson was a former marine with a Ph.D. in educational administration. He had chaired between twenty-five and thirty teams that had evaluated programs in higher education for the Middle States Association and North Central Association, including one that assessed West Point in 1989. He had also testified for the United States in desegregation cases, and the Justice Department team was bewildered and rather appalled to find him on the other side.[20] In fact, as the court would learn, Richardson saw racial integration and gender integration as very distinct issues.

He was particularly concerned that the admission of women to VMI would change barracks life dramatically, primarily the lack of privacy and total equality. Richardson's point, and that of the Institute and its alumni, was that treatment that not only *was* the same but also was *seen* to be the same was one of the things that made VMI great. The cadets knew that there was no favoritism because every student at the Institute, with its general communal existence, windowed bedroom doors, and unpartitioned bathrooms, could quite literally see how every other student was treated. Privacy was not stripped away mindlessly; it was deliberately eliminated to maintain equality. Absolute equality was designed to send the cadets an unmistakable signal that it was up to them to invent themselves. Success or failure became a matter of will rather than extraneous characteristics such as wealth, as Patterson's career there demonstrated.

Richardson compared VMI to a medieval cloister, saying that its isolation was typified by the honor system. "Institutions that have existed for character building," he reflected, "have tended to seclude themselves from the world, to seek isolation . . . a place where moral development can proceed unimpeded by the distractions of the outside world." The honor code was

> a symbolic way of emphasizing the absolute boundaries of this association from the rest of the world. . . . The honor code does that. . . . You either follow the behavior that the institute requires or you report that you have not followed that behavior with all the consequences that that implies . . . there is only one sanction, and that sanction is your removal from . . . the community. So it marks the absolute boundaries between what is and what is not VMI, and it adds to that sense of isolation from the rest of the world.[21]

In every way, Richardson concluded, VMI was a world apart: "the emphasis that VMI places on character development, on honor and integrity, on these kind of values is extremely unusual, and it is unique in terms of the institutions that I have visited." He added, "The Commonwealth of Virginia and this nation will never have too many educated and honorable men who are able to behave on the basis of the values that VMI seeks to inculcate," and he lamented the fact that the "male" model of education "has almost been allowed to disappear."[22] He explained what he meant by a male model:

> The single gender environment allows for an experience that is designed around male values, male tolerance, to exist in a virtually pure form. That is, it is not altered by the need to consider cross sex relationships . . . [and] it seems to be that the advantage of that is just intricately related to the quality of the outcome in terms of the building of character and the inculcation of leadership in men.[23]

There was no doubt in Richardson's mind that, given the "nurturing" environment necessary to women, they could not do well at VMI. The result would be the destruction of the adversative model. Ironically, by insisting on access to the VMI experience, women would make that experience disappear.

What might seem to be a fairly obvious line of questioning about the VMI experience went unasked. The Justice Department never honed in on the question of what evidence VMI had to show that the more rigorous aspects of "the VMI experience as it now exists"—the rat line, the lack of privacy—were related to the ability of the less than 20 percent of VMI graduates who joined the armed forces to function well there, or how those same rigors contributed to the success of the more than 80 percent of VMI students who did not choose military careers. It was such a glaring omission that it renewed the speculation, mentioned earlier, that federal politicians were limiting the attorneys' ability to present their case.

William Broaddus rose to present VMI's star witness. The video monitor was turned on, and the court watched the testimony of sociologist David Riesman. It would be invoked repeatedly when Kiser wrote his decision.

Riesman's may have been the only name in the case to be recognized by everyone in the courtroom. His *Lonely Crowd* had been required reading for college students since its publication in 1950. The general public was less aware of his numerous influential books on higher education—*The Academic Revolution, On Higher Education, Choosing a College President,* and *Constraint and Variety in American Education* were just a few of them—his clerkship for Justice Louis Brandeis after graduation from Harvard Law School, or the twenty or so honorary degrees he had received since then.

His doctors had forbidden the eighty-two-year-old Harvard professor to travel, so Broaddus, Boland, and Moore taped Riesman's deposition at his home in Cambridge. Riesman prepared for it by watching what he described as three "extremely vivid and dramatic" VMI videotapes and by reading materials provided by the Institute: its catalog, the leading history of VMI, Richardson's deposition, the 1990 alumni survey, and statements by black alumni.[24] The result, as the lawyers discovered, was a man who had come to view VMI as a fortunate relic of a happier age.

Broaddus asked Riesman to describe his ideal college. "As I've sometimes put it," Riesman replied, "I'd like everyone who graduates from college to know two foreign languages, two lifelong sports, two musical instruments, to have read things about many parts of the world, to have lived in some other part of the world, to have experienced a different culture."[25] (One can imagine people in the courtroom mentally comparing their college days with Ries-man's more demanding ideal.)

> Q: If you would, continue on with respect to your comments on personal values. . . .
>
> A: I think that I just can't emphasize enough the importance of discipline, not only in the affluent portions of society, but because they set the model, because the popular culture supports hedonism, supports early gratification. Young people don't develop as they should. . . . Young people don't test themselves. They don't climb moral or physical mountains. . . . There's hardly a college in the country where it's impossible to get an education, but there are many that certainly make it easy to get by, and I think getting by has become the American norm. . . .
>
> One more thought about that, which is that the extracurricular life is quite out of control, and diagonally across from this house where we're having this hearing is one of the Harvard houses, and I don't have to walk very far to hear Rock Around the Clock and loud student rooms with music at all hours.[26]

VMI, in contrast, seemed to him to be "the strongest assault that I'm fa-miliar with in this country at the college level on the rating, dating, mating, youth culture." He was particularly impressed by the Institute's egalitarian ethos, its absence of "cross sex relations [that] get in the way of the same sex friendships that would have been formed in an earlier day," and its "total en-vironment."[27]

> Q: Is the absence of privacy an important part of the VMI system?
>
> A: It's an essential part of the VMI system because it is part of the way the honor code is monitored. It's part of the way in which the students are made to feel part of an institution. . . . The status, the wealth, the physical attraction, the ethnicity, whatever, is irrelevant in the VMI system; and, therefore, the most complete equal-ity, as against the coed system where the dating and the aspirations for, now less common, but still in the south . . . young women are thinking of marriage even very early.[28]

He thought that there was evidence "as to the negative effects of coedu-cation for many people who experience it, both women and men," although he did not indicate where that evidence could be found. "For many boys," he believed, "a single sex school . . . is optimal."[29]

> There are certain things that boys will do in the absence of girls . . . boys will learn a foreign language more readily in the absence of girls, will draw more readily than they will. They will dance, do all sorts of things that seem girlish where girls are better at it earlier. . . . In a boys' school or a men's college, men can write poetry, esoteric, exotic, erotic, what have you, and extend themselves in some ways that can happen in the optimal men's colleges, coed colleges, but somewhat less likely.[30]

If women were admitted to VMI, not only would a single-sex institution be lost; the VMI culture would be lost as well. Asked by Moore where a female student in Virginia could go for an education comparable to that at VMI, Riesman remarked, "the irony of your question is that by attaining what she wants she would lose what she wants because it wouldn't be there anymore."[31]

> I've tried to imagine several scenarios. One was I tried to imagine a women's VMI, wholly women. Inconceivable to me even the most, those women who, as I sometimes put it, are more macho than thou would not make up a cohort who would be able to deal with rats in the invariant way that VMI now deals with rats.
>
> I think that if women were admitted to VMI the whole program would collapse. I cannot imagine . . . that women would, for example, treat rats as rats are treated now at VMI. They simply wouldn't.
>
> Women would not go through the shaving of the head, the other reductions of previous attributes. They can't shed their gender. They can't shed their physical attributes.[32]

He apparently assumed that coeducation would mean integrated nudity. "There's still in the south and in Virginia, there are still men who divide the women into classes, the good girls and the bad girls and who are not used to seeing nude women on a daily basis, let alone a roommate basis."[33]

The loss of the VMI ethos would be doubly tragic: because of the way women learn, they could never have benefited from it, so it would have been destroyed for nothing. VMI concentrated on breaking students down, but "women do need more support, lose self-confidence earlier."[34]

> A: It begins, I would say, in middle school. Women become oriented to cheerleaders. . . .
>
> Q: Does the VMI system, as it presently operates, present an environment in which women could succeed?
>
> A: I don't see how they could succeed because they're not capable of the ferocity requisite to make the program work, and they are also not capable of enduring without—how should I say—I would fear, I would fear really psychological trauma if they went through the rat program. . . .
>
> Q: How would VMI have to change, sir, if women were admitted in order to create an environment in which women would be able to succeed?
>
> A: VMI would have to change so much that it would be hard to see what would be distinctive about it . . . not only would it be destructive for VMI and, therefore, for what VMI contributes to the country through its graduates and through what it stands for, I think it would be destructive for the country in another way.
>
> It would be one more example of the homogenization process.[35]

Riesman had wondered for a while whether his views were influenced by stereotypes and was satisfied that they were not. Like VMI, he apparently thought of a stereotype as a false mental construct, rather than as a statement about averages that frequently was true. His mother, he noted, was a "feminist" Bryn Mawr graduate; his aunt had gone to Wellesley and become "an active woman late in life, after her children were grown"; a female cousin had been a commissioner of welfare in Pennsylvania. Riesman himself had "helped make Harvard co-residential as well as coeducational" and had "introduced the first woman tutor" into a Harvard dorm. "So I was, I guess, an early leader and supporter of the women's movements" and could not be guilty of stereotyping.[36] He added that his thinking about male and female learning patterns had been influenced by Carol Gilligan's work. Unlike Gilligan, however, he postulated that the different learning styles of men and women had biological roots: "I cannot conceive the social engineering and, to put it most dramatically, the genetic engineering that would be necessary to have the same program in the presence of women."[37]

At the end of the deposition, Riesman made it clear who *he* thought had been on the stand that day:

> THE WITNESS: I thought all three of you did very admirably and reflectively.
> MR. BROADDUS: Thank you, sir.
> MR. MOORE: Thank you.[38]

THE FIRST VMI WITNESS on April 11 was Dr. Paul O. Davis III, an expert in human physiology who had published extensively in the field and had done contract work for the Department of Defense on the implications of physiology for women in the military. VMI brought him in to reiterate the point that because of the physiological differences between men and women, an integrated VMI either would have to establish separate physical education requirements and activities or would condemn VMI men to a program that would hold no challenges for them. Among the VMI activities Davis called "incompatible . . . with female physiology" were rope climbing, incline sit-ups, giant steps, leg raises, military press, and log walk with cable. If women attempted them, they would have 300 percent more injuries than the men. The rat line would have to undergo such "significant alterations" that "it would lose its allure and subsequently lose a large portion of its attractiveness to the males who would attempt to take this course."[39]

VMI's final witness, and by far the most eloquent, was VMI alumnus and educator Josiah Bunting. William Broaddus began his questioning by asking Bunting about the mission of VMI. Bunting was still at Lawrenceville at the time, but he was very much a part of the effort to defend VMI's admissions policy. In light of the fact that he would be the superintendent of VMI when the first female cadets arrived on post, Bunting's view of the Institute's function is particularly interesting. He described its mission as "the education of the citizen soldiers" who would "regard and esteem public service in positions of trust and leadership, public service broadly conceived to include not only the armed forces, but government, politics, community service, local boards."[40]

> Q: Now, does the concept of public service embody certain personal characteristics that are inculcated at the Institute?
>
> A: Yes, it certainly does. One might identify quickly a number of those characteristics. Pertinacity, character, resolution, self-reliance, moral courage, and then on a slightly lesser plane, the habitual willingness to work very, very hard over long periods of time, whatever obstacles may intervene. All of those are subsumed under the general heading of the quaint Victorian word "character," by which I understand is meant the willingness to do what you think is right under all circumstances, no matter what obstacles may interpose themselves.[41]

Broaddus asked what role barracks life played in developing these characteristics.

> A: I think it's important, whenever you talk about our subject this morning, to distinguish between education and training. . . . When we talk about education, we are talking about equipping people with intellectual self reliance, with confidence in their own intellectual judgments, with habitual willingness to study the evidence for a long time before reaching judgments fairly and indispassionately [sic]. . . .
>
> Training, on the other hand, implies habituation to a certain kind of conduct. It implies the inculcation of those qualities of human character which help the human appetite, the human will to subordinate themselves to the proposition of intellect. In the barracks, it seems to me, we enter the problems more of training than of education, various usages of barracks life tend to inculcate those principles which serve as the logical or useful concomitant of intellectual education outside the barracks.[42]

Bunting went on to explain the role of induced stress, egalitarianism, and lack of privacy in the cadets' training. He called induced stress "in many ways . . . its most important component" and said that he understood it as creating

> a holistic life . . . in which people are required to answer a number of obligations, a number of responsibilities almost at the same time. And through that kind of immersion in a closed system, they develop over a period of time during the rat year and during the rest of the cadetship, a certain ability to function effectively under conditions of stress and demands and challenge later on in life.

He considered egalitarianism to be a key element in American life ("we are a country which has achieved all its greatest traits as a result of the fact that we have had equal kind of opportunity") and in life at VMI:

> A: In barracks, you are exactly what you are without any baggage—social, financial, whatever—that you may have brought with you. . . .
>
> Q: The lack of privacy?
>
> A: The lack of privacy . . . is equally important. You basically must function as part of a community and the lack of privacy, it seems to me, drives home the lesson, hour after hour, day after day, that you are ultimately part of a community and that your value to the community depends on how willing and how able you are to contribute to it and to subsume your own ego in its larger purposes.[43]

The end result of the VMI experience was a cadet who was not only public spirited but also a whole and highly independent human being. When Broaddus asked if the VMI system produced "a monolithic product" or allowed "for creativity, perhaps even eccentricity," Bunting replied:

> The extraordinary beauty of this system is that by eliminating all of the normal signs of social distinction or achievement or wealth or merit or anything else, it throws the cadets completely upon their own interior resources. These are the kind of things, these kinds of challenges which tend to produce people later on of extraordinary self reliance, I might almost say eccentricity. A willingness to speak up, a willingness to say one thing, a willingness to pursue one's own line of endeavor, without any particularly solicitude for public opinion. So that the paradoxical result, it seems to me, of a good VMI education, is to create just the opposite of what a superficial examination might lead one to believe.[44]

He considered an institution like VMI to be of great importance in the United States. Although they were of different generations, Bunting's emphasis on character and public service echoed Riesman's concern about a decline in the American moral fiber.

> A: Perhaps at no time in American history with the conceivable exception of the Roaring Twenties has American culture put a higher premium on quick gratification of, of selfish impulses and desires, a higher premium on the rapid achievement of material success and the appurtenances of material success. And a heavier premium on doing what one can do to achieve those kinds of status symbols that elevate the bearer of those status symbols in his own estimation.
>
> It seems to me in a culture like this, VMI and the very few institutions that share its notion of mission, such as The Citadel, perform an exemplary role in standing up for those qualities which are perdurable to all of our history as a Republic and to all of our future.[45]

His sense of what was perdurable, or permanent and constant, in American society was perhaps somewhat idealized.

If I can hark back just for a moment to the period in our country between 1960 and 1965, the period of the so-called New Frontier in politics. Typically, college graduates of that era . . . went into the military or became priests or went off to get Ph.D.'s, or went into the service or joined the Peace Corps, they did the kind of things which fertilized the commonweal. You had a mixture of idealism, of a sense of obligation and duty. . . . Nowadays, it seems to me, in our society, such pursuits have a much lower standing in the minds of young people and relatively few are attracted to them.[46]

Bunting was passionate in his conviction that women had to be kept out of VMI; that their admission "would represent the complete disruption of, if not its purposes, of its abilities to deliver on its stated purposes and mission." He was convinced that women could not be successfully assimilated into a formerly all-male college unless they constituted a "critical mass," which he defined as at least 40 percent of the student body. That was the goal he had achieved at Briarcliff. He was absolutely certain, however, that VMI "couldn't even come close" to attracting such a number. Even if it did, things would be no better. "You would have a movement towards a relaxed, much more relaxed military culture. It would certainly be the end of the rat line and all of the closed disciplinary systems that we have talked about."[47]

If VMI attracted only 10 percent women, Bunting thought,

it would be cost ineffective . . . in terms of education, in terms of the moral make up and character of the institution. You would have an overwhelming dispropor- tionate amount of energy and solicitude flowing to the care and concern and needs of that very small minority group. . . . It would be a brutal disservice to young women. . . . It would be to make a mockery of sound educational philosophy in a residential setting.[48]

Women, Bunting said under John Moore's cross-examination, could acquire the same education and character building—but at Virginia Tech, not at VMI.[49]

WHEN THE LAST WITNESS was excused, Judith Keith began her closing argument with a firm reiteration of the points the government had been trying to make throughout.

This case is about the denial of the equal protection guarantees of the United States Constitution to female students. . . .

VMI is a fine school, but that is precisely the point. It is a fine, indeed, a unique school. The unique opportunities it offers should be open to everyone without re- gard to gender. . . .

The evidence plainly shows that there is nothing inherent in VMI's unique educational experience that precludes the admission and matriculation of qualified female students. Superintendent Knapp testified that there was no VMI admissions criterion that women could not meet. . . . Dr. Richardson testified that there will be no effect on academic or military programs at VMI. Colonel Bissell . . . testified that no determination has been made that female students could not satisfactorily and successfully perform in the systems and programs at VMI. . . . Dr. Richardson confirmed that there was nothing about the rat line or honor system that women could not do.[50]

If VMI based its argument on its past, Keith was willing to dip into history as well, but she drew on another text. VMI's assertions about "the alleged inability of female students to deal with stress generated by the VMI system" represented "nothing more than gender based stereotyping." It was a familiar phenomenon, she said. Both West Point and the University of Virginia had fought to keep women out, but women were now functioning there successfully, and neither institution had suffered as a result of their admission. VMI would not have to "abandon its mission and goal of producing educated and honorable citizen soldiers" if women were admitted, and it was ludicrous to say that VMI would attract none. Testimony at the trial had shown that in spite of its well-known policy of accepting only men, VMI had received 347 inquiries from women in the past two years alone.[51]

Keith's final peroration was, on paper, an impassioned statement of the law's rejection of discrimination, although some reporters wrote that she delivered it in a semimonotone.[52]

Female students have the Constitutional right to attend VMI. They have the right to benefit from public funds and from this unique public educational opportunity. They have the right to choose whatever school in the Commonwealth of Virginia they want to attend. No group of people, whether it is VMI students, administrators, alumni, or the Board of Visitors, can continue to deny the constitutional rights of female students simply because they fear change and because they just do not want women. These reasons cannot be translated into important governmental objectives and completely fail to demonstrate an exceedingly persuasive justification for the discriminatory admissions policy.

Your Honor, VMI may change, but change does not mean the end of tradition, and more importantly, change should not be feared or resisted when it vindicates the constitutional rights of those for whom tradition has meant exclusion.[53]

Griffin Bell rose to present the first of two closing statements for Virginia, focusing on the argument that the federal government was charging into Virginia to destroy one of its special institutions. There were echoes of litigation for racial integration in his rhetoric; in fact, Bell accused the government of harking back to an earlier and unloved era.

> As I say, every case is going to be fact driven. I don't know what regulations they have in the Department of Justice for bringing these cases, if they intend to bring any more. Ordinarily, our policy in this country is set by legislative bodies or groups to whom they have delegated part of their legislative power. . . . There is no delegation from Congress to the Justice Department to bring these kinds of cases, so I don't know where we are going to end up, they can just bring a case, or they have taken the position, as has been taken here, that every single sex school is doing something wrong, that they can't exist, then we have got a policy that is all sail and no anchor. They can just do as they believe, they have a roving commission to make the world over in their own image.[54]

Bell was factually incorrect; as we saw in chapter 4, the Civil Rights Act of 1964 specifically authorizes the Justice Department to bring "these kinds of cases" when an individual alleges discrimination on the basis of sex or race or religion.[55] Patterson, making the last statement, echoed Bell's attack on the Justice Department. He did so in a voice that contrasted sharply with Keith's calm manner, looking up from his handwritten notes to glare at the opposing lawyers, sometimes bellowing at them, occasionally pounding his fist.[56]

Patterson's presentation tracked VMI's tactics outside the courtroom. Bell had briefed the media throughout the trial, sometimes holding informal sessions during the morning and afternoon breaks, as well as at lunchtime. VMI had in fact hired a public relations firm to join its lawyers in daily press briefings.[57] (Justice Department policy at the time of the trial precluded the attorneys from discussing the case.) The strategy worked. Media accounts reflected the VMI team's assertion that the case was about the future of single-sex education. Patterson warned that VMI "should be saved from the government's desire for 'needless conformity' and given 'the same protection as the spotted owl and six-legged salamander.'"[58] Whittemore was quoted as saying, "There are differences between men and women. The cutting edge of feminist theory recognizes that. The focus is not on equal treatment but equitable treatment."[59] The result of the two lawyers' accessibility was favorable articles about them in otherwise unsympathetic places such as the *Washington Post*. Patterson was betting reporters steak dinners that his team would win.[60]

Now Patterson brought the war of the image into the courtroom. In doing so, he returned to the theme of a besieged VMI valiantly staving off an invading federal government.

Your Honor, I may be a little emotional, I am speaking for a long line of VMI men, and I hope I'm speaking for a long line yet to come. What we have here, Your Honor, is an amorphous thing called the United States Government.

Referring to the Justice Department lawyers, he told Kiser, "we don't have anybody in this courtroom but these four, lady and three gentlemen, that we look upon as the plaintiffs." Patterson hinted broadly that the government's insistence on protecting the privacy of the purported young woman who wrote the original letter of complaint actually masked the fact that the entire case was something that had been dreamed up in the bowels of a huge Washington bureaucracy rather than a genuine complaint:

> Your Honor, they talked about these inquiries that we received for the last two years. We have been in the newspaper, Your Honor, virtually every day for the last two years. Some organizations in this country like to set people up, and I don't suggest, and have no evidence that we were set up, but what I'm saying to you, sir, those things could be set up.[61]

After all, Patterson asked rhetorically, what did the government's case consist of? VMI had drawn on David Riesman, "the most respected sociologist in the country," as well as Richardson and Bunting. "When you compare Dr. Conrad, sir . . . it is like comparing a sparrow to eagles." "The government's experts, both of them, for that matter, Mr. Brewer and Dr. Conrad, have never spent one day in uniform of a soldier in the service of this country, and if you have not been in the military, sir, you cannot understand it. I do not know what the records of my friends from the Justice Department are." Conrad, he reminded the court, "has been a paid consultant for them for 10 years in the Civil Rights Division," again reminding Kiser of racial integration litigation— and throwing doubt on the reasons for Conrad's testimony. He implicitly accused Toffler of lying for personal gain: "And then we had Colonel Toffler, who I suggest to Your Honor is a fine soldier, he is following his orders, and I would suspect, without knowing, sir, that he is hoping that somewhere on the horizon there may be a star for him."[62]

Contrary to what Toffler said, West Point was in trouble because politicians similar to those in the Justice Department had made the school admit women:

> West Point, for whatever reasons it wants to change in their systems, and they have changed, has abandoned this system, think about it, because there is so much politics in it, has abandoned the system that produced Grant, that produced Lee, Jackson, Eisenhower, Pershing, MacArthur, Patton, and recently General Schwartzkopf.[63]

"Now, I asked Your Honor when we started this case," Patterson reiterated, "if we can't meet the test in *Hogan,* what institution can? And we start with *Hogan* and we know that the Constitution of the United States does not say that you can't have single sex institutions."[64] Why, as Patterson saw it, was the government so opposed to single-sex colleges? The answer could only be that the government was trying to create a unisex society.

> You know, sometimes in this case I feel like that the Civil Rights division thinks that God didn't create the differences between men and women, but VMI did. . . .
>
> The Department of Justice has tried from the day one in this case to make this a battle between men and women. It is not that. It has nothing to do with that. They make out like VMI men spring out of the earth, that we don't have mothers, that we don't have wives, that we don't have daughters, that we can't get along in the world with women, we can't live in a society with women.
>
> What they can't get straight in their mind and try as hard as they might, this is not a fight between men and women. This is a constitutional case. Your Honor rules on that.
>
> Your Honor, I have talked all I can, sir, I got to tell you I'm dead tired, this has been a tough run for me. I want to say in closing that in my 40 years at the bar, I do not believe I have ever seen a case as devoid of merit as the government's is here, that VMI ought to prevail and the record is convincing, and I urge you, sir, to find we met the test, and I say to you, sir, if the VMI we know and love, were to end, God forbid it won't, let it not be on the unfounded grounds that we are in violation of the Constitution of this land.
>
> Thank you, sir.[65]

Having cast aspersions on the honesty of Colonel Toffler, Clifton Conrad, and the federal government, as well as on the motivation and military records of the Justice Department lawyers, Patterson sat down. The *Washington Post* commented the next day that Patterson's argument was made "in tones reminiscent of the segregation battles of the 1960s."[66] Douglas managed to control his rage as he stood to say only, "Your Honor, we have nothing further. We will not engage in any personal attacks against the Commonwealth, against VMI or their attorneys."[67]

After six days of testimony from nineteen witnesses, court was adjourned.

The Judge and the Drummer

VMI truly marches to the beat of a different drummer.

—Judge Jackson Kiser

Judge Kiser handed down his decision two months after the trial ended. The opening lines of his opinion indicated that he viewed the case as the War Between the States revisited, and he knew which side he was on.

> It was in May of 1864 that the United States and the Virginia Military Institute (VMI) first confronted each other. That was a life-and-death engagement that occurred on the battlefield at New Market, Virginia. The combatants have again confronted each other, but this time the venue is in this court.

VMI, he continued, "claims the struggle is nothing short of a life-and-death confrontation,"[1] and Kiser agreed. The Institute would die if women were admitted to it, and he was not about to let that happen.

His decision rested on three propositions, all of which he drew from the testimony of expert witnesses. The first was that VMI's adversative method had proved over more than a century that it was a uniquely successful way to produce leaders. The government could hardly object to that finding, as it had made the questionable determination not to attack the method's value. The second proposition was that the method was inappropriate for women and would be harmful to them. A subset of this proposition held that the relevant question for the court was not whether there were *any* women who might succeed at VMI but whether *most* women could be expected to do so. That led Kiser to his final proposition, which was that VMI would be as harmed by the admission of women as women would be by attending VMI.

Kiser positioned his holding in two lines of Supreme Court cases: academic freedom cases, which he read as establishing that diversity was a legitimate state goal, and gender equality cases, summarized in his view by *Mississippi v. Hogan*'s "exceedingly persuasive justification" doctrine. The combination of cases he chose made for two oddities.

The first was that the academic freedom cases he cited were of questionable utility for the point he wanted to make. He named *Regents v. Bakke*, Felix Frankfurter's concurring opinion in *Sweezy v. New Hampshire, Williams v. McNair*, and *United States v. Mabus. Bakke* was the affirmative action case in which the Court held that a medical school could make the achievement of a diverse student body one of its admissions goals,[2] which seemed to support the Justice Department's point in *United States v. Virginia* rather than Kiser's conclusion that women should be kept out of VMI. The same was true of Frankfurter's opinion in *Sweezy*, which, in affirming institutional autonomy, said that "attainment of a diverse student body . . . is a constitutionally permissible goal for an institution of higher education."[3] In *Williams v. McNair*, the Supreme Court upheld a South Carolina tribunal's decision that an all-women's college did not have to admit men. No allegation was made in that case, however, that the college offered any programs or courses that were unavailable elsewhere or that there were no single-sex men's colleges.[4]

In the first two cases, the passages cited referred specifically to the benefits of having a diversified student body, which was precisely what VMI did not have. In *McNair*, the state provided one single-sex college for men and one for women (the college for men was The Citadel). All the Supreme Court had done in *Mabus* was agree to hear a case in which both the district court and the Fifth Circuit Court of Appeals had ruled that Mississippi had no obligation to eliminate the vestiges and effects of overt racial discrimination in its system of public higher education, as long as it had ended formal segregation.[5] (In 1992 the Supreme Court held that the lower courts had misinterpreted the law and sent the case back to be heard again.)[6] Kiser nonetheless cited the cases as indicating that diversity in an educational system was a legitimate goal, and he referred to *McNair* as establishing the pedagogical legitimacy of single-sex colleges.[7]

It was odder still that Kiser omitted any reference to the Supreme Court's substantive gender equality cases other than *Hogan*. There was no *Reed v. Reed*, no *Frontiero v. Richardson*, no *Weinberger v. Weisenfeld*—no judicial notice, in other words, of the Court's repeated insistence that depriving women of equal opportunity was both unconstitutional and a reflection of outmoded stereotypes. Kiser briefly mentioned Supreme Court cases ordering universities to admit African Americans[8]; Supreme Court decisions mandating equal treatment of men and women went largely unnoticed. Kiser's reliance on racial equality cases and his tacit dismissal of relevant Court holdings in the field of gender equality may not have been good law, but it signaled once again his perception of the case as reflecting the federal government's assault on the South.

While ignoring the other gender equality cases, Kiser announced that his decision was based on *Hogan,* which he interpreted as requiring him to undertake "a fact-intensive examination of the practical considerations underlying the challenged policy."[9] If he considered the policy to be based on the "practical considerations" cited by VMI rather than on ideas about sex roles and the differing abilities of each gender, it was unsurprising that the Institute won.

To Kiser, the overriding question was whether "diversity in education" was a "legitimate object" of governmental action, and he viewed it as having been recognized as such "both judicially and by education experts"[10] —hence his invocation of *McNair*. He did not ask the corollary question of *why* the creation of diversity was legitimate. It was, in fact, not a question that had received much discussion at trial.

If diversity was a legitimate governmental objective, and the option of going to a single-sex school was considered a subset of the academic diversity the government had the power to institutionalize, then VMI's exclusion of women *might* be legal—assuming, of course, that "diversity" was not used as an excuse for excluding some people from equal educational opportunity. The question of what made diversity a legitimate objective still remained.

It seems obvious that the goal of a system of higher public education—or any educational system, for that matter—is to educate its students. Administrators may well decide that different students learn best in different environments and therefore decide to diversify their offerings. They may establish four-year colleges, two-year junior or community colleges, universities with graduate departments, institutions focusing on agriculture or engineering or the performing arts, and so on. Different institutions may have different admissions standards.

From a pedagogical standpoint, however, the diversity of institutions cannot be regarded as a goal; it is a *means* to the end of education. And, as Kiser had noted in discussing the academic freedom cases, the Supreme Court had found that policies that diversified by segregating students in an unconstitutional manner were illegal. A state could not decide, for example, that the goal of diversity was best served by the establishment of institutions that accepted students of only one race. Presumably, public institutions could not admit students of only one religion or ethnic background either, although the existence of such institutions alongside mixed-religion or mixed-ethnicity schools certainly would add to the diversity of the state's offerings. That particular form of diversity was nonetheless impermissible because the Constitution, in holding the states to the standard of providing all citizens with "equal protection of the laws," eliminated their power to diversify in ways that served no legitimate educational objective or negated the equality that was an underlying goal of the Constitution.

Kiser's manifest desire to keep VMI as it was seems to have been behind his unexplained declaration that diversity in and of itself was a legitimate governmental goal. The only way "to attain single-gender diversity," as he correctly said, was "by admitting only one gender to an institution."[11] But how or why did attaining single-gender diversity constitute a legitimate governmental objective? In addressing that query, Kiser stated that "a substantial body of 'exceedingly persuasive' evidence supports VMI's contention that some students, both male and female, benefit from attending a single-sex college" and would achieve better academically and professionally because they attended a single-sex school.[12]

As the authority for that statement, Kiser turned to Astin's *Four Critical Years,* noting that Justice Powell had relied on the book when he dissented in *Hogan.* Astin was a "very substantial authority" whose study was "not questioned by any expert."[13] Kiser's reliance on Astin is worth remembering, because, as the next chapter shows, Astin took such strong issue with the way VMI and Kiser used his work that he would join a brief asking the court of appeals to overturn the lower court decision. For the moment, however, Astin's star was ascendant in at least one Virginia courtroom.

That compared sharply with the comments Kiser had for the United States' expert witness, Clifton Conrad. Although Conrad had testified that he was a "believer in single-sex education," he had also offered what Kiser considered the ludicrous opinion that public institutions should be open to everyone to the extent possible and that single-sex education therefore should be confined to the private sector. Conrad thought that single-sex education worked, but he also believed that it was unfair for taxpayers to support schools from which their children could be excluded on the basis of sex. That was too much for the judge. "An opinion based on equity rather than appropriate educational methods is entitled to little weight," stormed Kiser, adding in a footnote that if Conrad was consistent in his egalitarianism he would have objected to the fact that VMI's academic standards kept out some men as well.[14]

Among the "practical considerations" that VMI could legitimately consider was the potential effect of coeducation. "As West Point's experience in converting to coeducation bears out, the presence of women would tend to distract male students from their studies," Kiser wrote.

> It would also increase pressures relating to dating, which would tend to impair the esprit de corps and the egalitarian atmosphere which are critical elements of the VMI experience. . . . Allowance for personal privacy would have to be made. Doors would have to be locked, and the windows on all of the doors would have to be covered. . . . The introduction of women into VMI would add a new set of stresses on the cadets, of a very different kind than the cadets now face.[15]

The young men, as well as VMI, had to be protected from women.

But it was not only the men who needed the protection of the court; it was also the misguided women who thought they wanted to attend VMI. Sadly, they did not realize the dire consequences of their mistake. Kiser drew copiously on David Riesman's testimony to find that the adversative method "is simply inappropriate for the vast majority of women," and their admission would result in its being dropped.[16] Recognizing that "some women . . . would want to attend the school if they had the opportunity" and that *Hogan* "seems to teach that the court must consider the constitutionality of the policy without regard to the size of the available applicant pool," Kiser nonetheless upheld the exclusion of women because their admission would cause the demise of VMI: "Even if the female could physically and psychologically undergo the rigors of the life of a male cadet, her introduction into the process would change it. Thus, the very experience she sought would no longer be available."[17]

Kiser felt strongly that women were indeed different, and in ways that were relevant to VMI. He accepted Riesman's statement that the adversative method was "inappropriate for the vast majority of women."[18] He did not indicate why he considered it appropriate for the vast majority of men, a contention that seemed to underlie his opinion but that seemingly was contradicted by VMI's difficulty in attracting adequate numbers of male applicants. For him, the combination of the Board of Visitors' 1986 mission study findings and the evidence offered at trial sufficed to justify VMI's decision not to admit women.

The remaining issue was that women were deprived of VMI's "absolutely unique" military program. This was true, Kiser said, but he agreed with Riesman that if women were admitted to VMI, they would destroy the program from which they were currently excluded. And, he added, very few women would apply. He thought the Justice Department had picked the wrong target. "It seems to me that the criticism which might be directed toward Virginia's higher educational policy is not that it maintains VMI as an all-male institution, but rather that it fails to maintain at least one all-female institution."[19]

Whether Virginia chose that option or not, VMI and the "measure of diversity" it added to the state's educational system had to be left alone. Holding that the "virtually uncontradicted" evidence "supports Virginia's view that substantial educational benefits flow from a single-gender environment" and that gender discrimination therefore "serves an important state educational objective," Kiser concluded with a rhetorical flourish that would be repeated in virtually all accounts of the decision: "VMI is a different type of institution. It has set its eye on the goal of citizen-solider and never veered from the path it has chosen to meet that goal. VMI truly marches to the beat of a different drummer, and I will permit it to continue to do so."[20]

Kiser appended twenty-six and a half pages labeled "Findings of Fact" to the opinion. Both sides had presented him with their own proposed findings of facts and conclusions of law, which ran to 137 pages for the government and 119 for VMI.[21] The government might as well have saved itself the effort. Kiser accepted almost none of its suggestions.

The government noted, for example, that Richardson had testified that he had not examined detailed data about women who had indicated interest in VMI, while admitting that "it is extremely difficult to judge something about a nonexistent data base . . . if I thought there was some very large number of women who were being denied an opportunity to attend VMI, that would probably affect that judgment that I had mentioned."[22] VMI, by contrast, ignored Richardson's remarks in the comparable section of its suggested findings, which it entitled "Negligible Demand Among Females for Military Education."[23] Kiser referred to the testimony by VMI administrators cited by VMI and concluded about the 347 inquiries the Institute had received from women in the 1988 to 1990 period, "the seriousness of these inquiries cannot be determined."[24]

The Justice Department proposed that "it is one thing for the State to accommodate diverse modes of private education in its funding; it is something

quite different for the State itself to bar women from public state and federally funded institutions of higher education because of their gender."[25] The
comparable section in VMI's document was entitled "Virginia's Sensitive Balance." It began, "The Commonwealth has struck a sensitive and prudent balance among competing policy considerations in an effort to maximize diversity and educational opportunity." It continued, "Females are not denied
access to a single-gender experience as a result of VMI's admission policy. . . .
Nationally, approximately two percent of females are enrolled in single-sex
institutions, compared to less than half of one percent for males."[26] Kiser acknowledged that "no defense witness in this case offered to explain why Virginia provides the option of single-sex public education to men but not to
women," but he attributed that absence of diversity to "the consequence of
individual decisions by each public college in Virginia to admit men."[27] It was
neither Virginia nor VMI that denied women the option, in other words, but
one of the side effects of academic freedom and institutional independence.

Kiser's findings included a lengthy section summarizing average physical
differences between men and women, but there was no suggestion that some
women could do as well at VMI as many men. It was followed by another extensive set of statements about "Gender-Based Developmental Differences,"
which reflected the very stereotypes Kiser purported not to use. Kiser announced, as a finding of fact, that "males tend to need an atmosphere of ad-
versativeness or ritual combat in which the teacher is a disciplinarian and a
worthy competitor." Women, he asserted, learned differently. "Females tend
to thrive in a cooperative atmosphere in which the teacher is emotionally connected with the students."[28]

For all their length, the court's findings of fact omitted a great deal. Even
if one accepted a difference in male and female "averages" as dispositive, for
example, nothing was said about any average physical differences between
VMI men and those women who might be expected to apply to VMI, such as
the women typical of West Point or Annapolis applicants, rather than the average physical differences between *all* men and women. The lead lawyer in
The Citadel case, reflecting on *United States v. Virginia,* commented that
Hogan's acceptance of an "exceedingly persuasive justification" for discrimination, as long as it did not rely on traditional stereotypes, "assumes—in-
correctly—that individual judges are able to see and understand stereotypes
of gender. As the VMI decisions demonstrate, the myth of difference is so
powerful that discrimination against women often appears natural."[29] Certainly Kiser found it to be unobjectionable. As scholar Kenneth Karst has

noted, most men cannot help but be influenced by "the traditional construct of women." Male judges do not "consciously *choose* to define the idea of woman around their own needs for masculine self-identification." Like everyone else, they are socialized into a culture that teaches that women are different, and threateningly so. "Some of us may ultimately come to see the nature of woman as a social construct."[30] Others may not. Judge Kiser and VMI placed themselves firmly in the second camp.

Judge Kiser accepted VMI's dismissive depiction of the federal military academies as having a different mission from that of VMI. In a section entitled "Contrasting Mission of Federal Service Academies," he found that whereas the academies' goal was "to prepare cadets for career service in the armed forces," VMI's mission was "very different" in being "directed at preparation for both military and civilian life." He did not explain how that mission, which resulted in more than 80 percent of VMI's graduates choosing civilian careers, depended on such physical traits as upper body strength, body fat ratio, or performance "in activities which require explosive power, e.g., sprinting, basketball throw, medicine ball put, and jumping events."[31] One can only imagine the denizens of the country's corporate boardrooms and legislative assemblies performing pull-ups or providing medical proof of their low body fat ratio in order to demonstrate their ability to lead.

One section of Kiser's findings reviewed the VMI mission study. He noted that during the committee's interviews, "West Point provided generally favorable information concerning coeducation," including the fact that "gender integration has been successful." The testimony from Annapolis was equally positive, and the University of Virginia's programs were described as having been strengthened by the admission of women. Nonetheless, the only comment during those visits that he found "significant" was one made by the president of Washington and Lee University, to the effect that "if women were admitted [to VMI], the system would have to be modified." The court implicitly praised the Board of Visitors' conclusion that the admission of women "would alter the mission of VMI" and held that the deliberations of the study committee and the board "amply supports a finding that VMI's mission was established early in the life of the institution, and has been continued only after reasoned and careful analysis by the Board of Visitors."[32]

The "Findings of Fact" thus became the basis for Kiser's holding that Virginia had an "exceedingly persuasive justification" for keeping the Institute all male. Kiser differentiated the situation in *Hogan* by saying that the plaintiff there had been a resident of the town in which Mississippi University for Women was located, there was no other nursing school within commuting distance, and it would have been a hardship for him to move to another community. VMI, by contrast, required all students to live on the post, so residential convenience was not an issue—although why he thought that matter had been central to *Hogan* was unclear. Kiser added that VMI's admissions policy did not deny women access to particular academic programs because Virginia Polytechnic Institute offered the same courses, as well as optional military instruction, to both male and female students.[33]

VMI cheered the ruling. Patterson called Kiser's ruling a "victory for single-sex education, educational diversity and common sense."[34] The Citadel's president, Lieutenant General Claudius "Bud" Watts, expressed relief that "a very, very dark cloud has been lifted" from both military schools by the ruling.[35] A *Washington Times* editorial commented, "For Justice officials, the ruling is a timely reminder that its brand of social engineering, however lauded in elite circles, is not the law of the land."[36]

Others were less delighted. Ellen Vargyas, senior counsel with the National Women's Law Center, called the decision "an outrage." "This comes on the heels of the Persian Gulf war, where women performed admirably, where women were killed, where women were prisoners," she told the press. "And this court says blatant discrimination against women is all right."[37] John F. Banzhaf III, a professor at George Washington University Law School who had been involved in other sex discrimination cases, blamed the decision on the government's "bad and indifferent lawyering," which had "doomed a case that everyone thought was unbeatable."[38] A *New York Times* editorial entitled "Wrong Gray Line" chastised Kiser, saying, "The Virginia Military Institute may indulge its pride in uniqueness, but not at taxpayer expense. Let the college buy its own drum."[39]

In August, Attorney General Dick Thornburgh, about to leave the Justice Department to campaign in Pennsylvania for a seat in the U.S. Senate, announced that the Department would appeal. Some months later, the Department, by then in the hands of the Clinton administration, said that it would do so in cooperation with groups such as the American Civil Liberties Union, the National Women's Law Center, the American Association for University Women, and the National Organization for Women. Lawyers for the groups told the media that VMI's arguments were strikingly similar to those that had been made forty years earlier in defense of segregated public universities. Patterson's partner William Broaddus countered, "The apparent attempt of the A.C.L.U. to equate this with racial discrimination indicates they are unable to meet the issue head on."[40]

And so both sides, one of them backed by a federal district court and the other now augmented by public interest groups, prepared for a second battle in a second court.

In a Higher Court

> As a practical matter and commonsense matter, we know that
> women can't endure the type of first-year or maybe even second-
> year training that VMI offers, just as most women can't go
> through Camp LeJeune in the hot summertime.
>
> —Comment from the bench, U.S. Court of Appeals for the
> Fourth Circuit

Robert Patterson had faced off against one woman lawyer from the Justice Department in Judge Kiser's courtroom. When the U.S. Court of Appeals for the Fourth Circuit heard oral arguments in *United States v. Virginia* on April 8, 1992, his opponent was another, Jessica Dunsay Silver. There were, in fact, quite a few women lawyers working to overturn Judge Kiser's decision, doing the kind of gender equality litigation that Ruth Bader Ginsburg and other women of her generation had pioneered. Patterson and his peers had commanded the nation's courtrooms until the 1970s. Now it was a very different group's moment in the sun.

Most of the women who became involved in the case after the trial worked for public interest groups. Many of them were unaware of the litigation until Kiser's decision was handed down. Isabelle Katz Pinzler, then the director of the ACLU's Women's Rights Project, which Ginsburg had founded, was one of the few who did know about it. In many ways, she was typical of the attorneys who filled the burgeoning field of pro bono work (done on behalf of the general public) in the 1960s and 1970s.

Pinzler studied at Boston University School of Law after graduating from

Goucher College in 1967. She was not particularly attracted to litigation but went to law school because she wanted to help change the world for the better and believed that law would be a useful tool. While at Boston University, she began working with a publicly financed housing services center that, like many underfunded social services agencies, turned to law students for additional personnel. After graduation, Pinzler worked in the field of employment discrimination, where her path crossed that of an ACLU lawyer. He was impressed, and in 1978, when the WRP had an opening, Pinzler was hired as its new director.[1]

Pinzler was neither involved in *United States v. Virginia* at the trial level nor particularly concerned about its outcome. She considered the case to be a straightforward one involving "one of the few remaining Fourteenth Amendment gender discrimination issues out there—single-sex education—sex segregation in any kind of public education," and she had no doubt that the government would win at trial. To the WRP and other women's litigation groups, the case was about the kind of stereotyping that had been resoundingly rejected by the Supreme Court. The whole lesson of gender discrimination cases in the 1970s and 1980s had been that rights inhered in the individual, who did not necessarily conform to "average" abilities and propensities. Pinzler thought that VMI's stance reflected erroneous and outworn attitudes. "Attitudes: attitudes . . . toward women, attitudes . . . pervaded the case."[2]

Even given what they saw as that outmoded thinking, lawyers at the WRP and elsewhere were certain that the law would be followed. They "couldn't imagine that it wouldn't be a fairly quick win," Pinzler remembered. "We were all shocked when we saw the district court opinion." The shock came from Judge Kiser's reliance on averages, his assumption that women would neither want nor be capable of completing a VMI education, and his acceptance of the idea that a state could provide a program for men but not for women. "It was such a bad decision, so completely contrary to law." The WRP knew as soon as the decision was handed down that it would write an amicus curiae brief for the court of appeals.[3]

An amicus curiae (friend of the court) brief typically comes from individuals or groups that have a specific interest in the outcome of a case and believe that they offer a viewpoint or expertise beyond that of the parties. The National Association of Manufacturers, for example, is a frequent amicus before the Supreme Court; so are the AFL-CIO, the National Association for the Advancement of Colored People, governors, and state attorney generals.[4]

The group that appears as amicus in American courts more frequently than any other, aside from the solicitor general of the United States,[5] is the American Civil Liberties Union. The WRP was the ACLU unit whose "original and continuing mission," defined in the days when Ginsburg ran it, was to persuade the nation's judiciary that gender-based differentiations were presumptively unconstitutional.[6]

The WRP went into the case to make certain that the appellate judges had before them "some arguments about what the proper evidence was—what the [trial] judge admitted and shouldn't have admitted, and some military stuff that really wasn't in there." Pinzler, like others, felt that VMI's "expert witnesses" should not have been permitted to qualify as such under federal law and that the trial record lacked adequate refutation of testimony by VMI's expert witnesses about women's abilities and the history of women at the service academies. She rejected VMI's assumption that women could not handle the adversative method of leadership training and was eager to show that women both at the academies and in actual combat had demonstrated more than sufficient toughness. VMI's stereotypical depiction of women had to be countered, she thought, by an explanation of "what a stereotype is and what the problem with it is. In fact, a stereotype reflects something that often *is* true, but not as applied to every member of the group." The line of argument she favored was, "Yes, it's true that men are on the average stronger; no, it's not true" that women have different learning styles. The curves for male and female learning styles and abilities overlap; "there's a tiny bit on each end that doesn't," but for the most part, the curves are similar.[7]

Pinzler's concerns were shared by other women's rights groups and by attorneys for them, such as Marcia Greenberger of the National Women's Law Center in Washington. Greenberger had founded the Center in 1972 after Title IX, forbidding discrimination in education, was added to the Civil Rights Act of 1964. The organization quickly became a key player in education litigation. When the VMI litigation began, the Center had been a party or an amicus curiae in every Title IX case heard by the Supreme Court.[8]

Greenberger was delighted when the Justice Department brought the case, because she felt that the Department had not been putting adequate resources into educational gender equality litigation. She was less pleased, if unsurprised, at the way the trial was handled. What she saw as the Department's disinterest in cases involving educational gender discrimination had, she believed, resulted in a telling lack of expertise in the area. She considered the VMI case a "terrific" one in its stark presentation of core constitutional principles and the way they affected practical opportunities for women.[9]

The Center had written the only amicus brief submitted to the Supreme Court in *Hogan*. Greenberger had thought then that both the parties' briefs and the lower court decisions concentrated too heavily on the lack of an equal male school. The Center's contribution, echoed in Justice O'Connor's opinion for the Court, was to emphasize how the exclusion of men from the nursing school perpetuated the stereotypes that hindered gender equality. Greenberger fully expected that the VMI case, too, would go to the Supreme Court, and the Center was eager to bring its expertise to the table.[10]

Pinzler and Greenberger, along with other women from the WRP and the Center, had worked together before. So had lawyers from gender equality organizations such as NOW, the NOW Legal Defense and Education Fund (NOW LDEF), and the Women's Legal Defense Fund. The phone lines were busy in the days and weeks after Kiser's decision came down, as old and new allies called one another to express their dismay and decide what they should do.[11] Eventually the groups submitting or signing onto the amicus briefs before the court of appeals included all of the above organizations plus the American Association of University Women (AAUW), the Center for Women Policy Studies, the Women's Law Project, and the Older Women's League. A number of Virginia organizations joined in: the Virginia Federation of Business and Professional Women's Clubs, Friends of VMI for Equality, the Virginia Women Attorneys Association, and the Virginia branches of NOW, NOW LDEF, the ACLU, and the AAUW. The names on the joint brief included some of the country's most prominent female attorneys engaged in gender equality litigation: Pinzler, Greenberger, Ellen Vargyas, Shirley Sagawa, and Joan E. Bertin.[12]

Pinzler remembers the joint amicus brief as being "unusual" in the cooperation it generated among the participating groups. When organizations combine on a brief, personalities can clash, and the somewhat differing ideologies of the groups can present difficulties. That was not the case here. The fact that the women had worked together in the past and had come to trust one another was important; so was their sense that they were all in the trenches together. In addition, they shared the same kind of time and energy pressures endemic to organizations whose resources in no way match their influence in policy-making arenas. When one of the participants was so overloaded with other work that she could contribute only minimally, it was understood that her group's name would be added to the brief nonetheless.[13]

The groups' complementary emphases also helped. The WRP's constitutional expertise meshed nicely with the Center's experience in educational cases. When Pinzler heard about the decision, she knew "right away" that she had to get on the telephone with lawyers at the Center. They talked about a brief and, later, "We divided it up and we [WPR] took three sections of it. The Center took a section."[14]

The key factor uniting the groups was their outrage at Judge Kiser's decision. "It was such a huge target, such an easy target . . . the [case and issues weren't] difficult, complicated . . . there were no ideological differences," Pinzler recalled. To the women from the amicus groups, Kiser had simply misread the law of the land that had been firmly established when Ruth Bader Ginsburg was still arguing cases before the Supreme Court.[15]

There were no amici on the other side. The VMI team, however, assumed that it had all the heavy hitters it needed. Patterson's firm accounted for six participants, including three of his partners and H. Alexander Wise, the namesake and descendant of a family that had produced VMI students and VMI historians since the Institute's earliest days. In addition to Griffin Bell, there was William A. Clineburg, Jr., from Bell's Atlanta firm, and William B. Poff of Roanoke.

As the briefs were being written, a relative newcomer to women's rights litigation spoke up. It was the Virginia Women Attorneys Association. One of its leaders was Sylvia Clute, a partner in a two-woman Richmond law firm. Having heard that an amicus brief was being written, she and another Virginia lawyer decided to hold a meeting at the University of Richmond's T. C. Williams School of Law to explore the issues with interested students and discuss their possible involvement in the case. Only one student showed up. So, however, did T. C. Williams Professor John Paul Jones, who felt strongly that public funds should not be used to discriminate against women and was ready to advise a group of students willing to work on the case if such a group came together.[16]

It did, largely because of Eileen Wagner. Wagner was a former professor of rhetoric and mother of three who had decided to retool and get her law degree. She had rubbed shoulders with members of the Virginia establishment since moving to the state in the 1950s and was sympathetic to VMI's desire to remain as it was. She believed that it was illegal, however, for a state-supported institution to discriminate against women. She therefore became the leader of the three-woman, two-man student team. (Another member was a great-granddaughter of Confederate army general Jeb Stuart.)

"Our argument was not necessarily a 'feminist' argument," Wagner said, and that accounted in part for the decision to file a separate brief.

We based our challenge to VMI on Virginia laws which govern colleges and universities. We analyzed VMI's situation from the view of strategic planners in higher education. We knew, for example, that VMI was in trouble in recruitment before the lawsuit. We knew that VMI with all its financial bluster could not sustain the operating budget without tripling tuition if the school went private. We knew that widening the recruiting pool was VMI's only hope of surviving into the 21st century. So we side-stepped the emotional battle of the genders which allowed us to praise the VMI experience at the same time we pierced the fallacies of its boosters.[17]

They did so by concentrating on Virginia statutes. Viewing the case as primarily about the issue of who had the power to set educational policy for the state, they sought to show that single-sex diversity was not an important state interest.

Under state law, articulation of Virginia's higher education goals lay with the state's Council of Higher Education and the governor, but neither had been heard in the case because they had been removed as active parties to it.[18] What both VMI and the district court had ignored was the 1987 Virginia Plan for Higher Education, which set the state's goals as access, excellence, and accountability. That, Professor Jones's team argued, did not include diversity. Although the word "diversity" was mentioned in the plan, the context indicated that it denoted a variety of institutional structures such as state supported, independent, having selective admissions policies, and offering open admissions.[19] Diversity of student body meant heterogeneity, as indicated by the council-approved gender integration of the formerly single-sex University of Virginia, Mary Washington College, James Madison University, and Radford University.[20] And the 1990 report of the state Commission on the University in the Twenty-first Century had specifically stated that "faculty, staff, and students" of colleges and universities were to be dealt with "without regard to sex, race, or ethnic origin."[21]

Both VMI and Judge Kiser had relied on Alexander Astin's *Four Critical Years: Effects of College on Beliefs, Attitudes, and Knowledge*[22] to show that a desire for single-sex education met the *Hogan* "exceedingly persuasive justification" standard.[23] Astin's 1978 book detailed the success of all-male elite colleges of the 1970s, attributing much of it to the schools' single-sex policies. He had found students there to have higher involvement in academic subjects, athletics, and honors programs, and he had discovered greater verbal aggressiveness and student-faculty interaction than in coeducational institutions.

But in 1991, Astin noted that his research dated back to an era "when many of the most elite colleges in the country admitted only men" and that "the faculty and students who work and study at men's colleges today may be very different from their counterparts who participated in the research two decades ago."[24] The implications were, first, that changing societal mores might have altered the picture substantially, and second, that Astin's work had drawn conclusions from students at *elite* colleges and universities rather than at the decidedly nonelite VMI. His research could not be extended to justify an assertion that the adversative model had to be all male.[25] In fact, Astin was so distressed at the use of his work in the trial that he published an article about it in the *Chronicle of Higher Education*[26] and, at Wagner's invitation, signed onto her brief.

The contribution of the Wagner-Astin brief was the argument that VMI's single-sex admissions policy was illegal under state law, and it was a point that the court of appeals would make its own. That was not all the brief said, however, and although Wagner described the brief's argument as "not necessarily a feminist" one, its language was fairly strong. Under the heading "The Trial Court Erred by Accepting Evidence Tainted with Fixed Notions of Females' Inherent Handicaps and Innate Inferiority," the students condemned the district court's reliance on average differences in the physical strength of men and women, its acceptance of the assertion that women were too psychologically weak to manage the adversative system, and its assumption that the presence of women would interfere with an education for men.

> Thus, does the trial court impose upon females the ultimate handicap, the ancient role of the passive temptress. In this role, a female's personhood and abilities become irrelevant. Her very existence condemns her. Not only is she held liable for the inappropriate behavior of the males in her environment but she must be restrained or excluded from the normal course of daily living in order to reduce the incidence of such inappropriate male behavior.[27]

"Feminist" was still close to a dirty word in Virginia. The Wagner-Astin brief nonetheless reflected a key tenet of feminism in its insistence that women could do whatever men could do. The brief of the national women's organizations went further to emphasize that, as far as the law was concerned, most women did not *have* to be able to do what most men could do. Under the equal protection clause, if *some* women could succeed at VMI, they could not be excluded from it simply because of their sex—particularly when the state offered them no equivalent educational opportunity.

That would be part of the Justice Department's argument as well. The amicus organizations could not find out whether their thinking was in line with the Justice Department's approach, however. The Department was under orders throughout the Bush administration not to interact with the civil rights community and not to speak with the amicus groups. But although there was no communication between them, the groups' "take" on the case was in fact very similar to that of Jessica Silver, the Justice Department attorney who argued it before the Fourth Circuit.

Silver had a string of credentials and a substantial number of years in appellate litigation when she turned her attention to VMI. After graduating from George Washington University Law School in 1971, she clerked for New York federal district court judge Orrin Judd, practiced private law for a year, and then became counsel to Senator Edward Kennedy's subcommittee on health. She moved to the Department of Justice's Appellate Section in 1975 and became its deputy section chief in 1978. By 1992, she was supervising fifteen line attorneys in the appellate section of the Civil Rights Division, which handles all appeals in cases brought by the CRD's trial lawyers.

One of Silver's responsibilities was assigning cases to the division's attorneys. That permitted her to take the VMI case herself. She found it fascinating. Her first reaction was that, important as the case was, it revolved around the simple legal issue of whether women could be excluded from a unique college-level program. As she began to receive VMI's papers and eventually heard its lawyers in oral argument, however, she realized that they viewed the case as going far beyond the legal issue. To the Institute, it was about saving a way of life.[28]

The problem any appellate lawyer has is that the factual record is established at trial. The rule in federal courts is that a court of appeals can overturn a district court's findings of fact only if those findings are clearly erroneous within the meaning of the federal rules of civil procedure.[29] Judge Kiser's extensive findings, clearly designed to prevent an appeals court from overturning his decision, could be backed up by the trial record—however incomplete or misleading that record was. One of the things Silver, like Pinzler and Greenberger, would have liked to see in the record was testimony countering VMI's claim that there was no critical mass of women who could succeed at the Institute.[30] But the necessary testimony from government expert witnesses was not there.

Silver had to focus on law, not facts. She therefore emphasized VMI's lack of authority to pronounce diversity as a goal of the state educational system; only the state itself could make that claim. Even if diversity was accepted as a goal, she would tell the appeals court, Virginia provided diversity in its public higher education system only for men, not for women. She acknowledged that VMI was indeed unique in its program, its wealth, and its well-connected alumni, which was why excluding women from all that necessarily violated the Constitution. Her plea was firmly centered in the equal protection clause.[31] The appeals court, however, was not likely to be particularly sympathetic.

THE FOURTH CIRCUIT COURT OF APPEALS hears cases from Maryland, Virginia, North Carolina, South Carolina, and West Virginia. The *New York Times* called it "the boldest conservative court in the United States" in the 1990s,[32] particularly notable for its attempts to return to an earlier view of federalism by invoking states' rights as a limitation on the government in Washington. It was also the only federal appeals court that had never had a person of color on its bench.[33] Two of its members had seen earlier service under Presidents Reagan and Bush, helping them select conservative lawyers to staff the nation's courts.[34]

The panel chosen to hear the VMI case was headed by Judge Paul V. Niemeyer, first appointed to a federal district court in Maryland by Reagan and then to the Fourth Circuit by Bush. The other members were Hiram H. Ward, senior district judge from Winston-Salem and a Nixon appointee, and senior circuit judge J. Dickson Phillips, a Carter appointee from North Carolina. The term "senior judge" indicates that a judge has retired from full-time work but occasionally sits on a case. Judge Phillips was seventy years old, and Judge Ward was sixty-nine; Judge Niemeyer, at fifty-two, was much their junior.

It was Niemeyer who directed Jessica Silver to open her argument for the Justice Department on the morning of April 8, 1992. With Judith Keith listening attentively from the audience, Silver began to speak.

> MS. SILVER: VMI provides a distinctive educational program unavailable anywhere else in Virginia and denies the benefit of that program to women. On its face then, VMI's policy violates the Equal Protection Clause of the Fourteenth Amendment and can be upheld only if, under the Hogan standard, it's supported by an exceedingly persuasive justification.[35]

There was no such justification, she argued, because Judge Kiser had been wrong in concluding that the admission of women would change VMI in the four areas of physical training, the adversative method, privacy, and cross-sex relationships. Some women could manage VMI's physical requirements well. One of the judges interrupted to ask how great a percentage would be able to do that and whether VMI would not have to create a two-track system. Silver's answer was firm: "The position of the US is that VMI has to admit women. It does not have to change its program at all. . . . The fact that many or even most women wouldn't be able to comply with the current requirements cannot be a justification for keeping out those women who can comply with them."[36] Judge Niemeyer repeatedly asked whether a parallel school would be acceptable. That was not at issue, Silver replied, but there would be no objection to a comparable physical training system within VMI.[37] The court was not ready to let the point go, however.

> THE COURT: Well, as a practical matter and commonsense matter, we know that women can't endure the type of first-year or maybe even second-year training that VMI offers, just as most women can't go through Camp LeJeune in the hot summertime.[38]

Silver did not accept that. She was equally adamant that the need for privacy would not create problems, because the only thing VMI would have to do is ensure that women and men used the bathrooms and dressing areas separately.[39] The court was not satisfied.

> THE COURT: Well, it would create a bifurcation . . . there would not be total confrontation.
> MS. SILVER: That's true, Your Honor, but we're talking about a few minutes a day. We're talking--
> THE COURT: Well, I understand, but now you and I are making judgments about the program.[40]

From the record, the court appears so unsympathetic to the Justice Department's case that it might have found VMI's asserted interest in the unchanging purity of its program to constitute the "exceedingly persuasive justification" required by the Fourteenth Amendment. In fact, the lawyers from the women's groups who were seated in the courtroom knew that the argument was not going well at all—but not because of any failure on Silver's part. The Justice Department was still under orders from the Bush administration to say that nothing at VMI would have to change if women were admitted, with the exception of the provision of separate dorm rooms and bathrooms. Silver was not permitted to argue, for example, that VMI might have to emulate the service academies in creating slightly different physical training requirements for men and women and that such differences had not affected the rigor of the academies' training.[41]

One of the judges seemed to indicate that he considered VMI's view of itself persuasive and that he could not imagine women fitting into VMI's mission of producing citizen-soldiers:

> THE COURT: Well, it seems to me that that just permeates everything that is said about the reason why the mission is unique. It all traces back to maleness, physical vigor, the ability to withstand adversity, the ability to withstand invasions of privacy. Everything that is said about the mission, it seems to me, comes back to the absolute necessity that it be male and all male and untraveled by anything not male.
>
> MS. SILVER: As I understand the mission, it is to educate citizen soldiers. That is a mission that women can take part in. . . . We would not concede that its mission is to only have men at the school.[42]

The judges continued to ask whether the Fourteenth Amendment mandated the admission of women even if the VMI system would be destroyed by their presence, and Silver finally retorted, "If the mission is one that can only be accomplished for one sex, then it is not a valid Virginia state interest to support the program."[43]

Whatever the predilections of the judges, they got little help from Patterson. As Patterson himself recognized, he did not handle the argument well.[44] He was good at the kind of factual discussion and rhetorical eloquence that worked at trial. The job of the appeals court, however, was to make a determination based on law, and Patterson was inexperienced at that kind of argumentation. He opened his remarks, for example, by reiterating, "The question here is whether or not we preserve single-sex education for both sexes."[45] But it was already clear that that was not the question. When the court had asked Silver earlier, "Do you think that single-gender education, per se, violates the Fourteenth Amendment?" she had replied, "No, Your Honor, we don't."[46]

It was downhill from there, with Patterson frequently misspeaking and referring, for example, to "the Virginia law that provides discrimination against women." "In the history of civilization," he told the court, "there has never, never been a college for women like VMI is for men," thereby underscoring the Justice Department's point that the continued exclusion of women was based on outmoded stereotypes. "Well," one of the judges replied, "you're telling me about the history, but I'm interested in the Fourteenth Amendment."[47] And as the court indicated, Patterson lacked a satisfactory answer to the question of how VMI's admissions policy could be defended under that part of the Constitution.

Griffin Bell interrupted at one point, apparently in an attempt to save the argument by telling the court that *Hogan* permitted discrimination that was "substantially related to achieving a legitimate and substantial goal." One of the judges commented that the only goal at issue seemed to be making a distinction between men and women. When the court wanted to know where in the record it could find a point that Bell referred to, he answered vaguely, "It is in the record somewhere." The court then asked Silver about *Hogan*. What the case made clear, she replied, was that "diversity and single sex education just for men cannot be a valid state interest to justify excluding women."[48]

The judges' questions seemed to suggest that they agreed with Kiser about the changes women would bring to VMI. As their decision would indicate, that was exactly what they thought—but they also agreed with Silver that the case was about gender discrimination.

On October 5, the court held that Virginia was in violation of the equal protection clause. The commonwealth had three options, the unanimous opinion said: it could admit women to VMI, it could turn the Institute into a private college, or it could create parallel institutions or programs for women.[49] That did not mean the government had won, however, for the court clearly indicated that it thought VMI should remain all male.

"We do not . . . order that women be admitted to VMI if adequate alternatives are available," Judge Niemeyer wrote for the panel. "We accept the district court's factual determinations that VMI's unique methodology justifies a single-gender policy and material aspects of its essentially holistic system would be substantially changed by coeducation."[50] Invoking the names of Stonewall Jackson and George C. Marshall, the court wrote a paean to VMI and its "success in producing leaders." It agreed with Kiser that the adversative system was responsible for that success and spoke glowingly about all its components: the rat line, the dyke and class systems, the honor code, the Barracks, and the military regime.[51]

The court took note of Kiser's statement that the case reflected the second historical confrontation between VMI and the federal government, but it added, "What was not said is that the outcome of each confrontation finds resolution in the Equal Protection Clause." The question the judges had to address was exactly what the clause meant in the context of the case. Niemeyer dismissed both Lincoln and Jefferson as irrelevant:

> The obvious appeal to fairness in requiring the equal application of law too often becomes entangled with generalized notions of equality as referred to in Lincoln's

Gettysburg Address and, before that, the Declaration of Independence, and these generalizations tend to overwhelm the difficult task of deciding what is meant by equal protection.[52]

The "generalizations" were not helpful because they ignored the fact that "persons are in many important respects different," and the equal protection clause was not meant to apply to all laws "without regard to actual differences." Differences among people could be taken into account by a state as long as the classifications in its regulations served "an adequate governmental purpose."[53]

The word "adequate" reflected the argument in equal protection jurisprudence about how important the governmental purpose had to be. Under the Supreme Court's gender discrimination decisions, Niemeyer said, the purpose of the classification did not have to be "compelling," but it did have to be more than "rational." Like Kiser, he would employ intermediate scrutiny and ask whether excluding women from VMI was "substantially related to an important policy or objective."[54]

Niemeyer then asked whose "policy or objective" was at issue. If it was VMI's policy alone, he held, it was constitutionally permissible. Like Kiser, the appeals court believed that "the physiological differences between men and women," "the question of a woman's ability to perform and endure the physical training included in VMI's program," the potential effects of "cross-sexual confrontations," and unspecified "psychological" differences validated VMI's desire to remain single sex.[55] Niemeyer drew on Alexander Astin's study of single-sex education, ignoring the fact that its author had called the study outdated in papers before the court. Niemeyer extolled single-sex education both for the enhanced learning environment such education provided and for its "salutary consequences for sexual equality in the job market." Referring to a scholarly article claiming that students in single-sex colleges were less likely to maintain "stereotypical job aspirations," he added, "The experts for both sides in this case appear to agree with the conclusions reached in these studies."[56] VMI, then, was not depriving women of equality; it was actually helping them achieve it.

That, however, did not answer the question of whether a VMI policy that was legal was equally acceptable if it was a *state* policy. "The decisive question" in the case, Niemeyer continued, was "why the Commonwealth of Virginia offers the unique benefit of VMI's type of education and training to men and not to women." VMI's physical training program, the "rigor" of which was "tailored to males," "could be adjusted without detrimental effect" if it was done "in the context of a single-sex female institution."[57] Who, then, was responsible for the absence of a VMI analog?

Niemeyer implicitly drew on Eileen Wagner's brief for the answer, pointing to the power given to the Council of Higher Education and to the policy adopted by the Commission on the University of the 21st Century. The council's biennial plans regularly called for diversity among the state's institutions of higher education, and the commission's report repeated that "autonomy" and "diversity" were the system's hallmarks. When Attorney General Mary Sue Terry withdrew from the case in 1990, she said that Governor Wilder correctly interpreted state policy to mean that "no person should be denied admittance to a State supported school because of his or her gender."[58] Diversity, rather than gender classifications, appeared to be state policy. "If VMI's male-only admissions policy is in furtherance of a state policy of 'diversity,'" the court complained, "the explanation of how the policy is furthered by affording a unique educational benefit only to males is lacking." VMI could not implement a policy of diversity throughout Virginia, but the state could. And at the moment, the state was supporting a men-only college but not one for women only.[59] In other words, Virginia had failed to articulate the kind of important government objective that was necessary under the equal protection clause to justify providing public single-sex higher education and a VMI type of program only to men.

The court therefore remanded the case to the district court, directing that the commonwealth be given "the responsibility to select a course it chooses . . . that conforms with the Equal Protection Clause of the Fourteenth Amendment," and charging the lower court with establishing "appropriate timetables" and overseeing the implementation of whatever plan was devised.[60]

VMI had assumed that it would be able to remain all male; the Justice Department had assumed that VMI's doing so violated the Constitution. Neither side had said anything about possible program alternatives or whether establishing them would fulfill the constitutional mandate. Perhaps picking up Judge Kiser's strong hint, the appeals court, without asking either party to address alternatives, in effect endorsed the idea of a female VMI. As one scholar commented, "On appeal, the Fourth Circuit held that VMI could march to a different drummer, as long as women had their own band."[61]

The decision pleased almost no one, with the possible exception of some of the lawyers for the women's groups, who were satisfied only in part. They were certain that Virginia would find it too expensive to set up an all-women's program and that, although the litigation was far from over, women would eventually gain admission to VMI.[62] The government, well aware that it still had not gotten women into VMI, was not as sanguine. Jessica Silver was surprised at all the options the court gave VMI, particularly the option of circumventing the constitutional requirement by going private.[63] VMI was afraid that it might not be able to keep women out after all. Patterson put the best possible face on the court's ruling by telling the press that the judges "accepted that the V.M.I. experience is not designed for women, and if women went there they wouldn't get what they want."[64] He and his colleagues were nonetheless furious at what they saw as Mary Sue Terry's undercutting of them with her "inaccurate and prejudicial" articulation of state policy during the course of "politically charged litigation."[65]

They said as much in the papers they filed immediately with the court of appeals. VMI asked the three-judge panel to rehear the case and also requested that the court rehear it en banc, with all twelve judges present. The decision, which VMI believed overlooked "critical points of law and fact," meant that "public single-gender education will be effectively banned in all but the highly theoretical circumstance where 'separate-but-equal' single-sex programs are provided to both sexes." VMI's rehearing petition went on to sound a call against federal imperialism: "This unwarranted and impractical federal imperative will place the states in an educational straight-jacket. It will impede the creative exercise of educational judgment at a time when this country's schools most urgently need innovation and improvement."[66] The Justice Department opposed the petition, no doubt thinking that a second decision from the court could be no better and might conceivably be worse.[67] Both the three-judge panel and the full court declined to hear the case, with only two judges voting for a rehearing en banc.[68]

The Institute suffered another blow in January 1993, when Bill Clinton was sworn in as president. Roughly 500 schools had applied to participate in the inaugural parade, and traditionally, the 125 that are chosen represent every state, the District of Columbia, and U.S. territories abroad. VMI cadets had participated in every presidential inaugural parade but two since 1949, and they had missed those of their own volition (one fell during exam week, and the other could not have included the entire corps). This time, although the Armed Forces Inaugural Committee had issued its usual invitation to VMI to apply, the Institute was turned down. It appealed the decision to no avail. What may have been even worse in VMI's eyes was that its place as the representative of Virginia was taken by the Denbigh High School Marching Patriots.[69]

But VMI had just begun to fight. On November 24, 1992, it had moved for a stay of the appeals court's first decision, which was granted; on January 19, 1993, it asked the Supreme Court to hear the case.[70] And, perhaps with the women's groups' amicus petition in mind, it began mustering supporters of its own.

Two amicus petitions were filed in support of VMI's request for a grant of certiorari (a place on the calendar) from the Supreme Court. One was submitted by three women's colleges: Mary Baldwin and Southern Virginia College for Women, both neighbors of VMI, and St. Mary's College of North Carolina. The Court had to act, it said, to protect the future of single-sex education. Colonel John W. Ripley, the president of Southern Virginia College and a former commanding officer of VMI's marine unit, warned, "Anyone who has the buffoonery to think that private [single-sex] colleges are protected is smoking dope."[71] The second brief, filed by Wells College in New York and three Virginia women's colleges (Hollins, Sweet Briar, and Randolph-Macon), argued that the suspicion thrown on single-sex programs by the appeals court could result in legal challenges to battered women's shelters and single-sex prisons.

A reporter for the *Chronicle of Higher Education* claimed that the amicus colleges had been pressured by wealthy VMI alumni into taking a stand "that they know is questionable." He quoted an unnamed president of another women's college as telling him, "They were pushed into it by wealthy alums who are married to VMI alums." Mary Baldwin's president, Cynthia Tyson, would not reply to the question of whether the first brief was a result of VMI pressure, but Patterson's partner Anne Marie Whittemore told the reporter that VMI had "advised" some women's colleges that the appeals court's decision had "potential implications" for their continued existence. Neither the Patterson firm nor a Los Angeles lawyer who worked on one of the briefs would say whether the legal bill had been footed by VMI.[72]

The United States' brief pointed out that the courts below had not finished thrashing the case out, as the government had never asked that a separate institution or program for women be created, and so the parties had not argued that issue.[73] The Supreme Court seemingly agreed and refused to grant certiorari.[74] (In fact, the Court usually grants certiorari to only about 100 cases out of the more than 7,000 appeals it receives each year.)[75] That sent the case back to Judge Kiser, who gave VMI until the fall to tell him how it planned to comply with the court of appeals' ruling.

The case continued to roil Virginia politics. Mary Sue Terry, now the leading candidate for governor, said that the response to the Supreme Court's action should be admission of women to VMI. The three candidates on the Republican side all retorted that it should not; instead, the state should create an alternative program for women.[76] At the beginning of June, VMI's Board of Visitors held a closed meeting in which it told its lawyers to draw up a proposal for an alternative plan.[77] The focus of attention was about to shift to Staunton, Virginia, the home of Mary Baldwin College.

14

In a Different Voice

Young men will paddle their pledges; they will brand them;

they will make them consume alcohol and will make them eat

disgusting things. . . . Young women will give flowers,

write poems.

—Heather Anne Wilson, dean of students, Mary Baldwin College

Three years after VMI opened its doors in 1839, a Presbyterian minister with degrees from Dartmouth College and Andover Theological Seminary founded Augusta Female Seminary in Staunton, Virginia, thirty-five miles away. It was the town that would fete the VMI cadets when they marched to the battle of New Market. The new school, situated on gently rolling green hills, was designed for genteel Christian ladies.

Its founder served as principal for ten years. One of his successors was the Reverend Joseph Ruggles Wilson, father of Woodrow Wilson. The future president of the United States, who would endorse Mary Munford's unsuccessful move to admit women to the University of Virginia, was born in Staunton.

During the Civil War, the seminary suffered the same kinds of economic stress that all Southern institutions experienced, and the same paucity of men to fill civilian offices. Mary Julia Baldwin, a former pupil of the seminary's founder, was chosen to become its principal. She determinedly raised the level of the school until its higher classes were doing the equivalent of college work. The grateful Board of Trustees eventually renamed the school Mary Baldwin Seminary in her honor. When she died in 1897, Baldwin left her substantial estate to the school, providing it with a comfortable endowment.

Mary Baldwin Seminary became a junior college in 1916 and a four-year women's college in 1923. It began buying adjacent property and eventually expanded to fifty-five acres. By the time of the VMI litigation, Mary Baldwin College (MBC) had over 2,000 students studying twenty-six majors and twenty-one minors. Over a thousand men and women were enrolled in an adult degree program held at five sites throughout the state. Forty-five women were in a program that enabled exceptionally gifted high school students to move directly into college from the eighth grade; about a hundred more were working toward a master of arts degree in elementary school teaching. The school emphasized liberal arts, but an arrangement with Washington University in St. Louis enabled students interested in engineering to take courses there.[1]

About 600 of the students lived in the manicured campus's sixteen residence halls. The gracious, classic white-columned buildings had black wire lounge furniture outside and brass chandeliers, mahogany furniture, and plush carpets inside. Gently banked steps led from each lush level of lawn to the next. There was a parking lot for the students' expensive cars (VMI students could not have cars until their senior year). It was, as one faculty member said, a "niche institution," providing upper- and upper-middle-class Virginia families with a competent liberal arts college to which they could safely send their daughters.[2] The visual contrast with VMI could not have been greater. As soon became apparent, there were other differences as well.

In the 1980s, two phenomena that would affect *United States v. Virginia* occurred at Mary Baldwin. The first was a decline in the level of applicants. The young women from the best Virginia families whose predecessors had filled colleges like Mary Baldwin were no longer interested in single-sex classrooms and were turning their sights instead on coeducational universities. The college had in fact begun offering more financial aid to prospective students than it could afford, diversifying its student body to keep its classes filled.

The second event was the arrival in 1985 of Cynthia H. Tyson, a new president with an English accent, a Ph.D. in English language and medieval English literature from the University of Leeds, and a fervent belief in the benefits of single-sex education. She quickly realized that in order to remain viable, MBC would have to make its offerings more exciting.

Exactly when Tyson and the college began thinking about creating a leadership program as part of its new offerings is unclear, and it would become a matter of contention during the second phase of the VMI litigation. MBC had long claimed to develop leaders, and some MBC courses had "leadership components."[3] Dr. James Lott, dean of the college, testified that MBC had been thinking about developing a leadership curriculum and possibly seeking a grant with which to do so during the 1992–1993 academic year. The goal of the program, Lott said, would be to develop citizen-soldiers.[4] Whether that language was used before the VMI case is uncertain, but there is agreement that whatever leadership institute MBC might have created without the VMI case, it would not have included ROTC or any other military components.[5]

In any event, when the court of appeals told VMI and Virginia that VMI or an equivalent had to be made available to women, VMI got in touch with its neighbor. The two schools' interests dovetailed so completely that there was no downside for either. If MBC agreed to design a curriculum for women citizen-soldiers, VMI could continue excluding women. Baldwin would benefit financially. The VMI Foundation, which offered to open its coffers to Baldwin, had sufficient clout in Richmond to get even more money flowing from the state. And MBC, its administration believed, had the expertise to develop a fine program.

Tyson and Richard Richardson, the educational expert who had testified against gender integration at the trial, first prepared a proposal for an MBC leadership institute. Lott then presented it to twelve faculty leaders late in the summer of 1993. Richardson sent drafts of the plan to the faculty group; they replied with comments, and an initial plan for approval by the entire faculty was put together.[6]

When, on September 24, Tyson presented the plan to the faculty and spoke about a program with a military emphasis at ladylike MBC, "the whole thing was fraught with humor"; some faculty members remember loud laughter.[7] It was nonetheless endorsed by the faculty and the Board of Trustees, and a task force was created to come up with a curriculum.[8] On September 25 the VMI Board and VMI Foundation also approved the plan and voted to provide the new Virginia Women's Institute for Leadership (VWIL) with an operating endowment of about $5.5 million, a scholarship endowment of $500,000, and a building renovation fund of $500,000.[9]

Dean Lott was assigned to cochair the task force. Other members included MBC's dean of students, its director of residence life, four faculty members (one of whom was also an alumna), and a student. The program presented to Judge Kiser two days later was only a draft, and it would be revised during the following months. But the assumptions and thinking behind the final plan drawn up by the task force were consistent with the earlier versions and are reflective of VWIL's ideas about how to educate women.[10]

Before articulating those ideas, the task force members embarked on what they described as an "in-depth study of the published literature on the developmental psychology of women and the cognitive development of women." They drew up a four-page bibliography and then divided it among themselves, with each member giving the group written summaries.[11]

Among the authors they read were Carol Gilligan, Rosabeth Kanter, Antonia Fraser, Nannerl Keohane, Marilyn French, and Deborah Tannen.[12] There were articles from the *Psychology of Women Quarterly, Education Digest, Working Women,* and the *Harvard Business Review.* The list included works such as Helen Astin and Carole Leland's *Women of Influence, Women of Vision;* Ann Morrison, Randall White, and Ellen Van Velsor's *Breaking the Glass Ceiling;* and Dorothy Cantor and Toni Bernay's *Women in Power.*[13] The task force members noted in their summaries the recurrent finding that "women tend to value cooperation and relationships" and that "leadership is a process of working with and through people," "women's identity is relationship," and leadership is either "interactive" or "command and control," with women preferring the former.[14]

Drafts of proposed goals, course lists, and co-curricular activities were circulated and rewritten. A number of the college's courses already had "leadership components," and ideas for new offerings were added to them.[15] The task force members came up with so many that MBC's dean of students recalls that their greatest challenge was to keep the academic segment of the program within the college's 132-semester-hour bachelor of arts requirement.[16] Some members visited VMI and, adding their on-site impressions to their reading, decided that VWIL would teach leadership quite differently.[17] The adversative system was out; a model based on cooperation was in. Lott completed a progress report reflecting that decision in November, and another in December. In January 1994 the group presented the faculty with "Virginia Women's Institute for Leadership at MBC: A Status Report." The final eleven-page "Virginia Women's Institute for Leadership at Mary Baldwin College" plan was ready in September 1994.[18]

The plan was based on four components: the academic curriculum, physical and health education, military leadership, and the co-curriculum. Its students would take nine hours each in the arts, humanities, and social sciences, along with six hours in writing, three each in calculus and statistics, eleven in the sciences, six in international education, four required interdisciplinary courses about leadership (Leadership Communications; History and Theories of Leadership; Ethics, Community, and Leadership; and a junior leadership seminar), and a three-hour leadership internship. (Three academic "hours" translate into a course, or about forty-two classroom hours.) They would be required to demonstrate proficiency in a foreign language and in computer skills. Their eight semesters of physical and health education courses would include self-defense training in addition to tennis, golf, and racquetball.

The co-curricular program would consist in part of a one-week wilderness program run by students, an honor system, and a twice-a-week "Cooperative Confidence Building" program. The last, which would put the students through "physically and mentally challenging events, including obstacle courses, rappelling, a ropes course, and team building activities," was clearly designed to parallel one element of the rat line; in fact, the final plan called it "analogous to the VMI 'rat challenge.'"[19]

The military segment of the VWIL plan consisted of four years of ROTC; students would take classes at MBC but be bused to VMI once a week for drills. They would study subjects such as development of airpower, air force (or army or navy) leadership and management, and national security forces. The two hours in freshman and sophomore year and the four hours in junior and senior year devoted to ROTC would be conducted in uniform.

VWIL had its own version of VMI's class system. Freshmen were to be mentored by upperclass students, who would lead the new Corps of Cadets, enforce behavior regulations, and play key roles in the wilderness orientation and the cooperative confidence-building program. Each VWIL class would have full responsibility during its second semester as juniors and first semester as seniors for organizing a leadership speaker series that would bring outstanding leaders to the campus, and every VWIL woman would be required each year to organize a community service project or campus activity that demonstrated leadership skills. A VWIL student would live with other VWIL students for two of her four years at Baldwin; the other two years would be spent in dorms with non-VWIL students. She would take classes with non-VWIL students but, as a freshman, would meet weekly with a VWIL group and its academic adviser.[20]

The kind of leadership training that the task force concluded was appropriate for women was defined in terms of the society at large and sharply differentiated from that offered by VMI.

> Young women . . . are products of a culture . . . which allows young women to perform at less than their optimum and, paradoxically, treats them condescendingly when they do so. Leadership development for women will be most effective, therefore, if it takes place in a single-sex environment of challenge and support in which

each student is pushed, by others and by herself, to perform at her highest level. We find no evidence that an extreme adversative environment . . . is appropriate for young women; we do find solid evidence, however, that an organized and disciplined environment which has as its purpose the building up of self confidence through mastery of physical, intellectual, and experiential challenges . . . is in fact the optimum environment for the education and training of women leaders.[21]

Though acknowledging that studies showed that women tended to follow "interactive" leadership models and men "hierarchical" models, the VWIL plan specifically rejected "the view that the models can only be gender specific." "There are in fact a variety of combinations," the plan stated, and the "successful leader" would be "one who is able to define the context, gauge the environment of any enterprise, clarify the purpose of any group task, and bring to bear the mode(s) of leadership appropriate to the group and to its purpose." Leaders were expected to have "a solid grasp of the theories of leadership" and to "possess the intellectual skills to practice it." They had to be able "to work constructively with a diverse population."[22]

The VWIL program would differ in important ways from VMI's, beyond its emphasis on cooperative leadership. Whereas VMI was run as a military base-in-training, VWIL women would not wear uniforms or be subject to a military regime on most school days. VMI cadets were issued M-14 rifles and bayonets; no arms would be issued to VWIL women. Although Kiser had said that "the most important aspects of the VMI educational experience occur in the barracks," where the Spartan living arrangements were meant to create an "egalitarian ethic,"[23] VWIL students would not live together or eat their meals together.[24]

VMI was the first college in the South to offer engineering courses, and in 1994 it granted undergraduate degrees in liberal arts, biology, chemistry, civil engineering, electrical and computer engineering, and mechanical engineering. The VWIL curriculum would include no courses in engineering or advanced math or physics, and any student who wanted engineering courses would have to go all the way to Washington University in St. Louis. The state was expected to contribute the same assistance for each Virginia student as it did at VMI—a third of the total (tuition and fees) of $19,100 at MBC—but it would contribute nothing for students studying in St. Louis.

The athletic program at VWIL would differ from that at VMI, not least because of the disparity in facilities. VMI boasted an NCAA competition–level indoor track and field facility; baseball, soccer, and lacrosse fields; multipurpose athletic fields; obstacle course, boxing, wrestling, and martial arts facilities; eleven-laps-to-the-mile indoor running course; indoor pool; indoor and outdoor rifle ranges; and football stadium with its practice field and outdoor track. MBC, in contrast, had only two multipurpose fields and an indoor gym. In addition, there would be no contact sports such as boxing at VWIL. VMI, however, promised VWIL students some access to its athletic facilities.

The minimum physical fitness requirement at VMI was sixty sit-ups and five pull-ups in two minutes, and a one-and-a-half-mile run in twelve minutes. VWIL's fitness standard, which was based on the military's standards for women, would be twenty-eight push-ups in two minutes, sixty full-body sit-ups in two minutes, a flexed arm hang of at least fifteen seconds, and a one-and-a-half-mile run in fourteen minutes twenty-four seconds.[25] The flexed arm hang was substituted for pull-ups because of concerns about the average woman's upper body strength. The unintended message was that women who wanted a military education could not keep up with men.

There would, of course, be no rat line. The rituals would be those that already existed at MBC, with its Freshmen Follies, Apple Day, and Peanut Day. President Tyson would testify that she had to reassure MBC alumnae that VWIL would fit into their old school.

> We have wonderful traditions here. They have, for example, Apple Day. The question, you know, is big in the minds of some alumnae. "Oh, my goodness, are we going to lose Apple Day?" "Of course not. Our college will remain with its traditions just as you have always known it."[26]

Faculty and funding also differentiated Baldwin from VMI. Eighty-six percent of VMI's faculty but only sixty-eight percent of MBC's faculty held Ph.D.s.[27] At MBC, the faculty's expertise was in the arts and humanities. Whereas VMI offered degrees in liberal arts, the sciences, and engineering, students at Mary Baldwin could earn only bachelor of arts degrees. VMI had the highest endowment per student of any public college in the nation, equal to $66,000 per student.[28] Virginia spent more on VMI per capita than on any other college or university in the state—$6,116 compared with, for example, $5,750 at the University of Virginia —with the exception of the medical school at Virginia Commonwealth University.[29] And state aid was supplemented by the VMI Foundation, which gave VMI an additional $7,703,775.

Faculty salaries at MBC were lower, which affected the college's ability to recruit. The authoritative *Barron's Guide* placed MBC faculty salaries in the nation's bottom 20 percent, whereas VMI's were in the top 8 percent.[30]

IT IS ENTIRELY POSSIBLE that the VWIL regime made more sense as a consciously designed leadership training program than did VMI's adversative system. The original goal behind the establishment of VMI, after all, was to combine a college education with guardianship of an armory by young men who would be somewhat less rambunctious than regular members of the Virginia militia. Whether the strict single-sex military atmosphere of VMI was the best way to train leaders for the twenty-first century—who are far more likely to find themselves in boardrooms and professional offices than in military positions, and working alongside women in all of them—was an open question. That is where VWIL, with its incorporation of modern knowledge about leadership, might have an edge. Its activities were indeed geared to leadership, and it is somewhat difficult to understand how the rat line contributed to leadership training.

The virtues of VWIL, however, were not the point. VWIL was proffered as a substitute for admitting women to VMI, and as Michael Maurer commented, "Giving someone an orange when she is not being given apples is not a remedy."[31] VWIL's problem was that, on the one hand, it had been fashioned in the heat of a lawsuit, and for litigation purposes, it had to conform to the norm established by VMI and show that it would achieve the same goals. Virginia would stress that VWIL's mission statement was "comparable to and derived from the mission statement of VMI."[32] On the other hand, there were two factors mitigating against designing VWIL as a female VMI. The first was that MBC administrators and faculty did not believe that the VMI method was the best way to produce female leaders—if, indeed, they considered it the most effective method of producing male leaders. Second, if VWIL merely replicated the VMI experience in an all-female setting, it would suggest that women were capable of succeeding in the VMI program, which would undercut VMI's and Virginia's position.

VWIL therefore adopted "certain VMI systems" to the extent that they were "educationally beneficial for women."[33] It was indisputable that women who wanted the VMI style of military training or meaningful access to the VMI alumni network (which VMI would solemnly tell the court would be available to VWIL graduates) or a military atmosphere combined with a scientific education were not going to get it at VWIL.

MBC's carefully phrased disclaimer about there being no one best leadership style was less than persuasive in light of its language that VWIL incorporated "the optimum environment for the education and training of women leaders." In that, it perhaps inadvertently led to perpetuation of the very stereotypes that had kept women out of VMI for over a century. Its emphasis on cooperation rather than competition, like its assumption that female students would neither want nor benefit from a strict military regime, was a bit too reminiscent of the image of woman as lady. However well-intentioned MBC's leaders were, they found themselves in a situation in which funding for their leadership institute was dependent on their playing VMI's political and legal game. Play it they did, and the result was continued litigation—for neither the Department of Justice nor the attorneys for the many concerned national women's law groups were about to accept Apple Day instead of the rat line.

Kiser had ruled on August 23 that Wilder had to tell the court by September 27 whether the VWIL plan had the backing of the state. The governor's political quandary was as great as ever, for he was planning to run for the Senate in 1994.[34] Wilder leaped at VWIL as a way of placating both VMI alumni and women. "I'm satisfied that this plan is educationally sound and will remedy all current discrimination," he said on September 25. "It is a plan that recognizes the physiological and psychological differences between men and women. And instead of drawing a middle ground that would not fully benefit students of either gender, it strives to reach the same results V.M.I. currently achieves so successfully with men."[35]

If there is any truth to the allegation that Charles Robb, the man who held the Senate seat Wilder wanted, had encouraged the Bush administration to bring the suit, Robb must have been smiling. He refused to comment about the plan.[36] Wilder infuriated some Virginians by pledging $6.9 million in state funds for VWIL's start-up costs, claiming that renovating VMI and beginning new programs for women there would have cost even more. The anger stemmed from the fact that funds for the state's colleges and universities had been cut by 18 percent over four years. So while he was promising massive state aid to a private college, Wilder was warning state universities that they would face another 15 percent in cuts over the next two years.[37]

Eileen Wagner, the lawyer who had submitted an amicus brief to the court of appeals, took to the pages of the *Richmond Times-Dispatch* to accuse "power-brokers" of "frantically scrambling to appease the whims of VMI's alumni and friends." "They should knock it off and come into the 20th century," she advised, writing that it was unacceptable for state funds to be used to exclude women.[38] Former senator Emilie Miller told the press, "I would be outraged by separate but equal. This is separate and unequal."[39] Some MBC students were quoted as saying that the college was being used to continue discrimination against women, and they threatened a sit-in to protest the way the decision to create VWIL had been made.[40] Many Baldwin faculty deplored both the exclusion of women from VMI and the extraneous military elements that would be brought to campus by VWIL.[41]

The Justice Department was quick to blast the VWIL plan, charging that the proposal "omits the essential components and benefits of the unique VMI experience; it designs programs based on gender stereotypes . . . [and] by almost every measure, the plan fails" to provide VMI's educational experience for women. VMI, unlike VWIL, was a complete leadership school.

> That Institute participants would be required to take "core and elective courses in leadership, equivalent to a minor," only underscores the profound contrast between the proposed Institute and the VMI experience. VMI does not offer "core and elective courses in leadership" because, according to the defendants . . . VMI's leadership training is a very conscious process that cuts across the curriculum.[42]

Richardson acknowledged advising that women should not be subjected to key aspects of the VMI method, such as induced mental stress, equality of treatment, absence of privacy, and minute regulation of behavior.[43] The government pointed out that the court of appeals had said that the adversative method was not inherently unsuitable for women and added, "The Equal Protection Clause does not permit the allocation of benefits between the sexes based on predominant group traits."[44] The plan's denial to women of "the unique holistic system of adversative education" was symbolized by its relaxed attitude toward uniforms. President Tyson had commented, "If they want to wear them, they can wear them; if they don't want to wear them, they don't have to wear them."[45]

The offers of support by VMI were misleading, the government continued. General Knapp admitted, for example, that only a few of VMI's physical education facilities would actually be shared, and they would be available only during the orientation period.[46] In short, the government stated, "the bottom line is, VMI is a military-type school and MBC is not."[47] "This is not a remedy," Maurer said. "It's a marriage of convenience."[48]

Whether that made the VWIL plan unconstitutional as a substitute for admitting women to VMI would be the subject of the next trial.

Back in Judge Kiser's Court

There are some average differences between men and women,

but the average differences between men and women are trivial

compared to the very large individual differences within the

group of men and within the group of women.

—Carol Nagy Jacklin

Many of the same players were in the courtroom when the second trial in *United States v. Virginia* began on February 9, 1994.[1] Judge Kiser was behind the bench, Barbara Taylor had her stenography pads ready, and an overflow of media representatives with pens and pencils in hand was once again ready to relay the two sides' more dramatic points to the nation. A computer screen showed the trial transcript as it was being made, to compensate for Robert Patterson's impaired hearing.

There were also some new faces. VMI's legal team was up to eleven and included recently elected Virginia attorney general James S. Gilmore III, who would tell the court that he, Governor George Allen, and Lieutenant Governor Donald Beyer—all three of the commonwealth's statewide elected officials—supported the VWIL plan.[2] The Justice Department contingent was again led by Judith Keith, Nathaniel Douglas, John Moore, and Michael Maurer—the last no longer such a junior member of the team and now ready to play an increasingly important role. There were, in addition, two new members from the Civil Rights Division, Gary A. Haugen and Dana R. Carstarphen, an indication of the greater resources allocated to the case by the Clinton administration.

For VMI, this was the beginning of its last possible legal campaign over gender integration. The case would continue in a higher court no matter which way Kiser decided, and the Institute knew that it had to make a record demonstrating that VWIL fulfilled the mandate of the court of appeals. Virginia would present a three-part argument, two prongs of which tracked the earlier trial. First, the adversative system required a single-sex setting. Second, opening VMI to the few women who might be able to manage the adversative system would destroy the Institute for naught.

The third point was that Virginia had complied with the court of appeals' suggestion that it create a different program for women who wanted an education similar to VMI's. "For Virginia to provide an educational opportunity for women to become citizen-soldiers comparable to that enjoyed by men at VMI," the Institute's attorneys said in the summary of the VWIL plan they submitted to Kiser, "the Commonwealth must establish a single-gender educational environment and program" that would provide "a parity of opportunities and results for both genders." A "parallel" program that fit the requirement of providing an equally good education for women could not be identical to VMI's, however, because women learned differently from men, and recognition of those differences had to be built into the new program. The constitutional mandate was that women be given equal opportunity, not identical opportunity; here, the equal protection clause would be violated if a program for women merely copied one for men that would not meet women's developmental needs.[3]

The trial started with the last point. Anne Marie Whittemore called MBC dean James Lott to the stand. After summarizing the VWIL plan's history, Lott laid out its rationale.

> A: We are convinced by all of the literature in the field that while there are no inherent differences between the way men and women learn, our society has encouraged young women . . . [to] define our sense of self in relationships so that leadership development in women will occur most effectively on building on that fact rather than building on another theory or hypothesis about the ways women learn.[4]

As Lott's statement indicates, he and other VMI witnesses did not claim that women's asserted differential learning patterns were the result of nature rather than nurture. Rather, they would suggest, society had shaped men and women in such opposing ways that in order to get them both to the point at which they could successfully exercise leadership, men had to be challenged and cowed, while women required gentle encouragement in the building of self-confidence.

VWIL administrators and Whittemore clearly believed at least the second part; that is, that female leadership was best developed through cooperation and mutual support rather than competition. Whether VMI officials and the other members of its legal team saw women's perceived need for a particular kind of education as reflecting difference rather than inferiority is less obvious. To the Justice Department team and the women's groups, it did not much matter. What was important to them was that Virginia was still denying a military-environment learning experience to those women who wanted it and believed that they could benefit from it. The government's task was to demonstrate that women could benefit and had in fact benefited from just such an education, so depriving them of that opportunity was a violation of the equal protection clause.

Lott and other witnesses were persuasive in arguing that the VWIL program was a good way to teach leadership skills—so much so that a listener might have wondered at VMI's continued insistence that the adversative method was either necessary or desirable. As Lott told the court, the task force had decided that "the best way to develop the curriculum was to concentrate on courses in leadership" and "situations in which the young woman herself can take on leadership roles in the classroom." He added that the externship component of the program, which already had some MBC students spending 150 hours at law firm jobs, was crucial.[5]

> A: Now what the leadership externship would do would be to require her beyond that to do some sort of activity, and we're just instancing keeping a journal, in which she analyzes leadership, effectiveness of leadership, ineffectiveness of leadership, within a . . . community like that.[6]

Asked how the physical fitness component would differ from VMI's, Lott replied:

> A: We make some slight differences where we think it's appropriate. We will not require boxing. We would have self defense built into this.
>
> We're requiring, as of now, tennis, golf and racquetball and that came from our physical education faculty. In the Task Force discussions they were asked why those three, they made the point that these are the sports used in corporate leadership, and being able to play golf, being able to play racquetball, being able to play tennis gives you a leg up, so I think that was clever thinking on their part.[7]

VWIL graduates apparently would be trained to do battle on corporate racquetball-playing fields, if not in the military. They would also get a healthy dose of discipline. Lott asserted that the VWIL student would find a regime that was much more disciplined, much more orderly, much more arranged, particularly in the freshman year than is true of almost any college in 1994. . . . She will not be allowed to smoke. She will be expected to keep her room neat and orderly. It will be subject to spot inspections. She will be required to participate in a study, organized study program each evening . . . we want to create an environment, a living environment, a residential environment, in which the student is presented with challenges, is presented with the need to stretch herself but is given the support to enable her to meet those challenges.

The goal, Lott said, was getting students to the point at which they would be "able to practice leadership roles in positions outside VWIL."[8]

Lott made it clear that the rejection of both the VMI adversative method and all other forms of military-based education was based on gender. "Nothing in the literature that we read suggested that a similar approach would be effective for young women. . . . We also considered the military model . . . and determined that our program should use a disciplined approach to that [developing leadership] but not a military approach."[9]

Gary Haugen's cross-examination of Lott focused on MBC's lack of experience in the two areas for which VMI claimed it prepared students: the military, and leadership in general.

> Q: Dean Lott, the fact is that Mary Baldwin, apart from not having any military tradition of leadership, it doesn't have a tradition of leadership that's comparable to VMI, does it?
> A: It does not have a tradition of military leadership. . . .
> Q: Do you think there is anybody comparable there in terms of national leadership to General Stonewall Jackson?
> THE COURT: Marshall.
> Q: General Marshall?[10]

Lott answered that no MBC alumna was comparable to Marshall. Haugen then focused on the differences in the proposed academic program.

> Q: Dean Lott, Mary Baldwin doesn't offer a bachelor of science degree, does it?
> A: No. It does not.
> Q: VWIL students won't have an opportunity to take engineering classes at Mary Baldwin unless they want to go to St. Louis; isn't that right?
> A: Yes.
> Q: And they won't have the opportunity to take chemical engineering, will they?
> A: That is true. . . .
> Q: They won't have the opportunity to take mechanical engineering?
> A: We don't offer engineering at Mary Baldwin.
> Q: Do you offer a physics major?
> A: We do not.

Q: The VWIL students won't have an opportunity to go to a school where the primary focus of the students and the faculty is on math and sciences; isn't that correct?

A: That is correct.

Q: The VWIL students also won't have an opportunity to go to a school whose faculty is paid at a rate that's comparable to VMI, will they?

A: That is correct.[11]

Haugen pressed the dean on what made him think VWIL would be comparable to VMI.

A: We think that the Institute for Leadership is the most effective model for developing leadership skills in women—

Q: Excuse me, sir?

A: Which is—

Q: For which women? . . . When you say the adversative model of education is not beneficial for women, do you mean from that that there aren't any women for whom the adversative model of education would be beneficial?

A: No, I do not mean that.

Q: So there are some women for whom the adversative model of education would be optimal; isn't that right?

A: There may be.

Q: But this program isn't designed for those women, is it?

A: No.

Q: Isn't it true that the VWIL won't employ a method of induced stress because women—because of the special way that you think women learn?

A: Yes, the special way I think most women learn.[12]

Haugen next got Lott to admit that MBC had not done its homework about women who wanted to attend VMI.

Q: But your Task Force brought in no outside experts apart from talking to some people from VMI, isn't that right?

A: That is right.

Q: The Task Force made no investigation of what is necessary for the development of military leadership; isn't that right, specifically military leadership?

A: That is right in and of itself. . . .

Q: In designing the program, Dean Lott, you never even tried to figure out what women were seeking by attending VMI, did you?

A: No. We did not.

Q: In fact, you have no idea why women would want a VMI type of program with a single-sex setting; isn't that right?

A: I don't know what motivates . . . such a woman to select such a program.[13]

VMI expected the Justice Department to charge that the Institute was resorting to stereotypical thinking in assuming that reasonable women would neither want to attend VMI nor benefit from its method. It therefore called Elizabeth Fox-Genovese to the stand.

Fox-Genovese, a professor of history and women's studies, was one of the country's leading academic feminists. She had developed women's studies programs at the University of Rochester, the State University of New York at Binghamton, and Emory University in Atlanta. As she said, "teaching and educating women has been at the center of my life's commitment."[14] Her books such as *Within the Plantation Household* and *Feminism Without Illusions*, along with her estimated forty-five articles on women's issues,[15] were highly regarded by many feminists. Many others were more skeptical, particularly in light of her volume entitled *Feminism Is Not the Story of My Life: How Today's Feminist Elite Has Lost Touch with the Real Concerns of Women*, which asserted that feminism had failed by ignoring the needs of children and poor women.[16]

As she stated under cross-examination and again in an article she wrote after the trial,[17] Fox-Genovese assumed that a decision against VMI would mean the end of single-sex education. The first sentences of the article, tellingly, were, "The end of single-gender education would drastically diminish the opportunities of young American women and men. . . . In fulfilling one woman's choice to attend an all-male college, we will deny all women and men the choice of ever again attending a single-gender college."[18]

The article expressed Fox-Genovese's concern about daughters of less affluent families, whom she considered in particular need of single-sex schools, for reasons not made entirely clear.[19] Her concern was reflected at the trial, where she described MBC as playing an important societal function by moving from its past of serving the elite to enrolling many first-generation college goers. In that, she said, it resembled VMI. She suggested that VWIL would be even better than VMI in attracting a diverse student body and contributing to multiculturalism on the MBC campus, while being "fully comparable" to VMI in instilling self-confidence and self-discipline.[20]

She also believed that a decision against VMI would mean that any institution geared to only one sex was against the law, no matter what the reason for its existence. She mentioned battered women's shelters and rape crisis centers as examples.[21] How she reached that conclusion, given *Hogan*'s "exceedingly persuasive justification" criterion, is unclear.

Whatever her reasons, and however impressive her feminist credentials, Fox-Genovese's testimony was replete with stereotypes.

> Q: Doctor, in your opinion, does a single gender educational program for women as VWIL need to use the same methodology as VMI uses with respect to the rat line and the adversative system in order to produce the outcomes?
>
> A: No, I don't believe it does . . . the overwhelmingly scholarly evidence, quite apart from my personal experience . . . suggests that young women by the time they reach college for whatever reason have less confidence in themselves than young men. In other words, we really don't need to beat uppityness and aggression and all of that out of young women.[22]

She agreed that women would not want VMI.

> Q: Doctor, based on your work with undergraduates, would you describe to the court your opinion of anticipated student demand for VWIL and compare it to the demand that you just indicated for an all-women's mirror image of VMI?
>
> A: Look, we haven't had studies of this but . . . based on my reading of the literature on young women in college education, my own experience interviewing, my knowledge of polling data and the amount of time I spent talking to students, my own and other people's, I would be very much surprised if there was very much demand for a female VMI and I would expect the demand for VWIL to be significant and to rise. . . . I would think that VWIL would be extremely appealing for all kinds of reasons.[23]

Perhaps a professor who had spent her career dealing with women's studies students had not had the opportunity to meet the kind of women who were attracted by the military or by military-type discipline. As both the armed services and the federal military academies had discovered, military women, by and large, were not feminists—and a good many of them could not have afforded to attend the universities at which Fox-Genovese taught.

VMI called Heather Anne Wilson, MBC's dean of students, as an expert witness on women's education and the psychology of gender. Judith Keith immediately challenged Wilson's qualifications. Under questioning, Wilson acknowledged that her master's and doctoral degrees were in counseling and higher education and that she had published no scholarly works on the development of college-age women. Kiser ruled that her lack of formal training was balanced by Wilson's more than twenty years' experience in women's higher education and accepted her as an expert.[24]

That kind of decision about VMI's expert witnesses in both trials was criticized by some observers. An expert on physiology and physical education, with no credentials in psychology, had been permitted to testify at the first trial about women's purported "fear of failure." Kiser allowed Colonel Bissell, with his army credentials, to speak about women's emotional makeup. Ries-man's only authority for comments about "the fate of women's colleges" was newspaper clippings and meetings with college presidents.[25] It was Wilson's testimony, however, that suggested most graphically that the critics may have had a point.

Wilson thought that the way to assess the interests of male and female col-lege students was to examine how they spent their leisure time, and "the best example I can think of for that is what young men and women do as part of preinitiation in fraternities and sororities."

> A: The young men will paddle their pledges; they will brand them; they will make them consume alcohol and will make them eat disgusting things, take them on rides—you get the picture.
>
> Young women will give flowers, write poems. In my own sorority every upper-classman wrote me a letter telling me how wonderful I was before I was initiated. And that's what students do when they are on their own time.[26]

Wilson did not indicate whether she believed that there were nonsoror-ity women—or any sorority women, for that matter—who did not spend most of their leisure time writing poems to one another, or that any college men concentrated on activities other than whacking one another with paddles. She firmly denied, however, that she was relying on stereotypes.[27] She de-scribed the socialization process as beginning early, drawing on anecdote rather than science.

> A: I can't even tell you when it starts except that I know that a friend of mine is [a] clinical psychologist [and] has a four year old daughter. . . . Her four-year-old's favorite movie is Aladdin. . . . In the movie Aladdin, and this is representative of what young children are taking in, the princess, even though she has a large tiger at her command, has to wait to be rescued by Aladdin. . . . Women internalize these messages; they should take the passive role not the active role.[28]

Kiser accepted the anecdote as expert testimony.

Whether or not it was their intention, Wilson's and Fox-Genovese's re-marks rang variations on the idea of woman as lady. The entire thrust of the argument presented by VMI was in fact an updating of the theme. VMI's introduction of Carol Gilligan's work at the first trial had been designed to show that the difference in male and female psychology and learning pat-terns was a matter of scientific truth rather than stereotyping. Woman as lady was given a late-twentieth-century twist: as presented to the court, she was dressed in sweatpants rather than crinolines. But ladies still had to be made to understand that they were different from men and that their physiology necessitated their being firmly set on a different track from that appropriate for their more aggressive male counterparts. "Physiology" had been replaced by "the effects of culture on psychology," and "aggression" had been transformed into "testosterone levels," but the message was as old as the nation's history.

The next theme was articulated by MBC president Tyson, whose appearance caused another clash about expert witnesses' credentials. Whittemore introduced Tyson as an expert in single-gender education for women and in leadership development. Maurer got Tyson to state that all her degrees were in English and medieval English literature and that she had published no studies on the education of women or educational methodologies. Tyson, however, was in her ninth year as MBC president, and Kiser permitted her to testify as an expert witness. She too indicated that the possible impact of the case on the future of single-sex education was much on her mind.

> Q: And didn't you write, didn't you say if we lost VMI, then the women's institutions are next; isn't that right?
> A: I did say that, and I did write that.
> Q: So you—you're afraid of losing VMI, right?
> A: I am afraid of losing the option of single-sex education.
> Q: Right, because you think that if VMI were to become coed, that would have effects for your college, isn't that right?
> A: That is correct.[29]

Maurer asked about Virginia's repeated assertion that only a few women would be interested in VMI.

> Q: Now, you would never employ an adversative kind of education either at Mary Baldwin or for the VWIL, would you? . . . you think that the system in place right now is appropriate for Mary Baldwin students, don't you? . . . the cooperative model of education . . . ?
> A: I do.
> Q: And don't you also believe that the—that a program for women with extreme adversative elements would attract fewer women?
> A: I have so testified.
> Q: But you've done no market study on that subject, have you?
> A: Nor has anyone.
> Q: Right, so you've made no determination as to what the demand would be either for an adversative model or for the VWIL, have you?
> A: Mr. Maurer, there has not been time.[30]

As the trial went on, Kiser continued to rule against the Justice Department, turning down the government's motion to strike material on the benefits of single-sex education as irrelevant. When he said that he would admit evidence to the effect that very few women had demonstrated an interest in VMI, Douglas objected. Back in August, when Kiser had set the rules for pretrial discovery, he had declined to permit the Justice Department to ask VMI for information about inquiries by women. Now Kiser dismissed that objection as well.[31] Given Kiser's decision after the first trial, it seems reasonable to assume that the government attorneys were making their motions without much hope that they would be granted, but with an eye toward an eventual appeal.

Another deposition from David Riesman was read, this one stating the elderly scholar's approval of the VWIL plan and its lack of "the ferocity that I associate with VMI."[32] Major General Robert E. Wagner, a VMI alumnus who had been the commanding general of army ROTC, was admitted as an expert in military leadership, leadership in general, and training of civilians for the military, again over Justice Department objections. Wagner stated that women did not need VMI because women in ROTC who went to nonmilitary colleges did as well as ROTC graduates who had attended military academies. His point was that women at VWIL would receive adequate military training.[33]

VMI's third outside educational "expert," after Fox-Genovese and Riesman, was Richard Richardson. As mentioned earlier, Richardson had been closely involved in the creation of the VWIL plan. He had advised VMI and MBC that the adversative system "did not incorporate mental models that are empowering for women," that there would be insufficient demand for a VMItype college for women, and that being a member of a small minority of students "in an environment that has not been designed around the needs and life experiences of that population" would not be "conducive to developing the self-confidence that we associate with leadership."[34] He thought that VWIL, with its "social influence theory" of "collegial," "interactive" leadership, offered a "comparable opportunity" to that at VMI without the Institute's "social power of leadership."[35]

Although it was not articulated particularly well at either trial, the two sides had sharply conflicting views of the demands of the equal protection clause. The VMI legal team argued, in effect, that the clause applied to groups. Women had to be given the same opportunities as men if women *as a group* were likely or able to take advantage of them. If only small numbers of women were interested in an opportunity, then the state had no obligation to provide it for women as a group. Richardson, Fox-Genovese, and the other VMI witnesses contributed to the effort by basing their testimony on beliefs about the "way women are." VMI said repeatedly that yes, some women might be interested in and could handle the adversative method, but the equal protection clause did not require that VMI be "destroyed" for the sake of that handful.

The Justice Department, returning again and again to the charge of stereotyping, did not deny that most women would be uninterested in VMI. Its somewhat understated premise was that the equal protection clause protected the rights not of "most" but of the individual. A woman denied an opportunity that the state offered a man could rightly claim that the equal protection clause had been violated. The clause prohibits a state from denying "any person" the equal protection of the laws. To argue from stereotype, however true of the majority that stereotype might be, was to violate the rights of the individuals who did not conform to the norm.

The contrast between the Justice Department's interpretation and that of VMI's witnesses was underscored by the testimony of Dr. Beverly Sgro, secretary of education for Virginia. Maurer asked her about the state's educational responsibility.

> A: The Commonwealth is tasked with the responsibility of developing educational programs that meet the needs of the students of the Commonwealth. . . .
>
> Q: Well, it certainly meets . . . the needs of men, right?
>
> A: Correct.
>
> Q: But if a woman is interested in a VMI type of education, the Commonwealth doesn't believe she should have that right. Isn't that right?
>
> A: That's correct. . . .
>
> Q: Doctor, do you know what the Commonwealth's position is on the fact that women who would go to the VWIL would not be able to get an engineering education on campus?
>
> A: Yes. The state has no obligation to provide an engineering degree for any student in Virginia on every campus. As a matter of fact, that works at odds with what the state's goal is which is not to have duplicative programs, so there would be no obligation to provide the exact academic programs in every institution [in] Virginia.
>
> Q: Yet, the Commonwealth sees you provide engineering at VMI for men; isn't that right?
>
> A: That's correct, but that doesn't necessarily mean it needs to be provided at every other institution in the state.
>
> Q: Right, just because it is provided for men, doesn't mean it has to be provided for women, isn't that right?[36]

WHEN THE COMMONWEALTH rested its case, John Moore asked the court to rule that the VWIL plan did not meet the requirements of the equal protection clause. "The evidence establishes that despite the Fourth

Circuit's conclusion that neither the goal of producing citizen soldiers nor VMI's implementing regulations or methodology is inherently unsuitable for women, the VMI defendants' Proposed Remedial Plan is premised on the opposite assumption," he charged, speaking as much for the benefit of the appeals court as for Kiser. "Indirect contravention of the Fourth Circuit's mandate establishes that VMI, with the concurrence of the Commonwealth, would establish a program at Mary Baldwin College that would omit, omit— omit, Your Honor, the very attributes of VMI that make the experience of men who go there unique and holistic." He reminded Kiser that there would be no military life or engineering courses at VWIL and objected to the assumption that women would not want the opportunity to attend VMI. "With regard to the issue of demand, Your Honor, we would note that the record is void of any evidence regarding any study that the defendants have done to substantiate their claim regarding the lack of demand for a female single-gender VMI."[37]

William Boland, asking Kiser to rule for VMI, argued that the state could offer gender-specific programs if it did so in pursuit of a legitimate governmental objective. The differences between VWIL and VMI were "based on the model of leadership that Dr. Lott, Dr. Wilson, Dr. Tyson, Dr. Fox-Genovese and Dr. Riesman testified to."[38] Boland, too, was speaking for the record and the future eyes of the court of appeals. He turned to the Shannon Faulkner case for support.

Faulkner had brought suit in 1993 against VMI's South Carolina analog, The Citadel. The school had admitted her, unaware of her sex, and then denied her entry when it realized that she was a woman. By the time of the second VMI trial, much of the country was familiar with the Faulkner case. The lack of a named plaintiff in the VMI case made it much less interesting to the media, which lavished breathless prose on Faulkner's efforts to gain admission and her eventual rapid departure from the school on health grounds. The district court judge hearing the case ordered her admitted as The Citadel's first woman day student while the lawsuit was pending. The order was confirmed by the Fourth Circuit Court of Appeals, which has jurisdiction over South Carolina as well as Virginia.[39] The appeals court would hold later, after the second VMI trial, that Faulkner's right to substantially equal educational opportunities had been violated and that the right was personal: the lack of other applicants was irrelevant. It ordered her immediate admission and the submission of a remedial plan for other women.[40] As recounted in chapter 21, the dispute was not finally resolved until after the Supreme Court decided *United States v. Virginia* in 1996.

Now Boland read from the court of appeals decision in *Faulkner v. Jones:* "analysis of the nature of the separate facility provided in response to a justified purpose, must take into account the nature of the differences on which the separation is based, the relevant benefits to and the needs of each gender, the demand both in terms of quality and quantity and any other relevant factors." VWIL, he said, stood up under that criterion. "The thing that we have presented to this Court is precisely that, a single-gender, publicly supported opportunity for women in Virginia to achieve virtually identical goals and benefits as that is accomplished by VMI-type education."[41]

The appeals court had referred to its decision in *United States v. Virginia* when it decided *Faulkner v. Jones.* Now Moore replied to Boland by quoting from that decision: "'While providing a single-gender military education was held to constitute an appropriately important state purpose, we could find no state policy justifying Virginia's decision to offer this unique,' *unique* 'type of education, only to men.'"[42] Repetition of the word "unique" was Moore's addition, designed to emphasize the difference between VMI and VWIL.

Kiser ruled as expected. Saying that the appellate court's decision could be read "both ways"—either to uphold or to strike down VWIL as an adequate alternative to VMI—he declared that his "major task in this case" was to "develop . . . a full record for the appellate courts."[43] The trial would continue.

THE NEXT STEP IN ESTABLISHING that record for the higher courts was to hear the Justice Department's side of the case. The Department's first witness was Dr. Larry L. Leslie, director of the University of Arizona's Center for the Study of Higher Education and an expert on higher education finance.

Leslie had toured VMI and MBC and was convinced that VWIL would not be adequately funded.[44] Referring to the "financial component" of the VWIL plan, Leslie commented, "it was hard for me to take this document seriously."[45] MBC was suffering from what he called "fiscal distress," including an accrued three-year deficit of $6.5 million. The Southern Association of Colleges and Schools had raised questions about MBC's financial situation three years earlier and had been told that MBC would take care of it, but nothing had been done, and Leslie said that the lack of dollars would affect MBC's educational program negatively.[46]

He noted that VMI faculty were paid between 22 and 24 percent more than MBC faculty and added that he considered faculty pay and the ability to attract better faculty "the most significant indicator of the quality of the educational experience that students enrolled in those institutions" were likely to have. He was dubious about the ability of VWIL, "a program that doesn't exist at this point," to generate VMI's extraordinary level of funding.[47]

Lott had tried to dismiss the deficit as "planned."

> Q: Did you hear Dean Lott refer to the four years of deficits as planned deficits?
> A: Yes. I did.
> Q: Have you ever heard that term referred to before?
> A: I immediately thought that it's a term [used by] someone at the federal level and working up federal budgets.
> [Laughter.][48]

Subsequent witnesses testified to the great physical difference between the two campuses, comparing MBC's "beautiful mahogany furniture for the students, Georgian columns," and "generously proportioned" dorm rooms "absolutely stuffed with all kind of personal belongings," such as televisions and stereos, with VMI's forbidding buildings and its rules on personal possessions: "They essentially allow almost nothing."[49] MBC's relative poverty of athletic facilities, classrooms, and laboratories was also detailed.[50] Then the government called its counter to Fox-Genovese.

Carol Nagy Jacklin was a professor of psychology and dean of social sciences and communication at the University of Southern California and an expert in the psychology of gender. Her coauthored *Psychology of Sex Differences* was considered a leader in the field. She had edited the four-volume *Psychology of Gender,* which brought together 146 of the most important papers on the psychology of gender that had been published between 1910 and 1990.[51]

Led by Gary Haugen, Jacklin told the court that neither David Riesman nor Richard Richardson was an expert on the psychology of gender and that the VWIL plan rested on erroneous assumptions about the differences in the ways men and women learned. "There are some average differences between men and women," she testified, "but the average differences between men and women are trivial compared to the very large individual differences within the group of men and within the group of women."[52] To illustrate, she turned to a chalkboard graph showing the frequency distribution of men and women when assessed for fearfulness, commenting that the distribution was pretty much the same for most traits.

> THE COURT: The point being that you can't generalize as to any one individual?
> THE WITNESS: That's exactly right and gender is used as if you could generalize.

Gender seems to be used to try to predict many things that aren't well predicted by gender.[53]

Haugen asked whether it was possible to predict which leadership development program would be most effective for women.

> A: I don't believe it is.
> Q: And why not?
> A: Because women are not a single group. Women vary. Women are different just as men vary and men differ from each other.[54]

Whittemore, aware of Kiser's sensibilities, asked if Jacklin called herself a feminist and was a member of the ACLU and NOW—nothing that would play well in that particular courtroom.[55] More to the point, Whittemore pointed out inconsistencies between Jacklin's testimony in the courtroom and at deposition. Jacklin had been more willing to specify differences between male and female learning patterns in deposition, Whittemore noted; Jacklin replied that she had been talking about averages. Jacklin also admitted that some experts in the psychology of gender would disagree with her dismissal of learning differences.[56] The strategy worked; when Kiser wrote his opinion, he dismissed Jacklin out of hand with a laconic, "Dr. Jacklin's testimony was contradicted by most of the evidence in the record."[57]

Kiser's predilections were apparent in a comment he made to Michael S. Kimmel, the next witness. Kimmel, an associate professor of sociology at the State University of New York at Stony Brook, was an expert in historical sociology—that is, the study of how historians use their materials and what they base their conclusions on. He was also an expert in the sociology of gender who had analyzed historical responses to women's demand for higher education. "In the nineteenth and twentieth century," he began, "the arguments to exclude women" from institutions of higher education always revolved around the claim that "they don't want it. If we build it, they will not come."

> THE COURT: But you've got a few crazies that might want it.
> THE WITNESS: That's right.
> THE COURT: But generally they don't.[58]

Maurer asked Kimmel what opinion he had formed after examining the VWIL plan.

> A: When I first read The Plan, my experience was one of familiarity, although I had never seen it before. I said, "My goodness, it sounds like so many things I've seen in archives in libraries around the country about the arguments about what would be appropriate for women as a group and what kinds of things women are

suited for." . . . In the guise of exempting women from the things for which they were not suited, women were being excluded from the opportunity of the kind of educational methodology that is used at VMI.[59]

The suitability of a military-style education for women was confirmed by Captain Tamara Frezell, who had graduated from West Point in 1989 and was now its equal admissions officer. She had served in Saudi Arabia during Operations Desert Shield and Desert Storm, supervising $300 million worth of combat equipment for 125,000 personnel. Her path was a family one: her father, her sister, and her four brothers all had army careers.[60]

The next witness would testify that VWIL women would not get the kind of training Frezell had experienced at West Point or that men were offered at VMI. James A. Peterson, formerly in charge of physical conditioning classes at West Point, dismissed MBC as imbued with a "finishing school environment."

> A: Prior to the admission of women to West Point . . . we did our research and we tried to identify what women should be required to do on the basis of information provided to us by textbook warriors. . . . When they got to the Academy, their achievement so far exceeded our expectations that, to a very, very significant degree it was the considered opinion of myself and many of the people who [were] within the West Point environment . . . that the West Point environment . . . the traditions of excellence that exist in an institution like VMI and West Point and the naval academy . . . [were] the primary factor that allowed these women to achieve more than what we expected them to do.[61]

The VMI team was as contemptuous of Peterson's testimony as he was of MBC, establishing on cross-examination that he had spent only an hour at MBC, had not seen some of its facilities, and had met with no students.[62]

Then the Justice Department rolled out its big gun: Alexander Astin, the scholar who had been so incensed by VMI's and Kiser's use of his work on single-sex men's colleges that he had joined an amicus brief at the court of appeals level. At the time of the second trial, his studies of college students, which had lasted for eighteen years, had surveyed 8 million of them and followed 500,000 more closely.

Astin joined Peterson in emphasizing the importance of environment, testifying that the climate established by peer groups is the "key factor in any undergraduate's development" and that the VWIL students, a small minority in the relatively unchallenging atmosphere created by other MBC students, would not have "comparable outcomes or comparable experiences" to those at VMI.[63] More importantly, he scoffed at the idea that women's developmental characteristics made any acceptable educational method inappropriate for them, or that women would respond differently from men to an educational environment of absolutely equal treatment.[64] But in Kiser's eyes, Patterson skewered Astin, as Whittemore had delegitimized Jacklin. Astin acknowledged participating in a brief urging the court of appeals to overturn Kiser's ruling; he had been an expert witness for the ACLU in The Citadel case and had received $200 an hour for his services; more damning, still, he supported the women's movement.[65]

Patterson was able to show that Astin's own work indicated that men and women had different aspiration patterns and that women were more likely to achieve leadership positions if they had attended single-sex colleges. Under redirect examination by Haugen, Astin argued that these figures referred to averages and that "there is more overlap between the sexes in all these qualities than there are differences." Nothing he had written, he insisted, showed that men and women learn differently.[66]

The trial concluded with the VMI legal team predicting victory and the Justice Department and its allies fearing the worst from Judge Kiser. Both sides were right.

16

The Fife and the Drum,
Separate but Equal

Several months ago, one of the first women fighter pilots was killed during a practice run. Anyone who is prepared to do combat for her country—indeed, to be killed in preparation for that combat—should be eligible to apply for what she perceives to be the best possible training.

—Judge Diana Gribbon Motz

Judge Kiser must have been chuckling as he wrote his second VMI decision. Slyly turning the tables on the U.S. government and tossing the language of racial equality litigation in its face, he accused the people in Washington of trying to impose "separate but equal" institutions of higher education on the sovereign state of Virginia.[1]

The Justice Department, noting that the court of appeals had referred to "the unique benefit offered by VMI's type of education," had attacked VWIL for not offering a similar benefit to women. "The United States urges that to comply with the instructions of the Fourth Circuit, the Commonwealth is required to produce a plan that will create a separate institution which closely resembles, if not clones, the physical plant, the curriculum, the methodology, the prestige, and many of the other attributes of VMI," Kiser now wrote. "In other words, the United States reads the Fourth Circuit opinion to require a 'separate but equal' institution."[2]

"The sophistry of the 'separate but equal' concept" had been "roundly rejected" by the Supreme Court, Kiser solemnly chastised the very Justice Department that had fought to eliminate the last vestiges of "separate but equal" educational institutions in the South. In any event, there could be no VMI clone, because everyone acknowledged that the Institute, with its "intangible qualities of history, reputation, tradition, and prestige," could not be replicated. And the government's continuing demand that VMI admit women was disrespectful of the appeals court, accusing the Fourth Circuit of suggesting "an exercise in futility" or "an impossible task" when it held that Virginia "was free to establish 'parallel programs' or to devise 'creative options or combinations'" that would comply with the court's decision.[3]

What the appeals court meant, Kiser wrote, was that an acceptable program could be single sex without following the VMI model. The Fourth Circuit had stated, "'the record supports the conclusion that single-sex education is pedagogically justifiable.'"[4] A single-sex program for women with *goals* similar to VMI's, in other words, fit the bill.

VWIL was the answer. The result of "intensive study and planning by professionals who are leaders in the field of designing and implementing educational programs for women," it would provide an "analogy to the holistic VMI program" without imposing impossible male standards on women. Elizabeth Fox-Genovese had testified that the adversative method "would be not only inappropriate for most women, but counter-productive," because women required a program "which reinforces self-esteem." It was "the opinion of the Task Force that the methods adopted for the VWIL will produce the same or similar outcome for women that VMI produces for men," and Kiser was prepared to accept the assessment of the people he considered to be experts.[5]

He then turned to the government's point-by-point objections that VWIL's offerings would not equal VMI's, and in each case he indicated that the VWIL program was what women needed. The lack of advanced math and physics courses and an engineering major was acceptable because it was reasonable for MBC to offer only programs for which there was sufficient demand, and "demand at present would not justify an engineering program at MBC." He did not discuss the issue of whether MBC's lack of engineering courses was perhaps responsible for the fact that women who wanted to study engineering were not applying there. The relaxed residential lifestyle at VWIL was reasonable because the VMI model "would not produce the same outcomes for the VWIL population as it does for the VMI population." The fears of the United States that VWIL would be financially unsustainable were misplaced.[6]

Kiser indicated that he did not consider all "experts" equal and dissected the testimony of the Justice Department's witnesses to prove his point. "Dr. Conrad testified on cross-examination that he does not consider himself an expert in single-sex education." Kiser found that "Dr. Astin's personal ethical opposition to VM's current all-male admissions policy impairs his objectivity in evaluating the VWIL program," and "Dr. Astin further testified that his conclusions regarding VWIL's future outcome are speculative, and that educators could reasonably disagree with his conclusion that the VWIL program will not be able to achieve its stated goals." Similarly, "Dr. Jacklin agreed that experts could reasonably disagree with her opinion."[7]

By contrast, VMI had called *real* experts, such as Fox-Genovese.

> According to Dr. Fox-Genovese, anorexia is rampant among young college women, in part because they doubt themselves and so they want to exercise control. The control they feel they can exercise is over their own bodies. This, testified Dr. Fox-Genovese, is a turning of energy inward instead of projecting it outward. She explained that anorexia is self-discipline turned pathological. What young women need to understand is the fit between a predictable order of the outside world and their own tendencies towards self-discipline. Thus, she concluded, the adversative model is not appropriate to accomplish this result.[8]

Young women, given to pathetic pathologies such as anorexia, needed to be taken in hand and prevented from manifesting their illnesses by applying to a place like VMI. Left undiscussed was the question of whether some young men's choice of the brutal adversative method as a way of proving their own self-control and manhood might not be a cause for concern.

Kiser regarded the testimony of Richard Richardson and David Riesman as complementing that of Fox-Genovese. Given those experts, "I find that the differences between VWIL and VMI are justified pedagogically and are not based on stereotyping."[9]

Like the VMI lawyers, Kiser did not deny that it was within the realm of possibility that some women might opt for and succeed at a VMI-like institution, although he was dubious that such women in fact existed. The Justice Department attorneys had tried to compensate for the absence of a named plaintiff by hypothesizing a "Jackie Jones," arguing that if she wanted the VMI experience and the Institute refused to accept her application, her rights would have been violated. Patterson and his allies had suspected since 1989 that the Justice Department's refusal to identify the woman whose complaint had led to the lawsuit meant that she did not exist. Kiser's decision referred pointedly to "the allegorical Jackie Jones." Her mythological desires did not rise to the level of a constitutional imperative.[10]

Because Kiser had indicated at the beginning of his decision that he saw no constitutional need to admit women to VMI, VWIL was the one option remaining. "VWIL is a good design for producing female citizen-soldiers," he wrote. "If VMI marches to the beat of a drum, then Mary Baldwin marches to the melody of a fife and when the march is over, both will have arrived at the same destination."[11]

Kiser again demonstrated his tongue-in-cheek familiarity with racial equality cases, employing the language of *Brown v. Board of Education* in ordering Virginia to set up VWIL "with all deliberate speed." The new program was to be in place in time for the 1995–1996 academic year, and he directed the commonwealth to present the court with progress plans every six months.[12] As he had in 1991, the judge appended to his opinion a "Findings of Fact" section, this one eighteen pages long. It began, "Because a great majority of these findings are historical facts and are essentially uncontroverted, I found it convenient to use the format and much of the substance of the Defendants' Proposed Findings of Fact," thereby dismissing out of hand the Justice Department's 112 pages of suggestions.[13]

The decision was announced on a Friday. Cadets at VMI learned about it when a loudspeaker in the Barracks boomed the good news. There were immediate ecstatic cheers and high-fives.[14] Students spent much of the rest of the weekend celebrating. Someone scrawled, "Judge Kiser has ruled in V.M.I.'s favor!!! No women for now!! Praise God!" on a Barracks chalkboard. Another hand crossed out "now" and substituted "ever."[15] A senior told the media, "The equal-rights people want V.M.I. as a trophy," but the Institute had made a last stand and beaten them back.[16] VMI heralded the decision as "a victory for single-sex education—for both all-male and all-female schools."[17] The Justice Department attorneys, following Department policy, could not comment.

The decision was viewed by some as a victory for states' rights. Governor Allen had a spokesmen tell the press, "If the federal pests will now stay off our backs and allow us to proceed with this Virginia solution . . . we can enhance the opportunity for both men and women."[18]

Allen elaborated at VMI's commencement on May 21, congratulating the Institute on its successful fight against an "opponent . . . possessed of vastly superior resources and numbers" and pledging that he would "stand up to the arrogant, meddling federal bureaucrats whenever Virginia's right and prerogative are threatened." "Given the philosophy of the crowd in control in Washington," he added, "that's just about a full time job." Comparing the fight with the battle at New Market, he told the cadets that the government's motive had been to destroy VMI because the bureaucrats hated the things it stood for: "the traditional American values and virtues of moral character, personal discipline, self-reliance and an unabashed and unashamed love of home, state and country, and the willingness to defend them."[19] Apple pie and fatherhood had won again.

A number of the nation's newspapers ran variations on Kiser's language in their editorials. The *New York Times* commented, "That is cute writing but terrible reasoning." It continued, "Both sexes not only have the right to march in the same band, but are quite capable of doing so."[20] The *Boston Globe* added its own literary flourish: "If a woman prefers drums, the law allows her that choice, at least at public institutions."[21] "The fife and the drum need not be played separately," the *St. Louis Post-Dispatch* counseled. "Together, neither instrument sounds the same as it does alone, but though the new sound is different, it also is better, not worse than before. So, too, would be a VMI with women."[22] The North Carolina *News & Record* accepted Kiser's constitutional analysis but wondered whether it made for good policy. "Things have changed since VMI was founded a century and a half ago," it ruminated. "Even if a constitutional argument can be made for maintaining a single-sex academy such as VMI, a practical case for it is more difficult to frame. Single-sex education is one thing; segregated training for an integrated military career is something else."[23]

Most of the relatively few newspapers that carried editorials expected the case to be taken to the Supreme Court. On May 16, beginning the appeals process, the Justice Department announced that it would file papers with the Fourth Circuit.

THE STRATEGY OF THE UNITED STATES in its appeal was to emphasize VMI's uniqueness and the consequent constitutional violation implicit in Virginia's refusal to extend the VMI experience to women. The adversative system was part of the uniqueness, making VMI "the most challenging military school in the United States," and a VWIL that lacked it did not fulfill the mandate of the equal protection clause.[24] Even the MBC faculty, the government reminded the court, had laughed at the notion of creating a military institute on the gracious campus.[25] Offering women only VWIL added insult to the injury caused by VMI's refusal to admit them and carried "the same stigmatizing message" that "women simply are not up to the challenge of VMI's demanding program."[26] The government reiterated that rights under the Constitution inhered in individuals, not groups.

> The fact that most women might choose a different type of educational program does not lessen the stigma and, in any event, is beside the point. . . . The Equal Protection Clause protects individuals, and prohibits the use of stereotypes and generalizations to deny women benefits and opportunities not thought desirable or suited for them.[27]

The Justice Department warned that to sustain Kiser's decision would be to echo the days of legal segregation. It reminded the court that back in 1951, the Fourth Circuit had rejected the argument that black students would be better off at a law school of their own than at an integrated institution. The kind of "impermissible stereotypes and generalizations" the court had declined to accept then were paralleled by those in the present case, which—and here the Department quoted *Hogan*—were based on "'fixed notions concerning the roles and abilities of males and females.'"[28]

If Kiser's reasoning was followed, states could exclude women "from jobs such as police officer, firefighter, or even lawyer . . . simply by showing that most women are not as strong in certain respects as most men."[29] The issue of whether each woman was to be given an opportunity only if most women were likely to be interested in availing themselves of it was crucial. VMI "was designed for the atypical man," and even David Riesman had testified that "VMI's hostile spartan environment is not appropriate for most men."

> Both the men and the women interested in a VMI-type education constitute a small, self-selected subset of all men and women and . . . neither are typical of their gender. . . . Indeed, if the Commonwealth were really concerned about offering educational programs based on average or generalized learning traits, VMI would not exist. Thus, the testimony of defendants' experts that a parallel program for women need not include the central attributes of VMI's rigorous program, since they would not be suitable for most women, is beside the point.[30]

Throughout the litigation, the government reminded the court, VMI had "repeatedly emphasized the uniqueness of its educational methodology." In defending VWIL, however, Virginia contended that a VMI-type program was not necessary for the production of citizen-soldiers. The Commonwealth could not have it both ways. If there was nothing unique about the adversative method, then fears that women would alter it were irrelevant.[31]

"It is simply not true," the government continued, "that VWIL was designed the way it was because of the intensive studying and planning by educational professionals."[32] MBC had hastily thrown together a military component for a leadership program that it had already been considering, in order to comply with VMI's legal needs. VWIL was a political ruse designed to circumvent the court's order, not the result of a pedagogical judgment.

VMI replied that VWIL was "an educationally meaningful and good faith remedy" that would "provide public support for single-gender education to both young women at VWIL and young men at VMI." The crucial factor was that VWIL would give women "the benefits of a holistic single-gender education with the same goals as VMI," in keeping with the court of appeals' finding that the constitutional violation lay in the state's failing to offer a single-gender program for them.[33]

Treating women differently was not the same thing as treating them as inferiors.

> Because of recognized differences between the sexes in a variety of contexts, the Supreme Court has "consistently upheld statutes where the gender classification is not invidious, but rather realistically reflects the fact that the sexes are not similarly situated in certain circumstances," [and] has disallowed gender classifications only where the classification was not based on legitimate gender differences.[34]

Far from representing a throwback to the days of stereotyping, VWIL was a taste of the future. It was "designed by experts in women's education" on the basis of "the increasingly sophisticated understanding of differences between late adolescent males and females." The fact that one woman may possess "individual, possibly exceptional, characteristics" did not invalidate a classification. On the contrary, "reliance on predominant group characteristics" was in keeping with the intermediate scrutiny standard.[35]

The VMI legal team hammered away at the benefits of single-sex education and charged that the United States, ignoring legal precedent, was attempting "to manufacture a constitutional imperative of coeducation . . . implicitly urg[ing] a constitutional prohibition on public single-gender education." The appeals court had ruled that "'single-gender education is pedagogically justifiable.'" In both that decision and *Faulkner v. Jones,* the court had acknowledged the physical and psychological differences between men and women and had held that single-sex education fulfilled an "important state purpose."[36]

The Justice Department had listed the ways in which VWIL differed from VMI. Yes, VMI now said, there were differences, and they were deliberate. They represented "the optimum methodology for providing education and training for civilian and military leadership positions to young women who also seek the benefits of single-gender education," as well as an awareness that the VMI system would not "attract a sufficient cohort of young women to provide an educationally viable and economically feasible program." The district court had "accepted the commonsense position of the Commonwealth that because it has limited resources, it must identify student demand for the various alternatives in higher education and allocate its resources accordingly."[37]

VWIL had received the blessing not only of the experts called at trial but also of the current and former governors of Virginia, its lieutenant governor, its attorney general, its secretary of education, and the chairs of the education committees of both houses of the legislature. The state legislature had already appropriated funds for it. The implicit argument was that reasonable people believed that the VWIL plan was both a good one and economically viable and that the court had no business substituting its judgment for that of experts and democratically elected state officials.[38]

Both parties' contentions were buttressed by amicus briefs. An array of women's and civil rights organizations, led by the National Women's Law Center, submitted a joint brief in favor of the government's position.[39] The list of organizations tells a story about the maturity of the women's movement and its drive for gender equality. It is in part a tale of the political savvy of pro bono groups, of their recognition that there is clout in numbers and that organizations that may be at odds on some issues can make a greater impact when they join together on an issue about which they agree. The sheer number of law-oriented women's groups on the brief (which did not begin to reflect the totality of women's organizations in the country) was an indication of how well women had followed the example of Ruth Bader Ginsburg and her colleagues in making the law their own.

It was also notable that black women's groups and those perceived as largely white were working together. Gender equality was not a one-race issue. The possible implications of the case for racial equality were also worrisome, as indicated in the brief's argument that "the rationale that sex segregation is somehow part of the natural order, benefitting the excluded class as well as the privileged, has also been pressed before to justify segregation on the basis of race."[40]

The joint brief, although couched in legal vocabulary, barely concealed the anger of the women who wrote it. "VMI is and always has been an exclusive men's club, and its members want to keep it that way. There is, however, no constitutional basis on which to deny state supported educational opportunities to women who, but for their sex, are qualified for admission."[41]

Drawing from the transcript, the brief repeated the stereotypes about women relied on by Virginia and VMI.

For example, women and men are said to have different "ways of knowing"; women are supposed to adhere to an "ethic of caring," while men adopt an "ethic of justice"; women are physically weaker and more emotional and cannot take stress as well as men; women are said not to be motivated by aggressiveness and fear of failure; and more than a hundred physiological differences are said to contribute to a "natural hierarchy" in which women simply cannot compete with men in both physical activities and mental fortitude. Indeed, one witness, while acknowledging "some contributions" to the ballet, expressed the view that women excel over men only in their ability to produce children and milk.[42]

The women knew about the use of such stereotypes in their own profession. "This is not the first time that theories of biological and social differences between the sexes have been used to justify discrimination against women. Such differences were cited to rationalize denying women the right to practice law and the right to work on terms equivalent to men."[43]

The brief accused the district court of allowing VMI "to use the power of the state to define a certain kind of education as 'off-limits' for women, because (reduced of all the verbiage) they are allegedly not tough enough."[44] To show how wrong that was, the brief devoted a number of pages to the story of women in the American armed forces, including their service in Operation Desert Storm.[45]

Mary Baldwin College submitted a brief on behalf of Virginia, arguing that, as its section headings indicated, "The VWIL Program at Mary Baldwin College Is Just as Good as the VMI Program," and "Mary Baldwin College Designed the VWIL Program to Suit the Needs and Abilities of Real Students, Not Stereotypes."[46] The second amicus brief for VMI, offered jointly by Wells College, Saint Mary's College, and Southern Virginia College, all private women's colleges founded in the nineteenth century, made only the argument that single-sex education provided substantial benefits to women.[47]

Back when Mary Sue Terry had been handling the case, her office had contacted women's college presidents and asked if they would be willing to testify about the value of single-sex education. As mentioned in chapter 15, the VMI legal team later joined in, warning the presidents that a decision against VMI would mean the end of single-sex colleges. Rumor in Virginia had it that the women's colleges that took VMI's side in the court of appeals and, later, in the Supreme Court, were compelled to do so by VMI alumni who sat on their boards and by alumnae of their own who were married to VMI graduates. The colleges reportedly went along in the belief that they could not afford to alienate financially powerful VMI alumni and that the Institute would lose the case anyway.[48] None of the better-known women's colleges joined the briefs, reflecting their anger at the continued exclusion of women from VMI and their conviction that the future of privately funded single-sex education was not at stake in the case.[49]

IN KEEPING WITH the Fourth Circuit's rules, the judges who heard the first appeal also heard the second. Jessica Silver again argued for the United States; Robert Patterson was replaced by Anne Marie Whittemore. Agreeing with the joint amicus brief, Silver attacked the idea embodied in VWIL that women could not be tough. "Men go to VMI for the challenge and the rigor of the program," she told the court. "When women choose a college, they may be looking for the same challenge and the same rigor,"[50] but the state of Virginia was "still saying women are not tough enough to make it at VMI."[51] VWIL was not the answer; it would lack precisely that kind of physical and mental challenge.[52] She acknowledged that "most women would not do well [at, or] want to attend" a military-style program. That, however, was not the point. The issue was one of equal opportunity, and because VWIL would not provide it, Virginia was still in violation of the equal protection clause.[53]

Not at all, Whittemore responded. VWIL fit the clause's demands by offering women an innovative program well suited to their needs. Judge Phillips asked her, "Can the board of trustees at Mary Baldwin College, under this arrangement, decide unilaterally that this thing, from their perspective, is not working—and bail out?" Judge Niemeyer also expressed doubt. "Is this just a storefront, or is this real?" he queried. "I don't know how we can tell this now." "This is something new," Whittemore replied. "It is something that is going to require vigilance." She assured the court that both Virginia and MBC were committed to the continued funding of VWIL and that Judge Kiser would retain oversight of the program's progress.[54]

Silver assessed the judges' demeanor as indicating that, however ludicrous she found VMI's arguments, the court agreed with them.[55] She was right. When the decision was handed down on January 26, 1995, it held that VMI could remain all male and that VWIL was an adequate plan for women.[56]

The first sentence of Judge Niemeyer's opinion for the court indicated why. "At issue," he wrote, "is the important question of whether a state may sponsor single-gender education without violating the Equal Protection Clause of the Fourteenth Amendment."[57] If that was indeed the issue, then the United States could only lose. As Kiser had noted, the same panel of judges had held in the first appeal that single-sex education was "pedagogically justifiable," and the Supreme Court had suggested in *Hogan* that it might be constitutional to separate the sexes if there was an exceedingly persuasive reason for doing so. Virginia had won by convincing the court that the case was about the legitimacy of any publicly funded single-sex college rather than about inequality and reliance on stereotypes.

Tellingly, Niemeyer discussed the mandate of *Hogan* without ever mentioning the "exceedingly persuasive justification" standard it established. Rather, he read *Hogan* as requiring an analysis of whether the state's objective was "'legitimate and important'" and whether "'the requisite direct, substantial relationship between objective and means is present.'"[58] As he interpreted those tests, they amounted to little more than a nod to legislative choice. In determining whether the state's goal was "legitimate and important," "a court should not substitute its priorities of value over those established by the democratically chosen branch. . . . A court should, at this step, deferentially consider only whether the regulation is important to a legitimate governmental purpose."[59]

That sounded very much like the rational relation test. The court tightened it somewhat by saying that the next step was to examine the state's means of achieving its objective, through "procedural equal protection analysis" (the court's own term). The court would give deference to the objective but would "scrutiniz[e] closely the procedural mechanism adopted by the legislature" and determine whether it bore "a direct and substantial relationship" to the goal.[60]

Niemeyer thought that this satisfied the *Hogan* test. The court would nonetheless take an additional step, "carefully weighing the alternatives available to members of each gender denied benefits by the classification" once a state had created single-sex institutions.[61] Niemeyer explained what he meant.

> To achieve the equality of treatment demanded by the Equal Protection Clause, the alternatives left available to each gender by a classification based on a homogeneity of gender need not be the same, but they must be substantively comparable so that, in the end, we cannot conclude that the value of the benefits provided by the state to one gender tends, by comparison to the benefits provided to the other, to lessen the dignity, respect, or societal regard of the other gender. We will call this third step an inquiry into the substantive comparability of the mutually exclusive programs provided to men and women.[62]

"Substantive comparability" became the Fourth Circuit's version of the intermediate scrutiny test. The question was how the court proposed to measure it. Niemeyer said that the state could not provide benefits to only one gender if they tended, "by comparison to the benefits provided to the other, to lessen the dignity, respect, or societal regard of the other gender." The court would now have to decide whether offering VMI to men and VWIL to women did precisely that.

It began its inquiry by reiterating that "providing a single-gender education was a legitimate and important governmental objective." The court had been impressed by the "multitude of professional articles" that had been submitted to it "describing the benefits of single-gender education, especially for late adolescents coming out of high school."[63] It cited a story in *U.S. News & World Report* that credited a renewed interest in single-sex education to "the disproportionate distinction achieved by women who are alumnae of single-sex institutions," to studies of how young women in coed classes have lower aspirations, to concern about alcohol and date rape, and to disenchantment with the way large universities educate undergraduates.[64]

Turning to the next prong of its test, the court stated that the great benefit of single-gender education was that "students are not distracted by the presence of the other sex."[65] It did not consider whether coeducation results only in distraction or whether its benefits, such as the availability of diverse viewpoints, might make coeducation at least as sound as single-sex schooling. Reading its opinion, one wonders why the court did not suggest that all the Fourth Circuit's schools become single sex. It had nothing good to say about coeducation, which appeared to cause not only distraction but also rape.

Niemeyer viewed the adversative method as "not designed to exclude women" but unable to work any other way. He noted that the method "has never been tolerated in a sexually heterogeneous environment; indeed, we condemn it [in a coed school] for a good reason." Ever the correct Southern gentleman, he added, "If we were to place men and women into the adversative relationship inherent in the VMI program, we would destroy, at least for that period of the adversative training, any sense of decency that still permeates the relationship between the sexes."[66]

To "allay any skepticism and assure eradication of the constitutional violation," the judges ordered the district court to make certain that VWIL was "headed by a well-qualified, motivated administrator" who was properly paid, that it was adequately publicized, that it continued to receive the necessary state funding, and that it was reviewed regularly by "qualified professional educators."[67]

Niemeyer had spoken for a unanimous panel in the first appeal, but that was not the case here. Judge J. Dickson Phillips dissented. Phillips had been part of the panel holding that there was no constitutional requirement that the Institute admit women if women were given an equal educational opportunity elsewhere. He now implied that he had given up hope that Virginia would create that opportunity and stated that he did not think the VWIL plan had "any real and effectively measurable capacity" to bring Virginia into compliance with the equal protection clause. He would give the commonwealth only two options: admit women to VMI or give up state financing.[68]

Noting that the question of the constitutionality of what he dismissively labeled "separate-but-equal" publicly funded single-sex institutions had been left open by the Supreme Court in *Hogan*, Phillips said that it was not necessary to answer it in this case, because VWIL was not equal. He was also skeptical of Virginia's motives in creating VWIL. The assumptions about the role of women that had existed when VMI was founded had been left unexamined by the state until the United States brought suit, he reminded the majority, in spite of the Supreme Court decisions about gender equality beginning in 1971 with *Reed v. Reed*.[69]

Phillips was troubled at the court's being asked to validate a plan that existed only on paper. And what, he asked, was the governmental objective that was sufficiently important to justify gender classifications? "There is a real problem of identification in this case, for the Commonwealth seems uncertainly to advance a number as alternative or cumulative free-standing possibilities." One was the "intrinsic value" of single-sex education, a second was the need for "gender-adapted leadership training" if such training was to succeed, and a third was "system-diversity" for the commonwealth's institutions of higher education.[70]

Phillips did not believe that any of them was the real reason behind VWIL. One of the lessons of *Hogan,* he said, was that courts had a responsibility to decide whether the alleged objectives were the "actual purposes" for gender classifications. Here, they "demonstrably are rationalizations compelled by the exigencies of this litigation rather than the actual overriding purpose of the proposed separate-but-equal arrangement." He referred to the history of the case in a passage that would be quoted by the Supreme Court.

> I think it would support a confident and fair conclusion that the primary, overriding purpose is not to create a new type of educational opportunity for women, nor to broaden the Commonwealth's educational base for producing a special kind of citizen-soldier leadership, nor to further diversify the Commonwealth's higher education system—though all of these might result serendipitously from the arrangement—but is simply by this means to allow VMI to continue to exclude women in

order to preserve its historic character and mission as that is perceived and has been primarily defined in this litigation by VMI and directly affiliated parties.[71]

He did not believe that Virginia really thought that the plan was constitutional, either. The commonwealth had declined to defend VMI officially—Phillips was referring to Mary Sue Terry's decision to pull out of the case once Governor Wilder said that gender segregation was not state policy—and the justification for keeping it all male "was exclusively shaped and actively conducted by VMI, its official board, that board's members, and . . . VMI alumni organizations." Phillips then turned to political realities. It was "common knowledge" that

> the prestige and influence of VMI and its justly loyal alumni and their organization in influencing any political decision affecting VMI's interests is sufficiently powerful to ensure that their overriding purpose in this matter effectively defines the actual governmental objective of the Commonwealth's proposed remedial plan. That overriding purpose remains the preservation of VMI as a state-supported educational institution for men only, with all other asserted purposes of the plan merely secondary means to that end.

The contrast between VMI and VWIL, Phillips continued, "is so palpable as not to require detailed recitation. . . . If every good thing projected for the VWIL program is realized in reasonably foreseeable time, it will necessarily be then but a pale shadow of VMI." He implied strongly that he would have given the government everything it asked for. "The proper perspective from which to measure substantial equality of available benefits is that of the potential student who could be admitted to either school and has a choice," he wrote. From that perspective, "No separate single-gender arrangement that involved VMI as the all-mens' school and any newly-founded separate institution . . . as the all womens' component could pass equal protection muster." His final word on VWIL: "It will not work."[72]

JUDGE PHILLIPS WAS SO CERTAIN that it would not work that he asked for a rehearing of the case en banc—that is, with all members of the court in attendance. His request won the support of the chief judge and five others. Four judges, including Niemeyer, voted against the rehearing, and three others disqualified themselves. According to the court's rules, a majority of seven was required, so the case would not be reheard.[73]

Diana Gribbon Motz, one of the judges who had voted for a rehearing, felt so strongly about it that she took the relatively unusual step of writing a dissent from the decision. It was joined by three other judges, and eventually it too would be cited by the Supreme Court. Justice Ginsburg commented later that she found Motz's opinion more useful than the briefs submitted in the case.[74]

Like Phillips, Motz was appalled that more than forty years after the Supreme Court had struck down "separate but equal" education for African Americans, a panel of the Fourth Circuit had held that separate and "concededly not even equal" education for women was constitutional.[75] She referred to Phillips's dissenting opinion and the concurring opinion of Judge K. K. Hall in *Faulkner v. Jones*.[76] Then, however, she added some words of her own.

Motz was willing to employ the court's tripartite test, even though she was skeptical of its validity. As she noted, the Supreme Court had said in *J.E.B. v. Alabama* a few months earlier that "whether classifications based on gender are inherently suspect and so subject to strict scrutiny is an 'open question.'"[77] But even under the Fourth Circuit's criteria, the opinion by Judge Niemeyer was "confused and contrary to both law and logic."[78]

Motz read *Hogan* as meaning that "a state-supported single-gender educational program" could not be constitutionally justified "simply because it is a single-gender program." Rather, there had to be a reason why the program was "necessary to further an important governmental objective." But there had been no evidence that a single-sex environment was necessary to the governmental objective of producing citizen-soldiers or, for that matter, that the adversative system was a requirement. On the contrary, the military academies produced citizen-soldiers in a coeducational setting. Indeed, the academies' abandonment of the adversative system suggested that perhaps "the provision of that training to VMI cadets, rather than preparing them to be leaders in today's Armed Forces, affirmatively disadvantages them for military leadership roles."[79]

But if the adversative method was truly necessary to the VMI program, as VMI alleged, what did that make of VWIL?

> If "adversative" training is so critical to the VMI program that it virtually defines it, then a program without "adversative" training can never be "substantively comparable." Conversely, if the proposed program at Mary Baldwin is truly "substantively comparable" to the VMI program, then "adversative" training must not be critical to the VMI program, and so there is nothing to prevent the abolition of "adversative" training and admission of women to VMI.[80]

Calling VWIL "feeble" as a substitute for VMI's reputation and networks, Motz suggested that VMI could constitutionally preserve the homogeneous environment it considered so important if it simply gave up public funds.

"Conformity with constitutional requirements would thus be immediately achieved," she wrote, without the kind of continuing judicial oversight contemplated by Niemeyer's decree, "and at a substantial saving of taxpayers' money."[81]

Motz dealt with the not-enough-applicants argument by saying that most women, and most men, probably would not want to attend VMI, and "no one is arguing that women—or men" had to go there. "The question is can they constitutionally be denied that opportunity when the Commonwealth—with tax dollars from men and women—supports the institution."[82]

Only recently, she noted:

> One of the first women fighter pilots was killed during a practice run. Anyone who is prepared to do combat for her country—indeed, to be killed in preparation for that combat—should be eligible to apply for what she perceives to be the best possible training. As long as the Commonwealth provides support for VMI, women should be given the opportunity to attend.[83]

VMI's invocation of the virtues of single-sex education was "a stratagem to achieve the Commonwealth's real objective—preservation of VMI . . . without the unwelcome intrusion of women," and the result was a violation of the Constitution.[84]

But Motz was speaking in dissent, and VWIL was about to be born. The two sides in the dispute turned their faces toward Washington and the Supreme Court. On October 5, 1995, the nation's highest tribunal announced that it would hear the case.

17

Anticipating the Justices

> In cases involving discrimination between men and women, the
> natural differences between the sexes are sometimes relevant and
> sometimes wholly irrelevant.
>
> —Justice John Paul Stevens

The American legal system is just that: a system based on law.
The relevant law in *United States v. Virginia* was the Constitution—specifically, the Fourteenth Amendment's equal protection clause. But the Constitution is full of wonderfully vague phrases that cry out for interpretation, and
it is the Supreme Court that does the interpreting. The phrase "equal protection of the laws," on which the government based its suit, is as amorphous
as any. Supreme Court decisions in constitutional cases would always be
unanimous if the import of the Constitution was absolutely clear, but few of
them are. The responsibility for parsing it falls to each justice, who must decide for himself or herself exactly what it means. Government may, as Chief
Justice John Marshall said, be a government "of laws, and not of men,"[1] but
the laws are interpreted by men—and by women.

Parties to a Supreme Court case, then, consider more than the law and
the arguments they made in lower courts as they prepare their briefs and oral
arguments for the High Court. In addition, they examine earlier written opinions and votes by the justices in the hope of being able to fashion an argument that will resonate with a majority of them, deciding in advance which
justices are likely to be unsympathetic and which should be mentally appealed
to as the attorneys shape their pleadings. The general assumption was that

in this case, the Justice Department could count on the votes of Justices Ruth Bader Ginsburg, John Paul Stevens, and David Souter.

Justice Stevens, almost seventy-six years old when the VMI case was argued, had sat on the Supreme Court since 1975. That made him the only current justice other than Rehnquist to have participated in some of the path-breaking gender equality cases of the 1970s. He had earned a reputation on the Court as an independent thinker who could not automatically be assigned to one side or the other in most cases. Both the Justice Department and VMI could take heart from his past opinions.

Stevens had accepted advocate Ginsburg's argument in *Califano v. Goldfarb* that granting automatic survivor benefits only to women was discriminatory, and he wrote in *Craig v. Boren* that sex-based categorization was "objectionable because it is based on an accident of birth."[2] He had taken the position that alimony could not be levied solely on men and that jury duty had to be shared equally by the sexes.[3] His dissent in *Michael M. v. Superior Court,* in which the majority validated a law holding men but not women accountable for statutory rape (sex involving a minor), was predicated on his belief that the law was based on "traditional attitudes toward male-female relationships," which reflected "nothing more than an irrational prejudice."[4]

But Stevens had voted with the majority in allowing Congress to limit military registration to men.[5] He said in *Michael M.* that when men and women were treated differently by law,

> the natural differences between the sexes are sometimes relevant and sometimes wholly irrelevant. If those differences are obviously irrelevant, the discrimination should be treated as presumptively unlawful in the same way that racial classifications are presumptively unlawful. . . . This presumption, however, may be overcome by a demonstration that the apparent justification for the discrimination is illusory or wholly inadequate.[6]

He wrote in *Caban v. Mohammed* that a New York law permitting an unwed mother but not an unwed father to block an adoption simply by withholding consent had overcome the presumption. The determination that unwed mothers and unwed fathers were differently situated required both "more than merely recognizing that society has traditionally treated the two classes differently" and an "analysis that goes beyond a merely reflexive rejection of gender-based distinctions."[7]

In other words, Stevens was skeptical of gender distinctions but prepared to accept them if a good enough argument could be made for doing so. In

Mathews v. Lucas, a case involving discrimination against illegitimate children, he stated:

> Habit, rather than analysis, makes it seem acceptable and natural to distinguish between male and female, alien and citizen, legitimate and illegitimate; for too much of our history there was the same inertia in distinguishing between black and white. But that sort of stereotyped reaction may have no rational relationship—other than pure prejudicial discrimination—to the stated purpose for which the classification is being made.[8]

The Justice Department could point to Stevens's dislike for stereotypes. VMI seemed favored by his willingness to accept justifiable distinctions, which VMI thought was the situation here.

Court watchers at least had some opinions by Stevens to go on, even if those opinions could be interpreted differently. That was not true of Justice Souter, who had moved from the New Hampshire Supreme Court to the U.S. Supreme Court in 1990—an unusual situation, as recent practice favored taking Supreme Court nominees from the federal rather than the state bench. (Souter had in fact been appointed to the federal First Circuit Court of Appeals in 1990 but had never sat on it, as the Supreme Court nomination intervened.) At the time, women's groups were among those concerned that the rather conservative opinions he had written in New Hampshire did not augur well. Judges on state courts do not spend a lot of time interpreting the U.S. Constitution, however, and their records there are not necessarily indicative of what they will do on the Supreme Court.

Souter's first major opinion on the Court was the one he coauthored with Justices Sandra Day O'Connor and Anthony Kennedy in *Planned Parenthood of Southeastern Pennsylvania v. Casey.*[9] Although their plurality opinion limited the constitutional right to abortion established by *Roe v. Wade,*[10] it confirmed the central holding of that case. In his few years on the Supreme Court, Justice Souter had demonstrated not only an unusually fine intelligence but also a growing protectiveness of individual rights. Like Justice Stevens, he had been part of the majority in *J.E.B. v. Alabama,* reaffirming the sex neutrality of the jury box.[11] Thus they had both added their names to the majority opinion by Justice Harry Blackmun, which said in part:

> Today we reaffirm what, by now, should be axiomatic: Intentional discrimination on the basis of gender by state actors violates the Equal Protection Clause, particularly where, as here, the discrimination serves to ratify and perpetuate invidious, archaic, and overbroad stereotypes about the relative abilities of men and women.[12]

Blackmun had added that there was a "real danger that government policies that professedly are based on reasonable considerations in fact may be reflective of 'archaic and overbroad' generalizations about gender."[13] And Stevens and Souter had signed onto that language. If the Justice Department showed persuasively that the case was about gender discrimination and stereotypes rather than about the future of single-sex education, Souter was a probable vote for the government.

Chief Justice William Rehnquist had voted against gender equality in almost every case decided while he was on the Court; he was expected to agree with VMI. Justice Antonin Scalia was another sure vote for that side. Scalia believed that the only standard that should be used in equal protection analysis was the rational relation test,[14] and VMI was certain that it had established a rational relationship between the commonwealth's objective of diversity and VMI's single-sex admissions policy. Scalia's probable position could also be gleaned from the typically caustic dissenting opinion he had penned in *J.E.B. v. Alabama,* excoriating the majority for what he described as the "anti-male-chauvinist oratory" that "obscured" the Court's legal reasoning.[15]

The most telling indication was Scalia's concurrence when the Supreme Court had denied certiorari to *United States v. Virginia* in 1993, after the first decision by the court of appeals, presumably to let Virginia decide what it would do and permit the case to be fully argued in the lower courts afterward. Scalia wrote then that he would have preferred for the Supreme Court to hear the case "before, rather than after, a national institution as venerable as the Virginia Military Institute is compelled to transform itself." The Court's practice, however, was to "await final judgment in the lower courts" before getting involved, and Scalia would adhere to that rule. It is relatively rare for a justice to write a concurrence when the Court denies certiorari, and the only reason for Scalia to do so seemed to be embedded in his final sentence: "Our action does not, of course, preclude VMI from raising the same issues in a later petition, after final judgment has been rendered."[16] The hint was unmistakable.

Justice Clarence Thomas's son was a cadet at VMI, so Thomas recused himself from the case. That left three justices not yet accounted for: O'Connor, Kennedy, and Stephen Breyer.

Many Court watchers considered Justice O'Connor a probable vote for the Justice Department. No one reading her language in *Hogan* could doubt her disdain for outmoded gender stereotypes. The problem for prognosticators in *United States v. Virginia* was that there was language in *Hogan* that could be read as favoring the other side as well.

The United States could point to passages such as the following:

> Rather than compensate for discriminatory barriers faced by women, MUW's policy of excluding males from admission to the School of Nursing tends to perpetuate the stereotyped view of nursing as an exclusively woman's job. . . . MUW's admissions policy lends credibility to the old view that women, not men, should become nurses, and makes the assumption that nursing is a field for women a self-fulfilling prophecy. Thus, we conclude that, although the State recited a "benign, compensatory purpose," it failed to establish that the alleged objective is the actual purpose underlying the discriminatory classification.[17]

That situation—claiming that a discriminatory policy was meant to compensate women when in fact it was based on stereotypes and was designed to circumvent the equal protection clause—was exactly what the government thought it had in VMI. There was nothing compensatory, it would tell the Court, about VWIL.

Conversely, O'Connor had noted that the record in *Hogan* showed that "admitting men to nursing classes does not affect teaching style," and "the presence of men in the classroom would not affect the performance of the female nursing students." She therefore found the record "flatly inconsistent with the claim that excluding men from the School of Nursing is necessary to reach any of MUW's educational goals."[18] VMI, however, thought that it had shown that the presence of women *would* affect the educational goals of its co-curricular programs, and the effect would be entirely negative. If the criterion was a lack of impact on current practices, then VMI seemingly would carry the day. In addition, the "exceedingly persuasive justification" standard suggested that publicly supported single-sex education was permissible in some instances, and VMI's argument was that the benefits of single-sex education and the adversative system constituted just such a persuasive justification.

Each party, then, would emphasize those sections of Justice O'Connor's opinion that seemed to support its view and tailor its briefs with her in mind. They would also concentrate on Justice Kennedy.

Kennedy had joined the Court in 1988, after the major gender equality cases had been decided, so there was little in his judicial record to suggest which way he would vote. He, like O'Connor, was considered a centrist whose

vote in most constitutional cases could go either way. Careful opinion readers noted, however, that Kennedy had concurred in *J.E.B.* and had indicated
that a gender-specific policy would bear a high burden of proof.

> In over 20 cases beginning in 1971, however, we have subjected government clas-
> sifications based on sex to heightened scrutiny. . . . And though the intermediate
> scrutiny test we have applied may not provide a very clear standard in all instances,
> our case law does reveal a strong presumption that gender classifications are in-
> valid. See, e.g., Mississippi Univ. for Women v. Hogan.[19]

Kennedy had also written in *J.E.B.* that the basic command of the equal
protection clause was, "'the Government must treat citizens as individuals,
not as simply components of a racial [or] sexual . . . class.'"[20] Another hint
might be extracted from Kennedy's having joined Souter and O'Connor as
coauthors of the plurality opinion in *Planned Parenthood v. Casey,* widely
viewed as a women's rights case.

The final vote would be cast by Justice Breyer, who had arrived at the
Court only two years before and had sat on no gender equality cases there.
The few gender discrimination decisions he had written as a member of the
First Circuit Court of Appeals contained no clear message.[21] But during his
confirmation hearings before the Senate, Breyer had been asked whether he
considered the intermediate scrutiny standard in gender discrimination cases
to be sufficient. "It may not be," he replied, adding that the question did "not
seem to me, as I read the cases, to be closed."[22] That augured well for the Justice Department: the tighter the standard for decision, the better its chances.

If Ginsburg, Stevens, Souter, and Breyer actually did decide for the United
States, the Justice Department had to pick up one more vote from either O'-
Connor or Kennedy to win the case. VMI could count on Rehnquist and
Scalia. In order for *it* to prevail, therefore, the Institute had to get the votes
of both O'Connor and Kennedy. The eight justices would then be evenly split,
and under the Court's rules, the lower court decision would stand. The VMI
attorneys had great hopes for O'Connor and Kennedy and thought that they
might persuade enough of the other justices to get a real majority. The record,
they believed, was strong enough for that.[23] The big question for them, as
for the government, was what strategy in their briefs and in their oral arguments would best serve their quest for votes.

ALTHOUGH THE PARTIES kept the perceived predilections of the
justices in mind, their briefs in many ways tracked those for the court of ap-

peals. The government framed the issue for the Supreme Court as "whether the exclusion of women from the Virginia Military Institute, based solely on their sex, violates the Equal Protection Clause of the Fourteenth Amendment."[24] Reminding the Court of its own approach to antidiscrimination law, the Justice Department wrote:

> All individuals belong to racial, gender, and ethnic groups. The "average" or "typical" aspirations of the members of those groups often differ. . . . Those differences raise the question whether an individual may be denied an opportunity because he or she has aspirations or abilities that differ significantly from those of the average member of the group. . . . Individuals have a fundamental right to be treated on the basis of their own abilities and capacities. They may not be denied opportunity because most members of their race have different characteristics from their own.[25]

The Court had said so, the Justice Department noted, as early as 1938. In *Missouri ex rel. Gaines v. Canada,* the justices had rejected the argument that there were not enough black law school applicants to warrant provision of a law school education for them, in a still-segregated educational system, because the right to equal protection was "'a personal one.'"[26] The Justice Department considered that directly on point. It repeatedly emphasized the case's similarity to situations involving racial discrimination.[27] VMI would reply that the race cases were irrelevant; whereas racial segregation of students provides no "meaningful or valid educational benefits," the record in the present case showed that "single-sex education at the college level does provide important pedagogical benefits that cannot be replicated in a coeducational setting."[28]

Although the Supreme Court is willing to overturn decisions made by lower courts, it also assumes that those courts should be treated with a degree of deference. Here, the United States had to respond to the fact that both the district court and the court of appeals had ruled against it. It did so by attacking the court of appeals' new standard of "substantive comparability" and its conclusion that the case was about the constitutionality of single-sex education.[29]

Again and again, the United States' papers reminded Justice O'Connor of her opinion in *Hogan*. *Hogan* had specifically rejected single-sex education as an end in itself; rather, it had held that "single-sex education for only one sex may be constitutionally justifiable *in order to compensate for discrimination that only one sex has suffered.*"[30] There was no such rationale in the VMI case, and *Hogan* taught that "the exclusion of one sex from an educational institution reserved for the other" is not an acceptable governmental objective.[31] *Hogan* held that a "sex-based classification must be evaluated with reference to the *actual* reason the State has chosen to employ it," but VMI's motives for its hasty establishment of VWIL were suspect.[32] *Hogan* rejected stereotypes; VMI relied on them.[33] Some of the government's prose, such as quotes from Justice Kennedy's concurrence in *J.E.B.*, was clearly directed at that justice.[34]

Virginia and VMI reiterated their belief that the real issue was the government's desire to destroy all public single-sex education.

> The central, though unspoken, premise of petitioner's brief is that the Constitution should be construed to forbid public single-sex education . . . petitioner seeks to impose on the Nation its dogmatic view that coeducation is the only permissible methodology for all public schools.[35]

Permitting it to do so would be a mistake. Single-sex education was a valid element of a system of "providing diverse and pedagogically beneficial opportunities at all educational levels," which in turn "constitutes a legitimate and important governmental objective."[36] Virginia was not alone in believing that. Experiments in single-sex education were taking place in inner cities and in states "across the nation," and single-sex classes already existed in New Hampshire, Illinois, New York, California, Maine, Michigan, Maryland, and New Hampshire, as well as the commonwealth.[37] Virginia's invocation of that list warned the justices that the issue was national as well as local.

The commonwealth asserted that it had not opted for the pedagogical methods of VWIL unthinkingly. Instead, VWIL was based on the "considered judgments of professional educators as to the most effective methods" for educating men and women and on a "reasoned analysis of modern scholarship and professional determinations," not on outmoded stereotypes.[38] The state, in fact, rejected those stereotypes.

> Unlike the archaic and harmful stereotypes condemned in this Court's cases, VWIL is not based upon any outdated notions about the proper role of women in society. Quite the contrary, VWIL is founded on the principle that women's place in "the marketplace and the world of ideas"—and in the military—is the same as that of men, but that student demand and developmental norms make VWIL's methodology a more effective and practicable means of maximizing opportunities for the development of confident and successful women leaders.[39]

It was "false," VMI said, to suggest that the differences between VMI and VWIL contained "the message that women are unfit for a rigorous military or similar career." Virginia believed "that women can and will attain leadership

positions both in the military and elsewhere." The demand of the equal protection clause was that a state treat students equally, not that it treat them
identically, and educators had an obligation to take differences among them
into consideration in fashioning educational programs and institutions.[40]

A MAJOR BONE OF CONTENTION between the two sides was the
standard the Supreme Court ought to use in deciding the case. The United
States argued for applying strict scrutiny, saying that this was "the correct
constitutional standard for evaluating differences in official treatment based
on sex."[41] In other words, the United States was asking the Court to change
its standard in gender discrimination cases from the intermediate one to the
more stringent criterion used in race discrimination cases, so that a gender-
specific law would be presumed unconstitutional. The call for strict scrutiny
reflected the urging of the women's rights community, but it was not without its problems.

Two years earlier, the Clinton administration had eliminated the Bush administration's ban on cooperation between Justice Department litigators and
civil rights groups, and the Department was working closely with the ACLU
Women's Rights Project and the other leading women's law groups as it prepared to argue the case. The Department lawyers were "collegial and ac-
commodating; they shared documents and the record," answered whatever
questions the women's groups had, and generally indicated that they were
glad the groups were on their side.[42]

By the time *United States v. Virginia* reached the Supreme Court, Isabelle
Pinzler had left the WRP and moved to the Justice Department as a deputy
assistant attorney general in the Civil Rights Division.[43] Because the Department's ethics rules prohibited the involvement of anyone who had worked for
either side in a case, even as amicus, she was initially kept off the case. Eventually, at the request of Assistant Attorney General Deval Patrick, she received
a waiver that allowed her to advise him on the VMI case as long as she had no
direct involvement in or supervision over decision making.[44] (Another former
ACLU staffer—holder of the prestigious one-year Karpatkin Fellowship that
the organization awarded to outstanding law school graduates interested in
civil liberties law—was working on the case for the solicitor general's office.)[45]

Part of Pinzler's role in advising Patrick involved dealing with the question of whether the Justice Department ought to include the argument for
strict scrutiny in its brief. The WRP, like the rest of the women's rights legal

community, had always hoped that the Court would adopt the higher standard, even though the WRP had argued the intermediate standard in recent years for strategic reasons. It was sometimes dangerous to argue for strict scrutiny before a hostile court, for example, because unfriendly judges could say, in effect, "Well, if you're arguing that the standard has to be strict scrutiny, that means you must believe your case can't win under intermediate scrutiny. We don't accept strict scrutiny as the standard, so you lose your case."[46]

In *United States v. Virginia,* however, many members of the women's rights community felt that strict scrutiny had found its moment: a gender equality case with Ruth Bader Ginsburg and Sandra Day O'Connor on the Court. Some strategists thought that other justices might be willing to adopt strict scrutiny now, because the Court had repeatedly referred to the question of what standard to apply in gender discrimination cases as an open one.[47] In addition, courts below were having difficulty figuring out exactly what intermediate scrutiny meant and how to apply it—a good reason for the Court to adopt a clearer guideline.

There were two potential problems with strict scrutiny, however, and the twenty-five or so people sitting around the attorney general's conference table began to wonder whether a strict scrutiny argument might someday hurt either affirmative action programs or the existing private women's colleges. The conferees agreed that VMI would have to admit women even under the intermediate standard. So if their case did not depend on strict scrutiny, should they take the chance that the higher standard might be interpreted to mean that affirmative action for women—programs designed to compensate women for past discrimination—was unconstitutional? The Supreme Court had invoked the strict scrutiny standard in striking down affirmative action programs for racial minorities, with Justice O'Connor writing the Court's opinion in two important cases.[48] But although the Court had condemned specific programs, it had not invalidated affirmative action as such. Marcia Greenberger of the National Women's Law Center argued that if affirmative action for race was upheld—with strict scrutiny as the long-established standard for examining race-specific policies—then affirmative action for women also would be constitutional under the higher standard. If the Court did not uphold affirmative action for racial minorities, it was unlikely to uphold it for women, so adoption of the strict scrutiny standard in gender discrimination cases would cost nothing. And if the Court chose not to change the standard, nothing would be lost.[49]

Although the government believed that the issue was whether *publicly* funded institutions could discriminate, everyone on both sides of the issue recognized the potential for the Court's decision to affect private colleges as well. Almost every educational institution in the United States gets money from the federal and state governments directly or indirectly, in the form of student scholarships and loans, faculty grants, grants and loans for constructing buildings, and so on. Would a victory for the Justice Department mean that private women's colleges, which of course discriminated against men, could no longer be permitted access to those funds? That was VMI's point in arguing that the future of all single-sex education hung in the balance.

The government and women's groups believed that the private women's colleges were safe, whatever the decision. Strict scrutiny meant that discrimination was permissible if it was *compellingly* necessary to achieve a legitimate governmental objective. Compensation for past unconstitutional discrimination was such a compelling reason, as the Court had indicated in upholding some affirmative action programs for women and racial minorities and as Justice O'Connor had seemed to suggest in *Hogan*.[50] Many of the women's colleges had come into existence to compensate for the exclusion of women from institutions and programs of higher education, so they ought to be able to meet that criterion. The Justice Department had never challenged federal aid to students or faculty grants at private colleges, and there was no reason to think that such financial support would be endangered by adoption of the strict scrutiny standard.[51]

The matter was resolved by Solicitor General Drew Days, who decided that the strict scrutiny argument would go into the brief.[52] (It is the solicitor general's office in the Justice Department that usually argues Supreme Court cases for the government.) But because the government had not mentioned strict scrutiny at the district and appeals court levels, the Supreme Court logically would ask why the Justice Department was introducing it at this stage. The government anticipated this query by writing that "this Court has not previously applied strict scrutiny to sex-based classifications," and lower courts were bound by the Supreme Court's rulings. The government had therefore used the High Court's intermediate standard in arguing before the lower courts. And though it remained convinced that the doctrine should be changed, it also believed "that cross-petitioners have not established that VMI's exclusionary policy satisfies intermediate scrutiny."[53]

VMI expressed astonishment that the United States would raise an issue that had not been addressed below and urged the Court to ignore it. If the Court chose to consider the question of the appropriate standard, however,

Virginia wanted it to remember that "intermediate scrutiny has achieved the worthy and balanced goal of invalidating most governmental line-drawing based on gender while preserving those relatively few gender distinctions that are supported by legitimate and important reasons." It warned that imposition of a strict scrutiny standard would raise questions about separate treatment of men and women not only in education but also in the military and in prisons, and it picked up on Elizabeth Fox-Genovese's somewhat quixotic assertion that strict scrutiny would mean that battered women's shelters would be unconstitutional if there were not also publicly supported battered men's shelters, whether they were needed or not. Finally, Virginia advised the justices to interpret the government's sudden reliance on strict scrutiny as tantamount to an admission that VMI and VWIL "can and should survive intermediate scrutiny."[54]

There were few surprises in the briefs the parties sent to the Court. But the government and VMI were not the only parties that felt strongly about the case, and other people were busy writing additional documents that the justices would need to peruse before deciding *United States v. Virginia*.

18

Other Voices

> If fear of "sexual distraction" were a valid reason for excluding
> women from public higher education, women would still be
> barred from all public colleges and universities.
>
> —Brief of Rhonda Cornum et al., *United States v. Virginia*

It takes particular skills to write briefs that go up to the Supreme
Court, and others to fashion language that comes down from that tribunal.
In the VMI case, three generations of women lawyers were involved in the
process.

Ruth Bader Ginsburg suggested that Pauli Murray and Dorothy Kenyon
were among the first generation of twentieth-century female attorneys who
used their talents for the benefit of other women.[1] Ginsburg herself and her
casebook coauthor Herma Hill Kay were examples of the second generation.
The women from the groups that cooperated with the Justice Department
as it prepared for the fight in the Supreme Court—Marcia Greenberger and
Joan Bertin, among others—followed in their footsteps, as did Justice Department lawyers Judith Keith, Jessica Silver, and Isabelle Katz Pinzler. A
fourth generation was represented by thirty-year-old Lisa Beattie.

Beattie had attended New York's Brearley School, a private single-sex institution that was also the alma mater of Ginsburg's daughter Jane. She received her bachelor's degree from Stanford University and spent two years
working for the ACLU's Public Education Department, Women's Rights Project, and Reproductive Freedom Project.

Beattie later went to Stanford Law School, where her outstanding grades
led to her being chosen to teach an undergraduate course on civil liberties

and civil rights, and where she was an editor of the prestigious law review. She wrote a paper about women in the military for the course she took on women and the law and also did research for Professor Gerald Gunther, the scholar who had recommended Ginsburg for a clerkship when Ginsburg was finishing law school.

Ginsburg was still on the court of appeals in 1993, when Beattie decided to apply for the position of her clerk. During the interview that followed, the student and the judge chatted at length about women and the law. Ginsburg liked the fact that Beattie had done work in the field and agreed to hire her.[2]

Then, however, Ginsburg was nominated to the Supreme Court, and she held off hiring a clerk while the nomination was pending. Supreme Court justices prefer their clerks to have worked for a lower court judge so that they will not spend any of their hectic time at the highest court learning what a clerk does. Chief Judge Harry T. Edwards of Ginsburg's court, the District of Columbia Court of Appeals, had a position open and agreed to take on Beattie for the 1994–1995 term. After her year with Edwards, Beattie moved on to Justice Ginsburg's chambers. She was working there when the Supreme Court granted certiorari in *United States v. Virginia* and set January 17, 1996, as the date on which oral argument would be heard.

Some justices assign one of their four clerks primary responsibility for a pending case. (Justices Rehnquist and Stevens employ only three clerks each.) The clerk frequently prepares a bench memo, which summarizes such things as the history of the case, the relevant laws and legal decisions in the field, and any particularly useful thoughts from amicus briefs. The bench memo may include quotes from the briefs, and it also indicates what legal tests the clerk believes the justice should use in deciding which way to vote. The justices may use the points in the memos as a basis for questions during oral argument.

Most justices allow the clerks to decide among themselves which clerk will handle a case, and most clerks use a lottery system. That was the practice in Ginsburg's chambers, where the clerks would do a blind pick of numbered pieces of paper to determine who would get the first choice of cases.

When the Court granted certiorari in the VMI case, it became one of the cases up for grabs. Lisa Beattie lost the ensuing lottery in Ginsburg's chambers, and another clerk got the assignment. Beattie tried unsuccessfully to persuade him that she was best trained to handle *United States v. Virginia*. It was an exciting case, and everyone wanted to help shape it, but Beattie was certain that her law school experience and her ACLU work had prepared her particularly well. Most unusually, Ginsburg herself stepped in and reassigned the case to Beattie. Ginsburg wanted "someone who had not only the insight but the background" for the case and was familiar with the basics of gender equality law.[3]

That meant that Beattie would have the job of going through the parties' briefs. But the paper flow, and her work, had barely begun.

THE WOMEN'S GROUPS were not only influencing the Justice Department papers; they were also writing and sharing the drafts of their own briefs as amici curiae.[4] The Supreme Court is not required to accept all amicus briefs from everyone interested in influencing its thinking, but it almost always does so if the requests are filed in a timely fashion. The amicus briefs can be useful when they come from individuals or groups particularly knowledgeable in the field who are likely to present a point of view or an argument that the justices would not otherwise see. All the groups supporting the government in the VMI case met that description, and most had submitted briefs to the Court in other cases.

The effort they undertook was both individual and communal, reflecting the path that had become the norm for the women's rights community. The organizations had different emphases; they formed new coalitions and abandoned old ones when a case was on appeal, and lawyers moved from one group to another. Sometimes one of the groups represented a party to a case but would share information and drafts with other groups expected to come in as amici. Sometimes, as in the VMI case, the parties would be represented by people outside the groups. The constant factor was the sense of community and the impulse to cooperate in the name of a cause that they were each a part of, no matter where each lawyer happened to be working.

Joan Bertin was an example. She had moved from the ACLU Women's Rights Project to direct Columbia University's Program on Gender, Science, and Law. During her last years at the WRP, she had been "the basic designated Supreme Court amicus brief writer for the women's rights groups," in part because the WRP had greater legal resources than the others. Other women's rights organizations were always welcome to join the briefs if they wanted to, Bertin recalled, and "they almost always did want to. Along the way we had the usual public interest community skirmishes over whether you say 'and' or 'or'" and some differences over strategy, but that was all relatively minor. The disagreements did not affect either the friendships among the women or their sense of community. She remembered few such differences in the VMI case.[5]

In *United States v. Virginia,* however, she did not sign onto the communal brief. Instead, she wrote one that went to the Court under the names of the Columbia program, the American Association of University Professors, the Center for Women Policy Studies, and twenty-five professors and educational consultants. She went to all the people who did research on sex differences and asked them to join in, and the result was a brief that emphasized the things Carol Gilligan had tried to point out at the court of appeals level: that the experts on the differences between the sexes on whom VMI and Judge Kiser relied were not expert at all, and that the scientific evidence did not show that men at VMI or anywhere else benefited from single-sex education.

The brief requiring the greatest cooperation was spearheaded by the National Women's Law Center (NWLC) and the ACLU's WRP. It eventually was signed by most of the organizations that had joined the amicus brief in the court of appeals, as well as by the American Jewish Committee, the Anti-Defamation League, the Coalition of Labor Union Women, the Mexican American Legal Defense and Educational Fund, the National Association of Social Workers, the National Council of Jewish Women, the Older Women's League, People for the American Way, Women Work! and the National Network for Women's Employment—an array of twenty-nine groups representing women (and men) who were Caucasian, African American, Mexican American, professionals, blue-collar workers, white-collar workers, and businesswomen.[6] They began by placing the case in historical perspective, which was crucial to their argument.

If the case was treated as part of a story about the country's historical discrimination against women, including the definition of women as lesser citizens who had to be excluded from the voting booth, the jury box, public office, and the military, then the Justice Department probably would win. Virginia's provision of public single-sex education for men but not for women, and VMI's insistence that women could not hack the adversarial method, became no more than a chapter in a centuries-long refusal to recognize women as equal. VWIL was yet another attempt to keep women out of a male preserve.

If, however, the case was taken out of the larger societal historical context and viewed as part of VMI's institutional history, the story was different. Then the Institute had to be seen as a place that fulfilled its mission of producing citizen-soldiers. The fact that citizen-soldiers had been successfully produced elsewhere by other methods was irrelevant. VMI worked for the students who attended it; it educated them successfully, and in a country whose public school system was in a state of disarray, where the new emphasis was on tailoring education to the needs of specific students, anything that might interfere with VMI's success could be depicted as foolish at best and evil at worst. VWIL was designed for other students with their own specific demands.

The NWLC-ACLU brief therefore situated the case in the broader societal narrative and analogized it to the story of racial discrimination.

> Virginia for 150 years has offered men a benefit it denies women—the opportunity to pursue an education at VMI. Virginia began excluding women from VMI when it founded the college in 1839—a time when Virginia considered African-American slaves to be property and subjected married women to the total control of their husbands.[7]

The remainder of the thirty-page brief was devoted to the argument for strict scrutiny, which was presented as a required corrective for historical wrongs. Women continued to be discriminated against. That they, unlike racial minorities, constituted a majority of the population did not negate their need for the protection of the higher standard, as "women remain severely underrepresented in the political process, and lack the power necessary to prevent sex-based discrimination like that at issue here. . . . As the historical record reflects, the percentage of women in the population has never prevented discrimination against them." The Court's attempts to undo the discrimination through intermediate scrutiny had resulted only in "an unworkable half-measure,"[8] generating confusion and conflicting decisions in the lower courts. One result of Court decisions sharply restricting affirmative action policies, the brief noted, was that "continued application of intermediate scrutiny creates a serious anomaly in equal protection jurisprudence." Under the decisions, "white men receive greater constitutional protection from race-conscious affirmative action plans, however benignly intended, than women receive from sex discrimination."[9]

A second brief in support of the government was submitted by a number of women's and civil rights groups in California.[10] Although it emphasized the need for the strict scrutiny standard, it also contained a lengthy section arguing that adoption of that standard should not be used to strike down "remedial and non-invidious classifications" that were designed "to assist persons in overcoming disparate burdens and to promote inclusion of all on an equal footing."[11] A third amicus brief, for the Lawyers' Committee for Civil Rights Under Law, avoided the debate over strict scrutiny and accused the court of appeals of having been overly deferential to the spurious claim that Virginia was interested in single-sex education; again, the historical record had to be examined closely.[12]

Nancy Mellette, the young woman who had become the lead plaintiff in the Citadel case after Shannon Faulkner dropped out, was another amicus. So were a handful of states, arguing that keeping VMI closed to women deprived their female residents of an equal opportunity for a military-style education. "Virginia's ostensible interest in single-gender education is a fiction," they declared.[13] Twenty-six private women's colleges told the Court that a decision in favor of the government would not threaten *private* women's colleges.[14]

The amicus brief that received the most attention from the press and would be cited in the Court's decision[15] bore the names of eighteen active and retired military officers.[16] The first name was Rhonda Cornum, the air force doctor who had been shot down and held prisoner during Desert Storm. Among the others were three generals and six graduates of West Point's first coeducational class. Army Brigadier General Evelyn P. Foote (retired) was a Vietnam veteran who had been commanding general at Fort Belvoir. Kristine Holderied, a Virginian, had graduated at the top of her U.S. Naval Academy class in 1984—the first woman to do so at any of the service academies. Major General Jeanne Holm (retired) had spent thirty-three years in the armed forces, beginning as a private in 1942, and had been the first woman promoted to major general. (She had also been helpful to Ginsburg and the ACLU's Women's Rights Project in the 1970s, when the WRP was fighting the automatic discharge of servicewomen for pregnancy.)[17] Major Lillian A. Pfluke (retired), a weapons system engineer, military parachutist, and former national military triathlon champion, had been number one in physical education while at West Point. (It was Pfluke whose op-ed column in the *Richmond Times-Dispatch* had drawn a reply from General Bunting.) Major Alison Ruttenberg of the Colorado Air National Guard was one of the first Titan II intercontinental ballistic missile launch officers. Their barely contained anger was evident in their opening sentences:

> Military members, female and male alike, swear an oath to defend the very Constitution which has been construed by the courts below to deem women unworthy to attend the Virginia Military Institute. . . . Women, who have participated in every American armed conflict, including many of the signatory amici curiae, have demonstrated with their lives that they can withstand the stress of combat situations, the challenges of military leadership and the physical challenges of mobilizing a fighting force. Yet, because of their gender, these Americans are not qualified to attend VMI.[18]

They drew on their military experience to address each of VMI's assertions. The "extreme" adversative method, based on "an artificial stress, not a real-life or combat-type stress," had no proven relationship to the goal of producing citizen-soldiers. The privacy issue was a "red herring," as the military academies had managed to accommodate privacy concerns with minimal impact on their programs.[19]

The claim that "cross-sex relationships" would destroy VMI was particularly infuriating. "If VMI is claiming a military mission," the brief said, "it should be preparing its cadets with the realities of a mixed gender military. If VMI's purpose is to train leaders in the community, it should be training its cadets to function in a mixed-gender social and political world."[20] Above all,

> VMI takes pride in the self discipline developed by cadets through its rigorous training program. This self discipline should enable the cadets to control themselves irrespective of "sexual distractions." Additionally, if fear of "sexual distraction" were a valid reason for excluding women from public higher education, women would still be barred from all public colleges and universities.
>
> Regulations concerning fraternization could be implemented to maintain good order and discipline within ranks. The court noted without elaboration that the introduction of women to VMI would create a "new set of stresses on the cadets." VMI has emphasized that mental stress is a key component of its adversative program, so any added stress might actually harmonize with this program goal.[21]

Most of the women would not have called themselves feminists. Cornum was typical. In her autobiography, describing her great-grandmother and other strong women in her family, she wrote, "Women in our family did not burn their bras, they just went out and did what they wanted to do."[22]

Mellissa Wells-Petry, retired army major and lawyer for the Washington-based Center for Military Readiness, joined the battle on the side of VMI. The amicus brief she helped write bore the names of groups that described themselves as "conservative, profamily" (Phyllis Schlafly's Eagle Forum) and their purposes as to "preserve, protect, and promote traditional and Judeo-Christian values" (Concerned Women for America) and to "promote conservative public policy" (Madison Project).[23] The culture wars were back in the Supreme Court. Arguing against adopting the strict scrutiny standard, the brief warned that "if the social consensus" about privacy "changed tomorrow— and [if] under this new contract, 'gender privacy' was deemed a social evil," the strict scrutiny doctrine might require the end of separate bathrooms for men and women. The signers worried that the higher standard might force total gender integration of school athletic teams, permit homosexual marriage, and require government funding of abortions.[24]

Anita Blair, a member of VMI's Board of Visitors and a partner in a Virginia law firm, submitted a brief for a number of other groups and individuals, including Lynne Cheney, former head of the National Endowment for the Humanities.[25] It too argued against strict scrutiny, claiming that "'boot camp' programs to rehabilitate criminals might be prohibitively expensive if they had to be duplicated for both men and women" and denying that women needed the Court's protection.[26] When a *Richmond Times-Dispatch* reporter called Blair for an upcoming story about the military women's brief, Blair commented that the female officers were "brave," "talented (and very admirable)," and said, "it's fascinating to read their stories." But she considered their brief to be about women in the military and therefore irrelevant. VMI was "intended not to create somebody who just can function in the military but to give the student, the cadet, an experience in which he has been tested to the limit, which he can use as his touchstone for the rest of his life. It's a test that needs to be conducted in a single-sex environment."[27]

A third amicus brief in support of Virginia was filed on behalf of seven outstanding educators, David Riesman among them.[28] A few of the signatories identified themselves as members of VWIL's External Advisory Council. They urged the Court to recognize that VWIL was "an important advance in women's education," based on "cutting-edge knowledge about leadership and character development and . . . enhanced by the single-gender setting." The brief defended both VWIL's offer of a "unique and valuable opportunity rather than a superficial equality" and the "well documented" benefits of single-sex education in general."[29]

Single-sex education was also the focus of a brief submitted by Wells College, Saint Mary's College, and Southern Virginia College. They, too, were concerned that strict scrutiny would mean the end of private women's colleges.[30] A group of educators represented by former senator John C. Danforth argued that states had an important governmental objective in providing an education that would lead to high academic achievement; that single-sex education was likelier to produce that result; and that, given their limited resources, states had to have the option of providing same-sex education for one sex without providing it for the other.[31] Some of the signers carefully distanced themselves from the Institute. The brief noted that "all of the amici do not necessarily endorse the overall educational philosophy at VMI," but wished only to express their interest in preserving single-sex education as "an important pedagogical alternative."[32]

South Carolina and The Citadel submitted a brief defending the court of appeals' "substantive comparability" standard.[33] Both would be directly affected by the outcome of the case, as the district court hearing the Citadel litigation had stayed the remedy trial pending the result of the Supreme Court's deliberations in the VMI case. The South Carolina Institute of Leadership for Women (SCIL), which had been set up in 1993 as South Carolina's response to the litigation about women's admission to The Citadel, wrote a brief supporting single-sex education for men as well as for women.[34] It demonstrated that SCIL could use caustic language of its own:

> Just as Nancy Mellette, in her amicus brief supporting the petitioner, asserts that she has a "very substantial" interest in the outcome of the Court's review of the VMI decision, the twenty-two SCIL students assert that they have an even stronger interest. . . . The twenty-two SCIL students, unlike Nancy Mellette, or Lieutenant Colonel Rhonda Cornum, USA, or the American Association of University Professors, are not prospective participants, past participants, or interested observers in an educational program, but are actual participants in an on-going educational program whose continued existence depends specifically on whether this Court affirms the VMI II holding that substantively comparable single-gender educational programs are constitutionally permissible.[35]

For emphasis, the names of the students were attached, along with a list of their activities and the languages spoken by each of them.[36]

The attorney generals of Wyoming and Pennsylvania made an argument for continuing to permit the states to serve as laboratories, "providing experimentation and diversity in the area of education." They feared that the "growing interest" across the country in experimenting with all-girl math and science classes and inner-city all-male academies would be stymied by the adoption of strict scrutiny, and they agreed with VMI that the Justice Department and its supporters were out to destroy private single-sex schools.[37]

Finally, Mary Baldwin College entered an impassioned plea for its new program. VWIL had been designed by "a task force of educators, not by lawyers" such as those writing the amicus briefs on the other side. The brief detailed the reasons for not replicating VMI, asserting that VWIL offered women "benefits that are at least as valuable as those offered to men by VMI." It summarized numerous scholarly works demonstrating the positive results of single-sex education, including greater academic achievement and self-esteem, career success, and entry into traditionally male professions.[38]

WHILE THEY WERE WRITING their briefs, the two parties had to decide who would handle the oral argument before the Supreme Court.

Each side is given only a brief half hour to speak, and the justices use much of that time to raise questions or make comments. Arguing before them is a job for only the most talented of advocates. Robert Patterson wanted Anne Marie Whittemore to represent VMI. She had won at the court of appeals level, and he thought that she had done a terrific job there. The clients, however, were the VMI Foundation and the VMI Alumni Association, and they wanted someone with Supreme Court experience.[39] They turned to Theodore B. Olson.

Olson had graduated cum laude from the University of the Pacific in 1962 and had been on the law review at the University of California at Berkeley (1965). By 1996, he was a Washington insider, having been chosen by the Reagan administration as an assistant attorney general and head of the Justice Department's Office of Legal Counsel from 1981 to 1984. The Office of Legal Counsel, which drafts the attorney general's official opinions, is also charged with preserving and enhancing the power of the president and advising both the White House and the attorney general on difficult legal questions. In 1982–1983 Olson advised the White House that it did not have to let Congress see certain Environmental Protection Agency documents the legislators had requested about the program to clean up toxic wastes. He was later accused of having lied to Congress about the matter and became the subject of an investigation by a special prosecutor.

Although no charges were ever brought, the investigation may have hurt Olson's hope for a seat on the Supreme Court. He returned from the Justice Department to the "inside the Beltway" offices of Gibson, Dunn & Crutcher, a firm with more than 700 lawyers that he had joined immediately after law school. By 1996, he had argued more than a dozen cases before the Supreme Court, most of them in the preceding few years. The Court included two other former heads of the Office of Legal Counsel who had held that post under Republican presidents: Chief Justice William H. Rehnquist, who had served under President Nixon, and Associate Justice Antonin Scalia, who had served under President Ford. At fifty-six, Olson was seven years younger than Paul Bender, who would appear for the Justice Department.[40]

Bender had his own distinguished professional record. He had graduated magna cum laude from Harvard Law School, where he was an editor of the law review. He had been selected to clerk for two of the country's most prestigious jurists: first Judge Learned Hand, on the Second Circuit Court of Appeals, and then Justice Felix Frankfurter, on the Supreme Court. (Bender, a classmate of Ruth Bader Ginsburg's at James Madison High School, was clerking for Frankfurter when Frankfurter refused to consider Ginsburg for the job.)[41] A constitutional law expert and civil liberties activist, he had taught at the University of Pennsylvania Law School until becoming dean of Arizona State University's College of Law. President Clinton named him principal deputy solicitor general of the United States in 1993. By 1996, Bender had appeared before the Supreme Court in some twenty cases.

Both advocates, then, were well-known and experienced Supreme Court litigators. While they were thinking and talking about the points they would make during oral argument, the justices of the Supreme Court and their clerks were doing their own preparations.

Lisa Beattie was busy fashioning the bench memo for Ginsburg. In it, she quoted language that had been used in other cases by various justices, particularly Sandra Day O'Connor. The goal, Beattie thought, was to make the memo so solid that it might be useful in the writing of an opinion, if Ginsburg ended up writing one. Ginsburg delighted Beattie by calling her up to say that the memo was terrific[42]—a coup for a Supreme Court clerk just a little more than a year out of law school.

The procedure in Justice Antonin Scalia's chambers was somewhat different. He too let his clerks choose their cases according to a lottery, "like the NFL draft," and he expected that all of them would want to work on VMI; it was, after all, "obviously one of the big cases of the term." The lucky clerk, however, was not asked for a bench memo, as Scalia considered such memos "a waste of time." Instead, Scalia wanted a one- or two-page description of the case, which he relied on to prevent him from overlooking any issues during oral argument. The justice was certain that he would not miss a major issue, but a lesser one might slip by.[43]

So, with Ginsburg armed with a bench memo (as well as her decades of advocacy for and writing about women's rights, and her strong desire to win the *Vorchheimer* case twenty years after the fact),[44] Scalia with a short summary, and the other justices with their own sets of papers, they stepped into the Supreme Court's impressive courtroom to hear oral argument in the case of *United States v. Virginia*.

Speaking to the Nation's Highest Court

My question is, what is it that's so important about this really

hard to grasp adversative thing?

—Justice Stephen Breyer

When Chief Justice William Rehnquist took a quiet stroll outside the Supreme Court building before nine o'clock on the morning of January 17, 1996, he encountered a long line of spectators hoping to get in for oral argument in *United States v. Virginia*. Demand was great; many of them would not be admitted. Even the media, which usually produced about twenty to twenty-five note takers, were out in force, and the eighty-six seats reserved for them were almost filled.[1]

Among those who did make it into the courtroom were many of the women amicus lawyers, who, as members of the Supreme Court bar, sat in a special section. Judith Keith got herself admitted to the Court bar that morning so that she could sit up front with the other lawyers from the Justice Department. The audience hummed with people from VMI, Mary Baldwin, and The Citadel: Josiah Bunting, VMI's highest-ranking cadet, MBC president Cynthia Tyson, three VWIL students, The Citadel's lawyer, and Shannon Faulkner's former lawyer. Lisa Beattie had secured a place for her mother. As Michael Maurer commented, "Everyone except my ex-girlfriend during the last five years was in that courtroom." Beattie sat on the side taking notes, because the transcript of oral argument did not reach the justices for some days.[2]

The Supreme Court's imposing four-story "Marble Palace"[3] is on First

Street, across from Congress. Its facade has become familiar to Americans as the imposing background for media shots of protesters admonishing the Court to do the right thing and lawyers commenting on what has gone on inside. For the visitor, however, the focal point of the building is the courtroom. It is reached by climbing majestically broad flights of white marble steps up to the sculpted bronze main doors, past marble statues entitled *Authority of Law* and *Contemplation of Justice*. Authority is male; Contemplation, female. The pediment above the main entrance, topping marble columns, bears nine symbolic figures. One is the "goddess of liberty," complete with the scales of justice. All the others are modeled after real people, all male. Below them is the inscription, "Equal Justice Under Law." The Supreme Court is remarkably like VMI in its statuary: the only women are stylized and mythical.

Inside, beyond the airport-like X-ray scanners and metal detectors, the vast, marble-columned Great Hall leads to the courtroom. Handbags are searched near its entrance, both for security purposes and to make certain that no pagers or cell phones disturb the judicial solemnity. Guards then usher spectators into the courtroom.

It is an awesome room, in the sense of creating a feeling of awe in the viewer, and it is therefore well suited to a house of justice. The first impression is of great size, as the courtroom measures ninety-one feet from front to back, eighty-two feet across, and forty-four feet high. The eye is drawn to the creamy marble columns on all four sides, following them up the soaring walls to the sculpted marble panels that circle the room. Mythical figures such as "Majesty of the Law," "Power of Government," "Defense of Human Rights," "Justice," and "Wisdom" grace the front and back panels. Historical figures associated with the law parade around the two sides: Moses, Hammurabi, Solomon, Confucius, Mohammed, Chief Justice John Marshall. Again, they are all male, although one can glimpse the winged female figures of "Divine Inspiration" and other embodiments of virtue and vice such as "Peace," "Corruption," and "Deceit."

The crimson of the long, gold-fringed drapes and the cushions of the spectators' benches is repeated in the gold, crimson, and black patterned carpet that draws one into the room and pulls one's attention to the raised mahogany bench in front. The justices reach it from behind another set of crimson and gold drapes. Between the spectators' rows and the bench is a bronze railing, marking off the section of mahogany seats reserved for members of the Supreme Court bar. There are tables for the two sets of lawyers and a central lectern with microphones for the attorney presenting an argument. A section for the press is off to the left; another set of pews on the right, each labeled with the name of a justice, is reserved for their guests.

The row of black leather chairs behind the bench is arranged according to seniority. The chief justice presides from the middle of the row, with the most senior justice seated to his right and the next most senior to his left. On the day the VMI case was argued, the audience saw Justice Ginsburg on the extreme left, followed by Justices Souter, Scalia, Stevens, Rehnquist, O'Connor, Kennedy, and Breyer (Thomas, having recused himself, was not present).

Over their heads hung a large clock; there is another on the back wall, where the justices can see it. The attorney's lectern has a microphone, and its start and stop lights are controlled by the chief justice. To waste time in this sanctum of the law would be unforgivable. The clock for the VMI case began ticking at 10:07 that day, when Chief Justice Rehnquist announced, "We'll hear argument first this morning in Number 94-1941, *United States v. Virginia,* and *Virginia v. United States.*"[4] The next hour no doubt felt both too short and too long for the attorneys who would step up to the podium.

The first was Paul Bender, speaking for the United States. The challenge for a lawyer arguing before the Supreme Court is that he or she has a mere thirty minutes in which to try to affect the justices' thinking, and it is not an uninterrupted half hour. The justices are free to inject questions or comments whenever they like, sometimes eliciting information from the lawyer, sometimes appearing to conduct a dialogue among themselves, and all the while the clock is running. An advocate has to decide precisely which points must be part of the presentation, which can be dropped under the pressure of time, and—the most difficult task—how to pick up a thread temporarily lost in the questioning or interpret the justices' questions so as to get in crucial points while appearing responsive. It is not an exercise for the fainthearted. Experienced advocates organize mock courts for themselves beforehand, with friends and colleagues shooting the kinds of questions that can be expected from the justices.

The point with which Bender chose to begin his argument was that VMI was a state-supported institution, and although it had seemed reasonable in 1839 for a military college to be all male, it was now almost the end of another century, and VMI's adversative method had become a "very valuable asset" in civilian as well as military life.

Justice Kennedy quickly interrupted, asking Bender to interpret the conclusions the lower courts had reached about "the extent to which the adversative method would be altered and affected by the admission of women."

Bender disagreed that the adversative method would have to be changed. Justice Scalia then picked up on one of the themes VMI had emphasized since the creation of VWIL and that Olson would repeat in his argument: that the difference between VMI and VWIL was validated by experts in education.

QUESTION (Scalia): Didn't both of the lower courts make that finding, that the effect of admitting women would be to destroy the adversative method?

MR. BENDER: Yes. I—

QUESTION: Now, you say that's wrong, but both of the lower courts found that, didn't they?

MR. BENDER: They—that finding was based entirely on a stereotypical view of women and men which says that women—men cannot administer the adversative method to women, women would not be able to survive with the adversative method.

QUESTION: It was not based on expert testimony?

MR. BENDER: Expert testimony was in turn based on—

QUESTION: But it was—

MR. BENDER: —exactly those characterizations.

QUESTION: I see. All of these experts are—can be dismissed as stereotypical.

Scalia went on to introduce another VMI theme: the Institute did not claim that no woman could manage the adversative method, but that too few could. Bender replied that that was not the point.

QUESTION (Scalia): As I recall the experts . . . it was not that women can't do it, it was that it would interfere with the kind of relationship among the students that produces the adversative method, that men and women would not engage in the same kind of adversariness that men and men or, perhaps, women and women would, that the sexual difference would make a difference. It has nothing to do with whether women can take the heat. That's not what the experts testified to.

MR. BENDER: It has to do with whether men will perceive that women can take the heat. . . . I think what this Court is called upon to decide is whether a State institution can model its program and its exclusion of women on the assumption that there are certain things that women can't do in general, there are certain things that men will not do with women because those men think that women are not capable of that, can model its institution and its educational method on the notion that this educational method, developed by men, emphasizing what they think of as manly qualities, is a place that women can't go, so that women cannot demonstrate that they have the same qualities.

Justice O'Connor jumped in to remind everyone that the case revolved around two questions: whether the appeals court was correct in saying that provision of a single-sex education for men but not for women violated the Constitution and, if it did, whether VWIL was an adequate remedy. "The discussion thus far doesn't really direct us to either of those questions," she chided Bender and Scalia, but then she turned to the matter that really concerned her. Why, she asked Bender, was the government urging the Court to adopt a strict scrutiny standard? Couldn't the case be decided using the intermediate test, as she had articulated it in *Hogan*?

Yes, Bender replied, but the Court had left open the question of what the appropriate standard was, "so we thought that the question might come up of asking us what we thought the right standard is."

"Well," an annoyed-sounding O'Connor commented, "it's not exactly an open question in the sense that the Court has decided a number of cases applying a sort of intermediate scrutiny."

"Right," agreed Bender, but he failed to note either in answer to O'Connor or in reply to Justice Kennedy's follow-up questions that the lower courts found intermediate scrutiny confusing and interpreted it in contradictory ways. Justice Scalia jumped in to comment that he failed to see how any single-sex school could meet the strict scrutiny standard. Missing another obvious opening, Bender made no mention of the passage in *Hogan* suggesting that programs serving a compensatory purpose rather than perpetuating outmoded stereotypes would pass muster.

There was no more discussion of the strict scrutiny standard, and the amicus lawyers in the audience squirmed at what they thought was Bender's failure to press for it.[5] A seasoned Court watcher commented, "Should a 'strict scrutiny' standard emerge in the end, it would have to be in spite of, not because of, its presentation to the Court by government counsel."[6] What the critics could not know was that, as the next chapter indicates, the Court would not have decided on the basis of strict scrutiny no matter what Bender did.

Justice Ginsburg presented Bender with a tacit invitation to explain why coed Virginia Tech, all-male VMI, and all-female VWIL would not fill the constitutional requirement of equal protection even if they were all funded equally. Bender replied that it was because the VMI degree was perceived as reflecting an ability to "survive the system" in an educational setting that was denied to women. Justice O'Connor asked whether parallel tracks within VMI would be sufficient.

MR. BENDER: That I don't think would work, because the thing that women, the opportunity that women are not given in Virginia is to show that they can do it on a level with men.

QUESTION (O'Connor): Oh, but just the same, the same requirements, and they get a degree from VMI.

MR. BENDER: But it's not with men. I think one of the powerful things that's going on here by excluding women from VMI is the message that women cannot compete in an—

Justice Scalia interrupted.

QUESTION (Scalia): I thought you said they could do it in a separate institution. I thought you said before if they had a fully adversative experience in a totally separate institution, that would be okay. . . . What is your basis for saying that the committee that set up this alternative institution, VWIL, decided not to have the same adversative method that VMI has because it thought women couldn't handle it, as opposed to the fact, which is what they said, that they thought not enough women would be interested in it?

MR. BENDER: They said that it would not be appropriate—

QUESTION: Which is not at all denigrating. It shows to my mind that they're pretty smart.

[Laughter.]

When he first became a judge, Scalia had been surprised at how often oral argument makes a difference. In many cases, he thought, a judge walked into oral argument on the knife's edge—willing to go either way and ready to be persuaded. Effective advocacy at oral argument could win a case.[7] But it was clear from his questioning that he was not open to persuasion in this case and, from the sharp tenor of his comments, that he suspected that his view would not prevail among his colleagues.

Bender finally got a bit of uninterrupted time when, turning to a field the justices knew well, he invited them to consider the analogy to legal education.

MR. BENDER: In thinking about this case . . . I've tried to relate it to something that I've had some experience with, which is legal education. And I thought, what if a State set up a State law school in 1839, all for men, because at that time only men could be lawyers, and over 150 years it developed an extremely adversative method of legal education, the toughest kind of Socratic teaching, tremendous time pressures, tremendous pressures in exams, tremendous combativeness by the faculty, tremendous competitiveness among the students, and developed a reputation for that.

And the graduates of that school . . . who survived that process became known as expert leading lawyers and judges in that State and Nationwide. And then as women came into the legal profession and started to apply to the school, to ask it to change its admission policy, the school made a judgment that most women really wouldn't be comfortable in this environment, and the faculty would have trouble cross-examining them in the same way they cross-examine men, and other students would have difficulty relating to them in the same competitive way, and so it's better not to let women into the school. What we'll do is, we'll set up a new women's law school, and it won't have the tough Socratic method, it will have a much warmer, a much more embracing environment, and it won't have large classes with a lot of pressure, it will have seminars, and it won't have tough exams, it will have papers, and things like that—

[Laughter.]

MR. BENDER: —and every woman has to go to that law school, and no man can, and no woman can go to the old law school. I think we all understand that that is not by any means equal treatment of women with regard to their access to the legal profession.

At least five of the justices must have recognized Bender's description of Harvard Law School, their alma mater. A journalist in the audience thought that Ginsburg was holding back a smile.[8] Justice Scalia, however, was not amused.

QUESTION (Scalia): It depends on whether, in fact, those findings that the law school would be destroyed, that it's—in the hypothetical you pose, those findings are obviously absurd. Those findings are not absurd in the context of VMI . . . it would destroy the nature of the institution.

MR. BENDER: I disagree with that.

Under questioning by Justice Stevens, Bender again denied that the adversative system would have to be altered if women were admitted. Justice Ginsburg raised another issue.

QUESTION (Ginsburg): Mr. Bender, one brief—the women in the military made a point that I didn't notice the Government making, and I'm wondering what your position is on it, and that concentration was on the men, not the women, and the point was that if women are to be leaders in life and in the military, then men have got to become accustomed to taking commands from women, and men won't become accustomed to that if women aren't let in.

MR. BENDER: And I think that's true not only in the military but it's true in the professions, it's true in corporate leadership.

Justice Souter put Bender on the spot by asking whether the government was arguing that the adversative method as currently constituted was not necessary for producing leaders. That was the point that the Bush administration reportedly had forbidden the Justice Department to make. Bender, indicating that he was not comfortable with the question even now, perhaps because the government had not made that argument below, hedged briefly and asked to reserve the rest of his time. Theodore Olson then stood up for VMI.

Olson's first sentence reflected the difference in the way the two sides saw the main question.

MR. OLSON: Mr. Chief Justice, and may it please the Court:

Although the Government has tried virtually everything in its power to deny it, this case involves the inescapable central question of whether the States can support single sex education. While 98 percent of Virginia's higher educational resources go into coeducation, educators are virtually united, both the Government's experts and the experts for the respondents, that many young men and young women significantly benefit from a single sex education.

Justice Stevens interrupted to ask what Virginia was doing for students "who would like single sex education but who would not like to go through the adversative method."

Olson replied, "You cannot create a school without an adequate student body, and resources are limited."

Stevens persisted: "Yes, but if most people who want single sex education don't want VMI, it's discriminating against them."

Olson repeated that Virginia had to consider its limited resources and the demand. "Virginia could not create a single sex educational school for young men that wanted an adversative system and a single sex education for young men who wanted a less than a co-adversative system." That bothered Justice Ginsburg.

> QUESTION (Ginsburg): But Mr. Olson . . . wasn't that what Virginia in fact had until 1972? It had [VMI and] the Charlottesville facility [the University of Virginia] virtually reserved to men. The curiosity is that you are defending single sex education when Virginia itself abandoned single sex education in all schools but one.

Justice O'Connor jumped in.

> QUESTION (O'Connor): We get back to the posture of this case, and one issue we have to decide is whether Virginia can provide single sex education to just one sex, to just men. That's one of these cases, isn't it?
> MR. OLSON: It—well—
> QUESTION: And you want to defend that.
> MR. OLSON: Well—
> QUESTION: You want to say it is not a violation of the Constitution to provide a single sex education just for men. . . .
> MR. OLSON: That's correct, Justice O'Connor . . . Virginia is providing public resources, pursuant to two constitutional amendments, to private schools. Five private schools in Virginia provide single sex education for women, and the State of Virginia is supporting those programs at that time, and there is not a sufficient demand at that point in time to create a separate institution. Now, Virginia is nonetheless, despite the fact that it feels that that program is defensible, because when the States choose to develop and finance a program that is for the benefit

of people of one gender, it doesn't necessarily have to create the exact program for the other gender if there isn't a sufficient demand or need for it.

QUESTION: Well, I guess that gets us into the second question, which is remedy.

MR. OLSON: Yes, it does, and there are essentially three choices here. What Virginia has chosen to do is to provide single sex education designed by experts to serve the people who need and want and would benefit from single sex—

That statement troubled Justice Ginsburg.

QUESTION (Ginsburg): Mr. Olson, just to clarify, Virginia didn't choose to do that, because you are, as Justice O'Connor pointed out, defending keeping things just as they were. You're defending the judgment that you wanted to get, which is VMI for all males, and no public program for women.

What she and Justice O'Connor were referring to was that the Court was hearing *United States v. Virginia* together with *Virginia v. United States.* In the first, the Justice Department was appealing the lower courts' acceptance of VWIL as an alternative to VMI. In the second, however, Virginia was still maintaining that it had no constitutional obligation either to admit women to VMI or to offer them a parallel program. Olson handled the question by turning it into one of procedure and by emphasizing Virginia's contention that educational experts had decided that a method different from VMI's was best for women.

MR. OLSON: What we are saying, however, because Justice O'Connor has asked the question, an entirely appropriate question, suppose you are not successful on that point [that Virginia could provide single-sex education for men only], and suppose that the court of appeals was correct and that there must be a remedy, what should that remedy be?

Olson said that Virginia could have deprived both men and women of the opportunity for single-sex education by admitting women to VMI; it could have created a VMI for women, thereby giving them a kind of education that the experts said would be wrong for them; or it could have eliminated Virginia's support for single-sex education by making VMI a private institution. Instead, Virginia was promoting diversity "by creating opportunities in a very, very large coeducational system for people of both sexes to make the choice of single sex education."

Justice Rehnquist questioned that.

QUESTION (Rehnquist): Well, Mr. Olson, when this lawsuit was brought Virginia funded VMI. Did it fund any single sex school for women?

MR. OLSON: Yes. Well, it provided tuition assistance grants to the five single sex colleges for women.

QUESTION: And what percent of a student's expenses in that case would be covered?

MR. OLSON: I'm not sure that the record is completely clear, but the single sex institutions for women in Virginia derive something—I believe the record indicates something between 5 and 10 percent of their resources from either the Federal Government or the State government, plus there's the factor that the Federal Government and the State government provide tax deductions—

QUESTION: Well, I know, but what I'm trying to get at is, is the assistance that is provided by Virginia to these private schools comparable in dollar amount to the assistance that is provided to VMI?

MR. OLSON: It was smaller in total amounts.

Justice Kennedy returned to the question of the need for the adversative system. Wasn't Olson saying that the adversative system was not absolutely necessary for the production of leaders, but simply "a good way to educate people"?

That was, of course, the heart of Virginia's dilemma in maintaining simultaneously that the adversative method had to be preserved and that women could be turned into leaders without it. Olson hedged. By that time, he clearly was flustered, and he fumbled under questioning from Justices Souter and Stevens about the asserted value of single-sex education, the reasons for denying women a VMI-type program, and, again, whether women would change VMI.

MR. OLSON: The experts know how best to educate young people. The experts that set up the VWIL program said we could have created an institution that looked very much like VMI. We did not feel it would be right to design a program based on litigation considerations because we know—and this is in the record—we know how best to design a program for young people. If we're going to have a single sex educational—

QUESTION (Stevens): Yes, but Mr. Olson, that didn't go to academics, because there's a square finding that the academic program would not be affected by—

MR. OLSON: The academic program itself is—would not be affected. . . . It's the environment in which the students learn . . . there's a finding in the record, and I can't give you the page number, to the effect that people succeed better in a single sex educational program across the board, both young men and young women. They do better, they achieve more, including the academics—

QUESTION: Academically or otherwise?

MR. OLSON: Academically and otherwise.

QUESTION: But the finding on page 212a of the appendix to the cert petition says squarely the presence of women in the institute would not alter the program academically.

MR. OLSON: I believe, Justice Stevens, that the evidence and the findings that are on page 168 of the appendix, 167, 176, pages 225, page 125—

QUESTION: You've given us four different pages.

MR. OLSON: I apologize.

QUESTION: Which one do you want us to read?

MR. OLSON: Well—

[Laughter.]

MR. OLSON: Let me start with page 176.

Ginsburg, demonstrating the same insistence on placing the case in a historical context that had illuminated her efforts as an advocate and become part of the technique used by the women's groups, returned to the matter of excluding women from prestigious institutions.

QUESTION (Ginsburg): I was struck by the resemblance of some aspects of this case to the case against the University of Virginia [in] Charlottesville . . . the three-judge court there did make two points, and one was that the University in Charlottesville couldn't continue all male because there were educational opportunities, opportunities for education at that facility uniquely that were not available to women in the women's colleges and elsewhere. And the second point that was made by that three-judge court in that litigation was that there exists, because of history, a prestige factor at the Charlottesville facility that was not matched by the other institutions.

MR. OLSON: And if I—if I may answer the latter part of that question first, one would hope that if single sex education can exist in this country and receive public support, that every single sex institution will have prestige, it will be unique. . . .

QUESTION: But this is all imaginary. What we have here and now is, we have two all male public colleges [VMI and The Citadel], they're both military schools. We have nothing comparable for women, with the exception of this program just started up in response to a court decree.

MR. OLSON: And this program, the courts below have examined this program and found that the goals are the same and that the outcome will be the same, and that this will be a successful program.

The exchange again highlighted the difference in approaches to the issue. Ginsburg, like the government, emphasized the lack of symmetry between VMI and VWIL; Olson, for VMI, concentrated on the similarity of goals.

Justices Kennedy and Breyer pushed Olson on the same thing that had caused Bender discomfort: the question of whether, given the absence of the adversative system at West Point and Annapolis, Virginia could credibly maintain that it was necessary to the production of leaders.

QUESTION (Kennedy): Does the adversative method produce a different product than the West Point method? I think the Government is in effect trying to say, don't worry about changing VMI because the product will be very good. It will be like

West Point and Annapolis, and those are marvelous products. Is there something in the adversative method that produces a different quality leader? . . .

MR. OLSON: I think that the answer to that question is best answered this way, is that because we are each different, we each respond to different educational methods and different educational stimuli. The West Point program is designed to create officers of the United States. The VMI program is designed to create leaders and adults who can operate in the civilian or in the military world, who have a sense of responsibility, the same goals, in other words, that the VWIL program is set up to do. The fact is that some young people do very well in a coeducational program, and come out the other end to be successful. Some young men and some young women aren't successful in coeducational programs. They are distracted. There's a million things that can go on in those programs—

QUESTION (Breyer): Mr. Olson, I think you're saying not that there is a distinctive difference in the product, but that there is a distinctive difference in the method of education which is suited to the people who go there, and that really does not answer the question. . . . Let me put the question, or subsume the question in something else.

It is—isn't it true that the district court judge never made any finding that there was a difference in the kind of leadership product, if you want to use that term, that VMI produces from what West Point or Annapolis or the other military schools—

MR. OLSON: That's correct, but it did make a finding that this system and this methodology works for the people that go to that school, and that—

QUESTION: Okay, which goes to the point which you made quite candidly, that you are resting your case essentially on the position that this is a valuable method of education because it serves a distinct group of people. You are not resting your case on the proposition that it is necessary to produce a distinctive kind of leader who is produced by it and can only be produced by it.

MR. OLSON: I agree with you, yes.

QUESTION: Well then, why couldn't you say exactly the same thing about ethnic or racial or any other kind of—religious, I mean, somebody could have a school, and they say, we're keeping a religious group, ethnic group or whatever, out of our public school because we have a certain unique kind of education that focuses on certain curricula in a certain way, and once they're in here they'll change the nature of that curricula because they won't have the same backgrounds, et cetera, and therefore we will use this unique kind of curriculum, method, et cetera, that we had in the past, and there would be some truth to that.

I mean, don't we have to look at the importance of this thing? It may be you don't have exactly the same rat line. Maybe you don't have exactly the same hazing type, but not complete hazing activity. That may be true with any ethnic group coming into a school, any religious group, any kind of a group.

Isn't the answer to that, so what? You'd have to show that it's important enough to maintain this adversative process, and what is it in this record that shows it's important enough to maintain that—

MR. OLSON: The evidence—

QUESTION: —to overcome the answer to a woman who says I want to go there? I want to go there. I want this.

MR. OLSON: The evidence is overwhelming that that system would not exist in the company of co—

QUESTION: Well, maybe it wouldn't. Maybe you wouldn't have precisely the same system with ethnic groups, racial groups, et cetera, but my question is, what is it that's so important about this really hard to grasp adversative thing that warrants saying—

[Laughter.]

QUESTION: I don't mean to be facetious about it, either. I want—I'm serious about it. What is it that is so important about it that enables you to say to a young woman I'm very sorry, even though you want to go there and you want this result, you can't?

MR. OLSON: The answer—the experts testified, and people who are professional educators, who have spent their life in education, saying that the system could not exist. It would fundamentally have to be changed.

QUESTION: I take that as a given. What I'm asking is, what's so important about that particular rat line?

Although the justices seem to delight in asking difficult questions of both sides, and their queries do not necessarily forecast their votes, many in the audience interpreted the preceding exchange to indicate that the swing justices were unconvinced about the importance of keeping VMI exactly as it was. Patterson and Whittemore had been hopeful about the Supreme Court because they thought the record was in VMI's favor. By the end of Olson's time, however, they thought the case had been lost. [9]

Bender stood up for his two minutes of rebuttal, which were immediately preempted by Justices Breyer and Scalia.

QUESTION (Breyer): I've a very quick question, which is, the main point, single sex education will disappear if we adopt your brief word for word. Suppose you decided that you needed single sex academies in inner cities. If we adopt your brief word for word, have we decided that case?

MR. BENDER: No, not at all. First of all, of course, you haven't decided the private single sex education for reasons that I think are clear, but even with regard to public single sex—

QUESTION (Scalia): Wait, only private single sex education that gets any assistance from the Government [meaning that the government would be prohibited from giving aid to private single-sex schools].

MR. BENDER: No, I don't think that's true, Justice Scalia. . . .

QUESTION: Can States give money to segregated schools, racially segregated schools, for example?

MR. BENDER: Can States give money—

QUESTION: Yes.

MR. BENDER: —to racially segregated schools? Under this Court's State action cases I think they can.

QUESTION: They can [sounding incredulous]? . . . That's the position of the Justice Department . . . that States can provide funding to racially segregated schools?

MR. BENDER: It depends on the circumstances. . . .

QUESTION: That's astounding.

[Laughter.]

Now the lawyers on the other side were dismayed. A lawyer for one of the amicus groups thought that her horror must have shown on her face. A reporter from *Law Week,* a legal newspaper, leaned over and, referring to Bender, said quietly, "He always screws up." She was not consoled. "I remember walking out of the courthouse feeling sick to my stomach and thinking that if I had ever heard an argument that could lose a winning case, I had just had that experience." Assistant Attorney General Deval Patrick told the media later that Bender had misspoken.[10]

Scalia had asked the hard two-part question that concerned many VMI watchers. First, if it was unconstitutional to use public funds to establish and maintain a single-sex educational institution in the absence of an equivalent institution for the other sex, could the state, for example, create separate math and science programs for girls and young women? Could the state argue that societal forces had made those fields so unwelcome and threatening to females that a kind of single-sex remediation was necessary? Second, if public money was not to be spent on single-sex education, did that limitation apply only to institutions or programs directly maintained by the government? Could the federal and state governments still provide textbooks and computers to *private* single-sex schools, and scholarships and loans to their students? Would those expenditures violate the Constitution?

Bender was backed into equating aid to single-sex schools with aid to single-race schools because the race-sex analogy had become traditional in American law since the 1970s, and because the Justice Department had emphasized the analogy in its briefs. If it was illegal for the government to separate the races in schools because such separation implied that one race was inferior—the holding of *Brown v. Board of Education*—then the same was true of the sexes. African Americans had been excluded from white institutions, which most of society viewed as the only "legitimate" ones, just as women had been excluded from male institutions.

That did not solve the problem of whether it was legal to provide a separate school, for example, for young African American inner-city men, on the premise that they might learn best in an institution tailored to their particular background and needs. If the answer was yes, how was that different from a state providing a separate school for young white men, as in the days of segregation? If such a school was privately funded, could the government give it books or student loans?

The issue was difficult, and the Justice Department and VMI disagreed about whether it was involved in the case at all. The VMI case was about the provision of a benefit for only one sex, the Department argued; it was about equality. The Institute replied that the basic questions underlying the present case and a projected challenge to an all-male inner-city school or an all-female math class were identical. Did the sexes—and perhaps the races—learn differently as a result not of biology but of diverse experiences? And if they did, wasn't an all-male VMI legitimate?

Bender had to deal with this complex matter in the face of a hostile interrogator, and he had only a few seconds remaining in which to do so. The pressure took its toll on his syntax.

> MR. BENDER: Coming back to your question, Justice Breyer, if I may, certainly a compensatory program that is—has a compensatory reason to compensate for prior discrimination, for example, could be a single sex program that would be for only that gender because only that gender has a need for that, so at least in those two areas . . . you could have that. . . . I think single sex education that a State proposes for single sex reasons, unlike this case, where this is done just to comply with a court decree, if a State proposes a single sex system, the issue then is, is it truly an equal system, and that would have to be decided.

At 11:08, Chief Justice Rehnquist announced, "The case is submitted." After six long years, the VMI litigation had been taken out of the hands of the lawyers and placed squarely in that of the justices.

20

The High Court Replies

However "liberally" this plan serves the State's sons, it makes no

provision whatever for her daughters.

—Justice Ruth Bader Ginsburg

There are only nine people in the Supreme Court's conference room when the justices sit down together to vote on a case. If they need any material during their deliberations, the most junior justice opens the door, summons one of the pages waiting outside, and takes the material into the conference room once it arrives. No one else is allowed in.

The purpose of the secrecy is frank deliberations. The justices want to be free to have honest, open exchanges—and, if it seems wise, to change their minds without fear of embarrassment. The second reason would prove particularly relevant to the VMI case.

As Alexander Hamilton noted in the *Federalist Papers*, the Supreme Court was designed to have neither the power of the purse nor that of the sword.[1] It cannot resort to arms, or to the withholding or bestowing of funds, to get its decisions enforced. The country's chief executive officers—the president and the governors—do not usually put their troops at the service of the Court. What the Court must rely on, if it is to remain an important part of the government, is the willingness of the American people in and out of office to follow even those decisions they dislike. This procedural consensus—the informal agreement by the people to abide by the judgments of legitimate policy makers, whether those policy makers are citizens voting in an election or duly elected or appointed officials—is one of the glories of American democracy.

The particular consensus at work in the case of the Supreme Court arises from public veneration of the Constitution. If the Constitution is treated by Americans like a secular Bible or Koran, a document that embodies absolute truth, the Supreme Court justices have become an analogous secular high priesthood. Only they understand the Constitution, as popular belief has it, though in fact, the vague phrases of that document are as comprehensible and mysterious to anyone else who bothers to read them. The meaning of an injunction such as "No state shall deny to any person within its jurisdiction the equal protection of the laws" is scarcely self-explanatory, nor is there anything in American history that provides an adequate road map. As Robert Patterson understood,[2] and as many lawyers and judges had proclaimed before him, however absolute the public may believe the Constitution to be, in reality, it means whatever the justices sitting on the Court at any given moment say it does.

Popular recognition of that fact, however, and of the reality that the justices do not pluck higher truths out of the tree of the Constitution but read its leaves differently and disagree about what they mean, would not serve the judicial mystique well. And since the judicial mystique is directly linked to continuation of the procedural consensus and acceptance of the Court's legitimacy, the justices do their arguing in private.

The chief justice opens discussion of each case in conference by laying out what he sees as the issues in it. The other justices then have the opportunity to present their views, in order of seniority. Justice Harry Blackmun liked to tell of the days when Chief Justice Warren Burger would introduce each case in conference. Justice Hugo Black, the senior judge who disagreed with Burger on almost every major issue, would listen patiently until Burger finished and then, with a reproachful "Oh, Chief Justice!" proceed to analyze the case in completely different terms.[3]

Something along the same lines happened when the justices conferred about *United States v. Virginia*. Chief Justice Rehnquist saw no constitutional reason to tell VMI to admit women, but Justice Stevens, the most senior judge, thought differently. As soon as the other justices began to speak, there was no doubt about the outcome. Only Justice Scalia agreed with Rehnquist. The vote was six to two. Justice Kennedy was with the majority, although his comments indicated that he might rethink his vote; the rest of the votes in the majority appeared solid.[4]

As noted earlier, when the chief justice is in the majority, he assigns the writing of the Court's opinion. Various chief justices have taken into account factors such as equitable distribution of the burden and different justices' expertise. Chief Justice Rehnquist bases his assignments largely on how up-to-date the justices are with their existing workloads. When the chief justice is in the minority, however, as happened in *United States v. Virginia,* the most senior justice in the majority chooses the opinion writer. It was therefore Justice Stevens who assigned the case to Justice Ginsburg.[5]

The justices returned to their chambers after conference, which is when Lisa Beattie learned that she would be expected to begin research for the Court's opinion and to draft possible language incorporating it. In fact, all the clerks in Ginsburg's chambers were mobilized for the research job, because there were so many areas to cover: the history of women in higher education, of women in untraditional professions, of women in medical school, of women lawyers, of laws respecting women, of what Ginsburg herself as well as the other justices had said about the matter. The other clerks funneled their research to Beattie.

Ginsburg gave Beattie a one-and-a-half-page memo indicating how she wanted the opinion written. The justice drew on a capacious memory to provide guidelines and suggestions. "Did you look at footnote 16 in *Frontiero?*" she asked Beattie, referring to a *Harvard Law Review* article about women and the equal protection clause. She remembered that while preparing for that case she had read the work of a nineteenth-century Harvard Medical School doctor whose textbook on gender and education had gone through seventeen editions, and she advised Beattie to find it.[6] Beattie did, and a quote from it was included in the final opinion.

With an eye both to keeping Ginsburg's majority and to acknowledging the work already done, Beattie made an effort to supply language that other justices, particularly O'Connor and Kennedy, had used in the past. There would be quotes from both in the opinion. It would draw on Kennedy's language rather than the majority opinion in *J.E.B. v. Alabama,* the jury selection case.

To Ginsburg and Beattie, the case was simply about equality in public institutions. It was not about the future of single-sex schools, as Ginsburg's opinion would make clear. There would also be no mention of strict scrutiny. Ginsburg recognized that a strict standard could create difficulties for affirmative action, as it had in the area of race, and that strict scrutiny was no longer "fatal in fact"; it created a presumption of unconstitutionality, but that presumption could be overcome. More important, perhaps, she wanted as many justices as possible signing onto her opinion for the Court. She was concerned that attempting any formula other than the now-established "exceedingly persuasive justification" criterion would undercut that effort. In any event, Ginsburg believed in judicial restraint and in using the most conservative method by which to reach a decision, and she thought that VMI's admissions policy was unconstitutional under an intermediate standard.[7]

Beattie circulated each of her drafts to the other clerks before they went to Ginsburg. They were the only people with whom she could discuss her work. She spoke to no clerk in the other justices' chambers about it, and Court secrecy meant that she could not mention it to any outsiders. Even her mother did not know what the decision was until it was announced by the Court.[8]

Ginsburg wrote most of her opinion from scratch and substantially recast those parts of Beattie's drafts that did appeal to her. As she commented later, "I literally worried over every word in the opinion."[9] The first draft was printed in the Supreme Court's basement, as is the custom, and circulated to the other justices. Each of the justices was then free to suggest changes. "When Kennedy came in and said, 'It's a wonderful opinion; I have a few suggestions for you,'" Ginsburg recalled, "then I knew that I had a Court."[10] The draft already quoted his language in *J.E.B. v. Alabama*.

In fact, Ginsburg knew she had a Court when the opinion was first circulated, but collegiality is one of her hallmarks as a judge. And the other justices had "all kinds of suggestions." "People cared a lot about what the VMI opinion said," and as a result, "I think we went to fifteen drafts, adjusting it for this one and for that." Several drafts "had an ending that I loved but we changed it because Justice Kennedy didn't like it."[11]

One suggestion came from Justice Scalia, although he had no intention of changing his vote. Ginsburg had drawn on the language of Judge James Braxton Craven, Jr., who had written the opinion in the University of Virginia lawsuit. Craven referred there to "the University of Virginia at Charlottesville" and to "the Charlottesville campus."[12] When Ginsburg's draft was circulated, "We had some wonderful back and forth between me and Nino [Justice Scalia]: the footnote about the University of Virginia at Charlottesville. 'There is no University of Virginia at Charlottesville [Scalia noted]; there is *the* University of Virginia.' I put 'University of Virginia at Charlottesville' in quotes, attributing it to Judge Craven, but Scalia still left his footnote," saying in his dissent, "The Court, unfamiliar with the Commonwealth's policy of diverse and independent institutions, and in any event careless of state and local traditions, must be forgiven by Virginians for quoting a reference to '"the Charlottesville campus' of the University of Virginia."[13]

All the clerks in Scalia's chambers were involved in the writing of the dis-

sent. After oral argument and before the conference at which the justices
voted on a case, Scalia's practice was to sit down with his four clerks. The one
assigned to the case would present the issues, and then Scalia and the others would discuss them. He would not follow that custom if the case was a
highly procedural one, in which the other clerks would not have the requisite knowledge, but they all understood the issues and the relevant law in the
VMI case.[14]

There was some gloom in Scalia's chambers when Justice Rehnquist announced that he was changing his vote and would write a concurrence. Interestingly, the clerk who would work on the concurrence had been a member of the first class of women to graduate from VMI's neighbor Washington
and Lee and had clerked at the Fourth Circuit Court of Appeals in Richmond.
Scalia was furious at the loss of Rehnquist's vote and reserved some of the
most scathing language in his dissent for the concurrence. Ginsburg had no
idea why Rehnquist changed his mind,[15] but it must have been a pleasant
surprise to the lawyer who had once been unsuccessful in convincing him
that gender discrimination was unconstitutional.

Ginsburg had heard about the VMI case relatively early, and it immediately reminded her of *Vorchheimer v. School District,* the Philadelphia single-
sex public school case.[16] "To me, it was winning the *Vorchheimer* case twenty
years later. It never took me so long to win a case as the *Vorchheimer* case."[17]
Even though VMI was a military school and Philadelphia's Central (all male)
High School was not, the principle involved was the same. In many ways, the
opinion she wrote in *United States v. Virginia* was the one she would have
liked to have seen in *Vorchheimer*.

Kenneth Karst wrote about *Brown v. Board of Education,* "the whole fab-
ric of Jim Crow was the Court's target, but you would never know it to read
the opinion. . . . What the Court did not do, and almost never does, was to
explain how its decisions fit into a larger social and political context."[18] The
Court in *Brown* spoke of the equal protection clause but not of the newly acknowledged history of racial subordination that was the Court's real target
and that constituted the context in which the justices wrote. Ginsburg would
not follow that precedent. Anyone who read her opinion for the Court would
come away with an understanding of the historical context.

The opinion began by crediting VMI with succeeding in its "mission to
produce leaders," noting that VMI alumni "overwhelmingly perceive that
their VMI training helped them to realize their personal goals." The key word
of that formulation appears to be "perceive," because the question of whether

the adversative method actually accomplished more than the nonadversative methods used in the federal military academies was an open one. In any event, the opinion continued, "Neither the goal of producing citizen soldiers nor VMI's implementing methodology is inherently unsuitable to women."[19] Ginsburg was signaling her rejection of the Institute's assumption that men and women invariably learn differently and that the overcoming of adversity is somehow "manly" and "unwomanly."

Although Supreme Court decisions refer to lower court rulings in a case, there is no reason to reproduce every word of the opinions of the courts below. The parts that are chosen are indicative of what the Court considers important. Ginsburg repeated Kiser's finding that VMI would be able to "'achieve at least 10% female enrollment,'" which would constitute the requisite "'critical mass,'" and his use of *Hogan* as the controlling precedent. She noted that in the first appeal, the appellate court had determined that the relevant part of Virginia's educational policy was in the 1990 report of the Virginia Commission on the University of the 21st Century, which Ginsburg also reproduced: colleges and universities were to "'deal with faculty, staff, and students without regard to sex, race, or ethnic origin.'"[20]

The second court of appeals decision was treated less favorably. Ginsburg observed that the appellate court had decided to review the commonwealth's objective in creating VWIL "'deferentially,'" "'determined deferentially the legitimacy of Virginia's purpose,'" and "'deferentially reviewed the Commonwealth's proposal.'"[21] The clear message was that in dealing with gender discrimination, courts had no business being overly deferential to legislative intent, and that the substitution of "substantive comparability" for *Hogan*'s "exceedingly persuasive justification" standard was unwarranted. To emphasize the point, Ginsburg quoted approvingly from the dissents, indicating that Judges Phillips and Motz got it right when they stated that Virginia's motives were suspect and that VWIL did not offer women an educational opportunity equal to that at VMI.[22]

The first question for the Court was whether keeping women out of VMI violated the equal protection clause. To answer it, Ginsburg turned to "the core instruction of this Court's pathmarking decisions" in *J.E.B. v. Alabama* and *Hogan,* both of which relied on the "exceedingly persuasive justification" standard.[23] She traced the development of the standard back to *Reed v. Reed* and the Court's other gender discrimination cases of the 1970s, noting that the historical context of the problem at issue included denying women the right to vote, the right to control property independently of their husbands, and the right to equal employment opportunity: "Today's skeptical scrutiny of official action denying rights or opportunities based on sex responds to volumes of history." Justice Kennedy's concurrence in *J.E.B.*, stating that the Court's earlier cases had created "a strong presumption that gender classifications are invalid"; Justice O'Connor's language in *Hogan;* and Justice Stevens's *Califano v. Goldfarb* concurrence, condemning reliance on overly broad generalizations about the sexes, were also cited.[24]

"Skeptical scrutiny" sounds very much like "strict scrutiny," but Ginsburg quickly added that "the heightened review standard our precedent establishes does not make sex a proscribed classification," for while no "inherent differences" justified racial or ethnic discrimination, "physical differences between men and women . . . are enduring." Those differences "remain cause for celebration, but not for denigration of the members of either sex or for artificial constraints on an individual's opportunity." Sex classifications could no longer be used "to create or perpetuate the legal, social, and economic inferiority of women," although they were legitimate if they compensated women for past discrimination.[25] Courts had an obligation to assess "actual state purposes" behind classifications.[26]

Taken together, these sentences result in the establishment of a standard that builds on and extends *Hogan* without either using the language of strict scrutiny or closing the door to the possibility of affirmative action for women. As Ginsburg commented later, the line between strict scrutiny and intermediate scrutiny was now blurred.[27] "Skeptical scrutiny" describes the new doctrine well. The rule of *United States v. Virginia* is that courts must approach every case of gender discrimination with an awareness of history and the benign-sounding but ultimately pernicious justifications used in the past for treating women differently. Ginsburg's jurisprudence, as illustrated earlier, is firmly based in a societal context. Law is about real-life people in real-life situations.

One of the great contributions of early-twentieth-century jurists and legal thinkers such as Oliver Wendell Holmes, Louis Dembitz Brandeis, and Roscoe Pound was to retrieve law from the dustbin of dry legal precepts to which it had been consigned by the nineteenth century and bring it into the daylight of the real world. Law was legitimate, they taught, only as it reflected social realities. The question they asked was, what was really going on out there, and how could law best deal with it? That illuminated Ginsburg's approach to the law as an advocate and remained her hallmark as a judge. Law is instrumental; it exists in order to get something done, and that "something" must be judged by the human result.

The bottom line was that Virginia and VMI lost their case. The commonwealth's sudden interest in single-sex education—and Ginsburg, no opponent of single-sex education, pointed to the "reality" that "single sex education affords pedagogical benefits to at least some students"[28] —was placed firmly in the context of other governmental policies designed to deny educational opportunities to women. Virginia's record throughout the nineteenth and twentieth centuries was one of continued deliberate discrimination: "First, protection of women against higher education; next, schools for women far from equal in resources and stature to schools for men; finally, conversion of the separate schools to coeducation."[29] VMI's 1986 decision not to admit women, placed in that context, hardly suggested "any state policy evenhandedly to advance diverse educational options. . . . However 'liberally' this plan serves the State's sons, it makes no provision whatever for her daughters."[30]

Although Virginia was among the worst offenders, it was not alone in its attitude toward women; again, the entire historical context had to be considered. The infamous Dr. Edward H. Clarke of Harvard Medical School and his seventeen-edition *Sex in Education* was cited to show that medical "experts" of the late nineteenth century had warned solemnly that "the physiological effects of hard study and academic competition with boys would interfere with the development of girls' reproductive organs" and that "'identical education of the two sexes is a crime before God and humanity, that physiology protests against, and that experience weeps over.'"[31] The analogy to VMI's "experts" was obvious.

Women had been kept out of law, medicine, and, more recently, the police because the experts said that they would undermine male solidarity. "Women's successful entry into the federal military academies, and their participation in the Nation's military forces," Ginsburg added dryly, "indicate that Virginia's fears for the future of VMI may not be solidly grounded," and she referred to the brief of Rhonda Cornum and the other military women.[32]

As for the fear voiced by Virginia and the court of appeals that a coed adversative system "would destroy . . . any sense of decency that still permeates the relationship between the sexes," Ginsburg commented, "It is an ancient and familiar fear" that had been heard as a reason for preventing women from entering the brutal world of law. The Supreme Court of Wisconsin had written in 1875, "'Discussions are habitually necessary in courts of justice, which are unfit for female ears. The habitual presence of women at these would tend to relax the public sense of decency and propriety.'"[33] Seven decades earlier Thomas Jefferson had told a correspondent, "Were our State a pure democracy . . . there would yet be excluded from their deliberations . . . women, who, to prevent depravation of morals and ambiguity of issue, could not mix promiscuously in the public meetings of men."[34] Ginsburg cited both.

She used quotation marks to heap a kind of restrained scorn on Kiser's pseudoscientific but otherwise similar "'findings'" about "'gender based developmental differences.'" The Court had repeatedly "cautioned reviewing courts to take a 'hard look' at generalizations or 'tendencies' of the kind pressed by Virginia." "The notion that admission of women would downgrade VMI's stature, destroy the adversative system and, with it, even the school, is a judgment hardly proved." *Hogan* was cited again, as was a speech entitled "Portia's Progress" that Justice O'Connor had given at New York University, recounting the history of women in the law.[35] Referring to VMI's goal of producing citizen-soldiers, Ginsburg ended her discussion of equal protection: "Surely that goal is great enough to accommodate women, who today count as citizens in our American democracy equal in stature to men."[36]

The next question was whether creation of VWIL was a constitutionally acceptable alternative to admitting women to VMI. It was not, because it was not a military institute and it enrolled students with lower grades, offered fewer curricular choices, had a lower funding level and a less well-prepared faculty, and did not place graduates in the powerful VMI alumni network.[37] Tacitly agreeing with the government, Ginsburg returned to an argument she had first made for the Court two and a half decades earlier in *Reed v. Reed:* classifications based on sex were as invidious as those based on race.

> Virginia's VWIL solution is reminiscent of the remedy Texas proposed 50 years ago, in response to a state trial court's 1946 ruling that, given the equal protection guarantee, African Americans could not be denied a legal education at a state facility. Reluctant to admit African Americans to its flagship University of Texas Law School, the State set up a separate school for Heman Sweatt and other black law students. As originally opened, the new school had no independent faculty or library, and it lacked accreditation. . . . This Court contrasted resources at the new school with those at the school from which Sweatt had been excluded. . . .
>
> More important than the tangible features, the Court emphasized, are "those qualities which are incapable of objective measurement but which make for greatness" in a school, including "reputation of the faculty, experience of the administration, position and influence of the alumni, standing in the community, tradi-

tions and prestige." Facing the marked differences reported in the Sweatt opinion, the Court unanimously ruled that Texas had not shown "substantial equality in the [separate] educational opportunities" the State offered.[38]

The opinion then expanded on one of the things Ginsburg had fought against as a litigator: "generalizations about 'the way women are,'"[39] and the way Virginia had used them to support offering women only VWIL. Shannon Faulkner's lawyer in the Citadel case had written that the opposition had done its best to turn Faulkner into a "gender outlaw" rather than a "real" woman.[40] Now Ginsburg wrote for the Court that such generalizations about "what is appropriate for most women, no longer justify denying opportunity to women whose talent and capacity place them outside the average description." Rights, in other words, inhered in the individual, not in the group of which she was a part, whether or not generalizations about the group were correct.

Additionally, the commonwealth was disingenuous in claiming that VWIL had no military regimen because it "'is planned for women who do not necessarily expect to pursue military careers.' By that reasoning, VMI's "'entirely militaristic' program would be inappropriate for men in general or as a group, for 'only about 15% of VMI cadets enter career military service.'"[41] Indeed, if VMI was based on assumptions about "most" men, then it had no justification at all. "Notably, Virginia never asserted that VMI's method of education suits most men," Ginsburg pointed out, and as Judge Motz had observed, "'many men would not want to be educated in such an environment.'"[42]

Ginsburg was not anxious to condemn VWIL; indeed, as she said later, she "felt kind of bad" about the criticism of the VWIL program that was a necessary part of her opinion. "I didn't want to put a bad face on the place [Mary Baldwin] because they do have another program which I think is wonderful." She was referring to MBC's Program for the Exceptionally Gifted, which permits carefully chosen young women to begin college anytime after the eighth grade.[43] But, as the decision concluded, "Valuable as VWIL may prove for students who seek the program offered, Virginia's remedy affords no cure at all for the opportunities and advantages withheld from women who want a VMI education and can make the grade."[44]

A prime part of the history of our Constitution, historian Richard Morris recounted, is the story of the extension of constitutional rights and protections to people once ignored or excluded. VMI's story continued as our comprehension of "We the People" expanded. There is no reason to believe that the admission of women capable of all the activities required of VMI cadets would destroy the Institute rather than enhance its capacity to serve the "more perfect Union."[45]

By situating the VMI case in its historical context, Ginsburg had eliminated the "gender outlaw" argument while using a Court opinion as an educational tool. Taken out of context, the VMI litigation might be seen as no
more than an attempt by unfeminine women to do something bizarre. After
all, as Judith Keith's colleagues had asked her, why would any woman want
to go to VMI? Placed in the framework of a society with a centuries-long history of underestimating women and then forbidding them to prove themselves, the dispute became simply one more instance of unwarranted discrimination. Even a younger David Riesman had agreed with the historical
analysis of gender relations. "The all-male college would be relatively easy to
defend if it emerged from a world in which women were established as fully
equal to men," he and Christopher Jencks had written in 1968, in a passage
quoted by Ginsburg. "But it does not. It is therefore likely to be a witting or
unwitting device for preserving tacit assumptions of male superiority—assumptions for which women must eventually pay."[46]

CHIEF JUSTICE REHNQUIST'S CONCURRENCE criticized what
he saw as the Court's introduction of "an element of uncertainty" about the
appropriate test in gender discrimination cases. He considered the intermediate standard set down in *Craig v. Boren* ("classifications by gender must
serve important governmental objectives and must be substantially related to
achievement of those objectives")[47] to be sufficient, and he expressed his inability to determine the "content and specificity" of the "exceedingly persuasive justification" standard.[48] Applying the *Craig v. Boren* test, he agreed
that Virginia's real goal in keeping VMI all male was not diversity, that VWIL
was not comparable to VMI, and that there was nothing in the record to show
that "an adversative method is pedagogically beneficial or is any more likely
to produce character traits than other methodologies."[49] As the method was
not necessary to fulfill VMI's mission, any changes in it that resulted from the
admission of women were of no constitutional significance.

His opinion differed from the Court's in two other major ways. First, he
thought that VMI had had insufficient notice before *Hogan* that its admissions policies were suspect, and he therefore would have limited the Court's
examination of the Institute's policies to the years after that decision had
been handed down. During that time, he noted, Virginia had done nothing to
provide women with the kind of equal education required by the rule in
Hogan: "Had the Commonwealth provided the kind of support for the private

women's schools that it provides for VMI, this may have been a very different case."[50]

Second, Rehnquist disagreed with the implication of the majority decision that VMI would have to admit women, believing that "it would be a sufficient remedy . . . if the two institutions offered the same quality of education and were of the same overall calibre." But he saw no possibility of VWIL being other than inferior to VMI "for the foreseeable future."[51]

Two passages refer specifically to negative statements about Rehnquist's opinion that appear in Justice Scalia's dissent. These can only be read as reflecting a dialogue between the two men[52]—albeit a hostile one, conducted through the medium of print. (As noted earlier, draft opinions are circulated to all members of the Court, so they can refer to one another's language in their final versions.) Scalia labeled Rehnquist's terminology "imprecise," his evaluation of the evidence "simply wrong," and his reasoning "a great puzzlement."[53] Scalia was angry at Rehnquist's withdrawal of his vote, Rehnquist was angry at the accusations in Scalia's opinion, and Scalia was angry at the chief justice's replies. In fact, judging from his forty-page dissent, Scalia was both extremely angry about and frustrated by the direction the Court was taking.

His ire was obvious from his first sentence, which was patently incorrect: "Today the Court shuts down an institution that has served the people of the Commonwealth of Virginia with pride and distinction for over a century and a half."[54] The decision, of course, did not shut down VMI; presumably Scalia meant that VMI would have to change, and he was not happy about that. He went on to accuse the majority of being "closed minded," "self righteous," "smug," "illiberal," antidemocratic, and dismissive of both Court precedents and American history.[55]

Scalia's dismay began with the majority's approach to the equal protection clause, which, he charged, "regards this Court as free to evaluate everything under the sun" by applying the rational relation, intermediate scrutiny, or strict scrutiny standard. The tests were "no more scientific than their names suggest," and the uncertainty was compounded by the Court's being able to pick whichever it liked for application to a particular case.[56] He was firmly opposed to "the Court's ability to invent degrees of proof." "What," he asked elsewhere, "gives the Court the power to do this? It is a con job," which results in the Court's saying that "this case requires 25 percent proof but that one, 50 percent." As there was only one equal protection clause, so there should be only one standard: rational basis.[57]

Although Scalia recognized that abstract tests "are essential" to evaluating whether the equal protection clause had been breached, "whatever abstract tests we may choose to devise, they cannot supersede—and indeed ought to be crafted so as to reflect—those constant and unbroken national traditions that embody the people's understanding of ambiguous constitutional texts."[58]

The justice had appointed himself the Court's guardian of American traditions soon after he reached the Court in 1986. He did not recognize a constitutional basis for the right to an abortion, to refuse life-prolonging treatment, or to be treated equally whatever one's sexual orientation.[59] "Tradition," to Scalia, stopped early in the twentieth century. The judicial role did not encompass protection of previously or currently disadvantaged groups when such groups' claims ran counter to long-enshrined majority beliefs. If a later generation rejected the traditions that were firmly in place at the time of adoption of the Fourteenth Amendment, it could direct the legislature to enact the new values into law.[60]

The tradition immediately at issue was "having government funded military schools for men," and although it was appropriate for "the people" to alter whatever tradition they liked "through democratic processes," it was not proper for the Court to preempt them by announcing that women had to be admitted to military colleges. VMI had been in existence and all male "for 200 years." "Who are the judges to say no?"[61]

Like VMI, Scalia thought that the case was about not gender equality but single-sex education, another American tradition. He read the majority opinion as eliminating it and chastised, "This is not the interpretation of a Constitution, but the creation of one."[62] There was no reasonable basis for saying that the Fourteenth Amendment extended special protection to sex.[63] In addition to misreading the Constitution, the Court was ignoring the evidence about developmental differences—"How remarkable to criticize the District Court on the ground that its findings rest on the evidence"—in favor of reliance on "a judge who merely dissented from the Court of Appeals' decision," irrelevant amicus curiae briefs, "various historical anecdotes designed to demonstrate that Virginia's support for VMI as currently constituted reminds the Justices of the 'bad old days,'" and "the Justices' own view of the world."[64]

Adopting VMI's line of reasoning, Scalia argued that a state with limited resources could "select among the available options," including that of providing single-sex education only to men. Women, he said, were already more than adequately served by the commonwealth's four private women's colleges, where Virginia residents were eligible for tuition assistance, scholarship grants, guaranteed loans, and work-study funds.[65]

Some of Scalia's most biting prose was reserved for Rehnquist's concurrence, "which finds VMI unconstitutional on a basis that is more moderate than the Court's but only at the expense of being even more implausible." What Rehnquist and the majority failed to see, he thought, was that "under the constitutional principles announced and applied today, single sex public education is unconstitutional . . . the Court indicates that if any program restricted to one sex is 'unique,' it must be opened to members of the opposite sex 'who have the will and capacity' to participate in it. I suggest that the single sex program that will not be capable of being characterized as 'unique' is not only unique but nonexistent." The high cost of potential litigation would keep public school officials from initiating or maintaining single-sex education: "single sex public education is functionally dead."[66]

Finally, quoting from the VMI "Code of a Gentleman," Scalia concluded, "I do not know whether the men of VMI lived by this code; perhaps not. But it is powerfully impressive that a public institution of higher education still in existence sought to have them do so. I do not think any of us, women included, will be better off for its destruction."[67]

SCALIA WAS RIGHT ABOUT ONE THING: the Court was reading its own values into the equal protection clause. Its values, however, paralleled those of a large part of the country, although not those of the minority who were on the other side of the culture wars and whom Scalia represented so eloquently. As noted earlier, the clause leaves open the meaning of the word "equal." The majority accepted the idea of a living Constitution designed to be sufficiently open-ended to embody the basic beliefs and needs of "We the People" at any given moment. Scalia relied on a jurisprudence known as "original intent," which holds that the courts are bound by the ideas of the people who wrote the phrases they interpret.

Women were not considered equal when the Fourteenth Amendment was ratified in 1868. Scalia was therefore correct in saying that, as written, it provided them with no protection. The Court had been holding since 1971 and *Reed v. Reed,* however, that the values of the people in the late twentieth century included at least a modicum of gender equality. If the actions of the country's elected representatives were any guide to the meaning the people wished to give to their Constitution, the passage of the 1964 Civil Rights Act, the 1972 Education Amendments (Title IX), and other legislative and executive actions indicated that gender equality had become a firm part of the American ideology. VMI and Justice Scalia had lost the culture wars. The new "tradition" of gender equality was now firmly entrenched—even at the Supreme Court.

That was clear from a dramatic moment on June 26, 1996, when Ruth Bader Ginsburg read parts of her opinion in *United States v. Virginia*—technically the Court's opinion, but most definitely hers—to a packed courtroom. She spoke in what one journalist described as "slow, firm tones,"[68] and the first time she mentioned the *Hogan* case, "she lifted her eyes from the memo she was reading and gazed for a moment at Justice O'Connor. With just the barest hint of a smile, Justice O'Connor stared straight ahead."[69]

THE FACT THAT THERE WERE two women on the Court, both of whom had had difficulty getting jobs when they graduated from law school, and that Ginsburg had written the majority opinion certainly shaped the Court's holding. As legal scholar Mark Tushnet commented about the case, "'This is Ruth Bader Ginsburg's vindication for her legal career. . . . This is the opinion she had hoped the Court would one day arrive at when she first started arguing cases of discrimination in the 1960s.'"[70]

Decision day was heady for others as well. "The Supreme Court overwhelmingly has given life to the promise in the Constitution that all of us deserve an equal shot at educational opportunity," Attorney General Janet Reno stated.[71] "This is a great win for women," Marcia Greenberger exulted.[72] Judith Lichtman, president of the Women's Legal Defense Fund, called the decision "a tremendous and historic victory for women because it unequivocally outlaws the use of gender-based stereotypes," and Janet Gallagher, one of Ginsburg's successors as director of the WRP, commented that it made "the Constitution's guarantee of equality real for women because it toughens significantly the standard of review" in sex discrimination cases.[73]

The nation's press backed the Supreme Court's decision and told their readers that they should, too. "The Supreme Court, on solid legal grounds, ended a century and a half of all-male tradition at the Virginia Military Institute,"[74] the *Houston Chronicle* reported. "The ruling was right on target," the *San Francisco Chronicle* commented, adding that the decision "was narrowly focused and did not discount the appropriateness of all single sex education."[75] "The admission of women to VMI is a victory for equality, not 'political correctness,'"[76] declared the *Chattanooga Times*. Referring to both VMI and The Citadel, the *Phoenix Gazette* chided, "Not since Alabama Gov. George Wallace stood in the schoolhouse door to block the admission of black students to the University of Alabama, have two state-funded universities exerted so much effort to pursue a discriminatory course."[77]

Even closer to VMI's home, the *Roanoke Times* scolded that "the millions spent by VMI's private foundations in fighting the coeducation lawsuit would have been better spent improving VMI" and that the Institute "should have welcomed women and invested those millions in curriculum, with the idea of enhancing Marshall's legacy."[78]

To Robert Patterson, however, the opinion was "a great tragedy."[79] He was "'shocked" that Ginsburg wrote the opinion. "Anyone who could conclude that she would have viewed this matter objectively would be clearly erroneous in my judgment,'" he told the media.[80] Bunting called the decision "a killer. . . . You have no idea how much of myself I have thrown into this for six or seven years, how terribly I wanted to avoid this result."[81] But, he added, "the institute teaches respect for duly constituted authority, and we shall discharge our responsibilities under the court's order."[82] He nonetheless noted correctly, "Many alumni will be heartbroken when they hear it."[83] Whether they would triumph in their desire to "save" the all-male Institute by taking it private remained to be seen.[84]

In 1997, after the Supreme Court decision and the transition year: female rat memorizing the *Rat Bible*. Andrew R. Alonso.

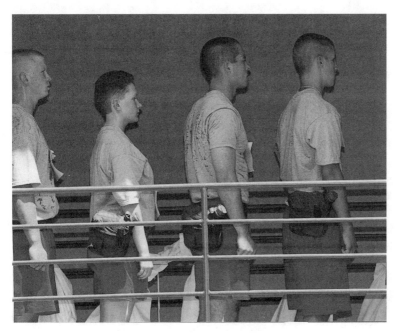

Coed rats. Nathan Beck.

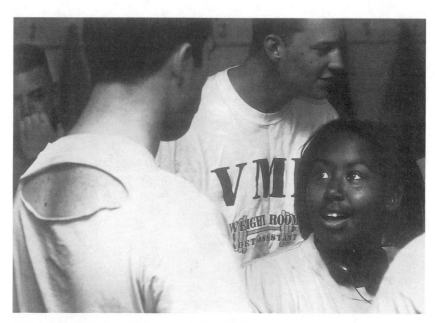

Rats no longer: in the weight room. Andrew R. Alonso.

Dressed for parade. Sam Dean, *Roanoke Times and World News*.

Training in fatigues. Andrew R. Alonso.

In fatigues. Andrew R. Alonso.

In formation. Andrew R. Alonso.

After the first year: woman upperclass cadet instructing male rats. Nathan Beck.

Erin Claunch and other cadets with the horse formation revived by Claunch. Sam Dean, *Roanoke Times and World News.*

Claunch and roommate studying for finals before graduation. Sam Dean, *Roanoke Times and World News.*

On the way to graduation 2001. Sam Dean, *Roanoke Times and World News*.

At graduation. Sam Dean, *Roanoke Times and World News*.

Bringing Women into the Choir

> When you are given a lawful order, you must execute it.
>
> Professionals may not allow their resentments to affect
>
> their work.
>
> —Josiah Bunting

A few days before *United States v. Virginia* was argued at the Supreme Court, Josiah Bunting told the media that admitting women to VMI "would be like bringing women into an all-male choir. We could still produce beautiful music, but quite different music."[1] But that music would never be heard at VMI, he implied the following month, stating that in only ten telephone calls to wealthy alumni he would be able to raise the $150 million to $200 million necessary to turn VMI into a private college.[2]

Bunting was in Canada giving a speech about the value of all-male schools when the decision was handed down. He found out about it as he was leaving the podium and was handed a note saying, "Too bad."[3] Although he made no secret of his disappointment at the news conference he held that afternoon, he called the prospect of VMI going private "very problematical" and added, "I must discourage speculation about that."[4] The braggadocio that was possible when VMI's lawyers were predicting victory had begun to dissipate in the harsh light of fiscal realities.

Technically, the Supreme Court returned the case to the lower courts, which would have the task of overseeing whatever decision VMI made. The state had the option of closing VMI down or permitting it to be privatized by the Board of Visitors or some other entity. That was why Governor George Allen could tell the press that "the nation's highest court has spoken, and we need to bring Virginia into compliance," without specifying what form that compliance would take.[5]

In reality, however, the handwriting was not only on the wall; it might as well have been posted on great billboards around VMI. Bunting had estimated that a private VMI, deprived of $9 million to $10 million a year from the state, would have to double its over $90 million endowment.[6] The Virginia Division of Risk Management assessed the value of VMI's land, eighty-one buildings, and their contents, currently owned by the state, at $175 million.[7]

The alumni had already kicked in more than $14 million for legal fees, public relations, and payments to VWIL—over $6 million to Patterson's firm and other lawyers alone[8]—but even their deep pockets could be stretched only so far. Two days after the Supreme Court ruling, Bunting commented, "I'm very conscious of what we have to do when the dust settles: to admit women, or to raise 10 zillion dollars and keep it all male."[9]

There were problems with privatization that went beyond dollars. Would the Department of Defense allow an ROTC program to continue at a college that the Supreme Court said was discriminating against women? Would the Justice Department regard privatization as an end run around the decision and mount a legal challenge against it?

The Citadel suggested the answer when, two days after the Court spoke, it announced that it would begin accepting female applicants. "There wasn't a lot of wiggle room in that decision," a Citadel spokesman commented. "It was 7–1. The only thing to do is turn to and march."[10] This led the Greensboro, North Carolina, *Record* to ask, "If The Citadel Can Do It, Why Can't VMI as Well?"[11] Bunting reported that the VMI Board of Visitors would meet in mid-July to consider its options.[12]

In fact, Bunting was maneuvering between a rock and a hard place. He knew that VMI would soon welcome female cadets, even though the advocates of privatization had to be given a hearing if the transition was to take place without damage to the Institute. Shortly after the Supreme Court decision was handed down, he held a meeting on the post to consider how to handle planning for gender integration, and the *Roanoke Times* reported that "in his 'heart of hearts,' he thinks VMI ultimately will go coed."[13] But the more vocal alumni, who were also active in making sure VMI stayed afloat financially and who played a major role in recruiting new students, were still determined to keep women out of VMI. They had to be convinced that the Institute was not beating a dishonorable retreat.

The board of the VMI Alumni Association met in Richmond on June 30 and voted to recommend a fund-raising drive for privatization but to hold off on implementation until it received approval from the Board of Visitors. Some alumni, such as association president Edwin Cox III, whose great-grandfather, father, and three sons had attended the Institute, were adamant about going private.[14] Others were more realistic. A few days later, board president William W. Berry told the *Richmond Times-Dispatch*, "Most people I've talked to say that if we're going to have to admit women, let's do it in the VMI way. In other words, let's do a hell of a good job." Aware that VMI's slow pace was being compared with the quick response of The Citadel, Bunting added, "It's not heel-dragging. This is a bunch of guys trying to come to grips with a topic that threatens something very close to their hearts."[15]

It was the discussion of privatization that got the headlines, however, and exacerbated the already substantial lack of trust that existed between the Institute on the one hand and the Justice Department and its allies on the other. Judith Lichtman, president of the Women's Legal Defense Fund, protested that VMI "seems to be devising methods so they can honor this court order in the breach."[16] Kent Willis, executive director of the ACLU's Virginia affiliate, agreed that VMI was stalling: "Among traditional Virginians, there's this secessionist notion that if they dig their trenches deep enough, the feds will go away."[17] Former attorney general Richard Thornburgh, who had presided over the Justice Department's early involvement in the case, said that although he understood the alumni's feelings about the Institute, "When those run up against the Constitution, it's the feelings, and not the Constitution, that has to give."[18]

Bunting was attempting to reassure the alumni with statements that VMI would not alter its standards if women were admitted, and Berry acknowledged that "a very small segment of alumni" were telling him, "'Shave her head. Put her in a rat line. She won't last long.'"[19] Marcia Greenberger was prompted to warn, "Arbitrary physical standards that are designed to keep VMI closed to women could be in conflict with both the letter and spirit of the Supreme Court decision."[20] Berry characterized the alumni's comments as, "that's emotion talking, not logic."[21] And Bunting lamented that the college's reaction was being misunderstood. The regularly scheduled meeting of the Board of Visitors would take place in mid-September, he noted, and "members of the VMI family—as well as our critics and enemies and friends—are quite properly using the interlude to express their opinion." He lambasted the "culture of Washington and New York" that "sees VMI as brutal, anachronistic, reactionary. They have it wrong. We're really nothing of the kind. This is a place of dignity and honor."[22]

In mid-July the seventeen-member Board of Visitors met on the post for the better part of three days and voted unanimously to develop a provisional plan for gender integration but turned down a plea by one of its members to put the formal imprimatur on admitting women. Bunting said that he would prepare an integration plan for the board's interim session on July 30. The final decision would not be made until the September meeting, which would give the alumni two months to come up with a privatization formula if they chose to do so. Bunting defended the slow pace: "The issue of co-education is not a simple one, and its implementation will require careful planning in order to serve the best interests of Virginia's young men and young women." He wanted time to consult with other formerly all-male colleges, including the federal academies and institutions in Virginia, so as to decide how to use "VMI's legacy . . . as a means of ensuring that young women would have the same kind of opportunities as young men."[23]

Journalists noted that there seemed to be a growing rift between the Board of Visitors and the alumni organizations.[24] Planning for the admission of women continued on July 30, when the Board of Visitors held a closed-door meeting at which it heard not only from Bunting but also from Major Rebecca Ray, a specialist on gender integration who had helped smooth the path when Texas A&M University admitted women to its cadet corps.[25]

There were nonetheless reasons for outsiders to suspect VMI of continued resistance. The alumni organizations were still intent on raising funds for privatization. The Board of Visitors meeting was closed to the public. A suspicious Justice Department feared that VMI would skew the results of any meetings it had with the service academies to justify maintaining its men-only policy, as had been the case back in 1986. The Department sent VMI's attorneys a demand that it be given an explanation of any contacts with officials or cadets at the academies or with the Department of Defense and that any future contacts be cleared ahead of time with the Justice Department. VMI officials, knowing that a carefully thought out campaign was being mounted to pave the way for gender integration without losing alumni support, were outraged. "The Justice Department appears to believe that [VMI] is incapable of producing a good-faith effort to comply with the laws of the United States," Bunting complained, but his plan was not at all evident to those who had reason to be wary of VMI's motives.[26]

On September 10, the Justice Department filed an emergency motion with the court of appeals, saying that VMI was "continuing business as usual in the face of the SC's decision" and demanding that it begin admitting women immediately. Assistant State Attorney General William Hurd replied that the federal government was trying to "hound and harass" the Institute.[27] On the same day, VMI's director of admissions sent a letter to Lauren Ashley Wagner, the daughter of attorney Eileen Wagner. Lauren, a Virginia high school senior, seemed a logical candidate for a coed VMI. She had sent the Institute a picture of herself in her Civil Air Patrol uniform posed in front of her helicopter, along with a request for an application. The admissions office hedged carefully, saying that its policy was currently under review. It would be "in touch with you in the near future regarding our admission procedures," it added, and gave her a toll-free telephone number if she had any questions.[28]

While the Justice Department's motion was pending and the Wagner family and others waited to see which way VMI would go, the Board of Visitors gathered on September 18 for four days of meetings. Board president Berry said that his mail was running "very close to 50–50, with privatization slightly ahead"[29] —a clear indication that the alumni's reaction was not as monolithic as the media portrayed it. The board's initial session, scheduled for three hours, lasted more than seven. Bunting reported on the progress of a committee he had put together to review every aspect of cadet life, in preparation for gender integration. "This is one of those subjects in which God is in the details," he warned, urging the board to take the time to do it right. "Do not each one of these little plans—where you're going to house them, how you're going to admit the women, physical training requirements—represent some particular evidence of good faith, goodwill and a willingness to really do it right?"[30]

Part of the board's time was allocated for public comment, and twenty-three speakers presented their thoughts. Only three argued against privatization; others, both speakers and audience, wore "Go Private" buttons. A survey of 1,000 alumni conducted by phone and mail had shown overwhelming support for going private. Those who spoke pledged their contributions. Bunting charged that alumni sentiment was in part a response to the Justice Department's motion in the Fourth Circuit for immediate admission and its insistence on monitoring VMI's contacts with the academies. "They must really think we're a bunch of redneck reactionaries who really hate them," he complained.[31] He was quite right.

But at the end of the meeting on September 21, the board voted to admit women. Bunting pledged that the changes to VMI would be minimal. Ginsburg's opinion, Bunting noted, "says some women have the will and the capacity to succeed in the training and attendant opportunities that VMI uniquely affords," and Berry added, "We are going to take her at her word."[32] A request from the alumni for another year in which to negotiate with the state about privatization was turned down.[33]

The vote was nine to eight.[34] Berry told the press that the dividing line seemed to be somewhere around the class of 1970, with earlier graduates voting for gender integration and more recent alumni favoring privatization. The two women on the board split. Anita Blair, the Independent Women's Forum leader who had submitted a Supreme Court brief on behalf of VMI, was against admitting women; Anne C. Woodfin, the head of a Richmond company whose husband and son were VMI alumni, was for it, reluctantly. (Woodfin later helped in the transition planning.) Robert C. Bobb, the African American Richmond city manager who had asked the board in mid-July to vote immediately for gender integration, said that he would have preferred VMI to remain all male but had to cast his ballot for the law and for equality. Some of the board members left the room with tears in their eyes. Bunting blamed Justice Department maneuvering and anti-Department sentiment for the closeness of the vote.[35]

Virginia officials were full of praise, with Governor George Allen, Lieutenant Governor Donald S. Beyer, and Attorney General James S. Gilmore III leading the chorus.[36] Others were more cautious. State senator Janet D. Howell was pleased that VMI had "entered the 20th century." But "we will be watching them very closely to see if it works for the women who enter," she warned. Bunting stated on NBC's *Today* that "the message we want to send to young women is that we are here as we are. If you choose to meet this challenge, you will be given the same help, the same support, but also the same difficulties that we put in front of young men." Ann MacLean Massie, a Washington and Lee University law professor, commented that VMI officials "came across as caving in, not liking it, and almost defiantly throwing out what amounted to a dare of, 'No, we're not going to change a thing, let's see how they really like it.'"[37] Assistant Attorney General Deval Patrick commented dryly that "after six years of litigation" and many years of gender integration at the service academies, "we are gratified that women will now be able to benefit from the unique educational opportunities that VMI has long offered to men." He too cautioned that the Justice Department would "work with school officials to ensure that women are successfully integrated into VMI."[38] Emily McCoy, an official of the Virginia chapter of NOW, approved of the Justice Department's caution. "It's important that they be closely watched, because there is clearly a hostility toward women," she said. "They need extra scrutiny."[39]

Bunting did not think so. "There are a lot of very bright people here determined to do things as well as they can be done, and who, in the old-fashioned sense of the word, are kind of liberal and open-minded," he said, reflecting his own military-style commitment to carrying out orders.[40] "When you are given a lawful order, you must execute it. Professionals may not allow their resentments to affect their work."[41] Acknowledging his past opposition to admitting women, he pledged to fight "with the same efficiency, and with elegance" to make the transition a smooth one,[42] promising that "none of the individual women will be made to feel any more unwelcome than any of the young men."[43]

VMI promptly mailed applications to high school seniors such as Lauren Wagner who had requested them after the Supreme Court decision.[44] But it was already September, and VMI's academic year, like most others, was well under way. Admission of women would not begin until the 1997–1998 school year. Bunting was convinced that it would take that long to plan well, and he was not about to invite the Justice Department to participate in the process. By the time of the Board of Visitors' vote, the court of appeals had sent the case back to Judge Kiser for supervision.[45] Bunting announced that he hoped to avoid having to give Kiser a formal plan rather than a "document that says we will comply with the Supreme Court order and admit women in 1997. Trust us," he advised, "we will do it—we're not going to give you a plan."[46]

That was the kind of language certain to raise Justice Department hackles. The Department had gotten the South Carolina district court to back up its requests to The Citadel, which had admitted women in the fall of 1996, for documentation about recruitment policies, housing, participation in extracurricular activities, scholarships, numbers of male and female faculty, and so on.[47] Now the Department asked Kiser to order VMI to provide it with an integration plan. VMI resisted. "When the Citadel submitted its 57-point plan," spokesman Mike Strickler said, "they immediately started taking potshots at it. They wanted a detailed plan from us of everything we were doing. If they wanted that, you gotta believe if there's something they don't like, they'll want it changed."[48] In a reply to a Justice Department request for information, Virginia Assistant Attorney General Maureen Riley Matsen suggested that if the Department wanted details about the Institute's application process, it could check out its Web site.[49]

Bunting continued to insist that women would have to meet the same standards, including physical requirements and buzz cuts, as men. When reporters asked if he expected that kind of treatment to land the Institute back in court, he replied tersely, "I do. . . . We expect the criticism and we welcome it, and we're ready to deal with it."[50]

The criticism came quickly. Lawyers on the other side, noting that The Citadel permitted women longer haircuts than men and had adopted a modified set of physical requirements for them, called Bunting's comments a thinly veiled warning to women to stay away. University of Virginia law professor Mary Anne Case remarked, "Their motive is not an egalitarian one, it is an exclusionary one. VMI is still re-fighting its own bizarre version of the Civil War here." Val Vojdik, Shannon Faulkner's lawyer, called VMI's position on physical education requirements similar to the massive resistance to racial integration forty years earlier. "The myth of total equality is just an excuse to exclude women, just as it was to exclude blacks."[51] Karen Johnson, a retired air force colonel who was vice president of NOW, called VMI "poor losers" and added, "The haircut is just a way of being vindictive. In Nazi Germany, they shaved the heads of female prisoners to shame them."[52]

The language was strong; so were the emotions. The two sides had had six years in which to learn not to trust each other. The Justice Department trial-level attorneys who had dealt closely with VMI were particularly skeptical of its intentions and wanted a tight watch kept on the implementation process. Michael Maurer thought that the burden was on VMI to show that women were welcome and that all vestiges of discrimination had been eliminated. That was the standard for race cases; that was the standard for gender cases. Marcia Greenberger worried about foot-dragging on VMI's part and what she expected to be Kiser's ignoring of it. Like the attorneys in the Justice Department's appellate division, she was willing to give VMI a planning year before women appeared on the post, but she had a "high degree of skepticism" about the purposes to which that year would be put.[53] Bunting accused the Justice Department of "an unwillingness which is unbecoming and in my view unworthy and certainly illiberal on their part to engage as colleagues concerned with a common enterprise in these issues," along with an "unwillingness to engage—to want to know how things work—'Yes, that's a good point; let us see if we can do this'—that kind of thing: the imputation of good will to one's adversaries."[54] But VMI still refused to turn over the kind of basic information about transition planning that would have been needed if the process was to become a "common enterprise."

Bunting appointed Mike Bissell, the commandant of cadets, to oversee the planning process. Bissell had also been serving as the commandant of VWIL, coordinating the two colleges' programs. Now he became chair of an executive committee made up of seven subcommittee heads, seven cadets, and a few specialists that met once a week all year (the subcommittees met separately, and frequently). Each subcommittee consisted of eighteen to twenty faculty, staff, alumni, and cadets. Together, they covered recruiting, facilities, academics, athletics, orientation, public relations, and co-curricular activities. Bissell shared Bunting's belief that cadets were the key to successful integration and insisted that a cross selection of them be involved; in one way or another, over 100 were.[55]

The range of problems studied by the committees would be legion, but perhaps the enormity of the cultural engineering that was being attempted was best reflected in the matter of language. There was, first of all, the question of what the new cadets would be called: "girls"? "females"? "ladies"? The fact that "women" was not the immediate and obvious choice is indicative of VMI's mind-set. Then there was the distaste for describing the committees' goal as "coeducation." "Integration" carried too much political baggage; the winner was "assimilation." Bissell's lair was dubbed the "Assimilation Office."[56]

The word was a dead give-away. Mary Anne Case commented that throughout the litigation, there had been an unspoken assumption of the "correctness of a masculine male standard," and the only question being asked was "whether women could fit it, not whether it was an appropriate standard for either sex."[57] Now, with Bunting insisting that nothing basic at VMI would change, the problem was posed as how to squeeze women into a male institution, and the opportunity to either revisit VMI's basic assumptions or reconstruct a military college equally geared to both sexes was lost.

Female applicants were telling VMI that they chose the Institute in order to test themselves against all its rigors, and they did not want changes made just because women were coming. They were seeking the rat line, breakout, and all the other hurdles that constituted so much of the VMI ethos. So were the young men who would apply in ever-increasing numbers, perhaps because all the publicity brought VMI to the attention of high school students who otherwise might not have known about it. From the point of view of the applicants' desires, VMI was doing the right thing by refusing to change.

Colleges have never constructed themselves solely or even primarily on the basis of student wishes, however. Instead, they have been geared toward a specific mission and have assumed that faculty and administrators were there because they knew what a college should be. Sufficient questions had been raised during the long litigation about the connection between VMI's goal of producing leaders and the training methodology it employed. Since the federal military academies had given up their versions of the adversative method but continued to function successfully, and since the overwhelming majority of VMI graduates went into civilian rather than military life, might the time be right to undertake the periodic review of practices that wise institutions engage in?

VMI was not interested in questions about its methods. What mattered was how women could fit into VMI life as it already was. There would be no reexamination of basic assumptions. Had they been revisited, those assumptions might well have been reconfirmed, or they might have been altered, but VMI presumably would have emerged as stronger and more secure at the end of the self-examination process. That, however, did not occur.

IT WAS DECIDED THAT the female cadets would be referred to as "brother rats." The word "dyke" would continue to be used for the reciprocal rat-upperclassman relationship. But the gender-specific profanity etched by generations of cadets into the classrooms' wooden desks would be sanded away. References to "men" in official college publications would be changed into the neutral "cadets" or "students" or enhanced with "and women." After consideration of adding a new wing for women, a consensus was reached on housing them in the existing Barracks. Shades would be added to the doors; regulations would forbid their being pulled down except when someone was dressing. There would still be no locks on the doors, but security lighting and emergency call boxes connected to the local police were installed around the post. Women would get their own locker and shower facilities in the physical education building, and for the first time, the post hospital would have private rather than mass examining rooms.

The media focused on the question of bathrooms, and so did some of the planners. Would the new women's toilets have stalls? The decision was that they would, but then the question of showers arose. Would women have the same kind of communal showers as the men? The matter of feminine hygiene seems to have been excruciatingly painful for some involved in the planning process. There was talk about "blood pathogens" and "special hygienic needs" and the perceived inability of women to clean themselves properly in the company of others, with the fearsome specter of menstruation lurking in the background.[58] Women would have individual shower rooms.

It said something about the perception of woman as "other" that VMI saw nothing inconsistent about treating women exactly like men when it came to academics and physical education but shied away from similar treatment when intimate details of the female body were involved. The planners focused on whether they would be acting unfairly by treating women as if their bodies were quite as normal as men's, without asking themselves if young women were any more or less embarrassed or free with their bodies than their adolescent male counterparts, or why a lack of bathroom privacy was considered both necessary to male bonding and unacceptable for females. Although the post hospital would now have private examining rooms, there was no suggestion that VMI's ability to train leaders would be impaired as a result. If that was true, what became of the assumption that the least possible amount of privacy was crucial to its methodology, even for men?

Yet VMI was able to break through stereotypes and old preconceptions in other ways. The difference between VMI's physical training demands—the minimum necessary to get a grade of D in the Institute's physical fitness test—and those of the service academies can be summarized as follows:

	Push-ups	Sit-ups	Run
West Point:			
Men	42 in 1 min.	52 in 2 min.	2 mi. in 15:54 min.
Women	18 in 2 min.	50 in 2 min.	2 mi. in 18:54 min.
Academy:			
Men	40 in 2 min.	65 in 2 min.	$1\frac{1}{2}$ mi. in 10:30 min.
Women	18 in 2 min.	65 in 2 min.	$1\frac{1}{2}$ mi. in 12:40 min.
Air Force Academy:			
Men	24 in 2 min.	49 in 2 min.	300 yd. in 1:05 min.
Women	9 in 2 min.	46 in 2 min.	300 yd. in 1:19 min.
VMI:			
Men	None	60 in 2 min. (+ 5 pull-ups)	$1\frac{1}{2}$ mi. in 12:00 min.[59]

After consulting with Washington and Lee's female assistant director of athletics and three female cadets from the cadet corps of Texas A&M University, among others, the final decision was made to hold men and women at VMI to the same physical standards.[60] Again, unlike the service academies, the Institute would require women to participate in boxing and wrestling as the men did, although the sexes would be separated for those activities. VMI had decided to operate on the assumption that VMI women could match VMI men athletically as well as academically.

Agonized attention was given to questions of clothing and jewelry. An institution that both regulates every aspect of a student's life and attempts to do so fairly must make its standards clear. That requires a lot of regulations. No jewelry would be permitted until after breakout, but then modest earrings could be worn. Female rats could wear colorless nail polish and "noneccentric" lipstick for formal occasions, and female cadets could do so at any time after the rat line ended. The skirts they would be supplied with for social occasions—knee length—had to be accompanied by seamless panty hose in neutral shades. Their swimsuits would be more daring than old-fashioned but more conservative than fashionable. The proper procedure for the placement and folding of brassieres was codified.[61]

The "dating question" was answered with a rule that it was permissible, but not along the chain of command—meaning that the regimental commander, the top cadet who had substantial power over all the others, could not date cadets at all. In April, all the cadets and staff attended workshops on sexual harassment and hazing. Twenty cadets, staff, and faculty were trained to deal with complaints of sexual harassment. Male cadets, who formerly had to tip their hats to all women, would have to do so only if the women were out of uniform. Yogurt and more dairy products would be available at every meal so that women's calcium requirements would be met. Bathroom mirrors were lowered. In addition to the regulation panty hose, the bookstore would carry VMI sweatshirts in pastel colors, VMI caps with a hole in the middle for ponytails, hair spray, specified brands of women's deodorant, and tampons.[62]

The day that the Board of Visitors voted to admit women, Terri Reddings, the African American assistant director of admissions at Virginia's Radford University, got a call asking her to come to the post. She was hired by VMI's admissions office and would telephone or meet with every woman who applied that year. By the end of September, VMI had begun a massive campaign to attract women, sending 31,000 letters to female high school seniors whom the Defense Department reported had applied to ROTC. There were four weekend coed open houses between October and April, with women permitted to stay in rooms on the post—although not in the Barracks. But the first woman who would ever live in the Barracks was about to arrive, and in March 1997 VMI's new female assistant commandant moved in. Every human being on the post—cadets, faculty, secretarial staff, administrators, buildings and grounds personnel, cafeteria workers, security officers—was assigned to sensitivity training sessions, run by a firm hired for that purpose.[63]

One of the people who came to VMI during the transition year was General Willard Scott, superintendent of the Air Force Academy. He urged drawing the entire community into the planning process. Under Bunting's direction, VMI personnel had visited about twenty other formerly all-male institutions (but not the service academies, as the Justice Department had forbidden unapproved contact between them and VMI). Bunting summarized the advice they received as, "'You really should work very hard to ensure that your own male undergraduates try to understand how difficult this will be for the first few cohorts of women who come in, who will be entering a closed system about which they're going to feel a lot of fear, they probably will sense a lot of hostility.'" The real job of integration would in fact have to be done by the students

> and not by administrators . . . because the culture of the Barracks is essentially hermetic. There are officers who walk around Barracks all the time, there are professors who go in and out, there's a commandant's staff, but it's organized almost like a nineteenth-century English public school and the prefects—the cadet captains and people like that—they're the ones who have to make it work. They are with the girls, they're with the other male cadets, twenty-three hours a day. . . . So for the culture to work properly, the students have to be its custodians.[64]

Student responsibility for the transition had been the key to success at Lawrenceville.

Mike Bissell put his own spin on that, arguing that not only the committees but the entire VMI "family" had to be resocialized. And so the community was broken up into sixty groups of twenty to thirty people, and Bunting decreed that one of the first things each group would do was watch a devastating 60 *Minutes* segment on the brutal treatment of the first female cadets at The Citadel.[65] He was insistent that VMI not repeat the mistakes of The Citadel. Shannon Faulkner, finally admitted as a full student there in August 1995 by court order, had been forced out within a week by cadet hostility.[66] Two of the four women who followed her once The Citadel decided to admit women had left after male cadets taunted and beat them and set their clothes on fire.[67] That story was in the minds of Bissell and others as VMI began planning for women. The Institute would do the job properly.

It nonetheless remained difficult for Justice Department lawyers to learn anything about VMI's plans. When Judge Kiser responded to a Department motion in December 1996 by ordering VMI to submit quarterly progress reports, he commented, "The problem at this point in the case seems to be a lack of meaningful communication. . . . It appears to me that, had the United States been kept informed as to what Virginia was doing to comply with the mandate of the Supreme Court, the present motion would not have been necessary."[68]

And perhaps if the Justice Department and the women's groups had been involved, the result might have been not only a transition that put The Citadel to shame but also a truly welcoming atmosphere for women. That, as mentioned earlier, would have required a reconsideration of the first principles that had driven both the Institute and the United States throughout much of their history.

THE CULTURE WARS MAY APPEAR on the surface to have been, and to be, about exclusion and inclusion. And in part, they were and are. Would it become natural to see African American and Asian American faces in corporate boardrooms, along with white ones? Would it become common to find women occupying seats in legislatures along with their long-established male counterparts? In short, would bastions of power that had long been populated only by white males now be open to others? Would those others be recognized as citizens in the full meaning of that term, cherished for more than their ability to work at menial paid jobs or bear children or fit into a culture that did not belong to them? Would those who had only been done *to* become part of the group that could *do*?

But the culture wars were also in part about concepts, and the possibility of changing them. The question was not only who should have access to power, for example, but also how power should be exercised both in a democratic society at large and in the smaller arena of the home. The culture wars were about the very definition of culture. Was the American culture only its Anglo-Saxon origins, its English language, its male sports, its public face? Was it monolithic? Or was its essence the diversity of backgrounds, values, and lifestyles that had been celebrated for so long in politicians' rhetoric of inclusion but denied every day in practice?

The first part of the culture wars as waged at VMI was won. In a sense, that was both inevitable—however long the litigation might take—and the easy part. Women who could do so would be allowed to fit themselves into a mold designed for men, in the same way that non–white Anglo-Saxon Protestant immigrants had been permitted to become part of the United States. "Look as much as possible as we do," generations of newcomers had been told. "Speak only our language; celebrate only our culture and our holidays; make our values your own. We have decreed what the creature who emerges from the melting pot will look like, and his appearance is remarkably like ours. Pattern yourself on him, and we will accept you."

There would be female cadets at VMI. They would have the opportunity to be as short-shorn and harassed and filled with pride at having survived as the men. Hairspray would stand alongside shaving cream in the bookstore. But no one questioned the validity of the institution itself: not its outcome, not its ability to produce citizen-soldiers who would do their alma mater proud, not what it meant to be the best kind of citizen-soldier or what it took to produce one. Was the human suffering deliberately inflicted by the Institute a good way to proceed? Was it the best preparation for a socially responsible and humanly fulfilling life? Might less marching time and more classroom hours be a better alternative? Might the knowledge of how human beings work be as important a lesson as the technique for snapping out orders?

VMI's lawyers claimed throughout the litigation that women learned in a different way. The authorities on whom they relied for that assertion taught that there was more than one learning style; that different men and women responded best to different pedagogical methods, so that an education dependent on a one-size-fits-all approach would result in failure for many. As it prepared to enroll women, VMI might have looked inward. It might have asked why 4 percent of its rats left the school within the first week and almost 25 percent before the end of the first year.[69] Were they merely poor fits, or were they potentially as good at fulfilling the role of citizen-soldier as those who stayed behind? In asking these questions, VMI might have discovered the lessons to be learned from those formerly dismissed as the "other," as well as the reasons why relatively few high school seniors applied to the Institute.

But that would have meant understanding that women were more than lesser and incomplete versions of men—something that leaders of most other formerly all-male institutions failed to grasp. The people who planned VMI's transition were honorable; they were well-intentioned. The problem for most of them was that they simply had not spent enough time listening to women—or to the many men who existed out of sight of the Barracks.

The Fife and the Drum,
Together at Last

May all our Citizens be Soldiers, and all our Soldiers Citizens.

—Sarah Livingston Jay (1783)

When Colonel Mike Strickler, VMI's public relations director, walked out of his office on the morning of August 18, 1997, he found over 250 media people from fifty-five different organizations. The newspapers represented included the *New York Times,* the *Washington Post,* and the *Boston Globe,* along with the *Washington Times, USA Today, Atlanta Journal and Constitution,* and *St. Petersburg Times.* National Public Radio, CNN, CBS, Fox, and the other American television networks and major cable outlets were there; so were three journalists from abroad. They were waiting to document the arrival of the 30 women and 430 men in VMI's class of 2001, along with 2 female exchange students.[1] The media were so eager for stories that the VMI senior in charge of the cadet public relations team was interviewed by four national radio outlets before breakfast.[2]

Some of the new students were already well acquainted with the post. Nineteen of the women "rats" and almost 170 of their male classmates-to-be had attended the five-week orientation program designed back in 1986 to reduce the dropout rate for new students. The first class of women was impressive. Seventeen-year-old Angelia Pickett was an honor student, the daughter of a retired air force officer, and an aspiring pilot and astronaut.[3] Kelly Sullivan was a discus champion who piloted her own plane.[4] Angela Nicole Myers was the daughter of one of the first African Americans in the

Marine Corps, back in 1942. She would be the first woman to get to the top of the hill during breakout in March.[5]

Kendra Russell was another of VMI's recruitment successes. She had received a letter from VMI after being accepted at the Air Force Academy and had been sufficiently interested to attend one of VMI's first open houses. Knowing that the male cadets she met there had opposed gender integration, she was all the more impressed by their determination to make it work. Their self-discipline and sense of VMI as a special place made her decide to join the class of 2001. She described herself as having read physics textbooks in high school "for fun," and she intended to pursue a double major in physics and math.[6] Erin Nicole Claunch, who would be one of her roommates, had decided on VMI rather than the federal service academies because they required summer attendance, and she had wanted to work during those months. She liked the fact that she could house her horse in the Lexington horse center. She had been riding all her life, and she had been a cross-country runner since the sixth grade. A would-be astronaut, she had also gotten straight As in high school.[7]

When Kendra and Erin and the others marched off to have their heads shorn, they discovered that there would be no buzz cuts after all, although they would scarcely leave the barbershop with anything that could be called tresses. They had an inch of hair on top and a carefully measured three-eighths inch on the sides, compared with the men's half inch on top and a trace of hair on the sides.[8] They had braced themselves for the haircut but were surprised to find themselves even unhappier with their new uniforms. The gray coatees (short jackets) were tailored for men and did not fit properly. The white and gray uniform skirts they were given as an option for social occasions were so shapeless that most of the women refused to wear them, and those who did and sent the skirts to be laundered found that the linings turned yellow.[9]

Many of the upperclassmen were less than welcoming. The April before, with no advance warning to the school's administrators, VMI's last all-male cadet corps had held a solemn ceremony to bid farewell to the "old" VMI. The cadet officers stuck their sabers in the ground and hung their shakos (plumed helmets) on them. It is a tradition of mourning observed when a soldier is killed in battle.[10] The message was clear: VMI was dead, and three-quarters of the cadets who lamented its passing were still on post when the women arrived.

They made certain that the rat line was as daunting as ever, and by early September 1997, three female and twenty-eight male rats had left.[11] Another woman was suspended on September 9 for striking a male upperclassman. Neither the departures nor the punishment was unusual. The attrition rate followed the pattern of earlier years, and suspension was the standard penalty imposed by the student governing committee for hitting someone. Earlier that month, a male sophomore had been suspended for striking a male rat with a broomstick, and in fact, the woman who was suspended chose to return the following year.[12]

The suspension nonetheless highlighted the continuing distrust between VMI and the Justice Department. When the Department, given as little information about the incident as anyone else, asked the Virginia attorney general's office whether there had been allegations of sexual harassment, Deputy Attorney General William Hard branded the inquiry "yet another improper effort [by the Justice Department] to insinuate itself into the day-to-day administration of the institute." Bunting said that he was tempted to tell Justice Department officials, "There's a foolish person sending me letters and signing your name to them."[13] VMI's refusal to turn over details, of course, simply exacerbated the Department's fear that something was rotten down in Lexington.

Problems of cross-gender relationships did arise. In March 1998 a male and female rat were punished for having a sexual encounter in the Barracks. The woman had already come to the students' attention when she had been caught some months earlier kissing a male cadet in a darkened Barracks room; both rats had been punished then for violating the prohibitions against displays of affection on the post and entertaining members of the opposite sex with lights off and shades drawn. The student Executive Committee now recommended suspension for both students involved in the new incident, but to the anger of many cadets, the publicity-wary administration reduced the punishment to penalty tours and confinement to barracks. Later in the year, a similar encounter between a senior and a female exchange student resulted in their expulsion.[14] An additional paragraph about dating rules was added to the following year's student handbook.[15]

The feared plethora of sexual harassment complaints, however, did not materialize—whether because harassment of all kinds was already an integral part of the rat line, or because of fear of being branded a troublemaker. What many of the women seemed more concerned about, when their hectic schedules left them time to consider such things, was the definition of femininity and how to protect their identities in a male institution. When eighteen VMI women represented the Institute at the dedication of the Women in Military Service for America Memorial that fall, their shorn heads led to their being mistaken for men; they had to learn to cope with that, as did other women who got the same reaction when they left the post. Some of the women tried to outdo the men in cursing, and some shaved their heads. Faculty wife Laura Brodie considered calling her book about the transition year *Sister Rat,* but she gave up the title when the women begged her not to differentiate them from male brother rats.[16] The femininity dilemma was particularly dramatic because of VMI's culture, but it was typical of the difficulties women had in trimming themselves to fit any pattern designed for men, and it again raised the question of why formerly all-male institutions were so hesitant to examine their assumptions and customs and ask which of them were really related to getting the job done.

Twenty-three female and 361 male rats were still at VMI by the time of breakout in March 1998. (Beth Ann Hogan, the first woman to sign VMI's register, had left in January.)[17] They lined up behind Bunting on March 16 at midnight, hoisting their 11-pound rifles and trying not to shiver in the freezing cold, and then set out on a fifteen-mile forced march. Snow began to fall. The rats—and the administrators who marched with them—finally got back to the post at five in the morning, feet blistered and bleeding. A few hours later they were crawling and clawing their way up the traditional mud-covered hill, emerging at the top to be hustled into heating tents.[18] VMI's first female rats and their male classmates, one of Bunting's sons among them, had metamorphosed into fourth classmen.

Colonel Bissell, who had described breakout so vividly at the first VMI trial, had fought successfully to keep it exactly as it had been the year before. This had nothing to do with a fondness for the ritual but was based on the advice the Institute had gotten from administrators of the military academies and other formerly all-male schools. Do not make any major changes, the administrators had warned; if you do, the women will be blamed for them, and the integration process will be all the harder.[19] Many of the cadets and alumni complained nonetheless that VMI was not as tough as it used to be— a lament that was regularly heard at the military academies and, perhaps, from all survivors of other terrifying obstacle courses as well.[20]

The rats certainly found the Institute tough enough, but VMI's first female fourth classmen could point to impressive accomplishments by the time they left in May for the summer break. They had better grades on average than their male classmates. Eight of them achieved the 3.0 grade point average necessary to make the dean's list in their first semester; some of them earned 3.5 averages. More than half the women had participated in the track and field or cross-country women's varsity program. Five had run as a cross-country team in the Southern Conference championships.[21] Kelly Sullivan had won third place in the hammer throw at the Southern Conference outdoor track and field championships.[22]

That did not stop many of the upperclassmen from determinedly holding onto their vision of women as interlopers. The class of 2000 called itself VMI's "Last Class with Balls" and engraved "LCWB" on the inside of their class rings, which many VMI men wear for the rest of their lives. Even as a rising senior at the end of her junior year, Kendra Russell tensed when she caught sight of a member of that class—she had experienced three years of their hostility. Her survival mechanism, and that of Erin Claunch, was to be quiet and "keep your head down."[23] Claunch would be reminded throughout her VMI years that "there are a lot of male cadets who believe this isn't a place for women."[24] Russell found the children of alumni and of alumni friends to be the most hostile.[25] All the women were still subjected to antifemale remarks, and Kelly Sullivan commented, "I feel like we're still fighting the battle, and we will be until we graduate."[26] Claunch thought that the Institute's sensitivity training had only fed the resentment, because the male cadets blamed the women for having to sit through it.[27] Although six women reached the rank of corporal at the end of their first year, none was invited to join the prestigious training cadre.[28]

The support of the only female professor in the physics department was enormously important to Claunch and Russell, and Russell also had the benefit of a sympathetic woman math professor.[29] There were nonetheless too few such helpful role models. At the end of their junior year, VMI had ninety-one male but only ten female full-time faculty, along with twenty-seven men and sixteen women part-timers.[30] The female teachers had their own problems. In one department, the male faculty members routinely chatted and went out to lunch together but never asked the lone female member to join them. Another woman on the post was quietly keeping a list of what she and other female faculty and staff considered instances of discriminatory treatment.[31]

Whatever difficulties the women were having, VMI was thriving. The quarterly summary the Institute filed with Judge Kiser on September 15 reported that 3,219 high school students had asked for information about the Institute, compared with 1,688 the previous year.[32] Almost 1,100 men had requested admission, which was the highest number in VMI history. Women too were sending inquiries. Ninety-one had completed applications—far from enough, however, to reach the critical 10 percent mass spoken about at trial, much less the 40 percent that Bunting had stated was necessary for successful integration.[33] "We are recruiting faithfully, we're trying very hard to make ourselves not attractive but appealing to some young women," he would say, but he had no realistic expectation of women constituting more than 8 to 9 percent of the students in the foreseeable future.[34]

Money was pouring in. The VMI Foundation and VMI Alumni Association raised nearly $10.6 million in fiscal 1997, the school's third best year ever for fund-raising.[35] In early December Bunting told the VMI board that integration was "more successful, frankly, than I thought it would be. We appear to have attracted a type of young woman who tends to be self-reliant, athletic, conservative . . . not interested in making a political statement by coming here, and willing to succeed on VMI's terms." He credited the year of preparation with the relatively smooth transition but added, "I'm sure there still is some reluctance, on the part of some cadets, to fully subscribe to the fact that we're coed. At the same time, we had a great deal of time to prepare." The Virginia ACLU's Kent Willis commented, "Generally speaking, it appears that VMI has had a successful first [half] year."[36]

As impressed as he was by the female cadets, Bunting was still regretful that they were on the post. The ensuing years did not change his mind. He thought that a "seriously disproportionate amount of emotional and professional energy and resources of this school" had been and would continue to be "consumed by our attempts to comply faithfully with the order," to "ensuring that this thing is done honorably and efficiently." He believed that the same thing was happening at the federal service academies, which were "still very much the products of a fervid and constant fixation on making coeducation work," twenty years after women had arrived. But there was an up side.

> There is some good news, which is kind of the obverse of what I just said—that it's a good thing for the young men to learn to execute an order over time, and do it properly and honorably, with which they disagree. It's what the English call "hard cheese," and I'm very proud of the way the students have done it here. . . . You know, the presiding presence at VMI is George C. Marshall; this is a very Marshallian kind of thing that we're doing.[37]

It was an interesting comment, and it reflected an attitude that would continue to poison VMI's well. Bunting and other administrators were determined to make "it" work, but the nature of "it" created a problem. Viewing the arrival of women in terms of their impact on the men suggested a belief that the Institute was still a home for men and those few women who could emulate men, rather than an institution that framed its mission in terms of both sexes. The first years of gender integration demonstrated that Colonel Bissell's "Assimilation Office" had not been misnamed. Women could never fully assimilate themselves to a male model, although they could mimic it with great success. Unless and until the model changed, they would not be entirely at home at VMI. Many at VMI said that "it" would not be successful until the last group of cadets to remember an all-male had VMI graduated. The implication was that the turnover would bring cultural change. No one, however, wondered aloud whether the VMI alumni who made up the majority of the administrators were part of the problem—whether they could shed the more exclusionary aspects of the old culture and set a model for embracing the new.

BY THE END OF THE 1999–2000 academic year, the third to see women at the Institute, things had shaken down somewhat. The eyes of the female cadets as they walked around the post were still wary, still defensive—but then, so were those of the men. It seemed to come with the territory; it was part of the house culture. The women sitting in classrooms wore crisp uniforms rather than jeans, but their hair was coiffed in the usual collegiate multiplicity of styles, and the one or two women in each class seemed no more or less relaxed than the men. One of VMI's first female cadets had been expelled during the fall semester for violating the honor code. (Nine male cadets were dismissed that semester in unrelated incidents.)[38]

Some of the women were excelling beyond the Institute's expectations. Erin Claunch was fifteenth academically in her class of 298, in spite of having spent a great deal of time training and competing with the cross-country team. She had passed VMI's physical fitness test with flying colors: eighty-four sit-ups in one minute (sixty were required), fifteen pull-ups (five required), and a run of one and a half miles in ten minutes forty-three seconds (less than twelve minutes required).[39] That was not only better than the average for the women; it was better than the average for the men.

Claunch was headed for a postgraduation commission in the air force. First, however, she had another job to do. A nine-member committee of administrators and students, which culled applicants based on grades, fitness, leadership, and extracurricular interests, chose Claunch as one of VMI's two 2000–2001 academic year brigade commanders—the students who bark out orders during dress parades and serve as liaisons with the commandant's office.[40] It was the second highest rank a cadet could achieve, just under the position of regiment commander. One of the things Claunch hoped to accomplish in her position was to organize early-morning workout groups for female cadets in order to improve their performance on the fitness test. Her own record was not typical. VMI had reported to Judge Kiser that the women were having trouble with the Institute's physical fitness test, particularly the pull-up requirement and finishing the mile-and-a-half run in twelve minutes.[41]

The recognition of Claunch's accomplishments and talents told an ironically double-edged story. VMI took due note of her abilities, but she still considered the Institute a pretty unfriendly place for women. Like so many other women pathbreakers, she had to be better than the men.

But she was, and so was her roommate. Kendra Russell would graduate as a physics and math major and with four minors: computer science, English, philosophy, and writing. She had a 3.5 average and was quietly taking more credits per semester than the Institute allowed; she simply had too much time on her hands, in spite of the additional energy spent studying Chinese with a faculty member, playing in the band, and participating in rugby and soccer. During her junior year, she had become disgusted with all the spelling and language errors in the school newspaper and had gone to the editor in chief, asking for and receiving permission to create and fill the position of copy editor.[42]

Her energy was rewarded by her being chosen as the first woman editor of the newspaper for the 2000–2001 academic year.[43] She was eager to take it in new directions, expanding it to cover not only VMI news but stories about the diverse communities in the Lexington area as well. She planned to give up physics when she left VMI, joining the air force as a language specialist and doing graduate work in languages.[44]

Bunting, who took pride in the women's accomplishments, told the media that he was surprised that a woman had been able to scale the ranks at VMI and become a brigade commander so early in the history of gender integration. He was not at all surprised, however, that Claunch was the one to do it. "She has really set the gold standard," he said, "not only for a female cadet but for any cadet at VMI."[45] But, as the previous year's graduation ceremonies had indicated, VMI's values did not yet reflect the reality of women's achievements there.

The two female transfer students who had arrived at VMI for the 1997–1998 academic year had gone through the rat line with the others. They became the first women to receive VMI degrees, at a graduation ceremony in

May 1999. VMI's senior class traditionally chooses the speaker for the ceremony. To the dismay of some in the VMI family, the class of 1999 voted to invite G. Gordon Liddy, who had gone to prison in the aftermath of the Watergate affair but was known to most of the young cadets only as a radio talk-show host.[46] Liddy acknowledged in his commencement address that "the issue of women at VMI is closed" but added, "the issue of women in the armed forces is open for debate." The military "had it right" during World War II, he continued, when women served in the rear to "free a man to fight."[47]

The female cadets stood up to cheer when the two transfer students were handed their diplomas. Most of the others in the audience stood and applauded Liddy, although some sat conspicuously still. Melissa Graham, one of the graduates, was about to receive a commission in the army field artillery. Liddy, who had served in the artillery, opined after the ceremony that she should rethink her plans. "There's such a thing as counter-battery fire, and she's liable to have her guts splattered all over her," he warned. Graham, metaphorically shrugging her shoulders, commented, "Knowing what he has done in the past, I'm not surprised by what he said."[48]

During his remarks from the stage, Bunting praised the graduating class for executing the order to accept women in their ranks "efficiently, gracefully and nobly."[49] Just how noble most of the seniors had been was an open question. Certainly, the leaders among the first classmen who had been charged with making integration work did their best, and some of the younger male cadets were less resistant to women as fellow students. Claunch and Russell, for example, were grateful for the friendships they had made with male cadets in their physics classes.[50] Perhaps, as the years went on, the presence of an entire student body that had known only a gender-integrated VMI would become an easier place for women to be. Or perhaps, as Bunting feared, the minimal number of female cadets would result in their continuing to be treated as interlopers. That remained to be seen.

AS OF THE YEAR 2000, it appeared that VMI would muddle through, with some tinkering still to be done. The administration had been worried about hypothermia during breakout in 1998, for example, given the freezing weather. The senior class, traditionally in charge of breakout, decided to do it differently in 1999. Early in the school year, the rats were taken halfway across the field at New Market and told that they could go the rest of the way when they had earned the honor. On February 15, they began a "leadership reaction course," which was a polite title for three days of sweat parties, teamwork exercises such as getting themselves and their supplies over a ten-foot log barrier and scaling an "electric fence" without touching it, and a five-mile march. Then, on February 18, they marched the eighteen miles between Harrisburg and New Market in a drizzle and restaged VMI's storied battle. It was so arduous an exercise, particularly after three days of constant testing and minimal sleep, that at least one senior volunteered to march with the rats in case there were medical emergencies.[51] Some disgruntled male cadets and alumni nonetheless viewed the change as a watering down and blamed the women.[52]

VMI experienced a major sexual harassment scandal in the spring of 2000. The male cadet chosen for VMI's highest position in the 2000–2001 academic year was discovered to have demanded sex from three female cadets. He was expelled, and VMI quickly informed both Judge Kiser and the Justice Department.[53]

Women continued to sign up for the rat line nonetheless—seventy-five applied for admission in 1998, eighty-four in 1999, and eighty-five in 2000[54]— and for VWIL as well. VWIL's first graduating class of twenty-two, down by almost half from the forty-two who had entered in the fall of 1995, left Mary Baldwin in May 1999. Eight of the graduates, or 36 percent, were headed for the military, as opposed to 29 percent of that year's graduating class at VMI. About forty to forty-five students were enrolling in VWIL each year, with no more than a handful of VWIL applicants seeking admission to VMI as well. The VMI Foundation had given VWIL about $200,000 a year for four years. Although that subsidy was ending, as had been agreed when VWIL was established, Virginia would continue to contribute about $200,000 a year and charge reduced tuition for Virginia residents. The VMI Foundation would go on providing $25,000 in scholarships, and Mary Baldwin had embarked on a major fund-raising campaign to ensure the continued existence of VWIL.[55]

VMI's coffers were fuller than ever. In October 2000 the Institute formally kicked off a $175 million fund-raising campaign at a gala 500-person black-tie dinner on the parade ground. Two alumni members of the Board of Visitors had each already donated $20 million toward the goal, and twenty additional contributions of at least $1 million each had been pledged or were in hand. Bunting announced that most of the money would go to academics, including a hoped-for center for international studies, a fine arts center, new faculty, scholarships, and upgraded technology.[56] The Institute's alumni were holding steady.

As the new millennium began, and after a decade of litigation, Virginia could bask in the knowledge that VWIL was a success. The Justice Department was vindicated by the clear indication that VWIL was no substitute for the VMI regimen, and the equally plain evidence that women could make it at VMI. And the women's legal groups might have noted that VWIL and the gender-integrated student body at VMI were each, in their own way, a reflection of a new societal reality.

"IT IS SOMETIMES DIFFICULT to remember," legal scholar Elizabeth Schneider wrote, "how visionary the notion of equality from a woman's perspective is—how much it really challenges."[57] Justice Ginsburg put it somewhat differently. "The VMI decision is a stunning change from the Court's rulings in 1873, in Myra Bradwell's case," she wrote, "that women could be excluded from the practice of law in Illinois, without offense to the Federal Constitution, and in 1961, in Gwendolyn Hoyt's case, that women in Florida need not be placed on lists from which jurors are drawn."[58] Taken together, the two comments point not only to the cultural and political revolution that was the major American story of the late twentieth century but also to the way the Supreme Court participated in and validated those changes.

The definition of community in America was permanently altered in the years following World War II, and *United States v. Virginia* can be seen as a battle in the continuing fight over the nature of that community. It was perhaps fitting that the battle ended in the U.S. Supreme Court, because that tribunal had contributed mightily to the dialogue with *Brown v. Board of Education* and the gender equality cases that preceded the VMI case.

The nonviolent demonstrators who took to the streets during the civil rights movement of the 1950s and 1960s had been asserting their equal membership in a national community—their right to be counted in elections, included in the halls of government, present in the boardrooms, seen in the media. Their membership was recognized by Congress when it passed the Civil Rights Act of 1964 and the Voting Rights Act of 1965, both of which said in effect, "Yes, you are an equal part of this community, and your rights as such must be respected." The Supreme Court, by legitimizing the demonstrations and holding that the statutes were constitutional, tacitly endorsed the politics of inclusion. Although the parameters of the right were somewhat unclear (Was affirmative action constitutional? Could a corporation be found liable because African American employees as a whole were paid less than white employees as a whole?), the Court told the country that some of the old values were no longer relevant.

That in no way eliminated the values from American life, nor did it satisfy those who saw the new regime as either a negation of basic values or a frightening challenge to their own dominance and privilege. When the cultural revolution went beyond matters of race to include even more threatening ideas about gender, it was viewed by some as tantamount to a collapse of morality and the respect for authority crucial to communal life. There went not only the neighborhood and the schools but also decency and the family.

By the 1990s, it was no longer respectable to question the inclusion of people of color in American institutions. Subtle and not-so-subtle means might be exercised to keep them out of some institutions, but in most parts of the country, a halt to mean-spirited racial rhetoric was respected. That left gender equality (and gender nonorthodoxy) as the focus of verbal resentment. Although many white critics had been angry at the inclusion of African Americans in the mainstream of American life, most did not see the new morality as a threat to what went on in their homes. At least there they could be safe from change, even if they were no longer safe from competition at school and in the workplace.

But that would not be true if the women in each household became full members of the community, endowed with the right to make equal demands and assume full responsibilities. It was the women's movement that literally brought the new culture home to many, so it is not surprising that it was the focus of fearful resentment. It was therefore important to the women's movement that the Supreme Court began to validate its goals in *Reed v. Reed* and in the other cases Ruth Bader Ginsburg and her colleagues argued, because the Court is seen as the final and legitimate arbiter in almost every area of life. That was all the more reason for some to assume that "even" the Court would not go as ridiculously far as to shoehorn women into one of the last remaining male bastions down in Lexington, Virginia.

In 1981, ten years after *Reed v. Reed,* six years after *Weinberger v. Wiesenfeld,* and three months before Sandra Day O'Connor took her seat on the Supreme Court, that tribunal had told a group of male plaintiffs that there was no constitutional violation in Congress's excluding women from compulsory military service and requiring only men to register for the draft.[59] The Court cited its traditional deference to congressional decisions about the military and said that Congress was acting within its power in excluding women from combat. (Equally, it was not acting unconstitutionally in putting the

whole burden of combat on men.) Given that exclusion, there was no reason
to have women register. Even the dissenters either agreed that there was
nothing wrong with excluding women from combat or ducked the question.[60]

In other words, the prospect of women as powerful rather than under control remained frightening to many and inconceivable to many more, and the
Court reflected the societal ambivalence about women as full citizens. It came
back to the question of community. Community, after all, is easily defined as
a negative as well as a positive: we are not "them," and that tells us who we
are. Our self-definition depends in part on the concept of the other. In the
larger society, defining women as other was a psychologically comforting tool
as well as a method for retaining political, economic, and social power. VMI
would fight for control over the definition of its community and the power to
determine access to it. Women were fine in their place, but women demanding entry into "man's place" were not. And VMI, and particularly VMI's
lawyers, came out of a tradition of fighting both new social forces and the federal government over how community was to be defined. The South had always practiced the politics of exclusion.

That insistent exclusivity, however, ran counter to what was happening in
American history, in the South as elsewhere. The civic culture had changed,
whatever pockets of resistance remained. The idea of equal citizenship was
now embedded in the country's value system. It had been validated and furthered by the Supreme Court's decisions and had become an element in the
lives of the justices. "Time was on the side of change," Ginsburg reflected
about the cases she had won. "Several men on this Court had daughters.
They were experiencing in their own lives the changes in attitudes about what
women should be doing."[61] With Ginsburg and O'Connor to guide them, and
with the experience of the Gulf War fresh in their minds, they could recognize an outmoded stereotype when they saw it.

What the old VMI and its partisans failed to recognize was that they had
stereotyped men as badly as women. Men were simultaneously exemplars of
aggression and so fragile in their identities that they could not be themselves
in the presence of women. They were incapable of treating women as equals;
they would not know who they were if women were their companions. The
men who fought to get women into VMI, along with their women companions in arms, were harbingers of a new culture. Men and women could oc-
cupy society together rather than in parallel and rigidly differentiated spheres.
Women could be full citizens, and both men and women would benefit. Societal togetherness, as Ginsburg wrote in the VMI decision, was not a nega-

tion of difference but a recognition that in some areas of life those differences were simply irrelevant.

"Going to court to claim a right under the United States Constitution is an assertion of membership in the national community," Kenneth Karst wrote.[62] So is serving on juries and in the military; so is demanding equal access to whatever a school such as VMI may have to offer. If General Bunting's fantasy of strolling on the post with Justice Ginsburg were to come true, the conversation probably would not follow his script. Instead, it might well become the story of how women became full citizens of the United States, and why the nation's daughters had as much right to be at VMI as did its sons.

Epilogue

"You are women and men both," Josiah Bunting solemnly informed VMI's graduating class of 2001 and the dozens of journalists gathered to record the occasion, "but VMI graduates first."[1] Kendra Russell apparently disagreed. "This is still very much a boys' locker room," she commented quietly, seemingly differing with General Bunting's assessment of whether gender identity or collegiate identity came first. "This institution still incubates a lot of resentment toward women."[2]

Thirteen women stood alongside 220 men as VMI's first coed class received its diplomas on May 19, 2001, a clear indication that the Institute had "assimilated" women into the corps. Whether that meant it had accepted them as well, however, was an open question. Just a week earlier, a male cadet went up to graduating senior Kim Herndon in a Lexington bar and announced, "I don't hate you personally, but I hate you as a whole."[3] VMI's commandant admitted in February 2001 that some male juniors were waging what he described as a "guerrilla campaign" against women juniors, and in fact almost 65 percent of the women in the class of 2002 had dropped out.[4]

The continuing mixed prospects for women at VMI were apparent in the Institute's attempts to cope with the phenomenon of pregnancy. When a junior became pregnant during the 2000–2001 academic year, the administration gave her the option of going on leave, moving to separate quarters on post, or continuing to live in the Barracks. She chose the last, and it appeared that the Institute had finally begun to think of itself as a community for women as well as men.[5]

Some of the male cadets, however, posted such vicious comments about the pregnancy that the Institute blocked access to the web site on which the worst remarks appeared.[6] And in July 2001, when the Justice Department thought it might join VMI in appearing before Judge Kiser to request that he officially close the books on *United States v. Virginia*, the Board of Visitors passed a resolution that changed the department's mind. The board ordered VMI administrators to promulgate rules requiring cadets who were pregnant or caused a pregnancy to leave. The resolution seemed to conflict with regulations under the federal Education Amendments of 1972 that forbid exclusion from educational programs on the basis of pregnancy. Because there is no way of knowing what unreported off-post pregnancies involve male cadets, the policy appeared to violate the equal protection clause as well. The ACLU, the National Right to Life Committee, and the Justice Department protested.[7] More litigation loomed.

But however mixed the "assimilation" picture, by the summer of 2001 twenty-one women had made it through the Institute. VMI now numbered among its alumni the two transfer students who graduated in 1999, six more who received their degrees in June and December 2000, and the thirteen present at commencement in Cameron Hall in 2001.[8] Another two of the original group of thirty women were scheduled to graduate in 2002. Two more had been "drummed out" for honor code violations and thirteen others had chosen to leave.[9]

Kendra Russell was on her way to the air force as a weapons control officer, having graduated with a 3.5 grade point average and awards for Superior Performer and Expert Marksman in Air Force Field Training. Erin Claunch had stood at the dais of the Virginia Senate three months earlier as it honored her and her fellow brigade commander Charlie Bunting. Now, the new recipient of VMI's prestigious Society of the Cincinnati Medal, Claunch was deciding whether to study astrophysics at the Johns Hopkins University or accept an officer's commission in the air force and help design and launch rockets.[10]

Down the road in Staunton, twenty-four seniors at the Virginia Women's Institute for Leadership were also acquiring diplomas. Forty-five percent of them had accepted commissions in the armed forces—a much higher percentage than the VMI graduates. Fifty-four students had just been admitted to the class of 2005 and what Mary Baldwin's web site boasted was "The Only All-Female Corps of Cadets in the World."[11] VWIL and its nonconfrontational style of leadership training seemed to have taken root.

So had coeducation at VMI. Brett Carter, one of the male graduates, was the first VMI student in sixteen years to win a Fulbright scholarship. "He's going to be a better son and a better husband and a better father because he knows how to treat women," his proud mother told reporters. "If I were going to marry, I would want to marry a VMI grad who graduated with women."[12]

New alumna Kelly Sullivan put it a bit differently. Most of the graduating women cadets wore their uniform pants; a few, Sullivan included, wore skirts.

"You're making quite a statement with that," one of her classmates commented. "It represents everything we stand for here," Sullivan replied. "I'm a girl."[13]

ON DECEMBER 6, 2001, with the somewhat reluctant agreement of the Justice Department, Judge Kiser declared the case of *United States v. Virginia* closed. Two days later Josiah Bunting announced that he would resign at the end of the 2001–2002 academic year so as to devote more time to his writing. It was impossible to know what would happen in the next chapters of the story about gender integration at VMI. What was clear, however, was that the tale had not yet ended.

Notes

Introduction

1. Author's interview with Josiah Bunting.

2. Henry A. Wise, *Drawing Out the Man: The VMI Story* (University Press of Virginia for the VMI Alumni Association, 1978), p. 14; John Hope Franklin, *The Militant South, 1800–1861* (Harvard University Press, 1956), p. 150; Peter Finn, "Year of the Female Rat," *Washington Post,* August 19, 1997. In fact, her hair was cropped but her head was not shaved.

3. Madelyn Rosenberg, "Changes Won't Reveal a Softer Side of VMI," *Roanoke Times and World News,* August 20, 1997.

1. A Crowd of Honorable Youths

1. One quote from an alumnus was typical of many printed by the media during *United States v. Virginia.* Sam Witt, class of 1958, described his emotions upon returning to VMI: "I still get a strange and empty feeling in my stomach. It's hard to explain to someone what it was like as a young man to arrive at that place. You knew you were facing an almost medieval ordeal. And you asked yourself, were you up to it? Your father was up to it. Your uncle was up to it. Now were you going to be able to make it?" Peter Finn, "Former Rats Remember Tortuous Times at VMI," *Washington Post,* April 20, 1997.

2. VMI Class of 1999, Office of Cadet Affairs, Office of Public Relations, *The 1999 Bullet: The Rat Bible for the Rat Mass of the Virginia Military Institute* (student handbook for new students published annually), p. 31. When the Virginia Society of the Cincinnati was dissolved, its funds went to Washington College for use in military training. The college employed Smith as its professor of military tactics until 1846. Henry A. Wise, *Drawing Out the Man: The VMI Story* (University Press of Virginia for the VMI Alumni Association, 1978) pp. 16–17.

3. *1999 Bullet,* p. 64.

4. *1991 Bullet,* p. 51

5. H. Wise, *Drawing Out,* p. 516.

6. Ibid., p. 517.

7. John White Pendleton (class of 1928) was a Rhodes scholar. Ibid., p. 551.

8. Laura Fairchild Brodie, *Breaking Out: VMI and the Coming of Women* (Pantheon, 2000), p. xi.

9. Adjutant General, Report, December 1, 1841, VMI Archives; Report of the Board of Visitors, July 4, 1848, incorporating Report of the Committee on Public Arms and Arsenal, p. 9, VMI Archives; Col. William Couper, *One Hundred Years at V.M.I.,* 4 vols. (Garrett and Massie, 1939), 1:9.

10. John Hope Franklin, *The Militant South: 1800–1861* (Harvard University Press, 1956), p. 172. See William Armstrong Crozier, *Virginia Colonial Militia, 1651–1776* (Genealogical Publishing, 1973).

11. Franklin, *Militant South,* p. 170.

12. Ibid., p. 236.

13. Ibid., p. 190.

14. Ibid., pp. 177, 185.

15. Ibid., p. 185.

16. Ibid., pp. 7–10.

17. Couper, *One Hundred Years,* 1:13.

18. Jennings C. Wise, *The Military History of the Virginia Military Institute from 1839 to 1865* (J. P. Bell, 1915), p. 31. Also see H. Wise, *Drawing Out,* p. 11. The VMI Catalog of 1999, p. 4, comments that the men "were lacking in self-discipline, and their leisure-time activities upset the decorum of Lexington."

19. Jennings C. Wise, *Sunrise of the Virginia Military Institute as a School of Arms: Spawn of the Cincinnati* (Jennings C. Wise, 1958), p. 303.

20. Quoted in J. Wise, *Military History,* p. 33. All the letters are in Couper, *One Hundred Years,* 1:17–21.

21. Couper, *One Hundred Years,* 1:17–21; see also J. Wise, *Military History,* pp. 32–33.

22. Petition dated January 13, 1836, cited in Couper, *One Hundred Years,* 1: 24.

23. Ibid., 1: 25–27; H. Wise, *Drawing Out,* pp. 9, 11.

24. J. Wise, *Military History,* p. 40.

25. H. Wise, *Drawing Out,* pp. 16–17.

26. Couper, *One Hundred Years,* 1:29. Students at either college could go to classes at the other. VMI students would go to Washington College for natural science studies, and VMI's professor of military science was automatically a professor at Washington College as well. Ibid., 1:38, 64.

27. Col. J. T. L. Preston, emeritus, "Historic Sketch of the Establishment and Organization of the Virginia Military Institute, Prepared at the Request of the Board of Visitors, July 4, 1889," quoted in Francis H. Smith, *The Virginia Military Institute, Its Building and Rebuilding* (J. P. Bell, 1912), pp. 23–24. Although the Institute's name generally is attributed to Preston, Jennings Wise thinks that it may have originated in part with Crozet. J. Wise, *Military History,* p. 41.

28. J. Wise, *Military History,* pp. 28–30; H. Wise, *Drawing Out,* p. 11.

29. Couper, *One Hundred Years,* 1:13, 96; H. Wise, *Drawing Out,* p. 17; Wes Allison, "Bunting Casts VMI in Feisty Beacon's Light," *Richmond Times-Dispatch,* May 16, 1996.

30. *1999 Bullet,* p. 50.

31. H. Wise, *Drawing Out,* p. 406. Wise notes that Catholic students would have been to early mass already and that religious attendance continued to be "encouraged." There had been complaints about this after World War II. As of 1958, cadets were of-

fered nondenominational services conducted by various local ministers as an alternative to marching to one of Lexington's churches. Ibid., p. 234.

32. Smith, *Virginia Military Institute,* p. 242; emphasis in original. J. C. Wise has commented that Smith was "a disciplinarian" by virtue of his West Point training and experience and "did not have to learn how to handle recalcitrant youths" (*Sunrise,* p. 329).

33. Smith, *Virginia Military Institute,* pp. 243, 246.

34. *Regulations of the Virginia Military Institute at Lexington* (Shepherd and Colin, 1839), p. 10.

35. H. Wise, *Drawing Out,* p. 12.

36. *Regulations of VMI,* pp. 5–7, 9.

37. Ibid., pp. 8–9, 19.

38. Couper, *One Hundred Years,* 1:42–43, 54, 57; Franklin, *Militant South,* pp. 150, 167; H. Wise, *Drawing Out,* p. 14.

39. *Regulations of VMI,* pp. 20, 22–23, 28, 30; Thomas W. Davis, "The Initial Corps: An Overview of VMI's First Cadets and Their Subsequent Careers," *VMI Alumni Review* (spring 1987), p. 22.

40. H. Wise, *Drawing Out,* pp. 17–18.

41. J. Wise, *Military History,* 49; Franklin, *Militant South,* p. 151; Couper, *One Hundred Years,* 1:282.

42. H. Wise, *Drawing Out,* p. 19.

43. Manuscript #0071, VMI Archives. The number of stands of arms was stated more authoritatively as 30,000 in Smith, *Virginia Military Institute,* p. 12.

44. Virginia statutes, March 29, 1839; *Regulations of VMI,* p. 4.

45. Couper, *One Hundred Years,* 1:93; H. Wise, *Drawing Out,* p. 20; J. Wise, *Military History,* pp. 50–52, Franklin, *Militant South,* p. 168.

46. J. Wise, *Military History,* p. 52.

47. *Lexington Gazette,* July 4, 1842, quoted in Couper, *One Hundred Years,* 1:100. Sixteen students were graduated. Thomas W. Davis, "The Initial Corps: An Overview," in *A Crowd of Honorable Youths: Historical Essays on the First 150 Years of the Virginia Military Institute,* ed. Thomas W. Davis (VMI Sesquicentennial Committee, 1988), p. 4.

48. Couper, *One Hundred Years,* 1:34–35.

49. Franklin, *Militant South,* pp. 138–139, 145.

50. Edward L. Ayers, *Southern Crossing: A History of the American South, 1877–1906* (Oxford University Press, 1995), p. 33; Franklin, *Militant South,* pp. 129, 138–139, 166–167.

51. H. Wise, *Drawing Out,* p. 475.

52. Ibid., p. 17.

53. Couper, *One Hundred Years,* 1:139–147; H. Wise, *Drawing Out,* pp. 16–17; J. Wise, *Military History,* p. 54.

54. H. Wise, *Drawing Out,* p. 17; Couper, *One Hundred Years,* 1:311, 4:382.

55. Davis, *Crowd of Honorable Youths,* p. 149.

56. Dianne Avery, "Institutional Myths, Historical Narratives and Social Science Evidence: Reading the 'Record' in the Virginia Military Institute Case," 5 *Southern California Review of Law and Women's Studies* 189 (1996), p. 203.

57. Couper, *One Hundred Years,* 1:85.

58. J. Wise, *Military History,* p. 48.

59. The slave, who became the VMI baker and was known to cadets as "Old Judge," was sufficiently attached to VMI to return and continue working there after the Civil War. H. Wise, *Drawing Out,* p. 50; Couper, *One Hundred Years,* 3:240

60. J. Wise, *Military History,* p. 124; Davis, "Initial Corps," *VMI Alumni Review,* p. 22.

61. Couper, *One Hundred Years,* 1:298, 335.

62. Smith, *Virginia Military Academy,* p. 138; J. Wise, *Military History,* p. 87; Couper, *One Hundred Years,* 1:263.

63. H. Wise, *Drawing Out,* p. 28.

64. From Charles M. Barton, September 28, 1955, Manuscript #020, VMI Archives.

65. H. Wise, Dr*awing Out,* p. 28; VMI Catalog, 1989, p. 8; Franklin, *Militant South,* pp. 18–19.

66. H. Wise, *Drawing Out,* p. 35.

67. Couper, *One Hundred Years,* 1:318–319.

68. Ibid., 2:11–21; J. Wise, *Military History,* p. 110; John G. Barrett and Richard M. McMurry, "VMI in the Civil War," in Davis, *Crowd of Honorable Youths,* p. 35.

69. Order Book, April 21–30, 1861, pp. 43–49, VMI Archives.

70. Order Nos. 66 and 67, April 22, 1861, in ibid., pp. 43–49.

71. J. Wise, *Military History,* pp. 114–115, 141. The manual was also used by the U.S. Army for a short time. Couper, *One Hundred Years,* 2:26.

72. Couper, *One Hundred Years,* 2:105. Barrett and McMurry ("VMI in the Civil War," p. 36) estimate that the cadets trained 25,000 to 50,000 soldiers over four years.

73. J. Wise, *Military History,* p. 145; Couper, *One Hundred Years,* 2:101.

74. J. Wise, *Military History,* p. 496; Davis, "Initial Corps," *VMI Alumni Review,* p. 25. A complete list of VMI students who participated in the war is in Couper, *One Hundred Years,* 2:70–72. The camp was named after Gen. Henry ("Light Horse Harry") Lee.

75. Davis, "Initial Corps," *VMI Alumni Review,* p. 24.

76. J. Wise, *Military History,* 139; H. Wise, *Drawing Out,* p. 35. The relevant order is in the VMI Archives:

> April 30th, 1861, Order No. 69
> The following order has been received from the Gov. of Va.
> Executive Dept. Richmond, Va.
> April 28th, 1861. The Superd't of the Va. Military Institute is authorized & instructed to afford facilities at the Institute for the discipline & instruction of volunteer companies, so far as the same may be effectively done without sacrificing the interests of the school. It is to be understood that the state shall bear no charge for the support of such volunteers until they are called into the service of the state, & they are to be regarded as fully under military control & subordination in all respects as if they were in service, & will obey all orders of the Superintend't or acting Supt., and officers attached to the Institute.
> [Signed] John Letcher, Gov. of Va., by order of Majr. Crutchfield, Act'g Supt.

77. Jackson was buried on May 15, 1863. H. Wise, *Drawing Out,* pp. 36–37; J. Wise, *Military History,* pp. 220–231; Couper, *One Hundred Years,* 2:172, 187, 190–191.

78. H. Wise, *Drawing Out,* pp. 37, 39.

79. Ibid., p. 37; J. Wise, *Military History,* pp. 330–331; Couper, *One Hundred Years,* 2:270–273, 306–307; Davis, "Initial Corps," in *Crowd of Honorable Youths,* p. 9.

80. J. Wise, *Military History,* pp. 293–295.

81. Ibid., pp. 296–297.

82. H. Wise, *Drawing Out,* p. 40; Barrett and McMurry, "VMI in the Civil War," p. 40.

83. H. Wise, *Drawing Out,* pp. 39–43; J. Wise, *Military History,* pp. 337, 339; Couper, *One Hundred Years,* 2:328–329. There are numerous accounts of New Market, some of them including extensive information about various cadets. Among them are William Couper, *The VMI New Market Cadets* (Michie Company, 1933); William C. Davis, *The Battle of New Market* (Doubleday, 1975); and John S. Wise, Jr., *The End of an Era* (Houghton Mifflin, 1899).

84. Couper, *One Hundred Years,* 2:323–324; author's interview with Col. Michael M. Strickler, July 14, 1999.

85. Barrett and McMurry, "VMI in the Civil War," p. 32. J. Wise lists 1,781 VMI graduates and cadets in the Confederate army, 249 of them killed in service. *Military History,* pp. 432–461.

86. Barrett and McMurry, "VMI in the Civil War," pp. 31–32; J. Wise, *Military History,* p. 303.

87. Letter to *New York Times* from George S. Patton, Major General, U.S. Army (ret.), written April 8 and published April 24, 1991.

88. Material supplied by Diane B. Jacob, VMI archivist.

89. Letter from William Couper to Mrs. Wm. G. Robertson, December 1, 1930, VMI Archives.

90. Material supplied by Diane B. Jacob, VMI archivist.

91. H. Wise, *Drawing Out,* pp. 35–36.

92. Couper, *One Hundred Years,* 2:303, 3:30–42; Barrett and McMurry, "VMI in the Civil War," p. 41; H. Wise, *Drawing Out,* p. 43, J. Wise, *Military History,* p. 367. The moving force behind the restitution was Henry A. duPont, who had been one of the Union soldiers present at the destruction. DuPont's 1855 application to VMI had been rejected because the Institute did not yet accept non-Virginians, and he later become a senator from Maryland. Jackson Memorial Hall was built with the restitution funds. J. Wise, *Military History,* pp. 353, 367; also see pp. 464–484; H. Wise, *Drawing Out,* p. 94.

93. Wes Allison, "No Stranger to Battle, VMI Fights Feeling of Frustration," *Richmond Times-Dispatch,* May 12, 1996.

94. H. Wise, *Drawing Out,* pp. 44–45.

95. Letter from William Nalle, October 16, 1870, Manuscript #042, VMI Archives. H. Wise says that the entire corps volunteered to sit with the body. *Drawing Out,* p. 45.

2. From the Civil War to the Civil Rights Era

1. Francis H. Smith, *Special Report of the Superintendent of the Virginia Military Institute, on Scientific Education in Europe* (Ritchie, Dunnavant, 1859); Francis H.

Smith, *The Virginia Military Institute, Its Building and Rebuilding* (J. P. Bell, 1912), pp. 149–159, 219–220; Henry A. Wise, *Drawing Out the Man: The VMI Story* (University Press of Virginia for the VMI Alumni Association, 1978), pp. 47; William Couper, *One Hundred Years at V.M.I.*, 4 vols. (Garrett and Massie, 1939), 1:339–340.

2. Anne Firor Scott, *The Southern Lady: From the Pedestal to Politics, 1830–1930* (University of Chicago Press, 1970), pp. 111, 129.

3. Edward L. Ayers, *Southern Crossing: A History of the American South, 1877–1906* (Oxford University Press, 1995), p. 33; Scott, *Southern Lady,* pp. 112–113.

4. Only some of its graduates were awarded a bachelor's degree, but as of 1913, all VMI graduates would receive one. H. Wise, *Drawing Out,* p. 48.

5. Couper, *One Hundred Years,* 4:112, 122; George M. Brooke, *John M. Brooke, Naval Scientist and Educator* (University Press of Virginia, 1980), pp. 354–360.

6. Couper, *One Hundred Years,* 3:130–131, 245–255.

7. The musicians were replaced in 1906 by a professional bugler. Couper, *One Hundred Years,* 1:68; H. Wise, *Drawing Out,* p. 408.

8. Couper, *One Hundred Years,* 1:264–265; Abigail E. Adams, "The 'Military Academy': Metaphors of Family for Pedagogy and Public Life," in *Wives and Warriors: Women and the Military in the United States and Canada,* ed. Laurie Weinstein and Christie C. White (Bergin and Garvey, 1997).

9. Moses Jacob Ezekiel, *Memoirs from the Baths of Diocletian,* ed. Joseph Gutmann and Stanley F. Chyet) (Wayne State University Press, 1975), p. 104, quoted in H. Wise, *Drawing Out,* p. 57.

10. H. Wise, *Drawing Out,* pp. 77–78; Forrest C. Pogue, "George C. Marshall: Historical Significance," in *A Crowd of Honorable Youths: Historical Essays on the First 150 Years of the Virginia Military Institute,* ed. Thomas W. Davis (VMI Sesquicentennial Committee, 1988), pp. 273–301. The brother was Stuart Marshall, who became an ALCOA executive in North Carolina.

11. Pogue, "George C. Marshall," p. 274; *1999 Bullet,* p. 72; H. Wise, *Drawing Out,* p. 477.

12. In 1940, while he was serving as chief of staff, Marshall accepted an invitation to speak at VMI's graduation. The May ceremony turned out to coincide with the battle of Britain, and Marshall's speech was interrupted by an urgent summons to return to Washington. He nonetheless finished his remarks before leaving. The school responded to the man who is arguably its most distinguished son by building the Marshall Arch, identical in design to the 100-year-old Washington Arch, the entrance to a new wing of the Barracks. The bronze statue of Marshall is the only one of an alumnus on the post. His papers were installed in the Marshall Library, dedicated in 1964 at a ceremony attended by 15,000 people and featuring speeches by President Lyndon Johnson and former president Dwight Eisenhower and the reading of a third speech sent by Harry Truman. H. Wise, *Drawing Out,* pp. 211, 238, 532–534.

13. "The High Court Confronts Sex Bias," *New York Times,* January 17, 1996; Wes Allison, "VMI Mystique Resists Change," *Richmond Times-Dispatch,* January 14, 1996. Rear Adm. Richard E. Byrd, Jr., who made the first successful aeronautical trip to the North Pole, spent two years in the class of 1908 before transferring to Annapolis. The

Corcoran Gallery curator is William J. Cowart III. Other alumni include Brig. Gen. Frank McCarthy, who produced the movie *Patton;* television and film actors Dabney Coleman and Fred Willard; Detroit Lions football coach Bobby Ross; best-selling author Harold Coyle; Gen. Lemuel C. Shepherd, Jr., a commandant of the Marine Corps; Gen. J. H. B. Peay III, who commanded the army's 101st Airborne Division in Operation Desert Storm; and CEOs and other executives of corporate and financial institutions such as AT&T, Bell Atlantic International, Virginia Power, T. Rowe Price Associates, Ethyl Corporation, Saunders Karp & Company, and Wheat First Securities Financial.

14. Couper, *One Hundred Years,* 4:95.

15. "Ethnic Distributions, 1984–1996," courtesy office of Col. Michael Strickler, VMI.

16. One VMI historian described it as including group beatings known as "sheenies"; other particularly brutal beatings on "Bloody Sunday"; forced exercise done to the point of collapse, followed by revival with buckets of liquid filth; and upperclassmen throwing heavy water tumblers at rats during meals. H. Wise, *Drawing Out,* pp. 120–124; see also Adams, "The 'Military Academy,'" p. 66.

17. H. Wise, *Drawing Out,* pp. 85, 123.

18. Ibid., p. 91.

19. Jeff E. Schapiro, "Legislative Study of '27: Close VMI," *Richmond Times-Dispatch,* July 14, 1996; H. Wise, *Drawing Out,* p. 127.

20. *Report of the Commission to Survey the Educational System of Virginia, Submitted to the General Assembly January, 1928, House Document No. 4* (Davis Bottom, Superintendent Public Printing, 1928), pp. 23, 229. This is the report given by the entire commission to the state legislature; the earlier staff report to the commission is M. V. O'Shea, *Public Education in Virginia: Report to the Educational Commission of Virginia of a Survey of the Public Educational System of the State* (Davis Bottom, Superintendent Public Printing, 1928).

21. *Report of the Commission,* p. 230.

22. Ibid., p. 26; emphasis added.

23. Ibid., pp. 24, 230.

24. Ibid., p. 230.

25. H. Wise, *Drawing Out,* p. 120; Scott Reid, "Thank You, Sir. May I Have Another?" *Roanoke Times and World News,* February 25, 1999.

26. H. Wise, *Drawing Out,* p. 126; Schapiro, "Legislative Study of '27."

27. David Shribman, "There She Stands Like a Stone Wall, Battling the Federals," *Wall Street Journal,* February 26, 1990.

28. H. Wise, *Drawing Out,* p. 199.

29. Ibid., pp. 120–124, 199.

30. Adams, "The 'Military Academy,'" p. 66.

31. H. Wise, *Drawing Out,* p. 233.

32. *1999 Bullet,* p. 41.

33. H. Wise, *Drawing Out,* pp. 170–171.

34. Ibid., pp. 232, 482.

35. Ibid., pp. 102–103.

36. Liza Mundy, "'It Couldn't Be the Same Thing as VMI,'" *Washington Post Magazine,* March 10, 1996.

37. H. Wise, *Drawing Out,* pp. 223, 233, 307–308, 555.

38. Ibid., p. 286.

39. Ibid., pp. 277–278.

40. Ibid., p. 287.

41. Ibid.

42. Ibid., p. 288; Peter Finn, "At VMI, Pioneers Recall Breaking Earlier Barrier," *Washington Post,* October 5, 1997.

43. H. Wise, *Drawing Out,* p. 288.

44. Ibid., p. 289; Finn, "At VMI." A third cadet drowned in an accident after his first year, and a fourth dropped out for academic reasons, but three of the initial five graduated with their class.

45. Finn, "At VMI."

46. H. Wise, *Drawing Out,* p. 349; Finn, "At VMI."

47. The 1999 *Bullet* declares in bold type on p. 75, "THE CADET CORPS HAS TRADITIONALLY PAID RESPECT TO THE GREAT GENERAL BY RENDERING A HAND SALUTE WHEN PASSING THE FRONT DOORS OF THE CHAPEL. THIS TRADITION IS EXECUTED BY CADETS AT THEIR OPTION AND IS PURELY VOLUNTARY."

48. H. Wise, *Drawing Out,* pp. 289, 348.

49. Ibid., pp. 349–350.

50. Ibid., pp. 351–353.

51. Ibid.; Matt Chittum, "VMI, W&L Live with Confederate Legacy," *Roanoke Times and World News,* February 14, 2000.

52. Finn, "At VMI"; "Ethnic Distributions, 1984–1996."

53. H. Wise, *Drawing Out,* p. 341.

54. Ibid., p. 357.

55. *Mississippi University for Women v. Hogan,* 458 U.S. 718 (1982).

56. Ibid., p. 724.

57. *United States v. Virginia,* 766 F. Supp. 1407 (W.D. Va. 1991), Joint Appendix, pp. 949–950. The minutes of the committee's visit became government exhibit 67 in the case.

58. Ibid., government exhibit 69.

59. Mission Study Committee of the Board of Visitors, Virginia Military Institute, "Final Report," May 16, 1986, pp. 1–3.

60. VMI Catalog, 1989, pp. 29, 30.

61. "Male Bastion Finding Fewer Good Men," *New York Times,* October 20, 1993.

62. VMI Catalog, 1989, pp. 7, 13.

63. Ibid., pp. 7, 8. Under the 1912 amendment to Virginia's Militia Act, the VMI faculty constitutes the Virginia militia, unorganized; they carry military ranks from second lieutenant, first lieutenant, or captain for instructors through the superintendents' rank of general. Full professors are colonels. H. Wise, *Drawing Out,* p. 33.

64. Council of Higher Education for Virginia, *The Virginia Plan for Higher Education 1987,* p. 80. See also VMI Catalog, 1989–1990.

65. Council of Higher Education report, cited in Finn, "At VMI."

66. Felicity Barringer, "Academy's Tradition Goes on Trial," *New York Times,* April 4, 1991.

67. H. Wise, *Drawing Out,* p. 500.

68. Ibid., pp. 403–404.

69. "VMI Runs Rear-Guard Action Against Admitting Women," *Washington Post,* June 1, 1986.

70. Ibid.

71. Author's interview with Judith Keith.

3. Brother Rat

1. Donald P. Baker, "VMI's Leader into the Future," *Washington Post,* July 8, 1996.

2. Ibid.

3. Ibid.

4. Seymour M. Hersh, "33 Teachers at West Point Leave Army in 18 Months," *New York Times,* June 25, 1972.

5. Josiah Bunting, *The Lionheads* (Braziller, 1972).

6. Hersh, "33 Teachers at West Point Leave."

7. Allison Blake, "VMI Picks Leader," *Roanoke Times and World News,* August 2, 1995.

8. Author's interview with Josiah Bunting.

9. Ibid.

10. Quoted in Matt Chittum, "VMI out of Step with Academies," *Roanoke Times and World News,* August 30, 1998.

11. The quotes that follow are from the *Rat Bible (Bullet)* of 1990–1991 (the year the case was brought), pp. 2, 16, 3, 55, 13–14.

12. Nancy Chodorow, "Family Structure and Feminine Personality," in *Women, Culture, and Society,* ed. Michelle Zimbalist Rosaldo and Louise Lamphere (Stanford University Press, 1974), pp. 43–66.

13. Margaret Mead, *Male and Female* (Morrow, 1949), p. 175.

14. Norman Mailer, *Cannibals and Christians* (Dial Press, 1966), and *The Armies of the Night: History as a Novel: The Novel as History* (Weidenfeld and Nicolson, 1968); both cited in David D. Gilmore, *Manhood in the Making: Cultural Concepts of Masculinity* (Yale University Press, 1990), p. 19.

15. Kenneth L. Karst, "Woman's Constitution," 1984 *Duke Law Journal* 447 (1984), p. 453.

16. Gilmore, *Manhood in the Making,* pp. 110, 11.

17. Ibid., p. 223.

18. Ibid., pp. 223–224.

19. Karst, "Woman's Constitution," p. 453.

20. Arnold Van Gennep, *The Rites of Passage,* trans. Monika B. Vizedom and Gabrielle L. Caffe (Routledge and Paul, 1960).

21. Daniel S. Joseph, "First Class President's Letter," *Bullet,* 1990, p. 7.

22. Gilmore, *Manhood in the Making,* pp. 229, 221.

23. Josiah Bunting, "Making Room for Sister Rat," *Newsweek,* December 23, 1996.

24. *United States v. Virginia,* 766 F. Supp. 1407 (W.D. Va. 1992), Joint Appendix, pp. 101–102; hereafter Joint Appendix.

25. Warren Fiske, "Where Rites Make Might," *Virginian-Pilot* (Norfolk), September 1995; Donald P. Baker, "True to VMI Tradition," *Washington Post,* July 12, 1996.

26. Jeffrey Rosen, "Like Race, Like Gender? Separate but Equal at VMI," *New Republic,* February 19, 1996.

27. The situation described in these paragraphs is of the rat line as it existed in 1989 when *United States v. Virginia* began. As indicated in chapters 22 and 23, changes in the physical facilities have been made since women were admitted.

28. Richard C. Richardson, "A Comparison of the Educational Opportunities at the Virginia Military Institute (VMI) with Those at Virginia Polytechnical Institution and State University (VPI) with Comments on the Consequences of Admitting Women to VMI," March 13, 1991, *United States v. Virginia,* 766 F. Supp. 1407 (W.D. Va. 1992), defense exhibit 58, p. 3.

29. The description of the rat line is taken from testimony of Col. Norman M. Bissell, Joint Appendix, pp. 101–102, 118, 123–125; Kent Jenkins, Jr., "Candidates Lend an Ear to VMI Issue," *Washington Post,* October 2, 1989; Robert O'Harrow, Jr., and Stephanie Griffith, "VMI Case Sets off Debate," *Washington Post,* October 7, 1992; "Male Bastion Finding Fewer Good Men," *New York Times,* October 20, 1993; Peter Finn, "Former Rats Remember Tortuous Times at VMI," *Washington Post,* April 20, 1997; "VMI's Rat Line: Only the Fittest and Most Committed Endure," *Virginian-Pilot,* August 20, 1997.

30. Joint Appendix, p. 786.

31. Chittum, "VMI out of Step."

32. Liza Mundy, "'It Couldn't Be the Same Thing as VMI,'" *Washington Post Magazine,* March 10, 1996.

33. Charlotte Grimes, "Battle Idea of Women as Cadets Has VMI up in Arms," *St. Louis Post-Dispatch,* February 18, 1990.

34. Richard C. Richardson, Joint Appendix, pp. 684–685.

35. Joint Appendix, pp. 143–144, 781–787.

36. Ibid., p. 781.

37. Ibid., p. 783.

38. Ibid., pp. 143, 782.

39. Abigail E. Adams, "The 'Military Academy': Metaphors of Family for Pedagogy and Public Life," in *Wives and Warriors: Women and the Military in the United States and Canada,* ed. Laurie Weinstein and Christie C. White (Bergin and Garvey, 1997), pp. 64–69.

40. Chittum, "VMI out of Step."

41. Figures for the class of 2001 supplied by VMI; Wes Allison, "VMI Sees Normal Attrition Rate," *Richmond Times-Dispatch,* February 14, 1996; Peter Finn, "One

Woman, 13 Men Bow out at VMI," *Washington Post,* August 22, 1997. Figures for service academies from Chittum, "VMI out of Step."

42. Josiah Bunting, "VMI Marches to Different Drum," *Richmond Times-Dispatch,* December 21, 1995.

43. Blake, "VMI Picks Leader."

44. Author's interview with Bunting. George Patton's son, in the letter to the *New York Times* (April 24, 1991) referred to in chapter 1, said substantially the same thing: "I fail to understand why this truly great institution cannot be let alone to do its thing. . . . Why try to fix something that has done well by America for over 150 years?"

45. David Nakamura, "VMI Leader Still Prefers the Old Way," *Washington Post,* June 13, 1998.

46. Author's interview with Bunting.

47. Ibid. The attorney in the parallel Citadel case would comment later that there were indeed no studies of men's colleges, but they "have all but disappeared due to lack of demand." Valorie K. Vojdik, "At War: Narrative Tactics in The Citadel and VMI Litigation," 19 *Harvard Women's Law Journal* 1 (1996), p. 5.

48. Bunting, "Making Room for Sister Rat"; author's interview with Bunting.

49. Bunting, "Making Room for Sister Rat."

50. Bunting, "VMI Marches to Different Drum."

51. Lillian A. Pfluke, "VMI Should Follow West Point's Lead . . . ," *Richmond Times-Dispatch,* December 12, 1995.

52. Josiah Bunting, letter to the editor, *Richmond Times-Dispatch,* December 21, 1995; emphasis in original.

53. "U.S. Lawyer Fined in VMI Bias Case," *Richmond Times-Dispatch,* December 20, 1990.

54. Josiah Bunting, *An Education for Our Time* (Regnery, 1998), p. 124; emphasis added.

4. The Advocate

1. *Bradwell v. The State* (usually cited as *Bradwell v. Illinois*), 83 U.S. 130 (1873).

2. *Cummings v. Missouri,* 71 U.S. (4 Wall.) 277, 321 (1866).

3. *Bradwell v. The State,* at p. 141.

4. See, e.g., *Barber v. Barber,* 62 U.S. 582 (1858); *Pennsylvania v. Ravenel,* 62 U.S. 103 (1858); *Kelly v. Owen,* 74 U.S. 496 (1868); *Gridley v. Wynant,* 64 U.S. 500 (1859).

5. *Minor v. Happersett,* 88 U.S. 162 (1874). For a fuller account of the Court's decisions about the status of women, see JoEllen Lind, "Dominance and Democracy: The Legacy of Woman Suffrage for the Voting Right," 5 *UCLA Women's Law Journal* 103, 196–208 (1994).

6. Lockwood was admitted to the Supreme Court bar on March 3, 1879. The case she coargued with Michael L. Woods was *Kaiser v. Stickney,* 131 U.S. 187 (1880).

7. *Hoyt v. Florida,* 368 U.S. 57 (1961), at p. 62.

8. *Brown v. Board of Education,* 347 U.S. 483 (1954).

9. Jo Freeman, *The Politics of Women's Liberation* (McKay, 1975), pp. 53–54, 64; Barbara Sinclair Decker, *The Women's Movement: Political, Socioeconomic, and Psychological Issues* (Harper and Row, 1983), pp. 322–323; Cynthia Harrison, *On Account of Sex: The Politics of Women's Issues, 1945–1968* (University of California Press, 1988), pp. 177–178, 295n.

10. See Elizabeth M. Schneider, "The Dialectic of Rights and Politics: Perspectives from the Women's Movement," 61 *New York University Law Review* 589 (1986).

11. Federal Judicial Center, "Diversifying the Judiciary: An Oral History of Women Federal Judges," interview with Justice Ruth Bader Ginsburg conducted by Sarah Wilson for the Federal Judicial Center, July 5, 1995, pp. 3–4; hereafter Wilson I.

12. Ibid., p. 1.

13. Ibid., pp. 10–11.

14. Ibid., p. 14.

15. Ibid., pp. 17–18.

16. Ibid., p. 19.

17. Ibid.; Ruth Bader Ginsburg, comments on author's manuscript, March 2001; hereafter RBG comments on manuscript.

18. Wilson I, pp. 12, 21, 17.

19. Sandra Day O'Connor, "Portia's Progress," 66 *New York University Law Review* 1546 (1991), p. 1548; Ruth Bader Ginsburg, "Remarks on Women's Progress in the Legal Profession in the United States," 33 *Tulsa Law Journal* 13 (1997).

20. Wilson I, p. 22.

21. Ibid., pp. 26–27; Neil Lewis, "The Supreme Court: Woman in the News; Rejected as a Clerk, Chosen as a Justice: Ruth Joan Bader Ginsburg," *New York Times,* June 15, 1993; RBG comments on manuscript.

22. Wilson I, pp. 23, 28. Ruth Bader Ginsburg and Anders Bruzelius, *Civil Procedure in Sweden* (The Hague, Netherlands: M. Nijhoff, 1965); also see Ginsburg and Bruzelius, *The Swedish Code of Judicial Procedure* (F. B. Rothman, 1968).

23. Wilson I, pp. 31–32; oral history interview with Justice Ruth Bader Ginsburg conducted by Maeva Marcus for the D.C. Circuit Historical Society, August 8, 1996, p. 7; hereafter Marcus I.

24. Wilson I, pp. 29–31; Marcus I, p. 21; Ginsburg, "Remarks on Women's Progress," pp. 15–16; Ruth Bader Ginsburg, "Justice Ruth Bader Ginsburg Remembers," *Rutgers Tradition* (summer 1995), p. 10; RBG comments on manuscript.

25. Ginsburg, "Remarks on Women's Progress"; Ginsburg, "Justice Ginsburg Remembers," pp. 10–11; Wilson I, pp. 29–31, 34–37; Marcus I, p. 21.

26. Deborah Jones Merritt, "Hearing the Voices of Individual Women and Men: Justice Ruth Bader Ginsburg," 20 *Hawaii Law Review* 635 (winter 1998), p. 637; Marcus I, pp. 13–14; Kenneth M. Davidson, Ruth Bader Ginsburg, and Herma Hill Kay, *Text, Cases, and Materials on Sex-Based Discrimination* (West, 1974).

27. Wilson I, pp. 31–33; Marcus I, pp. 7–8; Ruth Bader Ginsburg, "Remarks at the Rededication Ceremony," University of Illinois College of Law, September 8, 1994, *University of Illinois Law Review* 11 (1995), p. 14.

28. See, e.g., Sara Evans, *Personal Politics: The Roots of Women's Liberation in the Civil Rights Movement and the New Left* (Vintage, 1980).

29. William H. Chafe, *The Paradox of Change: American Women in the 20th Century* (Oxford University Press, 1991), pp. 194–201; Betty Friedan, *The Feminine Mystique* (Norton, 1963).

30. William H. Chafe, *Women and Equality: Changing Patterns in American Culture* (Oxford University Press, 1977), pp. 120–123; Chafe, *Paradox of Change*, pp. 188–190, 200.

31. Ruth Bader Ginsburg, "Women at the Bar—A Generation of Change," 2 *University of Puget Sound Law Review* 1, 4 (1978).

32. Toni Carabillo, Judith Meuli, and June Bundy Csida, *Feminist Chronicles 1953–1993* (Women's Graphics, 1993), pp. 14–16, 25–26; Decker, *Women's Movement*, pp. 323–325.

33. Chafe, *Paradox of Change*, pp. 216–220; also see Jerry Falwell, *Listen America* (Doubleday, 1980), pp. 150–151; Phyllis Schlafly, *The Power of the Positive Woman* (Arlington House, 1977).

34. Author's interview with Ruth Bader Ginsburg, May 23, 2000; Federal Judicial Center, "Diversifying the Judiciary: An Oral History of Women Federal Judges," interview with Justice Ruth Bader Ginsburg conducted by Sarah Wilson for the Federal Judicial Center, September 25, 1995, p. 30; hereafter Wilson II.

35. Ginsburg, "Remarks on Women's Progress," pp. 16–17; Ginsburg, "Justice Ginsburg Remembers," p. 11.

36. Linda K. Kerber, *No Constitutional Right to Be Ladies: Women and the Obligations of Citizenship* (Hill and Wang, 1998), p. 202; Marcus I, p. 11. Pauli Murray and Mary O. Eastwood, "Jane Crow and the Law: Sex Discrimination and Title VII," 35 *George Washington Law Review* 232, 235 (1965).

37. Wilson I, pp. 39–40; Isabelle Katz Pinzler, introduction to *With Liberty and Justice for Women: The ACLU's Contributions to Ten Years of Struggle for Equal Rights* (American Civil Liberties Union, December 1982), p. 2.

38. *Reed v. Reed*, 93 Idaho 511, 465 P.2d 635; Marcus I, pp. 8–9. Section 15-324 of the Idaho Code provided that when a person died intestate, "of several persons claiming and equally entitled to administer, males must be preferred to females."

39. Ginsburg, "Justice Ginsburg Remembers," p. 11; Marcus I, pp. 8–9; Wilson I, pp. 39–41; *Reed v. Reed*, 404 U.S. 71 (1971), oral argument, p. 3. The attorney was Allan R. Derr.

40. Ginsburg, "Remarks on Women's Progress," p. 17; RBG comments on manuscript.

41. *Plessy v. Ferguson*, 163 U.S. 537 (1896).

42. *Brown v. Board of Education*, 347 U.S. 483 (1954).

43. See, e.g., *McLaughlin v. Florida*, 379 U.S. 184 (1964); *Loving v. Virginia*, 388 U.S. 1 (1967). The Court's first use of the suspect classification doctrine for race-based government action came in *Korematsu v. United States*, 323 U.S. 214 (1944), at p. 216. *Korematsu*, however, upheld the government's detention of Japanese Americans during World War II. For the most part, the doctrine was not developed until after *Brown*.

44. Brief for Appellant, *Reed v. Reed,* 404 U.S. 71 (1971), at pp. 15–16, quoting "Sex Discrimination and Equal Protection: Do We Need a Constitutional Amendment?" 84 *Harvard Law Review* 1499, 1507–1508 (1971).

45. Brief for Appellant, *Reed v. Reed,* pp. 11, 12.

46. Ibid., pp. 25, 62–66.

47. Ginsburg was following the lead of Louis D. Brandeis, who first used what became known as the "Brandeis brief" in *Muller v. Oregon,* 208 U.S. 412 (1908). In it, Brandeis drew on factual material from around the world to demonstrate that limiting the hours that women could work was a legitimate response by Oregon to the multiple duties shouldered by women. Ironically, the case was used to justify subsequent "protective legislation" that kept women out of jobs that legislatures considered dangerous or inappropriate and was sharply criticized by Ginsburg in her brief for *Reed.* See Brief for Appellant, *Reed v. Reed,* pp. 41–45.

48. Brief for Appellant, *Reed v. Reed,* pp. 9–10.

49. Ruth Bader Ginsburg, "Constitutional Adjudication in the United States as a Means of Advancing the Equal Stature of Men and Women Under the Law," 26 *Hofstra Law Review* 263 (1997), p. 267.

50. Author's interview with Ginsburg (2000); Wilson I, p. 41.

51. Author's interview with Ginsburg (2000). The case was *Minor v. Happersett,* 88 U.S. (21 Wall.) 162 (1874). On Burnita Shelton Matthews, see Ruth Bader Ginsburg and Laura W. Brill, "Women in the Federal Judiciary: Three Way Pavers and the Exhilarating Change President Carter Wrought," 64 *Fordham Law Review* 281 (1995), pp. 284–286.

52. *F. S. Royster Guano Co. v. Virginia,* 253 U.S. 412, 415 (1920).

53. Wilson I, p. 44.

54. Ibid., p. 50.

55. Marcus I, pp. 23–24.

56. Ginsburg, "Remarks on Women's Progress," p. 18.

57. *Goesaert v. Cleary,* 335 U.S. 464 (1908).

58. Angela Hunt, "Women Right Now: Meet Our New Supreme Court Justice," *Glamour,* October 1993.

59. Marcus I, p. 28.

60. Ibid.

61. Oral argument, *Kahn v. Shevin,* 416 U.S. 351 (1974), pp. 11–12.

62. Marcus I, p. 25.

63. Author's interview with Ginsburg (2000); RBG comments on manuscript, quoted in Deborah L. Markowitz, "In Pursuit of Equality: One Woman's Work to Change the Law," 14 *Women's Rights Law Reporter* 335 (1992), p. 97 n. 272; Wilson II, p. 6.

64. Author's interview with Ginsburg (2000).

65. *Frontiero v. Richardson,* 411 U.S. 677 (1973).

66. Brief for American Civil Liberties Union as Amicus Curiae in Support of Appellants, *Frontiero v. Richardson,* 411 U.S. 677 (1973), p. 45.

67. Wilson I, pp. 48–49; Marcus I, p. 33.

68. Marcus I, pp. 36–37.

69. Ibid., p. 38.

70. Ibid., p. 34.

71. Oral argument, *Frontiero v. Richardson,* pp. 17, 19, 20.

72. *Frontiero v. Richardson,* 411 U.S. 677 (1973), at p. 688.

73. Author's interview with Ginsburg (2000).

74. *Frontiero v. Richardson,* p. 691.

75. Because the case involved the federal government rather than the states, the Fourteenth Amendment's equal protection clause did not apply. The Court relied on the equal protection guarantee that it has held is implicit in the Fifth Amendment's due process clause and is binding on the federal government.

76. *Frontiero v. Richardson,* pp. 691–692 (Powell, concurring).

77. Author's interview with Ginsburg (2000).

78. Ruth Bader Ginsburg, "The Burger Court's Grapplings with Sex Discrimination," in *The Burger Court: The Counter-Revolution that Wasn't,* ed. Vincent Blasi (Yale University Press, 1983), p. 136.

5. Women Making Laws for Women—and Men

1. Section 202(g) of the Social Security Act, as amended, 42 U.S.C. §402(g).

2. Oral history interview with Ruth Bader Ginsburg conducted by Maeva Marcus for the D.C. Circuit Historical Society, August 13, 1996, p. 7; hereafter Marcus II.

3. Ruth Bader Ginsburg, "Constitutional Adjudication in the United States as a Means of Advancing the Equal Stature of Men and Women Under the Law," 26 *Hofstra Law Review* 263 (1997), p. 268.

4. Quoted in Ruth B. Cowan, "Women's Rights Through Litigation: An Examination of the American Civil Liberties Union Women's Rights Project, 1971–1976," 8 *Columbia Human Rights Law Review* 373 (1976), p. 396. The case was *Weinberger v. Wiesenfeld,* 420 U.S. 636 (1975).

5. Brief for Appellee, *Weinberger v. Wiesenfeld,* p. 17.

6. Ibid., p. 20.

7. Ibid., pp. 14–15, 17.

8. Author's interview with Ruth Bader Ginsburg (2000).

9. Oral argument, *Weinberger v. Wiesenfeld,* p. 21.

10. Ibid., p. 24.

11. *Frontiero v. Richardson,* 411 U.S. 677 (1973).

12. *Weinberger v. Wiesenfeld,* pp. 651–652, quoting *Stanley v. Illinois,* 405 U.S. 645, 651 (1972).

13. *Weinberger v. Wiesenfeld,* p. 645.

14. Ibid., p. 655.

15. Author's interview with Ginsburg (2000).

16. Ibid.; Ruth Bader Ginsburg, comments on author's manuscript, March 2001; hereafter RBG comments on manuscript. Jason Wiesenfeld eventually became a lawyer himself. Ginsburg officiated at his wedding. Oral history interview with Justice

Ruth Bader Ginsburg conducted by Maeva Marcus for the D.C. Circuit Historical Society, August 8, 1996, p. 8; hereafter Marcus I.

17. *Coffin v. Secretary of Health, Education and Welfare,* 400 F. Supp. 953 (D.D.C. 1975); *Hau v. Secretary of Health, Education, and Welfare,* Civ. No. 74-1016 (D.N.J. 1975); *Jablon v. Secretary of Health, Education, and Welfare,* 339 F. Supp. 118 (D. Md. 1975); and *Silbowitz v. Secretary of Health, Education, and Welfare,* 397 F. Supp. 862 (S.D. Fla. 1975).

18. *Califano v. Goldfarb,* 430 U.S. 199 (1977).

19. Oral argument, *Califano v. Goldfarb,* p. 22.

20. *Califano v. Goldfarb,* pp. 212, 214.

21. Ibid., pp. 217, 222 (Stevens, concurring).

22. Ruth Bader Ginsburg, "Sex Equality and the Constitution: The State of the Art," 4 *Women's Rights Law Reporter* 143, 146 (1978).

23. Ruth Bader Ginsburg, "The Burger Court's Grapplings with Sex Discrimination," in *The Burger Court: The Counter-Revolution that Wasn't,* ed. Vincent Blasi (Yale University Press, 1983), pp. 139–140.

24. *Califano v. Goldfarb* (Rehnquist, dissenting). Chief Justice Burger and Justices Stewart and Blackmun signed onto the dissent.

25. *Califano v. Goldfarb,* p. 204.

26. *Craig v. Boren,* 429 U.S. 190 (1976), at pp. 201–202, 203 n. 14.

27. Ibid., p. 197.

28. Ruth Bader Ginsburg, letter to Frederick P. Gilbert, January 26, 1976, cited in Deborah L. Markowitz, "In Pursuit of Equality: One Woman's Work to Change the Law," 11 *Women's Rights Law Reporter* 78 (1989), p. 93; *Reed v. Reed,* 404 U.S. 71, 76 (1971).

29. ACLU Amicus Brief, *Craig v. Boren,* pp. 11–19; Isabelle Katz Pinzler, introduction to *With Liberty and Justice for Women: The ACLU's Contributions to Ten Years of Struggle for Equal Rights* (American Civil Liberties Union, December 1982), p. 3; Marcus II, p. 9.

30. Ginsburg herself has written extensively about these topics. For a small sampling of her articles at different points in her career, see, "Sex and Unequal Protection: Men and Women as Victims," 11 *Journal of Family Law* 347 (1971); "Men, Women, and the Constitution," 10 *Columbia Journal of Law and Social Problems* 91 (1973); "From No Rights, to Half Rights, to Confusing Rights," 7 *Human Rights* 12 (1978); "Sex Equality and the Constitution: The State of the Art," 4 *Women's Rights Law Reporter* 143 (1978); "Women's Work: The Place of Women in Law Schools," 32 *Journal of Legal Education* 272 (1982); "Interpretations of the Equal Protection Clause," 9 *Harvard Journal of Law and Public Policy* 41 (1986); "Employment of the Constitution to Advance the Equal Status of Men and Women," in *The Constitutional Bases of Political and Social Change in the United States,* ed. Shlomo Slonin (Praeger, 1990); "Speaking in a Judicial Voice," 67 *New York University Law Review* 1185 (1992); and others mentioned in notes here. For a superb article about Ginsburg's life in the law, with citations to other articles, see Toni J. Ellington, Sylvia K. Higashi, Jayna K. Kim, and Mark M. Murakami, "Justice Ruth Bader Ginsburg and Gender

Discrimination," 20 *Hawaii Law Review* 699 (winter 1998). For the early years of the Women's Rights Project, see Cowan, "Women's Rights Through Litigation"; Margaret Berger, *Litigation on Behalf of Women* (Ford Foundation, 1980); Karen O'Connor, *Women's Organizations' Use of the Courts* (Lexington Books,1980).

31. *Edwards v. Healy,* 421 U.S. 772 (1975).

32. *Taylor v. Louisiana,* 419 U.S. 522 (1974), at pp. 533–535; *Hoyt v. Florida,* 368 U.S. 57 (1961). The Court stated in *Payne v. Tennessee,* 501 U.S. 808, 828, n. 1 (1991), that *Taylor* "in effect" overruled *Hoyt.*

33. Brief for Petitioner, *Duren v. Missouri,* 439 U.S. 357 (1979), p. 21, quoting John D. Johnston and Charles L. Knapp, "Sex Discrimination by Law: A Study in Judicial Perspective," 46 *New York University Law Review* 675, 718 (1971).

34. Brief for Petitioner, *Duren v. Missouri,* p. 22.

35. Oral argument, *Duren v. Missouri,* p. 19; Deborah Jones Merritt, "A Tribute to Justice Ruth Bader Ginsburg," *Annual Survey of American Law* (1997), p. xxix.

36. Marcus I, p. 42.

37. These included cases such as *Kahn v. Shevin,* 416 U.S. 351 (1974), and *Schlesinger v. Ballard,* 419 U.S. 498 (1975), arguing that women as a class merited compensation for past and continuing discrimination. Ginsburg saw them as interfering with the development of both the view that women were equal to men and the strict scrutiny doctrine. The ACLU affiliate in Florida began *Kahn v. Shevin* without the knowledge of the WRP, and Ginsburg felt that she had to take it on later in an attempt to save it. See Ginsburg, "Sex Equality and the Constitution"; Ginsburg, "Burger Court's Grapplings," pp. 141, 152; Federal Judicial Center, "Diversifying the Judiciary: An Oral History of Women Federal Judges," interview with Justice Ruth Bader Ginsburg conducted by Sarah Wilson for the Federal Judicial Center, July 5, 1995, pp. 46, 62–64; hereafter Wilson I.

38. *Williams v. McNair,* 316 F. Supp. 134 (D.S.C. 1970), at p. 136.

39. *Williams v. McNair,* aff'd, 401 U.S. 951 (1971).

40. *Vorchheimer v. School Dist.,* 532 F.2d 880, 888 (3rd Cir. 1976).

41. *Vorchheimer v. School Dist.,* aff'd per curiam, 430 U.S. 703 (1977). A Pennsylvania state court later found the system to be a violation of equal protection because of both tangible (e.g., number of library books) and intangible (e.g., prestige) benefits available only at Central High. *Newberg v. Board of Public Education,* 9 Phil. Cty. Rep. 556 (1983). The lawyers in *Newberg* did not make the same mistake as in *Vorchheimer* and did get information about lesser resources into the record.

42. *Vorchheimer v. School Dist.,* 430 U.S. 703 (1977); RBG comments on manuscript.

43. Ginsburg, "Sex Equality and the Constitution," p. 147; Ginsburg, "Burger Court's Grapplings," p. 144.

44. Author's interview with Ginsburg (2000).

45. Ginsburg, "Constitutional Adjudication in the United States," p. 268.

46. Roper Organization, *The Virginia Slims American Women's Opinion Poll* (Roper Organization, 1974); also see Karen Oppenheim Mason, John L. Dzajka, and Sara Arber, "Change in U.S. Women's Sex-Role Attitudes, 1964–1974," 41 *American Sociological Review* 573–596 (1976).

47. William H. Chafe, *Women and Equality: Changing Patterns in American Culture* (Oxford University Press, 1977), pp. 139–142; William H. Chafe, *The Paradox of Change: American Women in the 20th Century* (Oxford University Press, 1991), pp. 221–222; also see Lynn Weiner, *From Working Girl to Working Mother: The Female Labor Force in the United States, 1820–1980* (University of North Carolina Press, 1985).

48. Linda Greenhouse, "Justice O'Connor Seated on Nation's High Court," *New York Times,* September 26, 1981; Linda Greenhouse, "Sandra Day O'Connor: A Different Kind of Justice," *New York Times,* October 8, 1981; Fred Barbash, "O'Connor Proves Justices Can Be Popular," *Washington Post,* November 30, 1981.

49. Author's interview with Ruth Bader Ginsburg, July 28, 1994.

50. "Overheard," *Newsweek,* November 25, 1991.

51. *Mississippi University for Women v. Hogan,* 458 U.S. 718 (1982).

52. Ginsburg, "Constitutional Adjudication in the United States," p. 270.

53. *Mississippi University for Women v. Hogan,* pp. 721, 723, 724 n. 8, 727.

54. Ibid., p. 729.

55. Ibid., pp. 730–731.

56. Ibid., pp. 724–725, quoting *Wengler v. Druggists Mutual Ins. Co.,* 446 U.S. 142, 150 (1980), and citing *Frontiero v. Richardson,* pp. 684–685 (plurality opinion), among others.

57. In addition to *Frontiero v. Richardson, Weinberger v. Wiesenfeld,* and *Craig v. Boren,* see *Personnel Administrator of Massachusetts v. Feeney,* 442 U.S. 256 (1979); *Wengler v. Druggists Mutual Insurance Company,* p. 150; and *Kirchberg v. Feenstra,* 450 U.S. 455 (1981).

58. Ginsburg "Burger Court's Grapplings," p. 156.

59. *Hogan,* p. 724.

60. Ginsburg, "Burger Court's Grapplings," p. 156.

61. Pub. L. 92-318, 86 Stat. 373, 20 U.S.C. §1681(a), Education Amendments of 1972, Title IX, Section 901(a)(5).

62. *Hogan,* pp. 733–734.

63. Ibid., p. 735 (Powell, dissenting).

64. Ibid., p. 745.

65. Ibid., p. 738, quoting Alexander W. Astin, *Four Critical Years* (Jossey-Bass, 1977).

66. Kenneth L. Karst, "'The Way Women Are': Some Notes in the Margin for Ruth Bader Ginsburg," 20 *Hawaii Law Review* 619 (winter 1998), p. 619.

67. Marcus II, pp. 11–13; Wilson I, pp. 64, 67; Federal Judicial Center, "Diversifying the Judiciary: An Oral History of Women Federal Judges," interview with Justice Ruth Bader Ginsburg conducted by Sarah Wilson for the Federal Judicial Center, September 25, 1995, p. 32 (hereafter Wilson II); Ruth Bader Ginsburg and Laura W. Brill, "Women in the Federal Judiciary: Three Way Pavers and the Exhilarating Change President Carter Wrought," 64 *Fordham Law Review* 281 (1995), p. 188.

68. Wilson II, p. 13.

69. "Transcript of President's Announcement and Judge Ginsburg's Remarks," *New York Times,* June 15, 1993.

70. Marcus II, p. 32.

71. Wilson II, p. 22.

72. Ginsburg, "Remarks on Women's Progress," p. 14.

73. Author's interview with Ginsburg (2000).

74. Wilson II, p. 38.

75. *John Hancock Mutual Life Insurance Co. v. Harris Trust & Savings Bank,* 510 U.S. 86 (1993).

76. Author's interview with Ginsburg (2000); RBG comments on manuscript.

77. Author's interview with Ginsburg (2000).

78. Wilson I, p. 74.

79. Author's interview with Ginsburg (2000); RBG comments on manuscript.

80. Wilson II, pp. 30–31.

81. *City of Richmond v. J. A. Croson Co.,* 488 U.S. 469 (1989).

82. *Adarand Constructors v. Pena,* 515 U.S. 200 (1995), pp. 264, 269 (Souter, dissenting), 272, 275–276 (Ginsburg, dissenting).

83. *Harris v. Forklift,* 510 U.S. 17 (1993), at p. 26 (Ginsburg, concurring), citing *Hogan,* p. 724, n. 9.

84. *J.E.B. v. Alabama ex rel. T.B.,* 511 U.S. 127 (1994), at pp. 130–131.

85. Ibid., pp. 135, 136, 137.

86. Wilson I, p. 75.

87. Ibid.

88. *John Hancock Mut. Life Ins. Co. v. Harris Trust,* 510 U.S. 86 (1993); *United States. v. James Daniel,* 510 U.S. 43 (1993); *Barclay's Bank PLC v. Franchise Tax Bd.,* 512 U.S. 298 (1994); *BFP v. Resolution Trust Corp.,* 511 U.S. 531 (1994); *Campbell v. Wood,* 511 US 1119 (1994); *Central Bank v. First Interstate Bank,* 511 U.S. 164 (1994); *Chicago v. Environmental Defense Fund,* 511 U.S. 328 (1994); *Consolidated Rail Corp v. Gottshall,* 512 U.S. 532 (1994); *Dolan v. City of Tigard,* 512 U.S. 374 (1994); *Hess v. Port Authority Trans-Hudson Corp.,* 513 U.S. 30 (1994); *Holder v. Hall,* 512 U.S. 874 (1994); *Honda Motor Co. Ltd. v. Oberg,* 512 U.S. 415 (1994); *Ibanez v. Florida Dept. of Bus. & Prof. Reg.,* 512 U.S. 136 (1994); *McFarland v. Scott,* 512 U.S. 767 (1994); *Montana Dept. of Revenue v. Kurth Ranch,* 511 U.S. 767 (1994); *Nichols v. United States,* 511 U.S. 738 (1994); *NLRB v. Health Care & Retirement Corp.,* 511 U.S. 571 (1994); *Ratzlaf v. United States,* 510 U.S. 135 (1994); *Romano v. Oklahoma,* 512 U.S. 1 (1994); *Security Services Inc. v. Kmart Corp.,* 511 U.S. 431 (1994); *Stevens v. City of Cannon Beach,* 510 U.S. 1207 (1994); *Ticor Title Insurance Co. v. Brown,* 511 U.S. 117 (1994); *Adarand Constructors Inc. v. Pena,* 515 U.S. 200 (1995); *American Airlines v. Wolens,* 513 U.S. 219 (1995); *Arizona v. Evans,* 514 U.S. 1 (1995); *Capitol Square Review Bd. v. Pinette,* 515 U.S. 753 (1995); *Celotex Corp. v. Edwards,* 514 U.S. 300 (1995); *Commissioner v. Schleier,* 515 U.S. 323 (1995); *Florida Bar v. Went for It Inc.,* 515 U.S. 618 (1995); *Gustafson v. Alloyd Co.,* 513 U.S. 561 (1995); *Gutierrez De Martinez v. Lamagno,* 515 U.S. 417 (1995); *Hubbard v. United States,* 513 U.S. 1095 (1995); *Lebron v. National Railroad Passenger Corp.,* 513 U.S. 374 (1995); *Miller v. Johnson,* 515 U.S. 900 (1995); *Missouri v. Jenkins,* 515 U.S. 70 (1995); *Netherland v. Tuggle,* 515 U.S. 951 (1995); *Oklahoma Tax Comm'n v. Chickasaw Nation,* 515 U.S. 450 (1995); *Oklahoma Tax Comm'n v. Jefferson Lines,*

514 U.S. 175 (1995); *Parking Association v. City of Atlanta,* 515 U.S. 1178 (1995); *Plaut v. Spendthrift Farm Inc.,* 514 U.S. 211 (1995); *Rosenberger v. Univ. of Virginia,* 515 U.S. 819 (1995); *Sandin v. Connor,* 515 U.S. 472 (1995); *Shalala v. Guernsey Memorial Hospital,* 514 U.S. 87 (1995); *Shaw v. Hunt,* 516 U.S. 962 (1995); *Stone v. INS,* 514 U.S. 386 (1995); *Tome v. United States,* 513 U.S. 150 (1995); *United States v. Lopez,* 514 U.S. 1092 (1995); *United States v. Ntl Treasury Employees Union,* 513 U.S. 454 (1995); *US Term Limits Inc. v. Thornton,* 515 U.S. 646 (1995); *Vernonia School District v. Acton,* 515 U.S. 646 (1995); *Wood v. Bartholomew,* 516 U.S. 1 (1995).

89. Wilson II, pp. 33–35.

90. Author's interview with Ginsburg (2000); RBG comments on manuscript.

91. Wilson II, p. 34.

92. Author's interview with Ginsburg (2000).

93. *Shaw v. Reno,* 509 U.S. 630 (1993); Wilson I, p. 74.

94. Ginsburg, "Remarks on Women's Progress," p. 15.

95. Diana Gribbon Motz has calculated that the Supreme Court adopted Ginsburg's position, in whole or in part, in seventeen of the twenty-three cases in which Ginsburg filed briefs between 1971 and 1980. Motz, "Ruth Bader Ginsburg: Supreme Court Advocate 1971–1980," paper presented 1993, supplied by Judge Motz. Motz's list of cases in which Ginsburg wrote briefs but did not argue includes, in addition to *Reed v. Reed, Craig v. Boren,* and *Vorchheimer v. School District of Philadelphia, Pittsburgh Press Co. v. Pittsburgh Commission,* 413 U.S. 376 (1973); *Cleveland v. LaFleur,* 414 U.S. 632 (1974); *Corning Glass v. Brennan,* 417 U.S. 188 (1974); *Geduldig v. Aiello,* 417 U.S. 484 (1974); *Liberty Mutual v. Wetzel,* 424 U.S. 737 (1976); *Drew Municipal v. Andrews,* 425 U.S. 559 (1976); *Dothard v. Richardson,* 433 U.S. 321 (1977); *Coker v. Georgia,* 433 U.S. 584 (1977); *Nashville Gas v. Satty,* 434 U.S. 136 (1977); *Los Angeles v. Manhart,* 435 U.S. 702 (1978); *Regents v. Bakke,* 438 U.S. 265 (1978); *Orr v. Orr,* 440 U.S. 268 (1979); *Califano v. Westcott,* 443 U.S. 76 (1979); and *Wengler v. Druggists Mutual,* 446 U.S. 142 (1980). Two of the cases, *Coker v. Georgia* and *Regents v. Bakke,* did not involve gender equality.

96. See, e.g., Ginsburg, "Constitutional Adjudication in the United States," p. 270.

6. Birth of a Lawsuit

1. *United States v. Massachusetts Maritime Academy,* Civil Action No. 76-1696-Z, USDC-MS, 1984 U.S. Dist. LEXIS 16492; 762 F.2d 142, 1985 U.S. App. LEXIS 31207, 19 Fed. R. Evid. Serv. (Callaghan) 72 (1985).

2. 42 U.S.C. 2000c-6. The relevant sections read in part:

(a) Whenever the Attorney General receives a complaint in writing—

(2) signed by an individual, or his parent, to the effect that he has been denied admission to or not permitted to continue in attendance at a public college by reason of race, color, religion, sex or national origin, and the Attorney General believes the complaint is meritorious and certifies that the signer or signers of such complaint are unable, in his judgment, to initiate and maintain appropriate legal pro-

ceedings for relief and that the institution of an action will materially further the orderly achievement of desegregation in public education, the Attorney General is authorized, after giving notice of such complaint to the appropriate school board or college authority and after certifying that he is satisfied that such board or authority has had a reasonable time to adjust the conditions alleged in such complaint, to institute for or in the name of the United States a civil action in any appropriate district court of the United States against parties and for such relief as may be appropriate. . . .

(b) The Attorney General may deem a person or persons unable to initiate and maintain appropriate legal proceedings within the meaning of subsection (a) of this section when such person or persons are unable, either directly or through other interested persons or organizations, to bear the expense of the litigation or to obtain effective legal representation.

3. Author's interview with Judith Keith.

4. A journalist claimed in 1994 to have located the young woman at the Virginia Polytechnic Institute and State University (Virginia Tech). Steven Foster, "The Real 'Jackie Jones' Changed Mind, Not Beliefs," *Roanoke Times and World News,* February 12, 1994.

5. Although the letter said "Educational Opportunities Litigation Section," the formal name of the section was "Educational Opportunities Section."

6. Letter from Governor Gerald L. Baliles to VMI Board of Visitors, April 18, 1989, printed in *Richmond News Leader,* May 18, 1989.

7. Ibid.

8. Virginia Constitution, Article I, Section 2.

9. Baliles letter.

10. UPI, "VMI Policy Can Stand Court Test," May 5, 1989.

11. John W. Knapp to James P. Turner, April 23, 1989, exhibit D, *United States v. Virginia,* 766 F. Supp. 1407 (W.D. Va. 1992).

12. UPI, "VMI Policy Can Stand Court Test"; Jeff E. Schapiro, "Terry and VMI: Follow a Woman into Battle, Men!" *Richmond Times-Dispatch,* February 11, 1990.

13. UPI, "VMI Policy Can Stand Court Test."

14. Emilie F. Miller, "Equal Access to Virginia Higher Education: Co-Education at VMI," *Lex Claudia* (summer 1990), pp. 5–6.

15. Ibid., p. 7.

16. Kent Jenkins, Jr., "Candidates Lend an Ear to VMI Issue," *Washington Post,* October 2, 1989.

17. Author's telephone interview with Gordon Davies.

18. Ibid.

19. Ibid.

20. Jenkins, "Candidates Lend an Ear," quoting Larry J. Sabato.

21. Quoted in ibid.

22. Peter Baker, "VMI Bucking Invasion of Women," *Washington Post,* February 4, 1990.

23. Press release, "Majority of Virginians Believe that Women Should Be Admitted to VMI," Virginia Commonwealth University, Survey Research Laboratory, June 27, 1989.

24. Michael Hardy, "VMI Backers Contend Poll Was Flawed," *Richmond Times-Dispatch,* June 29, 1989.

25. "VMI and *Vox Populi,*" *Richmond Times-Dispatch,* June 29, 1989. The newspaper quoted one of the political scientists, Larry Sabato, as responding to the survey question with, "It was a stacked question" and "That's a loaded question in anybody's book." The question's language was as follows:

> As you may know, Virginia Military Institute, also called "VMI," is a state-supported college that admits only males. It is one of two military colleges in the U.S. that does not admit females.
>
> Some people say that VMI should be able to maintain its all-male tradition if it wants to. Others say that because the state provides over $6,000 per student in support for it, women should have the opportunity to attend if they meet the entrance requirements.
>
> What about you . . . do you think VMI should remain all male, or should it admit women?"

A follow-up survey by the Survey Research Laboratory in February 1990, showed that Virginians favored gender integration at VMI by a five-to-four margin. Press release, Virginia Commonwealth University, Survey Research Laboratory, February 13, 1990.

26. Tyler Whitley and Peter Hardin, "Wilder's VMI View May Aid Ambitions," *Richmond News Leader,* November 21, 1990; Michael Hardy and Jeff E. Schapiro, "Male-Only Admission Policy at VMI Illegal, Wilder Says," *Richmond Times-Dispatch,* November 21, 1990.

27. Peter Hardin, "Attorney Who Brought Suit Tells VMI Board to Join the Parade," *Richmond Times-Dispatch,* July 12, 1996.

28. Jenkins, "Candidates Lend an Ear"; Nell Henderson and Peter Baker, "For VMI Cadets, It's Still 'Better Dead than Coed,'" *Washington Post,* February 2, 1990; Jeff E. Schapiro, "Terry Says Duty to Defend VMI May Harm Her Political Ambitions," *Richmond Times-Dispatch,* February 14, 1990.

29. James J. Kilpatrick, "It's Time for Tradition to Yield," *St. Petersburg Times,* December 8, 1990.

30. *Archer v. Mayes,* 213 Virginia 633, 194 S.E.2d 707 (1973).

31. Letter from K. Marshall Cook, senior assistant attorney general, January 9, 1990, quoted in Miller, "Equal Access to Virginia Higher Education," p. 9.

32. Ibid.

33. Ibid., pp. 10, 11.

34. James P. Turner to Douglas Wilder, January 30, 1990.

35. *VMI v. Thornburgh,* Case No. 90-0126-R, 1990 U.S. Dist. LEXIS 19843 (November 2, 1990).

7. Countersuit

1. *VMI v. Thornburgh,* 1990 U.S. Dist. LEXIS 19843, Civil Action Nos. 90-0084 and 90-0126-R, voluntarily dismissed by Virginia October 19, 1990, 1990 U.S. Dist. LEXIS

19843 (November 2, 1990); Donald P. Baker, "Terry Says Alumni Suit Endangers Defense of VMI's All-Male Status," *Washington Post,* February 11, 1990; "Shame on You, Mary Sue," *Richmond Sun Gazette,* February 15, 1990; Denise Marois, "Beyer Hedges on VMI, but Locals Miffed," *Richmond Sun Gazette,* February 15, 1990.

2. Author's interviews with Isabelle Katz Pinzler, Robert H. Patterson, and Anne Marie Whittemore.

3. Rob Walker, "VMI Sues U.S. over Admissions, Seeks Quick Action," *Richmond Times-Dispatch,* February 6, 1990; John F. Harris, "Terry Asks Court to Approve VMI's Male-Only Admissions," *Washington Post,* February 6, 1990.

4. John F. Harris, "For VMI, an Unlikely Defender of Discrimination," *Washington Post,* April 11, 1991; see "VMI Case Becomes a Battleground for the Theory of Separate but Equal," *Washington Post,* April 11, 1991; Judy Mann, "Neanderthal Bonding," *Washington Post,* February 7, 1990.

5. Author's interview with Patterson and Whittemore.

6. Brief for Virginia, *VMI v. Thornburgh.*

7. Jeff E. Schapiro, "Terry Says Duty to Defend VMI May Harm Her Political Ambitions," *Richmond Times-Dispatch,* February 10, 1990; Jeff E. Schapiro, "VMI Lawsuits Incompatible, Terry Says," *Richmond Times-Dispatch,* February 11, 1990; Baker, "Terry Says Alumni Suit Endangers Defense"; "Ms. Terry's Worries," *Richmond Times-Dispatch,* February 13, 1990.

8. Emilie F. Miller, "Equal Access to Virginia Higher Education: Co-Education at VMI," *Lex Claudia* (summer 1990), p. 12.

9. Letter to legislators from Sharon R. Chickering, president, for the Virginia Women Attorneys Association, January 11, 1991.

10. Miller, "Equal Access to Virginia Higher Education," p. 15; Bob Brown, "Appeal to Governor," *Richmond Times-Dispatch,* February 20, 1990.

11. Tyler Whitley, "ERA Group Chides Wilder, Terry over VMI Issue," *Richmond Times-Dispatch,* February 15, 1990.

12. David Shribman, "There She Stands Like a Stone Wall, Battling the Federals," *Wall Street Journal,* February 26, 1990.

13. Charlotte Grimes, "Battle Idea of Women as Cadets Has VMI up in Arms," *St. Louis Post-Dispatch,* February 18, 1990.

14. Tyler Whitley and Peter Hardin, "Wilder's VMI View May Aid Ambitions," *Richmond News Leader,* November 21, 1990; Bill Lohmann, "VMI Board, Alumni Still Firm on Males-Only Policy," *Richmond News Leader,* November 21, 1990.

15. Brown, "Appeal to Governor"; "Nader Irks Democratic Chief in Va.," *Washington Post,* February 22, 1990.

16. Phyllis Schlafly, "Leave the Military Colleges Alone," *USA Today,* February 22, 1990.

17. Grimes, "Battle Idea of Women as Cadets."

18. Rob Walker, "Catapulted into Media Spotlight, VMI Tries to Preserve Reputation," *Richmond Times-Dispatch,* February 12, 1990.

19. Cindy Creasy, "Multifaceted Lawyer Leads State Charge in VMI Case," *Richmond Times-Dispatch,* February 25, 1990.

20. At its inception, of course, the case was called *VMI v. Thornburgh*.

21. Author's interview with Patterson and Whittemore; Harris, "For VMI, an Unlikely Defender"; Anne Marie Whittemore, remarks, ABA convention panel, August 6, 1994, printed as "Single Gender Education and the Constitution," 40 *Loyola Law Review* 259–267 (1994).

22. Harris, "For VMI, an Unlikely Defender."

23. Whittemore, remarks, ABA convention panel, pp. 261–264.

24. *United States v. Gregory,* 582 F. Supp. 1319 (W.D. Va. 1984), overruled and remanded, 84-1613 (4th Cir. October 1, 1985); memorandum and order entered July 18, 1986, overruled and remanded 818 F.2d 1114 (4th Cir.), cert. denied, 484 U.S. 847 (1987); *United States v. Gregory,* CA-83-94-D, overruled and remanded, 871 F.2d 1239 (1989); rehearing and rehearing en banc denied July 20, 1989.

25. *United States v. Morrison,* 935 F. Supp. 779; reversed, 132 F3d 949; affirmed en banc, 169 F3d 820; affirmed, 529 U.S. 598 (2000).

26. Author's telephone interview with Gordon Davies.

27. L. Douglas Wilder, "VMI Commencement Address," May 19, 1990, quoted in Miller, "Equal Access to Virginia Higher Education," p. 17.

28. Michael Hardy, "Justice Department Faults Wilder in VMI's 'Discriminatory' Policy," *Richmond Times-Dispatch,* May 2, 1990.

29. Peter Baker, "New VMI Chief Silent on Lawsuit," *Washington Post,* March 30, 1990.

30. Letter from John Knapp, March 13, 1990, quoted in Miller, "Equal Access to Virginia Higher Education," p. 12.

31. *United States v. Virginia,* motion of the United States for summary judgment, May 25, 1990, pp. 12, 13.

32. 20 U.S.C. §1681(a)(5) (1978).

33. Author's interview with Judith Keith.

34. Author's interview with Patterson and Whittemore; see also Harris, "For VMI, an Unlikely Defender."

35. Author's interview with Michael Bissell.

36. Alexander Astin, *Four Critical Years: Effects of College on Beliefs, Attitudes, and Knowledge* (Jossey-Bass, 1978).

37. Leslie Miller-Bernal, "Single-Sex Education: An Anachronism or a Beneficial Structure?" in *The Sociology of Gender,* ed. Laura Kramer (St. Martin's, 1991); Cornelius Riordan, *Girls and Boys in School: Together or Separate?* (Columbia University, 1990); Valerie E. Lee and Anthony S. Bryk, "Effects of Single-Sex Secondary Schools on Student Achievement and Attitudes," 78 *Journal of Educational Psychology* 381 (1986); M. Elizabeth Tidball, "Perspectives on Academic Women and Affirmative Action," 54 *Educational Record* 130 (1973); M Elizabeth Tidball, "Baccalaureate Origins of Recent Natural Science Doctorates," 57 *Journal of Higher Education* 606 (1986); M Elizabeth Tidball, "Women's Colleges and Women Achievers Revisited," 5 *Signs: Journal of Women in Culture and Society* 504 (1980).

38. Mary J. Oates and Susan Williamson, "Women's Colleges and Women Achievers," 3 *Signs: Journal of Women in Culture and Society* 95 (1978); Marvin Bressler and

Peter Wendell, "The Sex Composition of Selective Colleges and Gender Differences in Career Aspirations," 51 *Journal of Higher Education* 650 (1980); Sara L. Mandelbaum, "Single Gender Education and the Constitution," 40 *Loyola Law Review* 253 (1994); Herbert W. Marsh, "Effects of Attending Single-Sex and Coeducational High Schools on Achievement, Attitudes, Behaviors, and Sex Differences," 81 *Journal of Educational Psychology* 70 (1989).

39. American Association of University Women, *How Schools Shortchange Girls* (Center for Research on Women, 1992).

40. American Association of University Women (AAUW), *Separated by Sex: A Critical Look at Single-Sex Education for Girls* (AAUW Foundation, 1998).

41. U.S. Department of Education, Office of Educational Research and Improvement, *Single-Sex Schooling: Perspectives from Practice and Research*, vol. 1. (Department of Education, 1993). A good survey of the literature on both sides, concluding that the evidence is mixed, is Fred A. Mael, "Single-Sex and Coeducational Schooling: Relationships to Socioemotional and Academic Development," 68 *Review of Educational Research* 101 (1998).

42. Author's interview with Josiah Bunting.

43. Author's interview with Michael Maurer.

44. Michael Hardy, "U.S. Judge Keeps Wilder in VMI Suit," *Richmond Times-Dispatch,* November 6, 1990.

45. Peter Finn, "Leading the March into Coeducation—the Man Himself," *Washington Post,* August 15, 1997.

46. John F. Harris, "Top Va. Officials Assail VMI's All-Male Policy," *Washington Post,* November 21, 1990.

47. Thomas Heath, "At VMI, Disappointment in the Ranks," *Washington Post,* November 21, 1990.

48. Eric Sundquist, "Cadets Take Development in Stride," *Richmond Times-Dispatch,* November 21, 1990.

49. Jeff E. Schapiro, "Senator to Again Urge End of VMI Male-Only Rule," *Richmond Times-Dispatch,* November 24, 1990.

50. Quoted in Robert G. Holland, "Common Sense vs. Feminist Idiocy in the Assault on VMI," *Richmond Times-Dispatch,* November 28, 1990; see also Jeff E. Schapiro and Michael Hardy, "Attorney General Withdraws from VMI Discrimination Suit," *Richmond Times-Dispatch,* November 28, 1990.

51. Patrick J. Buchanan, "Scalawags of the Month," *Richmond Times-Dispatch,* December 1, 1990.

52. Tyler Whitley and Peter Hardin, "Wilder's VMI View May Aid Ambitions," *Richmond News Leader,* November 21, 1990; Michael Hardy and Jeff E. Schapiro, "Male-Only Admission Policy at VMI Illegal, Wilder Says," *Richmond Times-Dispatch,* November 21, 1990.

53. Schapiro and Hardy, "Attorney General Withdraws." The Civil Rights Act of 1990 would have mitigated six Supreme Court decisions that made it more difficult for employees to prove job discrimination or to invoke affirmative action principles. Congress failed by one vote to override President Bush's veto.

54. On December 6, Terry appointed Virginia lawyer Joel Klein, a former clerk for Supreme Court Justice Lewis Powell and a specialist in civil rights and constitutional law, and James Daniel, a partner in the Virginia firm of Daniel, Vaughan, Medley & Smitherman, as pro bono lawyers along with Patterson. The two later dropped out. Rob Walker and Michael Hardy, "Attorney General Asks 2 Lawyers to Represent VMI," *Richmond Times-Dispatch,* December 1, 1990; "Federal Judge Allows Terry to Bow out of VMI Case," *Richmond Times-Dispatch,* December 11, 1990; John F. Harris, "Private Lawyers Asked to Defend VMI in Suit," *Washington Post,* December 1, 1990; John F. Harris, "Terry Excused from Defending WMI," *Washington Post,* December 11, 1990; Jon Allyn Soderberg, "The Virginia Military Institute and the Equal Protection Clause: A Factual and Legal Introduction," 50 *Washington and Lee Law Review* 15 (1993).

55. "Around the Region: Women Supporting VMI," *Washington Post,* January 13, 1991.

56. Tyler Whitley, "Backers of All-Male VMI Policy Win Grass-Roots Battle at Rally," *Richmond News Leader,* January 15, 1991.

57. Laura Fairchild Brodie, *Breaking Out: VMI and the Coming of Women* (Pantheon, 2000), pp. 11, 159; author's interview with Maurer.

58. Faulkner, a high school student, was rejected by The Citadel on the basis of its men-only policy. The Citadel and VMI cases were fought along the same legal lines, and The Citadel eventually admitted women as a result of the Supreme Court's decision in *United States v. Virginia.* See Valorie K. Vojdik, "At War: Narrative Tactics in The Citadel and VMI Litigation," 19 *Harvard Women's Law Journal* 1 (1996).

59. Author's interviews with Pinzler and Keith.

8. GI Joe and GI Jane

1. Rhonda Cornum, "Soldier: The Enemy Doesn't Care If You're Female," in *It's Our Military, Too! Women and the U.S. Military,* ed. Judith Hicks Stiehm (Temple University Press, 1996), pp. 3, 13–14; see also Rhonda Cornum as told to Peter Copeland, *She Went to War: The Rhonda Cornum Story* (Presidio, 1992).

2. Peter Riesenberg, *Citizenship in the Western Tradition: Plato to Rousseau* (University of North Carolina Press, 1992), pp. 7–9, 20–21.

3. Morris Janowitz, *Military Conflict* (Sage, 1975), p. 435; Sebastian De Grazia, "Political Equality and Military Participation," 7 *Armed Forces and Society* (1981), p. 185.

4. *Dred Scott v. Sandford,* 60 U.S. (19 How.) 393, 520 (1857).

5. Billie Mitchell, "The Creation of Army Officers and the Gender Lie: Betty Grable or Frankenstein?" in Stiehm, *It's Our Military, Too,* p. 29. "Billie Mitchell" is the pseudonym of an officer who teaches at West Point.

6. Federal Judicial Center, "Diversifying the Judiciary: An Oral History of Women Federal Judges," interview with Justice Ruth Bader Ginsburg conducted by Sarah Wilson for the Federal Judicial Center, July 5, 1995, p. 56; oral history interview with Justice Ruth Bader Ginsburg conducted by Maeva Marcus for the D.C. Circuit Historical Society, August 8, 1996, p. 27.

7. *Olmstead v. United States,* 277 U.S. 438, 485 (1928) (Brandeis, dissenting).

8. Helen Rogan, *Mixed Company: Women in the Modern Army* (Putnam, 1981), pp. 120–123; Mattie E. Treadwell, *The Women's Army Corps* (Department of the Army, 1954), pp. 6, 50; see also Linda K. Kerber, *Women of the Republic: Intellect and Ideology in Revolutionary America* (University of North Carolina, 1980); Mary Beth Norton, *Liberty's Daughters: The Revolutionary Experience of American Women* (Little, Brown, 1980).

9. Maj. Gen. Jeanne Holm, USAF (Ret.), *Women in the Military: An Unfinished Revolution* (Presidio Press, 1982), pp. 10–11.

10. Merrianne E. Dean, "Notes: Women in Combat—The Duty of the Citizen-Soldier," 2 *San Diego Justice Journal* 429 (1994), p. 429.

11. Holm, *Women in the Military,* p. 12. For the periods of World War I and World War II, see Linda K. Kerber, *No Constitutional Right to Be Ladies: Women and the Obligations of Citizenship* (Hill and Wang, 1998), pp. 263–265; Rogan, *Mixed Company,* p. 124.

12. Holm, *Women in the Military,* pp. 19–24, 27; James D. Milko, "Comment: Beyond the Persian Gulf Crisis: Expanding the Role of Servicewomen in the United States Military," 41 *American University Law Review* 1301 (1992), pp. 1304–1305. For the history of women in the U.S. military, see Rosemarie Skaine, *Women at War: Gender Issues of Americans in Combat* (McFarland, 1999); Carol Barkalow, with Andrea Raab, *In the Men's House: An Inside Account of Life in the Army by One of West Point's First Female Graduates* (Poseidon Press, 1990); Missy Cummings, *Hornet's Nest: The Experiences of One of the Navy's First Female Fighter Pilots* (Writer's Showcase, 1999); Francine D'Amico and Laurie Weinstein, eds., *Gender Camouflage: Women and the U.S. Military* (New York University, 1999); Linda Grant De Pauw, *Battle Cries and Lullabies: Women in War from Prehistory to the Present* (University of Oklahoma Press, 1998); Jean Ebbert and Marie-Beth Hall, *Crossed Currents: Navy Women in a Century of Change* (Brassey's, 1999); R. Claire Snyder, *Citizen-Soldiers and Manly Warriors: Military Service and Gender in the Civic Republican Tradition* (Rowman and Littlefield, 1999); Susan Zeiger, *Battle Cries and Lullabies: Women in War from Prehistory to the Present* (Cornell University Press, 1999); Karen Zeinert, *The Valiant Women of the Vietnam War* (Millbrook Press, 2000).

13. D'Ann Campbell, "Combatting the Gender Gulf," 2 *Temple Political and Civil Rights Law Review* 63 (1992), p. 65, citing Treadwell, *Women's Army Corps;* D'Ann Campbell, "Women in Combat: The World War II Experience in the United States, Great Britain, Germany, and the Soviet Union," 57 *Journal of Military History* 301 (1993).

14. Holm, *Women in the Military,* pp. 28, 30, 56.

15. Ibid., pp. 59; Rogan, *Mixed Company,* pp. 133–134.

16. I am grateful to Judith Hicks Stiehm for this information.

17. Holm, *Women in the Military,* pp. 60–61.

18. Ibid., p. 62.

19. Georgia Clark Sadler, "Women in Combat: The U.S. Military and the Impact of the Persian Gulf War," in *Wives and Warriors: Women and the Military in the United*

States and Canada, ed. Laurie Weinstein and Christie C. White (Bergin and Garvey, 1997), p. 80; Holm, *Women in the Military,* p. 98.

20. Rogan, *Mixed Company,* p. 133.

21. Holm, *Women in the Military,* p. 105.

22. Women's Armed Services Integration Act of 1948 (Pub. L. 625—80th Congress), ch. 449, 62 Stat. 356-75, codified in 10 U.S.C. §§6015, 8549.

23. Judith Hicks Stiehm, *Arms and the Enlisted Woman* (Temple University Press, 1989), p. 120.

24. Betty Friedan, *The Feminine Mystique* (Norton, 1963).

25. Holm, *Women in the Military,* pp. 181–182; Stiehm, *Arms and the Enlisted Woman,* p. 39; Kerber, *No Constitutional Right,* p. 265.

26. Jill Laurie Goodman, "Women, War, and Equality: An Examination of Sex Discrimination in the Military," 5 *Women's Rights Law Reporter* 243 (1979).

27. Stiehm, *Arms and the Enlisted Woman,* p. 25. As Rhonda Cornum would write three decades later about her great-grandmother and other strong female relatives, "Women in our family did not burn their bras, they just went out and did what they wanted to do." Cornum as told to Copeland, *She Went to War,* p. 90.

28. Holm, *Women in the Military,* p. 249.

29. Donald G. Mathews and Jane Sherron De Hart, *Sex, Gender, and the Politics of ERA: A State and the Nation* (Oxford University, 1990), pp. 37, 222, 202, reporting the Louis Harris 1979 survey on the Equal Rights Amendment, no. 794022.

30. Hoisington served on the VMI Board of Visitors from 1985 to 1993.

31. *Struck v. Secretary of Defense,* 460 F.2d 1372 (9th Cir. 1971), judgment vacated, 409 U.S. 1071 (1972). The air force changed its policy before the Supreme Court handed down judgment in the case.

32. Holm, *Women in the Military,* pp. 273, 279; Stiehm, *Arms and the Enlisted Woman,* p. 39.

33. "Air Force Captain Battles Ban," *Evening Star* (D.C.), September 29, 1970.

34. Holm, *Women in the Military,* p. 305; Judith Hicks Stiehm, *Bring Me Men and Women: Mandated Change at the U.S. Air Force Academy* (University of California Press, 1981), pp. 11–13.

35. The cases, *Waldie v. Schlesinger,* no. 74-1636 (Naval Academy), and *Edwards v. Schlesinger,* no. 74-1637 (Air Force Academy), were filed on September 26, 1973. The plaintiffs—Representatives Jerome Waldie, Coralie S. Cross, Don Edwards, and Fortney Stark, Jr.—sought a permanent injunction requiring the Defense Department to process the applications of qualified female applicants and admit them, and a declaratory judgment that refusal to process women's application violated the equal protection clause of the Fifth Amendment by excluding women from educational and career opportunities and preventing members of Congress from fulfilling their statutory authority to nominate people to the academies in a nondiscriminatory manner.

36. H.R. 11268, 93d Cong., 1st sess. Representative duPont came from the same extended family as the duPont who had sponsored the bill to make federal reparations to VMI for damage suffered during the Civil War. See chapter 1, n. 92.

37. See *Waldie v. Schlesinger* and *Edwards v. Schlesinger,* 166 U.S. App. D.C. 175, 509 F.2d 508 (1974).

38. W. P. Clement to Hon. F. Edward Hebert, April 26, 1974; H.R. 11268, 93d Cong., 1st sess., Armed Services Committee Hearings, p. 20.

39. *An Appraisal of the Impact of Integrating Women into the U.S. Naval Academy and Aboard Ship,* printed as H.R. 9832, 93d Cong., 2d sess., "Regarding Equal Admission to the Service Academies," Subcommittee no. 2, Armed Services Committee, Hearings May 29–August 8, 1974, p. 120; hereafter Hearings.

40. Ibid., pp. 120–121.

41. Quoted in Stiehm, *Bring Me Men and Women,* p. 19.

42. Hearings, pp. 135, 137.

43. Ibid., pp. 165, 174.

44. Ibid., pp. 197–198.

45. Ibid., p. 174.

46. Ibid., p. 228.

47. Ibid., pp. 23–24.

48. Ibid., p. 235.

49. Obituaries in the *New York Times* and *Los Angeles Times,* September 15, 1990.

50. Hearings, pp. 35–39.

51. Testimony by Glenn Ellefson-Brooks, director, Veterans Affairs, Women's Lobby, Inc., in Hearings, p. 224.

52. Hearings, p. 213.

53. Ibid., pp. 214, 220.

54. Holm, *Women in the Military,* pp. 308–309.

55. Hearings, p. 224.

56. *Waldie v. Schlesinger, Edwards v. Schlesinger,* 166 U.S. App. D.C. 175; 509 F.2d 508 (1974).

57. Stiehm, *Bring Me Men and Women,* p. 38.

58. Ibid., p. 43.

59. Title IX, Pub. L. 92-318, 20 U.S.C. §1681:

Sex

(a) No person in the United States shall, on the basis of sex, be excluded from participation in, be denied the benefits of, or be subjected to discrimination under any education program or activity receiving Federal financial assistance, except that:

(1) . . . in regard to admissions to educational institutions, this section shall apply only to institutions of vocational education, professional education, and graduate higher education, and to public institutions of undergraduate higher education . . .;

(4) . . . this section shall not apply to an educational institution whose primary purpose is the training of individuals for the military services of the United States, or the merchant marine;

(5) . . . in regard to admissions this section shall not apply to any public institution of undergraduate higher education which is an institution that traditionally and continually from its establishment has had a policy of admitting only students of one sex. . . .

(c) . . . For purposes of this title an educational institution means any public or private preschool, elementary, or secondary school, or any institution of vocational, professional, or higher education, except that in the case of an educational institution composed of more than one school, college, or department which are administratively separate units, such term means each such school, college, or department. (June 23, 1972, P.L. 92-318, Title IX, §901, 86 Stat. 373; December 31, 1974, P.L. 93-568, §3(a), 88 Stat. 1862; October 12, 1976, P.L. 94-482, Title IV, §412(a), 90 Stat. 2234)

60. Hearings, p. 218.

9. The Lady and the Soldier

1. Anne Firor Scott, *The Southern Lady: From the Pedestal to Politics, 1830–1930* (University of Chicago Press, 1970), pp. x–xi.

2. Jacquelyn Dowd Hall and Anne Firor Scott, "Women in the South," in *Interpreting Southern History: Historiographical Essays in Honor of Sanford W. Higginbotham,* ed. John B. Boles and Evelyn Thomas Nolen (Louisiana State University Press, 1987), p. 458.

3. Virginia Kent Anderson Leslie, "A Myth of the Southern Lady: Antebellum Proslavery Rhetoric and the Proper Place of Woman," in *Southern Women,* ed. Caroline Matheny Dillman (Hemisphere Publishing, 1988), p. 19.

4. Scott, *Southern Lady,* p. 17.

5. "Prof. Dew on Slavery," in *The Pro-Slavery Argument* (Lippincott, Grambo, 1853), p. 338.

6. George Herbert Fitzhugh, *Sociology for the South, or the Failure of Free Society* (Burt Franklin, 1965), p. 214.

7. Ibid., p. 147. Also see William Harper, "Harper's Memoir on Slavery," in *Pro-Slavery Argument*. The works of Dew, Fitzhugh, and Harper are examined in Leslie, "Myth of the Southern Lady," pp. 19–29.

8. Jacqueline Jones, "The Public Dimension of 'Private' Life: Southern Women and Their Families, 1865–1965," in *A New Perspective: Southern Women's Cultural History from the Civil War to Civil Rights,* ed. Priscilla Courtelyou Little and Robert C. Vaughan (Virginia Foundation for the Humanities, 1989), p. 40.

9. Suzanne Lebsock, *"A Share of Honour": Virginia Women 1600–1945* (Women's Cultural History Project, 1984; Virginia State Library, 1987), p. 76; also see Catherine Clinton, *The Plantation Mistress: Women's World in the Old South* (Pantheon, 1982); Scott, *Southern Lady,* pp. 45–79; Marli F. Weiner, *Mistresses and Slaves: Plantation Women in South Carolina, 1830–1880* (University of Illinois Press, 1997).

10. Barbara Welter, "The Cult of True Womanhood: 1820–1860," 18 *American Quarterly* (Summer 1966), p. 171, quoting Daniel Webster, "The Influence of Woman," in *The Young Ladies Reader* (Philadelphia, 1851), p. 310.

11. Scott, *Southern Lady,* pp. 68–71; Lebsock, *"A Share of Honour,"* p. 61. Also see Fletcher Melvin Green, "Higher Education of Women in the South Prior to 1860," in

Democracy in the Old South and Other Essays, ed. J. Isaac Copeland (Vanderbilt University Press, 1969), pp. 199–219.

12. Scott, *Southern Lady*, pp. 106–129.

13. Edward L. Ayers, *Southern Crossing: A History of the American South, 1877–1906* (Oxford University Press, 1995), pp. 45, 158; Elna C. Green, *Southern Strategies: Southern Women and the Woman Suffrage Question* (University of North Carolina, 1997), pp. 156–157.

14. Ayers, *Southern Crossing*, p. 21; Joanne V. Hawks and Sheila L. Skemp, *Sex, Race, and the Role of Women in the South* (University Press of Mississippi, 1983), p. xv; also see Gerda Lerner, "Community Work of Black Club Women" in *The Majority Finds Its Past* (Oxford University Press, 1979), pp. 83–93.

15. Ayers, *Southern Crossing*, p. 162.

16. Ibid., p. 13. The Virginia General Assembly passed laws in 1900 and 1906 mandating separate railroad and streetcars for blacks and whites. Lebsock, "*A Share of Honour,*" p. 91.

17. Donald G. Mathews and Jane Sherron De Hart, *Sex, Gender, and the Politics of ERA: A State and the Nation* (Oxford University, 1990), p. 4.

18. Jean E. Friedman, "Women's History and the Revision of Southern History" in Hawks and Skemp, *Sex, Race, and the Role of Women*, p. 12.

19. Hawks and Skemp, *Sex, Race, and the Role of Women*, p. xiii, quoting from Friedman, "Women's History," in ibid. pp. 3–12.

20. Green, *Southern Strategies*, p. 152.

21. Ibid., pp. 154–155. Cott places the beginning of women's suffrage associations in the South in the 1890s. Nancy F. Cott, "The South and the Nation in the History of Women's Rights," in Little and Vaughan, *A New Perspective*, p. 15. Also see Charlotte Jean Sheldon, "Woman Suffrage and Virginia Politics, 1909–1920" (master's thesis, University of Virginia, 1969); Trudy J. Hanmer, "A Divine Discontent: Mary Johnston and Woman Suffrage in Virginia" (master's thesis, University of Virginia, 1972).

22. See, e.g., Lebsock, "*A Share of Honour,*" pp. 101, 120. Hawks and Skemp (*Sex, Race, and the Role of Women,* pp. xiv–xv) attribute the failure to develop a strong women's movement to the emphasis on race, which divided black and white women. Wheeler disagrees with Lebsock, calling the Southern suffrage movement "a full-fledged women's rights movement." Marjorie Spruill Wheeler, *New Women of the New South: The Leaders of the Woman Suffrage Movement in the Southern States* (Oxford University, 1993), p. 185. Unlike Hawks and Skemp, Lebsock views race as only a tangential issue in Virginia's suffrage movement. Suzanne Lebsock, "Woman Suffrage and White Supremacy: A Virginia Case Study," in *Taking off the White Gloves: Southern Women and Women Historians,* ed. Michele Gillespie and Catherine Clinton (University of Missouri Press, 1998).

23. Quoted in Scott, *Southern Lady*, p. 181.

24. Quoted in Wheeler, *New Women of the New South*, p. 78.

25. Green, *Southern Strategies,* p. 166; Lebsock, "*A Share of Honour,*" p. 122; Wheeler, *New Women of the New South*, p. 26; Dewey W. Grantham, *The South in Modern America: A Region at Odds* (HarperCollins, 1994), p. 71.

26. Wheeler, *New Women of the New South*, p. 23.

27. Ibid., p. 5.

28. Ibid., p. 32.

29. Ibid., p. 4.

30. Mathews and De Hart, *Sex, Gender, and the Politics of ERA*, p. 14.

31. Wheeler, *New Women of the New South*, pp. 4–5.

32. Scott, *Southern Lady*, pp. 200, 210.

33. Lebsock, *"A Share of Honour,"* pp. 128–129.

34. Grantham, *South in Modern America*, pp. 172–173.

35. Janowitz notes that between 1900 and 1940, a majority of officers were recruited from families in or from the South. Morris Janowitz, "The All-Volunteer Military as a 'Sociopolitical' Problem," 22 *Social Problems* 432–449 (1975), pp. 440–441.

36. Grantham, *South in Modern America*, pp. 272–273. In the 1990s, according to the Pentagon, 42 percent of the country's military and civilian personnel were stationed in the eleven states of the Old Confederacy. Kevin Sack, "Southerners in Conflict over Events," *New York Times*, December 18, 1998.

37. Grantham, *South in Modern America*, p. xv. The concept of the white South as constituting a distinctive subculture and even a separate "ethnic group," introduced by Lewis M. Killian in *White Southerners* (Random House, 1970), can also be found in George Brown Tindall, *The Ethnic Southerners* (Louisiana State University Press, 1976); Howard F. Stein and Robert F. Hill, *The Ethnic Imperative* (Pennsylvania State University Press, 1977); Carl N. Degler, *Place over Time: The Continuity of Southern Distinctiveness* (Louisiana State University Press, 1977); and John Shelton Reed, *The Enduring South: Persistence in Mass Society* (University of North Carolina Press, 1974) and *Southerners: The Social Psychology of Sectionalism* (University of North Carolina Press, 1983). The opposing view, that the South increasingly moved toward the rest of the nation in its values during the 1970s and 1980s, can be found in John C. McKinney and Linda Brookover Bourque, "The Changing South: National Incorporation of a Region," 36 *American Sociological Review* (1971); Gavin Wright, *Old South, New South: Revolutions in the Southern Economy Since the Civil War* (Louisiana State University Press, 1996); John Egerton, *The Americanization of Dixie: The Southernization of America* (Harper's Magazine Press, 1974); and Albert E. Cowdrey, *This Land, This South: An Environmental History* (University Press of Kentucky, 1983).

38. See, e.g., Karen M. Mason, John L. Czajik, and Sara Arber, "Change in U.S. Women's Sex Role Attitudes, 1964–1974," 41 *American Sociological Review* 573–596 (1976); Nan E. Johnson and C. Channon Stokes, "Southern Traditionalism and Sex Roles Ideology: A Research Note (paper presented to the Southern Sociological Society, Atlanta, 1979); Reed, *Southerners: The Social Psychology of Sectionalism*.

39. For upper- and upper-middle-class Southern women, see, e.g., Jacqueline Boles and Maxine P. Atkinson, "Ladies: South by Northwest," in Dillman, *Southern Women;* for blue-collar and pink-collar women, see Susan Middleton-Keirn, "Magnolias and Microchips: Regional Subcultural Constructions of Femininity," in Dillman *Southern Women*. Also see Suzanne Lebsock's seminal studies of Virginia women, particularly *"A Share of Honour."*

40. Lebsock, "*A Share of Honour,*" pp. 105–106, 131.

41. Patricia A. Stringer and Irene Thompson, *Stepping off the Pedestal: Academic Women in the South* (Modern Language Association of America, 1982), p. 6.

42. Lebsock, "*A Share of Honour,*" p. 136.

43. Marie T. Hough, Sarah Livermore, et al., eds., *The American Bench: Judges of the Nation, Fourth Edition, 1987–1988* (Reginald Bishop Forster and Associations, 1987).

44. Grantham, *South in Modern America,* p. 307.

45. Middleton-Keirn, "Magnolias and Microchips," p. 157.

46. Susan Gluck Mezey, "The Persistence of Sex Segregated Education in the South," 22 *Southeastern Political Review* 374 (June 1994), citing Stephen Earl Bennett and Linda L. M. Bennett, "From Traditional to Modern Concepts of Gender Equality in Politics," 45 *Western Political Quarterly* 93–111 (1992); the Virginia Slims polls of 1985 and 1989; and the Gallup polls of 1987 and 1988.

47. *United State v. Virginia,* 766 F. Supp. 1407 (W.D. Va. 1992), Joint Appendix, p. 21.

48. Quoted in Walter Russell Bowie, *Sunrise in the South: The Life of Mary-Cooke Branch Munford* (William Byrd Press, 1942), p. 21.

49. Quoted in Wheeler, *New Women of the New South,* p. 81.

50. Ibid., p. 81; Mary Gathright Newell, "Mary Munford and Higher Education for Women in Virginia" in Stringer and Thompson, *Stepping off the Pedestal,* p. 31; Lebsock, "*A Share of Honour,*" p. 116.

51. Green, *Southern Strategies,* p. 161.

52. Lebsock, "*A Share of Honour,*" p. 115.

53. Quoted in Anne Hobson Freeman, "Mary Munford's Fight for a College for Women Co-ordinate with the University of Virginia," 78 *Virginia Magazine of History and Biography* (October 1970), p. 481 n. 3.

54. Newell, "Mary Munford," pp. 27, 33; Lebsock, "*A Share of Honour,*" p. 116, Freeman, "Mary Munford's Fight," p. 481.

55. Freeman, "Mary Munford's Fight," pp. 484–487; Newell, "Mary Munford," p. 35.

56. Freeman, "Mary Munford's Fight," pp. 485–487, 487 n. 23.

57. Thomas Woody, *A History of Women's Education in the United States,* vol. 2 (Science Press, 1929), pp. 254–255.

58. Lebsock, "*A Share of Honour,*" p. 117; Newell, "Mary Munford," p. 37; Freeman, "Mary Munford's Fight," p. 483.

59. Newell, "Mary Munford," p. 37; Freeman, "Mary Munford's Fight," pp. 488–489.

60. Freeman "Mary Munford's Fight," p. 489.

61. *Kirstein v. Rector of Univ. of Va.,* 309 F. Supp. 184 (E.D. Va. 1970), p. 186.

62. Freeman, "Mary Munford's Fight," p. 481 n.1, citing *Richmond Times-Dispatch,* February 16, 1969, and *Richmond News Leader,* October 1, 1969. As indicated in *Kirstein v. Rector of Univ. of Va.,* the plan called for admission of 450 women in September 1970, 550 more in September 1971, and admission at the same rate as men beginning in September 1972.

63. *Kirstein v. Rector of Univ. of Va.,* p. 187.

64. Ibid.

65. *Owens v. Brown,* 455 F. Supp. 291 (D.D.C. 1978). The decision was made by district court judge John J. Sirica, who wrote in part that the legislative history "tends to suggest a statutory purpose more related to the traditional way of thinking of women than to the demands of military preparedness."

66. Pub. L. 95-485, Title VIII, §808, 92 Stat. 1623 (October 20, 1978).

67. *Women in the Military,* hearings before the House Committee on Armed Services, 96th Cong., 2d sess., November 13–16, 1979, and February 11, 1980, p. 231.

68. Maj. Gen. Jeanne Holm, USAF (Ret.), *Women in the Military: An Unfinished Revolution* (Presidio Press, 1982), pp. 367, 360.

69. *Rostker v. Goldberg,* 453 U.S. 57 (1981).

70. Judith Hicks Stiehm, *Arms and the Enlisted Woman* (Temple University Press, 1989), pp. 48, 55–56; Holm, *Women in the Military,* pp. xiv, 380–389.

71. 137 *Cong. Rec.* S5900 (statement of Senator William V. Roth, Jr., May 15, 1991).

72. Joan Hoff, *Law, Gender, and Injustice: A Legal History of U.S. Women* (New York University Press, 1991), p. 251; Charles Moskos, "Army Women: A Look at the Life, Sentiments, and the Aspirations," *Atlantic,* August 1990, pp. 71, 78. Also see Linda Bird Francke, *Ground Zero: The Gender Wars in the Military* (Simon and Schuster, 1997), pp. 50–51.

73. Francke, *Ground Zero,* p. 56.

74. Department of Defense, *Conduct of the Persian Gulf Conflict, Final Report to Congress* (1991), pp. 647–648; 137 *Cong. Rec.* S11,413–S11,435 (daily ed. July 31, 1991); D'Ann Campbell, "Combatting the Gender Gulf," 2 *Temple Political and Civil Rights Law Review* 63 (1992), pp. 69–70; Georgia Clark Sadler, "Women in Combat: The U.S. Military and the Impact of the Persian Gulf War" in *Wives and Warriors: Women and the Military in the United States and Canada,* ed. Laurie Weinstein and Christie C. White (Bergin and Garvey, 1997), pp. 79–97; Dana Priest, "Women at the Front," *Washington Post,* March 1, 1991; Molly Moore, "Women on the Battlefield," *Washington Post,* June 16, 1991; Capt. Carol Barkalow, "Women Have What It Takes," *Newsweek,* August 5, 1991.

75. Edward Walsh, "As Brave as Stallone . . . Beautiful as Brooke Shields," *Washington Post,* March 6, 1991; Amy Eskind, "A Post-Gulf Memorial Day, 1991: Arms and the Woman," *Washington Post,* May 26, 1991; Anna Quindlen, "Women in Combat," *New York Times,* January 8, 1992; Douglas Waller, "Women Can't Fly Jets and Other Myths," *Newsweek,* August 10, 1992; Melinda Beck et al., "Our Women in the Desert," *Newsweek,* September 10, 1990; Ellen Goodman, "Military Myths Meet Reality," *Boston Globe,* April 21, 1991; Guy Gugliotta, "Scuds Put U.S. Women on Front Line," *Washington Post,* January 28, 1991; Vaught quoted in Alan McConagha, "TV Channeled Women's Greater Role," *Washington Times,* June 18, 1991.

76. McConagha, "TV Channeled Women's Greater Role."

77. National Defense Authorization Act for Fiscal Years 1992 and 1993, Pub. L. No. 102-190, 105 Stat. 1290 (1991).

78. Roper Organization, *Attitudes Regarding the Assignment of Women in the Armed Forces: The Public Perspective* (August 1992).

79. Campbell, "Combatting the Gender Gulf," p. 86 n. 174.

80. *An Overview of U.S. Commitments and the Forces Available to Meet Them,* hearings before the Subcommittee on Military Personnel and Compensation of the House Committee on Armed Services, 98th Cong., 1st sess. 398 (1983) (statement of Richard Hunter, former staff director, military personnel policy, Office of Secretary of Defense); *Women in the Military,* hearings before the Military Personnel and Compensation Subcommittee of the House Committee on Armed Services, 100th Cong., 1st and 2d sess. 75 (1987 and 1988) (statement of Martin Ferber, senior associate director, National Security and International Affairs Division, General Accounting Office); Billie Mitchell, "The Creation of Army Officers and the Gender Lie: Betty Grable or Frankenstein?" in *It's Our Military, Too! Women and the U.S. Military,* ed. Judith Hicks Stiehm (Temple University Press, 1996), p. 39. See Mady Wechsler Segal, "The Argument for Female Combatants," in *Female Soldiers— Combatants or Noncombatants? Historical and Contemporary Perspectives,* ed. Nancy L. Goldman (Greenwood Press, 1982), pp. 267, 271, 272; Judith Hicks Stiehm, *Bring Me Men and Women: Mandated Change at the U.S. Air Force Academy* (University of California Press, 1981), p. 25.

81. James D. Milko, "Comment: Beyond the Persian Gulf Crisis: Expanding the Role of Servicewomen in the United States Military," 41 *American University Law Review* 1301 (1992), pp. 1314–1317.

82. Barkalow, "Women Have What It Takes."

10. In Judge Kiser's Court

1. Michael Hemphill, "She Wrote About It All with Paper, Pen, Accuracy," *Roanoke Times,* January 23, 1999. Kiser made the comment when Taylor retired in 1999.

2. *United States v. Virginia,* 766 F. Supp. 1407 (W.D. Va. 1992), Joint Appendix, p. 4; hereafter Joint Appendix.

3. Author's interview with Michael Maurer.

4. Author's interview with Judith Keith.

5. Author's interview with Maurer.

6. Matt Chittum, "VMI out of Step with Academies," *Roanoke Times,* August 30, 1998.

7. Joint Appendix, pp. 4, 6.

8. Ibid., pp. 7–8; emphasis added.

9. Ibid., pp. 8, 10.

10. Ibid., p. 9.

11. Author's interview with Robert Patterson and Anne Marie Whittemore.

12. Author's interviews with Maurer, Patterson, and Whittemore.

13. Author's interview with Maurer.

14. Author's interview with Patterson and Whittemore.

15. Joint Appendix, p. 19.

16. Ibid., pp. 22–23.

17. Liza Mundy, "'It Couldn't Be the Same Thing as VMI,'" *Washington Post Magazine,* March 10, 1996.

18. Joint Appendix, pp. 41, 54, 55.

19. Ibid., pp. 75–76.

20. Ibid., p. 71.

21. Author's interview with Norman M. Bissell.

22. Joint Appendix, p. 803.

23. Ibid., p. 802.

24. Ibid., pp. 163, 786, 129.

25. Ibid., pp. 781–783.

26. Author's interview with Bissell.

27. Joint Appendix, pp. 784–787.

28. Ibid., pp. 107, 109, 114.

29. Ibid., p. 810.

30. Ibid., pp. 810–812.

31. Author's interview with Bissell.

32. Author's interview with Keith.

33. Joint Appendix, p. 1065.

34. John F. Harris, "Letters from Women Entered at VMI Trial," *Washington Post,* April 6, 1991.

35. Joint Appendix, p. 971.

36. Ibid., pp. 308–312.

37. Ibid., pp. 315–318.

38. Ibid., pp. 332–339.

39. Ibid., pp. 344–350.

40. Ibid., p. 347.

41. Henry A. Wise, *Drawing Out the Man: The VMI Story* (University Press of Virginia for the VMI Alumni Association, 1978), p. 294.

42. Joint Appendix, pp. 332–339, 355–364, 363.

43. Ibid., p. 364.

44. Ibid., pp. 364–372.

45. Ibid., pp. 370–371.

46. Ibid., pp. 371–372.

47. Author's interview with Patterson and Whittemore.

48. Carol Gilligan, *In a Different Voice: Psychological Theory and Women's Development* (Harvard University Press, 1982). Gilligan's critics argue that speaking of a "feminine voice" contributes to the belief that women and men are different psychologically as well as physiologically and that treating them differently socially and legally is therefore justified.

49. Ibid., pp. 105, 8, 174.

50. Joint Appendix, p. 380.

51. Gilligan, *In a Different Voice,* p. 2.

52. Author's interview with Keith.

11. If Women Were Rats

1. *United States v. Virginia*, 766 F. Supp. 1407 (W.D. Va. 1992), Joint Appendix, pp. 424–430; hereafter Joint Appendix.

2. Ibid., pp. 433–439.

3. Ibid., pp. 443–469.

4. Ibid., pp. 471–474.

5. Ibid., pp. 483–485, 489, 491–492.

6. Ibid., pp. 493–494.

7. Ibid., pp. 494–496.

8. Ibid., pp. 508–509.

9. Ibid., pp. 522–523.

10. Ibid., pp. 532–535.

11. Ibid., pp. 555–556, 559–560.

12. Ibid., pp. 560–565.

13. Ibid., p. 570.

14. *Mississippi University for Women v. Hogan,* 458 U.S. 718 (1982), pp. 724, 726.

15. Joint Appendix, p. 652.

16. Ibid.

17. Ibid., pp. 655–656.

18. Ibid., pp. 657–659.

19. Ibid., p. 660.

20. Author's interview with Michael Maurer.

21. Joint Appendix, pp. 688–689.

22. Ibid., pp. 691–692.

23. Ibid., pp. 694–695.

24. Ibid., pp. 53, 79, 85, 109.

25. Videotaped deposition of David Riesman, February 21, 1991, p. 24; hereafter Riesman deposition.

26. Ibid., pp. 25–30.

27. Ibid., pp. 39–42, 45.

28. Ibid., pp. 59–61.

29. Ibid., pp. 31, 37–39.

30. Ibid., pp. 58, 94.

31. Ibid., p. 101.

32. Ibid., pp. 56–57.

33. Ibid., p. 61.

34. Ibid., p. 65.

35. Ibid., pp. 65, 66, 67, 73.

36. Ibid., pp. 72–73.

37. Ibid., p. 100.

38. Ibid., p. 110.

39. Joint Appendix, pp. 902–907, 901.

40. Ibid., p. 987.

41. Ibid., p. 988.

42. Ibid., pp. 990–991.

43. Ibid., pp. 992–993.

44. Ibid., p. 994.

45. Ibid., p. 1001.

46. Ibid., p. 1002.

47. Ibid., pp. 994, 999, 1000.

48. Ibid., p. 1000.

49. Ibid., pp. 1008–1011.

50. Ibid., pp. 1030, 1032–1033.

51. Ibid., pp. 1035, 1037–1038.

52. See, e.g., John F. Harris, "VMI Trial Is a Study in Contrasts," *Washington Post,* April 12, 1991.

53. Joint Appendix, pp. 1039–1040.

54. Ibid., pp. 1044–1045.

55. 42 U.S.C. 2000c-6.

56. Harris, "VMI Trial Is Study in Contrasts."

57. John F. Harris, "Ghosts of Old Virginia Haunt VMI Bias Trial," *Washington Post,* April 5, 1991.

58. Ellen Goodman, "VMI: Repository of Reaction . . . ," *Washington Post,* June 22, 1991.

59. John F. Harris, "For VMI, an Unlikely Defender of Discrimination," *Washington Post,* April 11, 1991.

60. Ibid.

61. Joint Appendix, p. 1058.

62. Ibid., pp. 1056–1057, 1053, 1054.

63. Ibid. p. 1063.

64. Ibid., p. 1059.

65. Ibid., pp. 1060, 1065.

66. Harris, "Ghosts of Old Virginia."

67. Joint Appendix, pp. 1065–1066.

12. The Judge and the Drummer

1. *United States v. Virginia,* 766 F. Supp. 1407 (W.D. Va. 1992), p. 1408.

2. *Regents v. Bakke,* 438 U.S. 265 (1978).

3. *Sweezy v. New Hampshire,* 354 U.S. 234, 263 (1957) (Frankfurter, concurring).

4. *Williams v. McNair,* 401 U.S. 951 (1971).

5. *Ayers v. Allain,* 914 F.2d 676 (5th Cir. 1990 en banc), cert. granted sub nom. *United States v. Mabus,* 499 U.S. 958 (1991).

6. *United States v. Fordice,* 505 U.S. 717 (1992).

7. 766 F. Supp. 1407, at p. 1410.

8. *Missouri ex rel. Gaines v. Canada,* 305 U.S. 337 (1938); *Sipuel v. Board of Re-*

gents, 332 U.S. 631 (1948); *Sweatt v. Painter,* 339 U.S. 629 (1950); *McLaurin v. Oklahoma,* 339 U.S. 637 (1950), cited in *United States v. Virginia,* 766 F. Supp. 1407, at p. 1409.

9. 766 F. Supp. 1407, at p. 1411.

10. Ibid.

11. Ibid.

12. Ibid., pp. 1411–1412.

13. Ibid. p. 1412.

14. Ibid.

15. Ibid., pp. 1412–1413.

16. Ibid., p. 1413.

17. Ibid., p. 1414.

18. Ibid., p. 1413.

19. Ibid., p. 1414.

20. Ibid., p. 1415.

21. United States' Proposed Findings of Facts and Proposed Conclusions of Law; VMI Defendants' Proposed Findings of Fact and Conclusions of Law, *United States v. Virginia,* Civil Action No. 90-0126-R (1991).

22. United States' Proposed Findings of Facts and Proposed Conclusions of Law, p. 20.

23. VMI Defendants' Proposed Findings of Fact and Conclusions of Law, pp. 102–105.

24. 766 F. Supp. 1407, at p. 1436.

25. United States' Proposed Findings of Facts and Proposed Conclusions of Law, p. 116.

26. VMI Defendants' Proposed Findings of Fact and Conclusions of Law, pp. 98–99.

27. 766 F. Supp. 1407, at p. 1420.

28. Ibid., pp. 1431–1434.

29. Valorie K. Vojdik, "At War: Narrative Tactics in The Citadel and VMI Litigation," 19 *Harvard Women's Law Journal* 1 (1996), p. 19.

30. Kenneth L. Karst, "Woman's Constitution," 1984 *Duke Law Journal* 447 (1984), pp. 468, 470–471.

31. 766 F. Supp. 1407, p. 1432.

32. Ibid., pp. 1428–1429, 1430.

33. Ibid., p. 1411.

34. John F. Harris, "VMI's Bar on Women Is Upheld," *Washington Post,* June 18, 1991.

35. Bob Dart, "Judge OKs VMI Ban on Women," *Atlanta Journal and Constitution,* June 18, 1991.

36. "One for the Cadets," *Washington Times,* June 19, 1991.

37. Felicity Barringer, "Banning of Women at Military College Is Upheld," *New York Times,* June 18, 1991.

38. Harris, "VMI's Bar on Women Is Upheld."

39. "Wrong Gray Line," *New York Times,* June 19, 1991.

40. John F. Harris, "Justice Dept. to Appeal VMI Ruling," *Washington Post,* August

13, 1991; "Appeal Sought in Ruling that Let Military Institute Exclude Women," *New York Times,* November 19, 1991.

13. In a Higher Court

1. For a short time during Ruth Bader Ginsburg's tenure at the Women's Rights Project, she had a codirector (Brenda Feigen Fasteau). Ginsburg was followed as director first by Kathleen Peratis and then by Pinzler.
2. Author's interview with Isabelle Katz Pinzler.
3. Ibid.
4. For a discussion of the history and possible impact of amicus briefs, see Joseph D. Kearney and Thomas W. Merrill, "The Influence of Amicus Curiae Briefs on the Supreme Court," 148 *University of Pennsylvania Law Review* 743 (January 2000); Samuel Krislov, "The Amicus Curiae Brief: From Friendship to Advocacy," 72 *Yale Law Journal* 694 (1963); Lee Epstein et al., *The Supreme Court Compendium: Data, Decisions and Developments,* 2d ed. (Congressional Quarterly, 1996), pp. 647–648.
5. Kearney and Merrill, "Influence of Amicus Curiae Briefs," p. 753 n. 25.
6. Author's interview with Pinzler.
7. Ibid.
8. Author's interview with Marcia Greenberger.
9. Ibid.
10. Ibid. The Center's brief in *Hogan* was filed by Zona Fairbanks Hostetler, Suellen Terrill Keiner, Phyllis N. Segal, Greenberger, and Judith L. Lichtman.
11. Author's interviews with Pinzler and Greenberger.
12. Brief Amici Curiae of the American Civil Liberties Union and ACLU Foundation of Virginia, National Women's Law Center, American Association of University Women, Center for Women Policy Studies, National Organization for Women, NOW Legal Defense and Education Fund, Virginia National Organization for Women, Virginia NOW Legal Defense and Education Fund, Women's Law Project, and Women's Legal Defense Fund, in Support of Appellant, *United States v. Virginia,* no. 91-1690, 976 F.2d 890 (1972).
13. Author's interview with Pinzler.
14. Ibid.
15. Author's interviews with Pinzler and Greenberger.
16. Author's interview with Eileen Wagner.
17. Letter from Eileen Wagner to author, March 10, 1999.
18. Brief Amici Curiae of the ACLU et al., pp. 6–11.
19. Brief Amici Curiae of Virginia Women Attorneys Association, Virginia Chapters of the American Association of University Women, Older Women's League, Virginia Federation of Business and Professional Women's Clubs, Inc., Friends of VMI for Equality, Dr. Alexander W. Astin, pp. 14–15; hereafter Wagner brief.
20. Ibid., p. 21.
21. Ibid., p. 16.

22. Alexander Astin, *Four Critical Years: Effects of College on Beliefs, Attitudes, and Knowledge* (Jossey-Bass, 1978).

23. Wagner brief, pp. 25–32.

24. Alexander Astin, "VMI Case Dramatizes Basic Issues in the Use of Educational Research," *Chronicle of Higher Education,* July 24, 1991, p. A36.

25. Wagner brief, pp. 36–37.

26. Astin, "VMI Case."

27. Wagner brief, pp. 38–44.

28. Author's interview with Jessica Silver.

29. Federal Rule of Civil Procedure 52(a). See *Anderson v. City of Bessemer,* 470 U.S. 564, 573, 576 (1985).

30. Author's interview with Silver.

31. *United States v. Virginia,* no. 91-1690, 976 F.2d 890 (1972), transcript of oral argument, pp. 3, 36, 42.

32. Neil A. Lewis, "An Appeals Court that Always Veers to the Right," *New York Times,* May 24, 1999.

33. President Bill Clinton would appoint the first African American to the court at the end of 2000, when Congress was out of session and Clinton could make an interim appointment. President George W. Bush reappointed the judge, Roger L. Gregory, to the usual federal lifetime term in 2001.

34. Lewis, "An Appeals Court." The two members in question were James Harvie Wilkinson III and J. Michael Luttig.

35. Transcript of oral argument, p. 3.

36. Ibid., pp. 6, 8.

37. Ibid., p. 10.

38. Ibid., p. 15.

39. Ibid., p. 16.

40. Ibid., p. 17.

41. Author's interview with Pinzler.

42. Transcript of oral argument, p. 42.

43. Ibid., p. 44.

44. Author's interviews with Patterson and Whittemore and Silver.

45. Transcript of oral argument, p. 19.

46. Ibid., p. 10.

47. Ibid., p. 21.

48. Ibid., pp. 31, 35, 36.

49. *United States v. Virginia,* 976 F.2d 890 (1992).

50. Ibid., p. 892; also see p. 900.

51. Ibid., pp. 893–894.

52. Ibid., pp. 894–895.

53. Ibid.

54. Ibid., p. 896.

55. Ibid., pp. 896–897.

56. Ibid., p. 897. The article is Marvin Bressler and Peter Wendell, "The Sex

Composition of Selective Colleges and Gender Differences in Career Aspirations," 51 *Journal of Higher Education* 650 (1980).

57. 976 F. 2d 890, at p. 898.

58. Ibid., p. 899.

59. Ibid., pp. 898–899.

60. Ibid., p. 900.

61. Jennifer R. Cowan, "Distinguishing Private Women's Colleges from the VMI Decision," 30 *Columbia Journal of Law and Social Problems* 137 (1997), p. 149.

62. Author's interview with Pinzler.

63. Author's interview with Silver.

64. Neil A. Lewis, "Court Tells Virginia to Give All Access to Military Training," *New York Times,* October 6, 1992.

65. "VMI Appeals Ruling on Admissions," *Washington Post,* October 20, 1992.

66. *United States v. Virginia,* Appellees' Petition for Rehearing and Suggestion for Rehearing en Banc, 1992 U.S. App. LEXIS 30490, pp. 1–2.

67. *United States v. Virginia,* US' Opposition to Appellees' Petition for Rehearing and Suggestion for Rehearing en Banc, submitted pursuant to Court's request, 1992 U.S. App. LEXIS 30490.

68. Ibid.

69. DeNeen L. Brown, "Final Cut Leaves VMI out of Inaugural Parade," *Washington Post,* January 5, 1993; George F. Will, "Government Coercion, VMI's Diversity," *Washington Post,* January 31, 1993.

70. 61 U.S.L.W. 3590 (February 23, 1993).

71. Scott Jaschik, "7 Women's Colleges Back VMI's Appeal to Retain All-Male Student Body: They Tell Supreme Court They're Threatened; Others Call Them Dupes," *Chronicle of Higher Education,* April 7, 1993.

72. Ibid.

73. *United States. v. Virginia,* Brief for the United States in Opposition, April 1993.

74. *Virginia Military Institute et al. v. United States,* 508 U.S. 946 (1993).

75. Certiorari statistics from the U.S. Supreme Court.

76. John F. Harris and Joan Biskupic, "High Court Rebuffs VMI Appeal," *Washington Post,* May 25, 1993; National Association of Attorneys General, "Supreme Court Denies Cert in Virginia All-Male School Case," *AG Bulletin,* May 1993.

77. John F. Harris, "VMI Working to Stay All Male, Sources Say," *Washington Post,* June 2, 1993.

14. In a Different Voice

1. Council of Higher Education for Virginia, *The Virginia Plan for Higher Education 1987,* p. 105; see also Mary Baldwin Web site, www.mbc.edu.

2. Author's interview with Gordon Bowen; see also *United States v. Virginia,* 852 F. Supp. 471, 501–502 (1994).

3. Author's interview with Brenda Bryant.

4. *United States v. Virginia,* 852 F. Supp. 471 (1994), Joint Appendix, pp. 419–420; hereafter Joint Appendix.

5. Author's interviews with Bryant and Bowen.

6. Joint Appendix, p. 421.

7. Ibid., p. 482.

8. Ibid., p. 422.

9. Ibid., p. 478; Peter Baker and Robert O'Harrow, Jr., "Wilder Considering Plan for Separate VMI Women's Program," *Washington Post,* September 24, 1993.

10. "The Virginia Women's Institute for Leadership at Mary Baldwin College," September 1994; hereafter VWIL Plan.

11. Joint Appendix, p. 428.

12. Carol Gilligan, *In a Different Voice: Psychological Theory and Women's Development* (Harvard University Press, 1982); Rosabeth Moss Kanter, *Men and Women of the Corporation* (Basic Books, 1977) and *When Giants Learn to Dance: Mastering the Challenge of Strategy, Management, and Careers in the 1990s* (Simon and Schuster, 1989); Antonia Fraser, *The Warrior Queens* (Knopf, 1989); Nannerl O. Keohane, "Educating Women for Leadership," 57 *Vital Speeches* (July 15, 1991); Marilyn French, *Beyond Power: On Women, Men, and Morals* (Summit Books, 1985); Deborah Tannen, *You Just Don't Understand: Women and Men in Conversation* (Morrow, 1990).

13. Helen S. Astin and Carole Leland, *Women of Influence, Women of Vision: A Cross-Generational Study of Leaders and Social Change* (Jossey-Bass, 1991); Ann M. Morrison, Randall P. White, Ellen Van Velsor, and the Center for Creative Leadership, *Breaking the Glass Ceiling: Can Women Reach the Top of America's Largest Corporations?* (Addison-Wesley, 1992); Dorothy W. Cantor and Toni Bernay, with Jean Stoess, *Women in Power: The Secrets of Leadership* (Houghton Mifflin, 1992).

14. Author's interview with Bryant; "Women and Leadership: A Selected Bibliography" and list of task force members supplied by Dr. Bryant.

15. Author's interview with Bryant; e-mail to author from Dean Heather Wilson, July 6, 1999.

16. Wilson e-mail.

17. Joint Appendix, pp. 430–431.

18. R. L. Owen, "MBC Program for Women and Leadership: 'A Modest Proposal'"; "Virginia Women's Institute for Leadership at MBC: Where We Are Now," November 22, 1994; Virginia Francisco/Carrie Douglass plan; Lott testimony, Joint Appendix, pp. 422–441.

19. VWIL Plan, p. 7.

20. Ibid., pp. 711.

21. Ibid., p. 2.

22. Ibid., pp. 1–2.

23. Joint Appendix, pp. 1423–1424.

24. MBC leaders said that VWIL women would live apart from other MBC students in the former barracks of the Staunton Military Academy once enrollment in the program reached fifty. Tyson's goal reportedly was 700 students. Debbi Wilgoren, "Plan

for Female VMI Splits Campus," *Washington Post,* September 29, 1993. It was unclear at the time when the more modest number of fifty would be reached—although, as it turned out, 141 women were enrolled for the 1999–2000 academic year. The separate quarters would not parallel the Spartan regime in VMI's Barracks.

25. Wes Allison, "No Stranger to Battle, VMI Fights Feeling of Frustration," and Pamela Stallsmith, "Mary Baldwin Looks to Future as VWIL Students Finish First Year" (articles combined as "Awaiting Washington's Word"), *Richmond Times-Dispatch,* May 12, 1996.

26. *United States v. Virginia,* no. 90-0126-R, 852 F. Supp. 471 (1994), deposition 255, quoted in U.S. Brief, p. 16.

27. *United States v. Virginia,* 852 F. Supp. 471, 502 (1994).

28. Ibid., p. 503.

29. Council of Higher Education for Virginia, "Total Appropriations for Operating Expenses at Public Institutions, 1990–91," January 10, 1991.

30. Joint Appendix, p. 156.

31. Author's interview with Michael Maurer.

32. *United States v. Virginia,* no. 90-0126-R, 852 F. Supp. 471 (W.D. Va. 1994), "VMI Defendants' Proposed Remedial Plan," September 27, 1993, p. 7.

33. Ibid.,

34. John F. Harris, "Judge's Order Throws Wilder into the Battle over VMI Policy," *Washington Post,* August 10, 1993.

35. Ibid.; John F. Harris, "Wilder Eyes a VMI for Women," *Washington Post,* September 26, 1993; "Military College to Start Separate Women's Course," *New York Times,* September 27, 1993.

36. Harris, "Judge's Order Throws Wilder." Robb was known in Virginia as a strong believer in equal protection of the laws and may well have supported the suit out of conviction, but he was unlikely to have regretted the political dilemma it created for Wilder.

37. Peter Baker and Robert O'Harrow, Jr., "Wilder Considering Plan for Separate VMI Women's Program," *Washington Post,* September 24, 1993; Harris, "Wilder Eyes VMI for Women"; "Military College to Start Separate Women's Course."

38. Eileen Wagner, "VMI Wants Taxpayers to Foot Bill to Protect It from Winds of Change," *Richmond Times-Dispatch,* February 24, 1994; "In Court, College Defends Separation of Sexes," *New York Times,* February 13, 1994.

39. "Virginia Military Institute to Establish Courses at Women's College."

40. Debbi Wilgoren, "Plan for Female VMI Splits Campus," *Washington Post,* September 29, 1993; Liza Mundy, "'It Couldn't Be the Same Thing as VMI,'" *Washington Post Magazine,* March 10, 1996

41. Author's interviews with Bowen and Bryant.

42. *United States v. Virginia,* 852 F. Supp. 471 (1993), United States' Opposition and Response to the VMI Defendants' Proposed Remedial Plan, p. 23.

43. Ibid., p. 8.

44. Ibid., pp. 7, 9–10.

45. Deposition of Cynthia Tyson, p. 222, quoted in ibid., p. 15.

46. Deposition of John Knapp, pp. 22–24, 27, quoted in ibid., p. 19 n. 6.

47. United States' Opposition and Response, pp. 1, 8, 15.

48. Quoted in David Reed, "Judge's Decision Keeps Women out of VMI at Least for Now," *Houston Chronicle,* May 2, 1994.

15. Back in Judge Kiser's Court

1. *United States v. Virginia,* 852 F. Supp. 471 (W.D. Va. 1994).

2. Peter Baker, "Va. Tries to Make Case for Keeping VMI All-Male," *Washington Post,* February 10, 1994.

3. "VMI Defendants' Proposed Remedial Plan," pp. 2–3; also see William Henry Hurd, "Gone with the Wind? VMI's Loss and the Future of Single-Sex Public Education," 4 *Duke Journal of Gender Law and Policy* 27 (Spring 1997). Hurd, a Virginia deputy attorney general, became part of the VMI team in 1994.

4. *United States v. Virginia,* 852 F. Supp. 471 (W.D. Va. 1994), Joint Appendix, p. 95; hereafter Joint Appendix.

5. Ibid., pp. 95–97.

6. Ibid., pp. 100–101.

7. Ibid., pp. 106–107.

8. Ibid., pp. 112–113, 115.

9. Ibid., pp. 124–125.

10. Ibid., pp. 149, 150.

11. Ibid., pp. 156–158.

12. Ibid., pp. 189–191.

13. Ibid., pp. 190–207.

14. Ibid., p. 217.

15. Ibid., p. 219; Elizabeth Fox-Genovese, *Within the Plantation Household: Black and White Women of the Old South* (University of North Carolina Press, 1988), and *Feminism Without Illusions: A Critique of Individualism* (University of North Carolina Press, 1991).

16. Elizabeth Fox-Genovese, *Feminism Is Not the Story of My Life: How Today's Feminist Elite Has Lost Touch with the Real Concerns of Women* (Nan A. Talese, 1996).

17. Joint Appendix, pp. 290–292; Elizabeth Fox-Genovese, "Strict Scrutiny, VMI, and Women's Lives," 6 *Constitutional Law Journal* 987 (1996).

18. Fox-Genovese, "Strict Scrutiny."

19. Ibid.

20. Joint Appendix, pp. 228–230, 232–233, 247.

21. Fox-Genovese, "Strict Scrutiny," p. 989.

22. Joint Appendix, pp. 249–251.

23. Ibid., p. 259.

24. Ibid., pp. 326–333.

25. For criticism of Kiser's rulings, see, e.g., Brief Amici Curiae of Carol Gilligan, Valerie E. Lee, Diane S. Pollard, Bernice Sandler, and the Program on Gender,

Science, and Law, *Shannon Richey Faulkner v. Jones,* no. 94-1978, 51 F.3d 440 (4th Cir. 1995), pp. 20–23. Testimony of physiology expert Paul Davis is in *United States v. Virginia,* 766 F. Supp. 1407 (W.D. Va. 1972), p. 939; Bissell, ibid., p. 910; Riesman, Joint Appendix, pp. 696–697. The rules governing admissibility of expert witnesses are in Federal Rules of Evidence, Rule 702 ("If scientific, technical, or other specialized knowledge will assist the trier of fact to understand the evidence or to determine a fact in issue, a witness qualified as an expert by knowledge, skill, experience, training, or education, may testify thereto in the form of an opinion or otherwise.") and Rule 703 ("The facts or data in the particular case upon which an expert bases an opinion or inference may be those perceived by or made known to the expert at or before the hearing. If of a type reasonably relied upon by experts in the particular field in forming opinions or inferences upon the subject, the facts or data need not be admissible in evidence."), and in *Daubert v. Merrell Dow Pharmaceuticals,* 509 U.S. 579 (1993).

26. Joint Appendix, p. 341.

27. Ibid., p. 342.

28. Ibid., pp. 595–597.

29. Ibid., p. 378.

30. Ibid., pp. 390–391.

31. Ibid., pp. 516–518.

32. Ibid., p. 480.

33. Ibid., pp. 554–570.

34. Ibid., pp. 611–614.

35. Ibid., pp. 616–623.

36. Ibid., pp. 680–681, 693–694.

37. Ibid., pp. 718–719, 721.

38. Ibid., p. 723.

39. *Faulkner v. Jones,* 10 F.3d 226 (4th Cir. 1993), affirming grant of preliminary injunction to Faulkner and ordering her admitted to day classes.

40. *Faulkner v. Jones,* 858 F. Supp. 552 (D.S.C. 1994). Faulkner reported to campus on August 12, 1995, but dropped out less than a week later, citing the stress of her long legal battle. In 1995 Nancy Mellette, the daughter and sister of Citadel men, joined the lawsuit. The Citadel decided to admit women immediately following the Supreme Court's 1996 decision in the VMI case (see chapter 21). Two of the four women who subsequently became students left in 1997 after male cadets set their clothes on fire and sprayed deodorant in their mouths on three occasions. See Catherine S. Manegold, *In Glory's Shadow: Shannon Faulkner, The Citadel and a Changing America* (Knopf, 2000).

41. Joint Appendix, pp. 722–724, 726.

42. Ibid., pp. 727–728.

43. Ibid., pp. 728–730.

44. Ibid., pp. 737–739, 742–760.

45. Ibid., p. 739.

46. Ibid., pp. 761–766.

47. Ibid., pp. 767–770.

48. Ibid., p. 772.

49. Testimony of James F. Brewer III, in ibid., pp. 823–824.

50. Ibid., pp. 837–842; testimony of Clifton Conrad, in ibid., pp. 1048–1067.

51. Eleanor E. Maccoby and Carol Nagy Jacklin, *The Psychology of Sex Differences* (Stanford University Press, 1974); Carol Nagy Jacklin, ed., *The Psychology of Gender* (New York University Press, 1992).

52. Joint Appendix, pp. 855–858.

53. Ibid., pp. 865–866.

54. Ibid., pp. 885–886.

55. Ibid., p. 924.

56. Ibid., pp. 910–921.

57. *United States v. Virginia,* 852 F. Supp. 471 (W.D. Va. 1994), at p. 480.

58. Joint Appendix, p. 943.

59. Ibid., pp. 944–945.

60. Ibid., p. 986.

61. Ibid., pp. 1122, 1128–1129.

62. Ibid., pp. 1139–1147.

63. Ibid., p. 1221.

64. Ibid., pp. 1225–1250.

65. Ibid., pp. 1252–1253, 1256, 1266.

66. Ibid., pp. 1305–1310, 1320.

16. The Fife and the Drum, Separate but Equal

1. *United States v. Virginia,* 852 F. Supp. 471 (April 29, 1994), aff'd, remanded, 44 F.3d 1229 (4th Cir. 1995).

2. *United States v. Virginia,* 852 F. Supp. 471 (1994), at p. 475.

3. Ibid.

4. Ibid.

5. Ibid., p. 476.

6. Ibid., pp. 477, 481–483.

7. Ibid., pp. 478, 479, 480 n. 8.

8. Ibid., p. 480.

9. Ibid., p. 481.

10. Ibid.

11. Ibid., pp. 478, 484.

12. Ibid., p. 484.

13. Ibid., p. 485.

14. "VMI, College to Proceed with Co-ed Alternative," *Legal Intelligencer,* May 3, 1994.

15. "Judge Endorses V.M.I. Plan on Excluding Women," *New York Times,* May 2, 1994.

16. Ibid.

17. "Military-Style Women's School Plan Approved," *Los Angeles Times,* May 1, 1994, quoting VMI spokesman Mike Strickler.

18. Martin Weil, "Judge Backs Males-Only VMI Policy," *Washington Post,* May 1, 1994.

19. Donald P. Baker, "Allen Assails Efforts to End VMI's All-Male Status," *Washington Post,* May 22, 1994.

20. "Judge Kiser Misses the Beat, Again," *New York Times,* May 9, 1994.

21. "Reveille for a Military School," *Boston Globe,* May 10, 1994.

22. "A Marriage of Convenience," *St. Louis Post-Dispatch,* May 5, 1994.

23. "VMI Plan May Work," *News and Record* (Greensboro, N.C.), May 9, 1994.

24. *United States v. Virginia,* 94-1667 (44 F.3d 1229), Opening Brief for the U.S. as Appellant, p. 6; hereafter Opening Brief.

25. Ibid., p. 15.

26. Ibid., p. 17.

27. Ibid., pp. 17–18.

28. Ibid., pp. 20–23, citing *McKissick v. Carmichael,* 187 F.2d 949 (4th Cir.), cert. denied, 341 U.S. 951 (1951), and quoting *Mississippi v. Hogan* at p. 725.

29. *United States v. Virginia,* 94-1667 (44 F.3d 1229), Reply and Answering Brief for the U.S., p. 24; hereafter Reply Brief.

30. Ibid., p. 7.

31. Ibid., p. 42.

32. Ibid., p. 5.

33. *United States v. Virginia,* 94-1667 (44 F.3d 1229), Brief for the Respondents, p. 2.

34. Opening Brief, p. 24, citing *Michael M. v. Superior Court,* 450 U.S. 464 (1981).

35. Ibid., pp. 3, 25.

36. Ibid., pp. 4; 7, quoting 976 F.2d 898; 8–9.

37. Ibid., pp. 11, 38.

38. Ibid., pp. 11–14.

39. *United States v. Virginia,* 94-1667 (44 F.3d 1229), Brief Amici Curiae of National Women's Law Center, American Association of University Women, American Civil Liberties Union, California Women's Law Center, Center for Women Policy Studies, Connecticut Women's Education and Legal Fund, Equal Rights Advocates, Federally Employed Women, Inc., Feminist Majority Foundation, Human Rights Campaign Fund, Lawyer's Committee for Civil Rights Under Law, National Association for Girls and Women in Sport, National Association of Commissions for Women, National Council of Negro Women, National Education Association, National Gay and Lesbian Task Force, National Hookup of Black Women, National Organization for Women, NOW Legal Defense and Education Fund, National Women's Conference Committee, National Women's Party, Northwest Women's Law Center, Trial Lawyers for Public Justice, Women Employed, Women's Law Project, Women's Legal Defense Fund, YWCA of the U.S.A., for Plaintiff-Appellant; hereafter Joint Brief.

40. Ibid., p. 3.

41. Ibid., pp. 1–2.

42. Ibid., p. 19. The testimony was that of Paul Davis, admitted as an expert on physiology and physical education. *United States v. Virginia*, 852 F. Supp. 471 (W.D. Va. 1994), Joint Appendix, pp. 932, 939–940.

43. Joint Brief, p. 23.

44. Ibid., p. 24.

45. Ibid., pp. 24–29.

46. *United States v. Virginia*, 94-1667 (44 F.3d 1229), Brief Amicus Curiae of Mary Baldwin College for Defendants-Appellees.

47. *United States v. Virginia*, 94-1667 (44 F.3d 1229), Brief Amici Curiae of Wells College, Saint Mary's College, Southern Virginia College for Defendants-Appellees.

48. Scott Jaschik, "7 Women's Colleges Back VMI's Appeal to Retain All-Male Student Body: They Tell Supreme Court They're Threatened; Others Call Them Dupes," *Chronicle of Higher Education,* April 7, 1993; author's interviews with Robert Patterson and Anne Marie Whittemore, Gordon Davies, Eileen Wagner, and Page Miller.

49. Jaschik, "7 Women's Colleges."

50. "Justice Department Argues Program for Women Unacceptable," *Legal Intelligencer,* September 29, 1994.

51. Associated Press, "U.S. Faults VMI's Plans for Women," *Virginian-Pilot,* September 29, 1994.

52. "Justice Department Argues Program for Women Unacceptable"; Associated Press, "U.S. Faults VMI's Plans."

53. Associated Press, "U.S. Faults VMI's Plans."

54. Allison Blake, "VMI Gender Flap Back in Court," *Roanoke Times and World News,* September 29, 1994.

55. Author's interview with Jessica Silver.

56. *United States v. Virginia*, 44 F.3d 1229 (1995).

57. Ibid., p. 1232.

58. Ibid., p. 1235, quoting *Hogan* at p. 725.

59. Ibid., p. 1235.

60. Ibid., p. 1236.

61. Ibid.

62. Ibid.

63. Ibid., pp. 1237, 1238.

64. Ibid., p. 1238, quoting "A Burst of Popularity," *U.S. News and World Report,* September 26, 1994.

65. Ibid., p. 1239.

66. Ibid.

67. Ibid., p. 1242.

68. Ibid., p. 1243.

69. Ibid., pp. 1245, 1244.

70. Ibid., pp. 1244, 1245, 1246.

71. Ibid., p. 1247; quoted in *United States v. Virginia*, 518 U.S. 515, 529 (1996).

72. Ibid., pp. 1247, 1250, 1251.

73. *United States v. Virginia,* 52 F.3d 90; 1995 U.S. App. LEXIS 9761 (April 28, 1995).

74. Ruth Bader Ginsburg, comments on author's manuscript, March 2001.

75. 52 F.3d 90, at p. 91.

76. Ibid., citing *Faulkner v. Jones,* 51 F.3d 440 (4th Cir. 1995).

77. Ibid., p. 92, citing *J.E.B. v. Alabama,* 511 U.S. 127 (1994), at p. 137 n. 6.

78. Ibid.

79. Ibid., pp. 92–93.

80. Ibid., p. 93.

81. Ibid.

82. Ibid.

83. Ibid., pp. 93–94.

84. Ibid., p. 92.

17. Anticipating the Justices

1. "The government of the United States has been emphatically termed a government of laws, and not of men." Chief Justice John Marshall, in *Marbury v. Madison,* 5 U.S. 137 (1 Cranch 137), at p. 163.

2. *Califano v. Goldfarb,* 430 U.S. 199 (1977); *Craig v. Boren,* 429 U.S. 190, 212 (1976) (Stevens, concurring); Ruth Bader Ginsburg, "Sex Equality and the Constitution: The State of the Art," 4 *Women's Rights Law Reporter* 143 (1978), p. 145.

3. On alimony, *Orr v. Orr,* 440 U.S. 268 (1979); on juries, *Duren v. Missouri,* 439 U.S. 357 (1979).

4. *Michael M. v. Superior Court,* 450 U.S. 464 (1981), at p. 501 (Stevens, dissenting).

5. *Rostker v. Goldberg,* 453 U.S. 57 (1981).

6. *Michael M.,* p. 497 n. 4 (Stevens, dissenting).

7. *Caban v. Mohammed,* 441 U.S. 380, 403 (1979) (Stevens, dissenting)

8. *Mathews v. Lucas,* 427 U.S. 495, 516, 520–521 (1976) (Stevens, dissenting).

9. *Planned Parenthood v. Casey,* 505 U.S. 833 (1992).

10. *Roe v. Wade,* 410 U.S. 113 (1973).

11. *J.E.B. v. Alabama,* 511 U.S. 127 (1994).

12. Ibid., p. 130.

13. Ibid., pp. 131, 135.

14. Author's interview with Antonin Scalia.

15. *J.E.B.,* p. 160 (Scalia, dissenting).

16. *Virginia Military Institute v. United States,* 508 U.S. 949 (1993).

17. *Mississippi v. Hogan,* 458 U.S. 718 (1982), at pp. 729–730.

18. Ibid., p. 731.

19. *J.E.B.,* p. 152.

20. Ibid., p. 153, quoting Justice O'Connor's dissenting opinion in *Metro Broadcasting, Inc. v. FCC,* 497 U.S. 547, 602 (1990).

21. *Stathos v. Bowden,* 728 F.2d 15 (1st Cir. 1984); *Lamphere v. Brown University,* 875 F.2d 916 (1st Cir. 1989); *Dragon v. Rhode Island Dept. of Mental Health,* 936 F.2d 32 (1st Cir. 1991).

22. "Nomination of Stephen G. Breyer to Be an Associate Justice of the Supreme Court of the United States," hearings before the Committee on the Judiciary, U.S. Senate, 103d Cong., 2d sess., July 12–15, 1994, p. 179.

23. Author's interview with Robert Patterson and Anne Marie Whittemore.

24. *United States v. Virginia,* Brief for the Petitioner, p. 1.

25. *United States v. Virginia,* Reply Brief for the Petitioner, pp. 1–2.

26. Ibid., p. 2, citing *Missouri ex rel. Gaines v. Canada,* 305 U.S. 337, 351 (1938).

27. See, e.g., Brief for the Petitioner, pp. 34–36.

28. Brief for the Respondents, LEXIS, p. 14.

29. Reply Brief for the Petitioner on a writ of certiorari, pp. 5–6; Brief for the Petitioner, pp. 45, 47; also see Reply Brief for the Petitioner, pp. 3–4.

30. Brief for the Cross-Respondent, pp. 10–11; emphasis added.

31. Ibid., pp. 11, 26; Brief for the Petitioner, p. 26.

32. *Virginia v. United States,* Brief for the Cross-Respondent, p. 18.

33. *United States v. Virginia,* Brief for the Petitioner, p. 40.

34. Ibid., pp. 35–36, 41.

35. Brief for the Respondents, p. 10.

36. Ibid.; Brief for the Cross-Petitioners, p. 13.

37. Brief for the Cross-Petitioners, pp. 19, 13.

38. Brief for the Respondents, p. 16.

39. Ibid., p. 34.

40. Ibid., pp. 35–36, 33.

41. *United States v. Virginia,* Brief for the Petitioner, p. 33; also see *Virginia v. United States,* Brief for the Cross-Respondent, p. 17.

42. Author's interview with Joan Bertin.

43. Pinzler assumed her new job in June 1994. In January 1997 she became acting assistant attorney general in charge, among other things, of the Educational Opportunities Section.

44. Author's interview with Isabelle Katz Pinzler.

45. Author's interview with Bertin.

46. Author's interview with Pinzler.

47. Author's interviews with Pinzler, Bertin, and Marcia Greenberger; *Mississippi v. Hogan,* 458 U.S. 718 (1982), at p. 724 n. 9; *Stanton v. Stanton,* 421 U.S. 7 (1975), at p, 13; *J.E.B. v. Alabama,* p. 127 n. 6; *Harris v. Forklift Systems, Inc.,* 510 U.S. 17 (1993), at p. 26.

48. *Richmond v. J. A. Croson Co.,* 488 U.S. 469 (1989) (also see *Wygant v. Jackson Board of Education,* 476 U.S. 267 [1986]); *Adarand Constructors v. Pena,* 515 U.S. 200 (1995).

49. Author's interviews with Bertin and Greenberger.

50. See, e.g., *University of California Regents v. Bakke,* 438 U.S. 265 (1978); *Fullilove v. Klutznick,* 448 U.S. 448 (1980).

51. Felicity Barringer, "Banning of Women at Military College Is Upheld," *New York Times,* June 18, 1991.

52. Author's interviews with Pinzler and Greenberger.

53. *Virginia v. United States,* Brief for the Cross-Respondent, pp. 16–17.

54. *United States v. Virginia,* Brief for the Respondents, pp. 22–23; *Virginia v. United States,* Brief for the Cross-Petitioner, p. 20.

18. Other Voices

1. Author's interview with Ruth Bader Ginsburg (2000); Ruth Bader Ginsburg, "Constitutional Adjudication in the United States as a Means of Advancing the Equal Stature of Men and Women Under the Law," 26 *Hofstra Law Review* 263 (1997), p. 267.

2. Author's interviews with Ginsburg and Lisa Beattie.

3. Ibid.

4. Author's interview with Joan Bertin.

5. Ibid.

6. Brief of Amici Curiae National Women's Law Center, American Civil Liberties Union in Support of Petitioner, American Association of University Women, The American Jewish Committee, Anti-Defamation League, Business and Professional Women/USA, Center for Women Policy Studies, Coalition of Labor Union Women, Connecticut Women's Education and Legal Fund, Feminist Majority Foundation, Federally Employed Women, Inc., Mexican American Legal Defense and Educational Fund, National Association for Girls and Women in Sports, National Association of Social Workers, National Council of Jewish Women, National Council of Negro Women, National Education Association, National Organization for Women, NOW Legal Defense and Education Fund, National Women's Conference Committee, National Women's Party, Older Women's League, People for the American Way, Trial Lawyers for Public Justice, Women Employed, Women's Law Project, Women's Legal Defense Fund, Women Work!, The National Network for Women's Employment; hereafter Joint Brief.

7. Ibid., p. 1.

8. Ibid., pp. 3, 2.

9. Ibid., pp. 2–3, citing *Richmond v. Croson,* 488 U.S. 469 (1989), and *Adarand v. Pena,* 515 U.S. 200 (1995).

10. Amicus Brief of Employment Law Center of the Legal Aid Society of San Francisco, Equal Rights Advocates, Inc., Chinese for Affirmative Action, the Women's Employment Rights Clinic of the Golden Gate University School of Law, National Economic Development and Law Center, Human Rights Advocates. It was also signed by three female law professors in the San Francisco area.

11. Ibid., pp. 25, 27.

12. Amicus Brief of Lawyers' Committee for Civil Rights Under Law in Support of Cross-Respondent United States of America.

13. Amicus Brief of Maryland, Hawaii, Massachusetts, Nevada, and Oregon, and the Northern Mariana Islands, p. 9.

14. Amicus Brief of Twenty-six Private Women's Colleges, p. 5. It was signed by Bennett College (N.C.), Brenau Women's College (Ga.), Chatham College (Pa.), Chestnut Hill College (Pa.), College of St. Benedict (Minn.), College of St. Catherine (Minn.), College of St. Elizabeth (N.J.), College of St. Mary (Nebr.), Columbia College (S.C.), Hartford College for Women (Conn.), Lesley College (Mass.), Marymount College–Tarrytown (N.Y.), Midway College (Ky.), Mount St. Mary's College (Calif.), Mount Vernon College (D.C.), Notre Dame College of Ohio, Pine Manor College (Pa.), Russell Sage College (N.Y.), St. Mary's College (Ind.), St. Mary-of-the-Woods College (Ind.), Seton Hall College (Pa.), Spelman College (Ga.), Trinity College (D.C.), Trinity College of Vermont, Ursuline College (Ohio), and Wilson College (Pa.).

15. *United States v. Virginia,* 518 U.S. 515 (1996), at p. 545 nn. 13, 14.

16. Brief Amici Curiae of Lieutenant Colonel Rhonda Cornum, USA; Brigadier General Evelyn P. Foote, USA (Ret.); Captain Patrician Murphy Gormley, JAG, USN (Ret.); Kristine Holderied; Major Andrea Hollen, USA (Ret.); Major General Jeanne Holm, USAF (Ret.); Major Pat Walker Locke, USA (Ret.); Danna Maller; Major Lillian A. Pfluke, USA (Ret.); Lieutenant Julie M. Roberts, SC, USNR; Major Alison Ruttenberg, COANG; Mary Rosinski Whitley; Brigadier General Roger C. Bultman, USA (Ret.); Dr. Margarethe Cammemeyer; Captain (SEL) Eileen L. O'Hickey, CHC, USN; Lieutenant Colonel Karen Johnson, USAF (Ret.); Major Jane McKeon, USA; Major Mary A. Finch, USA; and Women Active in Our Nation's Defense, Their Advocates and Supporters (WANDAS), Appendix, pp. 1a–11a. Seventeen of the signatories were women; the eighteenth was Brig. Gen. Roger C. Bultman (Ret.).

17. See, e.g., *Struck v. Secretary of Defense,* 460 F.2d 1372 (9th Cir. 1971), judgment vacated, 409 U.S. 1071 (1972). Holm also wrote one of the leading histories of women in the military: *Women in the Military: An Unfinished Revolution* (Presidio Press, 1982).

18. Brief, Cornum et al., pp. 2–3.

19. Ibid., pp. 5, 10–14.

20. Ibid., pp. 10–12.

21. Ibid., p. 15.

22. Rhonda Cornum as told to Peter Copeland, *She Went to War: The Rhonda Cornum Story* (Presidio, 1992), p. 90.

23. Brief Amici Curiae of the Center for Military Readiness, the Family Research Council, the Minnesota Family Council, Concerned Women for America, the Madison Project, the Eagle Forum, the Free Congress Foundation, and the Northstar Legal Center in Support of Respondent Commonwealth of Virginia, Appendix, pp. 1a–3a.

24. Ibid., pp. 5, 25–29.

25. Brief Amici Curiae of Independent Women's Forum, Women's Economic Project, Diana Furchtgott-Roth, Linda Chavez, Lynne V. Cheney, Christina Hoff Sommers, Abigail Thernstrom in Support of Respondents. Chavez was a former director of the U.S. Commission on Civil Rights; Sommers, a philosophy professor; and Thernstrom, coauthor of a book critical of affirmative action.

26. Ibid., pp. 8, 12–14.

27. Peter Hardin, "Female Officers Join VMI Legal Battle; Court Brief Cites Their Success Stories in Assailing Males-Only Admissions," *Richmond Times-Dispatch*, December 4, 1995.

28. Brief Amici Curiae in Support of Respondents by Dr. Kenneth E. Clark, Miriam B. Clark, Dr. James E. Colvard, Professor Susan Estrich, Sally Helgesen, Sara N. King, and Professor David Riesman. Clark was the psychologist whose work became the underpinning for *Brown v. Board of Education;* Estrich, the manager of Michael Dukakis's presidential campaign, was a former member of the ACLU Board of Directors.

29. Ibid., pp. 2–4, 5, 10.

30. Brief Amici Curiae of Wells College, Southern Virginia College, and Saint Mary's College Supporting Affirmance.

31. Amici Curiae Brief of Women's Schools Together, Inc.; Boys' Schools: An International Coalition; Robert Bobb; Thomas H. Butler, Ed.D.; Dr. Roy J. Dawson; Peter M. Flanigan; Dr. Richard Hawley; Frank Hayden; Dr. Spencer Holland; Nancy E. Kussrow; Professor Mary R. Lefkowitz; Kathleen S. McCreary; Joan S. McMenanim; Joseph W. McPherson; Dr. Angela Pienkos; Dr. Diane Ravitch; Dr. Cornelius Riordan; Dr. Joseph Spirito; Michael M. Uhlmann; and the Honorable Arnold W. Webster, Ph.D., in Support of Respondents, Cross-Petitioners.

32. Ibid., p. 2.

33. Brief of Amici Curiae the State of South Carolina and The Citadel, the Military College of South Carolina in Support of the Commonwealth of Virginia, et al.

34. Brief of Amicus Curiae South Carolina Institute of Leadership for Women in Support of Respondents.

35. Ibid., pp. 21–22.

36. Ibid., Appendix, pp. 1a–5a.

37. Brief of Amici Curiae States in Support of the Commonwealth of Virginia, p. 4.

38. Brief of Mary Baldwin College as Amicus Curiae in Support of Respondents, pp. 3, 7–8, 8–15.

39. Author's interview with Robert Patterson and Anne Marie Whittemore.

40. In 2001, Olson became solicitor general in the administration of president George W. Bush.

41. Ruth Bader Ginsburg, comments on author's manuscript, March 2001; hereafter RBG comments on manuscript.

42. Author's interview with Beattie.

43. Author's interview with Antonin Scalia.

44. RBG comments on manuscript; *Vorchheimer v. School District,* 532 F.2d 880 (3rd Cir. 1976), aff'd per curiam, 430 U.S. 703 (1977) (see discussion of the case in chapter 5).

19. Speaking to the Nation's Highest Court

1. Wes Allison, "Feisty Crowd Turns out to Watch Legal Serves," *Richmond Times-Dispatch*, January 18, 1996.

2. Author's interviews with Judith Keith, Robert Patterson and Anne Marie Whittemore, Lisa Beattie, Michael Maurer, Isabelle Katz Pinzler, and Joan Bertin; Peter Hardin, "VMI Prepares for Ultimate Battle," *Richmond Times-Dispatch,* January 14, 1996; Allison, "Feisty Crowd." The Supreme Court bar consists of lawyers permitted to argue before the Court. Membership is not exclusionary, and virtually any lawyer can be admitted in a simple ceremony held at the Court. Transcripts of oral arguments now reach the justices the following day.

3. The sobriquet probably was bestowed on the Court's home, completed in 1935, by John Paul Frank in *Marble Palace: The Supreme Court in American Life* (Knopf, 1958).

4. *United States v. Virginia,* 518 U.S. 515 (1996), oral arguments, p. 1.

5. Author's interviews with Pinzler, Bertin, and Marcia Greenberger.

6. Lyle Denniston, "The Center Moves, the Center Remains," 40 *New York Law School Law Review* 877, 884 (1996).

7. Author's interview with Antonin Scalia.

8. Margaret Carlson, "The Crying Game: No Female Stereotype Is Too Familiar or Out of Date for Virginia Military Institute, Fighting to Stay All Male," *Time,* January 29, 1996.

9. Author's interview with Patterson and Whittemore.

10. Author's interview; Allison, "Feisty Crowd."

20. The High Court Replies

1. "The judiciary . . . has no influence over either the sword or the purse; no direction either of the strength or of the wealth of the society; and can take no active resolution whatever. It may truly be said to have neither FORCE nor WILL, but merely judgment; and must ultimately depend upon the aid of the executive arm even for the efficacy of its judgments." *The Federalist Papers* no. 78.

2. Author's interview with Robert Patterson and Anne Marie Whittemore. See chapter 10.

3. Philippa Strum, "Change and Continuity on the Supreme Court: Conversations with Justice Harry A. Blackmun," *University of Richmond Law Review,* March 2000.

4. Author's interview with Ruth Bader Ginsburg (2000).

5. Ibid.

6. Author's interview with Lisa Beattie.

7. Author's interviews with Beattie and Ginsburg (2000); author's interview with Ginsburg (1994).

8. Author's interview with Beattie.

9. Ruth Bader Ginsburg, comments on author's manuscript, March 2001; hereafter RBG comments on manuscript.

10. Author's interview with Ginsburg (2000).

11. Ibid.; RBG comments on manuscript.

12. *Kirstein v. Rector,* 309 F. Supp. 184 (1970), at pp. 185–186.

13. Author's interview with Ginsburg (2000), citing her reference in *United States v. Virginia,* 518 U.S. 515, 538, 556 (1996), and that of Justice Scalia, dissenting, at p. 584.

14. Author's interview with Antonin Scalia.

15. Author's interview with Ginsburg (2000).

16. *Vorchheimer v. School District,* 532 F.2d 880 (3rd Cir. 1976), aff'd per curiam, 430 U.S. 703 (1977) (see discussion of the case in chapter 5).

17. Author's interview with Ginsburg (2000).

18. Kenneth L. Karst, "Woman's Constitution," 1984 *Duke Law Journal* 447 (1984), pp. 497–498.

19. *United States v. Virginia,* p. 520.

20. Ibid., p. 525, quoting *United States v. Virginia,* 976 F.2d 890, 899 (1992), in turn quoting from 1990 *Report of the Virginia Commission on the University of the 21st Century.*

21. 518 U.S. 515, at pp. 528, 546.

22. Ibid., pp. 529, 530.

23. Ibid., p. 530.

24. Ibid., pp. 531–533.

25. Ibid., pp. 533–534.

26. Ibid., pp. 535–536.

27. Author's interview with Ginsburg (2000). In 1997 Justice Ginsburg was quoted as having told a student audience, "There is no practical difference between what has evolved and the E.R.A." Quoted in Jeffrey Rosen, "The New Look of Liberalism on the Court," *New York Times Magzine,* October 5, 1997. Also see Kenneth L. Karst, "'The Way Women Are': Some Notes in the Margin for Ruth Bader Ginsburg," 20 *Hawaii Law Review* 619 (winter 1998), p. 621; Candace Saari Kovacic-Fleischer, "*United States v. Virginia*'s New Gender Equal Protection Analysis with Ramifications for Pregnancy, Parenting, and Title VII," 50 *Vanderbilt Law Review* 845 (1977).

28. 518 U.S. 515, at p. 535.

29. Ibid., pp. 535–538.

30. Ibid., p. 539.

31. Ibid., p. 537, quoting Edward H. Clarke, *Sex in Education; or, A Fair Chance for the Girls* (J. R. Osgood, 1873), pp. 38–39, 62–63, 127.

32. Ibid., pp. 544–545.

33. Ibid., p. 556, quoting *In re Lavinia Goodell,* 39 Wis. 232, 246 (1875).

34. Ibid., p. 532 n. 5, quoting letter from Thomas Jefferson to Samuel Kercheval (September 5, 1816), in *Writings of Thomas Jefferson,* vol. 10 (P. Ford ed., 1899), pp. 45–46, n. 1; also quoted in Ruth Bader Ginsburg, "Constitutional Adjudication in the U.S. as a Means of Advancing the Equal Stature of Men and Women Under the Law," 26 *Hofstra Law Review* 263 (1997), pp. 264–265.

35. 518 U.S. 515, at pp. 541–542, citing Sandra Day O'Connor, "Portia's Progress," 66 *New York University Law Review* 1546 (1991).

36. Ibid., p. 545.

37. Ibid., pp. 547–554.

38. Ibid., pp. 553–554, citing *Sweatt v. Painter,* 339 U.S. 629 (1950).

39. Ibid., p. 550.

40. Valorie K. Vojdik, "At War: Narrative Tactics in The Citadel and VMI Litigation," 19 *Harvard Women's Law Journal* 1 (1996), p. 7.

41. 518 U.S. 515, at p. 550, quoting 852 F. Supp., at p. 478, and 766 F. Supp., at p. 1432.

42. Ibid., pp. 550, 542, quoting 52 F.3d, at p. 93.

43. Author's interview with Ginsburg (2000).

44. 518 U.S. 515, at p. 555.

45. Ibid., pp. 557–558.

46. Ibid., p. 536 n. 8, quoting Christopher Jencks and David Riesman, *The Academic Revolution* (Doubleday, 1968), pp. 297–298.

47. *Craig v. Boren,* 419 U.S. 190, 197 (1976).

48. 518 U.S. 515, at pp. 558–559.

49. Ibid., pp. 560–562, 564.

50. Ibid., pp. 562–564; quote is at p. 564.

51. Ibid., pp. 565–566.

52. "The dissent equates our conclusion that VMI's 'asserted interest in promoting diversity' is not 'genuine,' with a 'charge' that the diversity rationale is 'a pretext for discriminating against women'" (518 U.S. 515, at p. 562, quoting pp. 579–580). "The dissent also says that the interest in diversity is so transparent that having to articulate it is 'absurd on its face'" (ibid., p. 562, quoting p. 592). "The dissent criticizes me for 'disregarding the four all-women's private colleges in Virginia (generously assisted by public funds)'" (ibid., p. 564, quoting p. 595).

53. Ibid., pp. 592, 593, 595.

54. Ibid., p. 566.

55. Ibid., pp. 566, 567, 570, 601.

56. Ibid., pp. 567–568.

57. Author's interview with Scalia.

58. 518 U.S. 515, at pp. 567–568.

59. *Webster v. Reproductive Health Services,* 492 U.S. 490 (1989), and *Cruzan v. Director, Missouri Department of Health,* 497 U.S. 261 (1990).

60. 518 U.S. 515, at p. 569.

61. Ibid.

62. Ibid., pp. 569–570.

63. Author's interview with Scalia.

64. 518 U.S. 515, at pp. 585, 586.

65. Ibid., pp. 578–579, 583.

66. Ibid., pp. 592, 596.

67. Ibid., p. 603.

68. Aaron Epstein, "High Court Knocks over Gender Wall," *Arizona Republic,* June 27, 1996.

69. Linda Greenhouse, "Military College Can't Bar Women, High Court Rules," *New York Times,* June 27, 1996. Repeated by Ginsburg in an interview with Lynn Sherr, Association of the Bar of the City of New York, November 15, 2000.

70. Quoted in Robert Marquand, "Male-Only Military School Must Admit Female Cadets," *Christian Science Monitor,* June 27, 1996.

71. Joan Biskupic, "Supreme Court Invalidates Exclusion of Women by VMI," *Washington Post,* June 27, 1996.

72. Ibid.

73. Lichtman quoted in David G. Savage, "Court Strikes Down VMI's All-Male Policy," *Los Angeles Times,* June 27, 1996; Greenberger quoted in Lyle Denniston, "Court: Women Can Go to VMI; 7–1 Ruling Is Based on Constitution's Guarantee of Equality," *Baltimore Sun,* June 27, 1996.

74. "Forward, March; Court Correct to Open VMI to Female Cadets," *Houston Chronicle,* June 28, 1996.

75. "VMI Long Overdue in Admitting Women," *San Francisco Chronicle,* June 28, 1996.

76. Michael Loftin, "Now, Women as VMI Cadets," *Chattanooga Times,* Aug. 20, 1997.

77. "Open Doors to Women, or Lose Your Funding," *Phoenix Gazette,* June 28, 1996.

78. Geoff Seamans, "VMI Shouldn't Treat Women Differently," and Roland Lazenby (VMI class of 1975), "VMI Is in Danger of Irrelevance," *Roanoke Times and World News,* September 29, 1996.

79. Judy Wiessler, "VMI Will Open Door to Women; Court Puts End to All-Male School," *Houston Chronicle,* June 27, 1996; Robert Marquand, "Male-Only Military School Must Admit Female Cadets," *Christian Science Monitor,* June 27, 1996.

80. Peter Hardin, "Court Shatters VMI System 7–1; Ruling Says Women Are Unfairly Excluded," *Richmond Times-Dispatch,* June 27, 1996.

81. Ibid.

82. Denniston, "Court: Women Can Go."

83. Allison Blake, "Court Rules Against VMI: The 7–1 Decision Means School Must Admit Women if It Wants to Remain Public," *Virginian-Pilot,* June 27, 1996.

84. David Reed, "VMI Says Going Private Would 'Save the Males,'" *Chicago Sun-Times,* June 27, 1996.

21. Bringing Women into the Choir

1. Aaron Epstein, "Separate but Equal?" *Atlanta Journal and Constitution,* January 14, 1996.

2. David Reed, "VMI Says Going Private Would 'Save the Males,'" *Chicago Sun-Times,* June 27, 1996; Jim Mason, "VMI's Leader: Rather Private than Mixed," *Richmond Times-Dispatch,* February 24, 1996.

3. Peter Finn, "Making Room for a New Breed of Rat," *Washington Post,* July 27, 1997.

4. Linda Greenhouse, "Military College Can't Bar Women, High Court Rules," *New York Times,* June 27, 1996.

5. Quoted in Reed, "VMI Says."

6. Ibid.; Peter Finn, "At VMI, Pioneers Recall Breaking Earlier Barrier," *Washington Post,* October 5, 1997.

7. Spencer S. Hsu, "'Rat Line,' Wrong Idea," *Washington Post,* July 9, 1996, including figures from a May 31, 1996, report of the Division of Risk Management.

8. Reed, "VMI Says"; "To Keep an All-Male V.M.I., Its Alumni Consider Buying It," *New York Times,* July 1, 1996; Mike Allen, "VMI Alumni Board Backs Privatizing," *Richmond Times-Dispatch,* July 1, 1996.

9. Allen, "VMI Alumni Board," quoting a June 29 article in the *Roanoke Times and World News.*

10. Statement quoted in Michael Janofsky, "Citadel, Bowing to Court, Says It Will Admit Women," *New York Times,* June 29, 1996; spokesman quoted in Mike Allen and Wes Allison, "VMI Vote May Be Delayed," *Richmond Times-Dispatch,* July 8, 1996; also see Chris Burritt, "About-Face; Citadel Says Women Are Welcome," *Atlanta Journal and Constitution,* June 29, 1996.

11. "If The Citadel Can Do It, Why Can't VMI as Well?" *Record* (Greensboro, N.C.), August 29, 1996.

12. Reed, "VMI Says"; Mike Allen, "V.M.I. Holding Back on Move to Obey Justices on Women," *New York Times,* July 11, 1996.

13. Finn, "Making Room for a New Breed"; Allen, "VMI Alumni Board," quoting *Roanoke Times and World News* of June 29.

14. "To Keep an All-Male V.M.I."; Allen, "VMI Alumni Board."

15. Allen and Allison, "VMI Vote May Be Delayed."

16. Ibid.; Mike Allen, "Allen Backs VMI on Delaying of Vote," *Richmond Times-Dispatch,* July 9, 1996.

17. Allen, "Allen Backs VMI."

18. Peter Hardin, "Attorney Who Brought Suit Tells VMI Board to Join the Parade," *Richmond Times-Dispatch,* July 12, 1996.

19. Hsu, "'Rat Line,' Wrong Idea."

20. Donald P. Baker and Tod Robberson, "Admit Women, Keep 'Rat Line,' VMI Alumni Say," *Washington Post,* July 2, 1996.

21. Hsu, "'Rat Line,' Wrong Idea."

22. Allen, "Allen Backs VMI."

23. Wes Allison, "VMI Board Ponders Options," *Richmond Times-Dispatch,* July 13, 1996; "V.M.I. Board Won't Rush Coeducation," *New York Times,* July 15, 1996; Wes Allison, "Alumni Are Given Deadline," *Richmond Times-Dispatch,* July 14, 1996.

24. See, e. g., Allen, "V.M.I. Holding Back"; Donald P. Baker, "In VMI Vote, Sex Barrier Starts to Fall," *Washington Post,* July 14, 1996.

25. Justin Pope, "VMI Board Hears from an Expert," *Richmond Times-Dispatch,* July 31, 1996; Justin Pope, "Message to VMI: Be Quick, Complete," *Richmond Times-Dispatch,* August 3, 1996.

26. Wes Allison, "VMI's Integration Inquiries Curbed," *Richmond Times-Dispatch,* August 18, 1996; Wes Allison, "Bunting Watching Citadel," *Richmond Times-Dispatch,* August 29, 1996.

27. Allison Blake, "State Pans Justice for Poking VMI; Feds: Let Women Apply Now,"

Roanoke Times and World News, September 19, 1996; Mike Allen, "Defiant V.M.I. to Admit Women, but Will Not Ease Rules for Them," *New York Times,* September 22, 1996.

28. Letter from Col. Vernon L. Beitzel, director of admissions, to Lauren Ashley Wagner, September 10, 1996, supplied by Eileen Wagner.

29. Wes Allison, "VMI Vote Split Along Age Lines," *Richmond Times-Dispatch,* September 24, 1996.

30. Wes Allison, "VMI Begins Decisive Talks on Its Future," *Richmond Times-Dispatch,* September 19, 1996; Wes Allison, "Plan to Take VMI Private Gains Credence," *Richmond Times-Dispatch,* September 20, 1996.

31. Rex Bowman, "Alumni Make Fiery Pleas to VMI Board to Privatize School," *Washington Times,* September 21, 1996; Donald P. Baker, "Grads Close Ranks for Final VMI Plea," *Washington Post,* September 21, 1996; Wes Allison, "Alumni Back Private Role for VMI," *Richmond Times-Dispatch,* September 21, 1996.

32. Baker, "Grads Close Ranks"; Donald P. Baker, "By One Vote, VMI Decides to Go Coed," *Washington Post,* September 22, 1996; Guy Friddell, "Ginsburg Sets the Standard as VMI Readies for Women," *Virginian-Pilot,* September 23, 1996.

33. Baker, "By One Vote."

34. See William Berry, "A Coed VMI Will Seek to Preserve What Is Central to VMI," *Richmond Times-Dispatch,* October 6, 1996.

35. Allison, "VMI Vote Split Along Age Lines"; Mike Allen, "Cadets and Others Say It's Time to March On," *Richmond Times-Dispatch,* September 22, 1996; Wes Allison, "Some Alumni Weep; Officials Promise Survival," *Richmond Times-Dispatch,* September 22, 1996.

36. Allison, "Some Alumni Weep."

37. Wes Allison, "VMI's Tough Talk Has Effects," *Richmond Times-Dispatch,* September 23, 1996.

38. Baker, "By One Vote."

39. Wes Allison, "U.S. to Shadow VMI as It Goes Coed," *Richmond Times-Dispatch,* September 23, 1996.

40. Sandra Brown, "VMI: Progress Has Price; School Wants $5.7 Million to Accommodate Women," *Roanoke Times and World News,* September 23, 1996.

41. Katherine Gazella, "VMI: No Longer Just for Men," *St. Petersburg Times,* August 18, 1997.

42. Brown, "VMI: Progress Has Price."

43. Gazella, "VMI: No Longer Just for Men."

44. Allison, "Some Alumni Weep." Although VMI offered Ms. Wagner a substantial scholarship, including a year of study in Europe, she chose to go to the Air Force Academy. Her younger sister eventually went to the Naval Academy. Author's interview with Eileen Wagner.

45. *United States v. Virginia,* Remand Order, 96 F.3d 114 (4th Cir. 1996).

46. Allison, "U.S. to Shadow VMI."

47. Ibid.; Allison Blake, "VMI Seeks to Go Coed on Its Own; Officials Try to Avoid Court Supervision," *Roanoke Times and World News,* September 24, 1996.

48. Rex Bowman, "Court Denies Justice Role in Planning of Coed VMI," *Washington Times,* December 3, 1996.

49. Allison Blake, "U.S. Asks Court for VMI Plan; Justice Department Told to See Internet," *Roanoke Times and World News,* October 22, 1996

50. Wes Allison and Paul Bradley, "Plan for Women Lists Buzz-Cuts, Barren Barracks," *Richmond Times-Dispatch,* September 22, 1996; Allison, "VMI's Tough Talk."

51. Eric Lipton, "VMI Cuts No Slack for Female Applicants," *Washington Post,* Sept. 24, 1996; "VMI Seeks to Go Coed on Its Own."

52. Associated Press, "Groups Blast Coeducation Proposal from VMI," *Virginian-Pilot,* September 24, 1996.

53. Author's interviews with Isabelle Katz Pinzler, Michael Maurer, and Marcia Greenberger.

54. Author's interview with Josiah Bunting.

55. Author's interview with Michael Bissell; Laura Fairchild Brodie, *Breaking Out: VMI and the Coming of Women* (Pantheon, 2000), chap. 2.

56. Author's interview with Bissell; Brodie, *Breaking Out,* pp. 73–74.

57. Mary Anne Case, "Two Cheers for Cheerleading: The Noisy Integration of VMI and the Quiet Success of Virginia Women in Leadership," 1999 *University of Chicago Legal Forum* 347 (1999), p. 363.

58. Brodie, *Breaking Out,* p. 113; author's interview with Mike Strickler.

59. "VMI Compliance Lacks Citadel Style," *Atlanta Journal and Constitution,* September 26, 1996.

60. Brodie, *Breaking Out,* p. 151.

61. See ibid., chap. 7.

62. Allison Blake, "VMI Women May Get Same Barracks, Different Coifs," *Roanoke Times and World News,* December 11, 1996; Donald P. Baker, "At VMI, Hats on, Skirts In," *Washington Post,* December 11, 1996; Madelyn Rosenberg, "Changes Won't Reveal a Softer Side of VMI," *Roanoke Times and World News,* August 20, 1997; Allison Blake, "'The Job's Not Done, It's Just Starting,'" *Richmond Times-Dispatch,* August 24, 1997; Allison Blake, "The Rat Line Is Alive and Well," *Richmond Times-Dispatch,* May 17, 1998; Brodie, *Breaking Out,* chap. 7.

63. Brodie, *Breaking Out,* pp. 93–94, 174–175; Robert O'Harrow, Jr., "For VMI, Going Coed Is a Tough Mission," *Washington Post,* October 24, 1996; Robert O'Harrow, Jr., "Girls Get a Glimpse of VMI," *Washington Post,* November 17, 1996; Robert O'Harrow, Jr., "VMI Accepts 33 Women so Far for Fall's 1st-Year Class," *Washington Post,* March 12, 1997; Betty Hayden Snider, "4 Women Get Invitations to Attend VMI," *Roanoke Times and World News,* December 8, 1996; Finn, "Making Room for a New Breed"; "First Female Cadets at V.M.I. Are in Class and in Uniform," *New York Times,* August 19, 1997.

64. Author's interview with Bunting.

65. Author's interviews with Bunting and Bissell; Brodie, *Breaking Out,* pp. 172–180.

66. See Catherine S. Manegold, *In Glory's Shadow: Shannon Faulkner, The Citadel and a Changing America* (Knopf, 2000), pp. 208–237.

67. Chris Sosnowski, "Abuse Probe at Citadel to Continue," *Post and Courier*

(Charleston, S.C.), December 16, 1996; Adam Nossiter, "Woman Who Left the Citadel Tells of Brutal Hazing Ordeal," *New York Times,* February 18, 1996; Associated Press, "F.B.I. Looking into Report of Hazing at Citadel," *New York Times,* December 14, 1996.

68. Allison Blake, "VMI Must Submit Plan," *Roanoke Times and World News*, December 3, 1996.

69. Figures for class of 2001 supplied by VMI; Wes Allison, "VMI Sees Normal Attrition Rate," *Richmond Times-Dispatch,* February 14, 1996; Peter Finn, "One Woman, 13 Men Bow out at VMI," August 22, 1997; Matt Chittum, "VMI out of Step with Academies," *Roanoke Times,* August 30, 1998.

22. The Fife and the Drum, Together at Last

Epigraph: This toast was drafted by John Jay's wife to celebrate the signing of the Treaty of Paris on September 3, 1783, quoted in Linda K. Kerber, *No Constitutional Right to Be Ladies: Women and the Obligations of Citizenship* (Hill and Wang, 1998), p. 2.

1. Author's interview with Mike Strickler. Two female transfer students also registered that day.

2. Laura Fairchild Brodie, *Breaking Out: VMI and the Coming of Women* (Pantheon, 2000), p. 213.

3. Michael Janofsky, "Military College Awaits Its First Female Cadets," *New York Times,* July 20, 1997.

4. "First Female Cadets at V.M.I. Are in Class and in Uniform," *New York Times,* August 19, 1997.

5. Wes Allison, "At Last: Rats No Longer," *Richmond Times-Dispatch,* March 17, 1998.

6. Author's interview with Kendra Russell.

7. Author's interview with Erin Nicole Claunch; Lynn Rosellini, "A Leader Among Men," *U.S. News and World Report,* April 10, 2000.

8. Robert O'Harrow, Jr., "VMI Report Sets Rules for Women," *Washington Post,* May 29, 1997; Jean Seligmann with Kimberly Martineau, "Hair Today and Gone Tomorrow," *Newsweek,* September 1, 1997.

9. Author's interview with Claunch; Brodie, *Breaking Out,* pp. 134, 237.

10. Richard Lowry, "Patriotic Bunting," *National Review,* September 1, 1998; Brodie, *Breaking Out,* pp. 191–193.

11. Peter Finn, "3rd Woman Decides to Leave VMI," *Washington Post,* September 2, 1997.

12. "V.M.I. Expels Woman for Hitting Male Student," *New York Times,* September 10, 1997; Peter Finn, "VMI Suspends Woman," *Washington Post,* September 10, 1997; Wes Allison, "Female Cadet Is Suspended," *Richmond Times-Dispatch,* September 10, 1997.

13. Matt Chittum, "VMI Superintendent Pleads for 'Source of Sanity,'" *Roanoke Times and World News,* September 26, 1997.

14. Peter Finn, "VMI's Intimacy Rule Is Put to the Test," *Washington Post,* March 7,

1998; Peter Finn, "VMI Won't Suspend 2 in Sexual Contact Case," *Washington Post,* March 13, 1998; Brodie, *Breaking Out,* pp. 267–270.

15. Rex Bowman, "Second Coed Class Arrives at VMI," *Richmond Times-Dispatch,* August 18, 1998.

16. Brodie, *Breaking Out,* pp. 278–280, 287; author's interviews with Strickler and Norman Bissell; author's conversation with Laura Brodie, VMI, July 14, 1999.

17. Peter Finn, "First Woman to Enroll at VMI Decides to Leave," *Washington Post,* January 17, 1998.

18. Allison, "At Last: Rats No Longer"; Matt Chittum, "Coed Class at VMI Are 'Rats' No Longer," *Roanoke Times and World News,* March 17, 1998; Brodie, *Breaking Out,* chap. 14.

19. Author's interviews with Bissell and Josiah Bunting.

20. Author's interviews with Robert Patterson and Anne Marie Whittemore, Andrew Kurt Clark, and Michael Maurer; Lynn Rosellini and David Marcus, "A Leader Among Men," *U.S. News and World Report,* April 10, 2000.

21. Author's interview with Strickler; Matt Chittum, "First Female 'Rats' Break Silence," *Roanoke Times and World News,* March 18, 1998; Mary Anne Case, "Two Cheers for Cheerleading: The Noisy Integration of VMI and the Quiet Success of Virginia Women in Leadership," 1999 *University of Chicago Legal Forum* 347 (1999), p. 371, citing N. M. Bissell, "Assimilation Plan for Women in the Corps: Status Report #1" (January 30, 1997); Brodie, *Breaking Out,* pp. 332, 334.

22. Vic Dorr, Jr., "End of Rat Line Bodes Well for Sullivan," *Richmond Times-Dispatch,* April 25, 1998.

23. Author's interviews with Claunch and Russell.

24. Rosellini, "Leader Among Men."

25. Author's interviews with Claunch and Russell.

26. Matt Chittum, "Banished Cadet to Return to VMI This Fall with the 35 Other Women Enrolled in Institute's Second Coed Class," *Roanoke Times and World News,* July 24, 1998.

27. Author's interview with Claunch.

28. Author's interview with Strickler, May 5, 2000.

29. Author's interviews with Claunch and Russell.

30. Author's interview with Strickler (2000).

31. Author's interviews with female faculty and staff, VMI.

32. Wes Allison, "VMI Rate of Attrition Is About the Same," *Richmond Times-Dispatch,* September 23, 1997.

33. Matt Chittum, "Today, First VMI Women Graduate," *Roanoke Times and World News,* May 15, 1999; author's interview with Strickler.

34. Author's interview with Bunting.

35. "VMI Groups Raise Nearly $10.6 Million in a Year," *Richmond Times-Dispatch,* July 18, 1997.

36. Wes Allison, "VMI Returns to Normal," *Richmond Times-Dispatch,* December 14, 1997.

37. Author's interview with Bunting.

38. Matt Chittum, "1 of 1st Female Cadets Dismissed from VMI," *Roanoke Times and World News,* December 15, 1999; Calvin R. Trice, "VMI Expels Female Cadet," *Richmond Times-Dispatch,* December 18, 1999.

39. Associated Press, "Woman Elected Battalion Leader," March 24, 2000.

40. Author's interview with Strickler (2000); John White, "Loudoun Woman, a Star Student, Athlete and Pioneer, Advances to a Top VMI Post," *Washington Post,* March 23, 2000; "Woman Rises to Top Post in VMI Corps," *Seattle Times,* March 23, 2000.

41. "Women Cadets Struggle with Fitness Test, Report Shows," Associated Press State and Local Wire, March 29, 2000; Matt Chittum, "Fitness Test a Hurdle for VMI Women; 23 Percent of Women Pass While 85 Percent of Men Do," *Roanoke Times and World News,* March 30, 2000; Kia Shant'e Breaux, "Women Appear to Be Adjusting Fine at Virginia Military Institute," Associated Press State and Local Wire, April 17, 2000.

42. Author's interviews with Russell and Strickler (2000); Matt Chittum, "Female Cadet Chosen VMI Newspaper Editor," *Roanoke Times and World News,* March 30, 2000.

43. Author's interview with Strickler (2000); "Metro in Brief: First Woman Chosen to Lead VMI Paper," *Washington Post,* March 30, 2000.

44. Author's interview with Russell.

45. Quoted in White, "Loudoun Woman."

46. Donald P. Baker, "Virginia Notebook: Cadets Like Liddy, the Radio Host," *Washington Post,* April 8, 1999; Scott Reid, "A Blot on Our Standard of Honor," *Washington Post,* April 18, 1999; Josh White, "Diplomas, Dreams and Dissent; First Female Cadets Graduate from VMI," *Washington Post,* May 16, 1999.

47. Matt Chittum, "Women Graduate from VMI," *Roanoke Times and World News,* May 16, 1999.

48. Matt Chittum, "Today, First VMI Women Graduate," *Roanoke Times and World News,* May 15, 1999; Rex Bowman, "A Historic VMI Graduation," *Richmond Times-Dispatch,* May 16, 1999; Gerald Mizejewski, "2 Women Graduate into VMI History," *Washington Times,* May 16, 1999.

49. Chittum, "Women Graduate from VMI."

50. Author's interviews with Claunch and Russell.

51. Megan Schnabel, "History Marches Anew at VMI," *Roanoke Times and World News,* February 28, 1999; Josh White, "Muddy Rite Ends at VMI," *Washington Post,* February 26, 1999; Calvin R. Trice, "VMI Cadets Retrace Path to Storied Battle," *Richmond Times-Dispatch,* March 1, 1999; Associated Press State and Local Wire, "No Muddy Hill Climb, but End of Breakout Still Grueling for VMI Rats," March 1, 1999; author's interview with Bissell.

52. Author's interview with Robert Patterson and Anne Marie Whittemore; Calvin R. Trice, "16 of VMI's 30 Original Females to Be in Senior Class," *Richmond Times-Dispatch,* July 17, 2000.

53. Author's interview with Strickler (2000).

54. Ibid.; "Report for the Period August 16, 1999 Through March 22, 2000," *United States v. Virginia,* C.A. No. 90-0126-R; Calvin R. Trice, "Student Interest in VMI Grow-

ing, Entry Applications Highest in 18 Years," *Richmond Times-Dispatch,* August 13, 2000.

55. Liz Seymour, "VMI Alternative Graduates 1st Class; Women Praise VWIL Program," *Washington Post,* May 22, 1999; Calvin R. Trice, "Discipline, Regimen: 22 of 42 Starters to Finish Women's Military Program," *Richmond Times-Dispatch,* May 22, 1999.

56. Calvin R. Trice, "VMI Marches Proudly Toward Campaign Goal," *Richmond Times-Dispatch,* October 22, 2000; Matt Chittum, "VMI Kicks off Capital Campaign in Big Way; 2 Pledges are 23 Percent of $175 Million Goal," *Roanoke Times and World News,* October 22, 2000; Philip Walzer, "Large Gifts Propel VMI's Fund-Raising Campaign," *Virginian-Pilot,* October 22, 2000.

57. Elizabeth Schneider, "The Dialectic of Rights and Politics," in *Feminist Legal Theory: Foundations,* ed. D. Kelly Weisberg (Temple University Press, 1993), p. 520.

58. Ruth Bader Ginsburg, "Constitutional Adjudication in the United States as a Means of Advancing the Equal Stature of Men and Women Under the Law," 26 *Hofstra Law Review* 263 (1997), p. 263.

59. *Rostker v. Goldberg,* 453 U.S. 57 (1981).

60. Ibid., pp. 70, 72, 74, 76, 77, 83 (White, dissenting), 87 (Marshall, dissenting).

61. Oral history interview with Ruth Bader Ginsburg conducted by Maeva Marcus for the D.C. Circuit Historical Society, August 13, 1996, p. 33.

62. Kenneth L. Karst, *Law's Promise, Law's Expression: Visions of Power in the Politics of Race, Gender, and Religion* (Yale University Press, 1993), p. 20.

Epilogue

1. Quoted in Calvin R. Trice, "VMI Celebrates 'Day for Everyone,'" *Richmond Times Dispatch*, May 20, 2001; Chris Kahn, "VMI Graduates Its First Class of Female Cadets," Associated Press, May 19, 2001.

2. Quoted in Chris Kahn, "First Class of Female Cadets Graduating from Virginia Military Institute," Associated Press, May 12, 2001.

3. Quoted in Lisa Rein, "Chance to Be Officers and VMI Alumnae: 13 Women to Graduate In First Coed Class," *Washington Post*, May 19, 2001.

4. Laura Brodie, "Pregnant on the Parade Ground: In Need of Corps Changes at VMI," *Washington Post*, April 2, 2001.

5. VMI, "Statement on Pregnant Cadet," February 20, 2001, http://web.vmi.edu/pr/pregnancy.htm; Steven Ginsburg, "Pregnant VMI Cadet to Remain on Campus," *Washington Post*, February 16, 2001; Matt Chittum, "VMI Acknowledges First Pregnant Cadet," *Roanoke Times and World News*, February 16, 2001. As of June 2001, it was unclear whether she would return for her senior year. E-mail to author from Col. Mike Strickler, June 20, 2001.

6. Laura Brodie, "Pregnant on the Parade Ground," op. cit.; Steven Ginsberg, "VMI Blocks Student Access to Web Site," *Washington Post*, March 8, 2001.

7. Daniel F. Drummond, "VMI Plans to Dismiss Cadets Who Become Parents,"

Washington Times, July 3, 2001; "VMI Drafts Pregnancy Policy," *Roanoke Times and World News*, July 6, 2001.

8. Strickler e-mail, June 20, 2001.

9. Rein, "Chance to Be Officers."

10. Rein, "Chance to Be Officers"; "VMI's New Era: Kendra Russell," *Roanoke Times and World News*, May 13, 2001; Matt Chittum, "A Graduation to Remember," *Roanoke Times and World News*, May 20, 2001; "Briefs and Notes from the General Assembly," Associated Press state and local wire, Feb. 15, 2001; "Cadet Claunch Honored by General Assembly," VMI web site, http://web.vmi.edu/pr/ir/mar01/claunch.htm.

11. E-mail to author from Brenda L. Bryant, July 2, 2001; http://www.mbc.edu/vwil/index.htm.

12. Michael D. Shear, "13 Women Join Ranks of VMI's Graduates," *Washington Post*, May 20, 2001.

13. Chittum, "A Graduation to Remember."

Selected Bibliography

Much of the information about the VMI litigation and the progress of gender integration at the Institute comes from newspapers. Scholars interested in doing their own research should refer to the notes.

Interviews

Lisa Beattie, June 17, 1999, New York City
Joan Bertin, December 11, 1999, New York City
Norman M. Bissell, July 15, 1999, VMI
Gordon L. Bowen, July 16, 1999, Mary Baldwin College
Laura Fairchild Brodie, July 15, 1999, and May 5, 2000, Lexington, Virginia
Brenda L. Bryant, July 16, 1999, Mary Baldwin College
Josiah Bunting III, July 15, 1999, VMI
Andrew Kurt Clark, April 26, 1999, Richmond
Erin Nicole Claunch, May 5, 2000, VMI
Gordon K. Davies, June 28, 1999, telephone interview
Ruth Bader Ginsburg, July 28, 1994, New York City; September 18, 1995, and May 23, 2000, Washington, D.C.
Marcia D. Greenberger, May 23, 2000, Washington, D.C.
D. Judith Keith, April 21, 1999, Washington, D.C.
Michael S. Maurer, April 20, 1999, Washington, D.C.
Page Miller, April 21, 1999, Washington, D.C.
Robert H. Patterson, Jr., and Anne Marie Whittemore, April 26, 1999, Richmond
Isabelle Katz Pinzler, March 17, 1999, New York City
Kendra Russell, May 5, 2000, VMI
Antonin Scalia, October 14, 1999, Washington, D.C.
Rose Mary Sheldon, May 4, 2000, VMI
Jessica Dunsay Silver, October 15, 1999, Washington, D.C.
Michael M. Strickler, July 14, 1999, and May 5, 2000, VMI
Eileen N. Wagner, April 26, 1999, Richmond

VMI

Adams, Abigail E. "Dyke to Dyke: Ritual Reproduction at a U.S. Men's Military College." In *Talking About People: Readings in Contemporary Cultural Anthropology,*

2d ed. Edited by William A. Haviland and Robert J. Gordon. Mayfield Publishing, 1996.

———. "The 'Military Academy': Metaphors of Family for Pedagogy and Public Life." In *Wives and Warriors: Women and the Military in the United States and Canada*. Edited by Laurie Weinstein and Christie C. White. Bergin and Garvey, 1997.

Avery, Dianne. "Institutional Myths, Historical Narratives and Social Science Evidence: Reading the 'Record' in the Virginia Military Institute Case." 5 *Southern California Review of Law and Women's Studies* 189 (1996).

Commission to Survey the Educational System of Virginia. *Report of the Commission, Submitted to the General Assembly January, 1928*. Davis Bottom, Superintendent Public Printing, 1928.

Couper, William. *One Hundred Years at V.M.I.* 4 vols. Garrett and Massie, 1939.

———. *The VMI New Market Cadets: Biographical Sketches of All Members of the Virginia Military Institute Corps of Cadets Who Fought in the Battle of New Market*. Michie Company, 1933.

Davis, Thomas W., ed. *A Crowd of Honorable Youths: Historical Essays on the First 150 Years of the Virginia Military Institute*. VMI Sesquicentennial Committee, 1988.

Davis, William C. *The Battle of New Market*. Doubleday, 1975.

Smith, Francis H. *The Virginia Military Institute, Its Building and Rebuilding*. J. P. Bell, 1912.

Wise, Henry A. *Drawing Out the Man: The VMI Story*. University Press of Virginia for the VMI Alumni Association, 1978.

Wise, Jennings C. *The Military History of the Virginia Military Institute from 1839 to 1865*. J. P. Bell, 1915.

Wise, John S. *The End of an Era*. Houghton Mifflin, 1899.

Women in the South

Bernhard, Virginia, et al., eds. *Southern Women: Histories and Identities*. University of Missouri Press, 1992.

Clinton, Catherine. *The Plantation Mistress: Women's World in the Old South*. Pantheon, 1982.

Dillman, Caroline Matheny, ed. *Southern Women*. Hemisphere Publishing, 1988.

Edwards, Laura F. *Scarlett Doesn't Live Here Anymore: Southern Women in the Civil War Era*. University of Illinois Press, 2000.

Fox-Genovese, Elizabeth. *Within the Plantation Household: Black and White Women of the Old South*. University of North Carolina Press, 1988.

Freeman, Anne Hobson. "Mary Munford's Fight." 78 *Virginia Magazine of History and Biography* 484 (October 1970).

Gillespie, Michael, and Catherine Clinton. *Taking off the White Gloves: Southern Women and Women Historians*. University of Missouri Press, 1998.

Hall, Jacquelyn Dowd, and Anne Firor Scott. "Women in the South." In *Interpreting*

Southern History: Historiographical Essays in Honor of Sanford W. Higginbotham. Edited by John B. Boles and Evelyn Thomas Nolen. Louisiana State University Press, 1987.

Hawks, Joanne V., and Sheila L. Skemp. *Sex, Race, and the Role of Women in the South.* University Press of Mississippi, 1983.

Lebsock, Suzanne. *"A Share of Honour": Virginia Women 1600–1945.* Women's Cultural History Project, 1984.

Little, Priscilla Courtelyou, and Robert C. Vaughan, eds. *A New Perspective: Southern Women's Cultural History from the Civil War to Civil Rights.* Virginia Foundation for the Humanities, 1989.

Mezey, Susan Gluck. "The Persistence of Sex Segregated Education in the South." 22 *Southeastern Political Review* 371 (1994).

Scott, Anne Firor. *The Southern Lady: From the Pedestal to Politics, 1830–1930.* University of Chicago Press, 1970.

Stringer, Patricia A., and Irene Thompson. *Stepping off the Pedestal: Academic Women in the South.* Modern Language Association of America, 1982.

Varon, Elizabeth R. *We Mean to Be Counted: White Women and Politics in Antebellum Virginia.* University of North Carolina Press, 1998.

Weiner, Marli F. *Mistresses and Slaves: Plantation Women in South Carolina, 1830–1880.* University of Illinois Press, 1997.

Wheeler, Marjorie Spruill. "Mary Johnson, Suffragist." *Virginia Magazine of History and Biography* (January 1992).

———. *New Women of the New South: The Leaders of the Woman Suffrage Movement in the Southern States.* Oxford University Press, 1993.

Wyatt-Brown, Bertram. *Southern Honor: Ethics and Behavior in the Old South.* Oxford University Press, 1982.

Women and Law in U.S. History

Berger, Margaret. *Litigation on Behalf of Women.* Ford Foundation, 1980.

Cowan, Ruth B. "Women's Rights Through Litigation: An Examination of the American Civil Liberties Union Women's Rights Project, 1971–76." 8 *Columbia Human Rights Law Review* 373 (1976).

Cole, David. "Strategies of Difference." 2 *Law and Inequality Journal* 33 (1984).

Ginsburg, Ruth Bader. "Gender and the Constitution." 44 *Cincinnati Law Review* 1 (1975).

Hoff, Joan. *Law, Gender, and Injustice: A Legal History of U.S. Women.* New York University Press, 1991.

Lind, JoEllen. "Dominance and Democracy: The Legacy of Woman Suffrage for the Voting Right." 5 *UCLA Women's Law Journal* 103 (1994).

Mezey, Susan Gluck. *In Pursuit of Equality: Women, Public Policy, and the Federal Courts.* St. Martin's, 1992.

Murray, Pauli, and Mary Eastwood. "Jane Crow and the Law: Sex Discrimination and Title VII." 35 *George Washington Law Review* 232 (1965).

O'Connor, Karen. *Women's Organizations' Use of the Courts.* Lexington Books, 1980.

O'Connor, Sandra Day. "Portia's Progress." 66 *New York University Law Review* 1546 (1991).

Rhode, Deborah L. *Justice and Gender: Sex Discrimination and the Law.* Harvard University Press, 1989.

VanBurkleo, Sandra. *"Belonging to the World": Women's Rights and American Constitutional Culture.* Oxford University Press, 2001.

Weiner, Lynn. *From Working Girl to Working Mother: The Female Labor Force in the United States, 1820–1980.* University of North Carolina Press, 1985.

Welter, Barbara. "The Cult of True Womanhood: 1820–1860." *American Quarterly* (Summer 1966).

Williams, Wendy W. "The Equality Crisis: Reflections on Culture, Courts and Feminism." 7 *Women's Rights Laws Reporter* 175 (1982).

The Women's Movement

Berry, Mary Frances. *Why ERA Failed: Politics, Women's Rights, and the Amending Process of the Constitution.* Indiana University Press, 1986.

Boles, Janet K. *The Politics of the Equal Rights Amendment: Conflict and the Decision Process.* Longman, 1979.

Chafe, William H. *The Paradox of Change: American Women in the 20th Century.* Oxford University Press, 1991.

———. *Women and Equality: Changing Patterns in American Culture.* Oxford University Press, 1977.

Decker, Barbara Sinclair. *The Women's Movement: Political, Socioeconomic, and Psychological Issues.* Harper and Row, 1983.

Evans, Sara. *Personal Politics: The Roots of Women's Liberation in the Civil Rights Movement and the New Left.* Vintage, 1980.

Freeman, Jo. *The Politics of Women's Liberation.* McKay, 1975.

Harrison, Cynthia. *On Account of Sex: The Politics of Women's Issues, 1945–1968.* University of California Press, 1988.

Mansbridge, Jane J. *Why We Lost the ERA.* University of Chicago Press, 1986.

Mathews, Donald G., and Jane Sherron De Hart. *Sex, Gender, and the Politics of ERA: A State and the Nation.* Oxford University Press, 1990.

Rhode, Deborah L. "Equal Rights in Retrospect." 1 *Law and Inequality* 1 (1983).

Rosen, Ruth. *The World Split Open: How the Modern Women's Movement Changed America.* Viking, 2000.

Schneider, Elizabeth M. "The Dialectic of Rights and Politics: Perspectives from the Women's Movement." 61 *New York University Law Review* 589 (1986).

Watkins, Bonnie, and Nina Tothchild, eds. *In the Company of Women: Voices from the Women's Movement.* University of Minnesota Press, 1997.

Women and Citizenship

Karst, Kenneth L. *Law's Promise, Law's Expression: Visions of Power in the Politics of Race, Gender, and Religion.* Yale University Press, 1993.

———. "The Pursuit of Manhood and the Desegregation of the Armed Forces." 38 *UCLA Law Review* 449 (1991).

———. "Women's Constitution." 1984 *Duke Law Journal* 447 (1984).

Kerber, Linda K. "May All Our Citizens Be Soldiers, and All Our Soldiers Citizens." In *Arms at Rest: Peacemaking and Peacekeeping in American History.* Edited by Joan R. Challinor and Robert L. Beisner. Greenwood Press, 1987.

———. *No Constitutional Right to Be Ladies: Women and the Obligations of Citizenship.* Hill and Wang, 1998.

Smith, Rogers M. *Civic Ideals: Conflicting Visions of Citizenship in U.S. History.* Yale University Press, 1997.

Snyder, R. Claire. *Citizen-Soldiers and Manly Warriors: Military Service and Gender in the Civic Republican Tradition.* Rowman and Littlefield, 1999.

Women in the U.S. Military

Barkalow, Carol, with Andrea Raab. *In the Men's House: An Inside Account of Life in the Army by One of West Point's First Female Graduates.* Poseidon Press, 1990.

Campbell, D'Ann. "Combatting the Gender Gulf." 2 *Temple Political and Civil Rights Law Review* 63 (1992).

———. "Women in Combat: The World War II Experience in the United States, Great Britain, Germany, and the Soviet Union." 57 *Journal of Military History* 301 (1993).

Cornum, Rhonda, as told to Peter Copeland. *She Went to War: The Rhonda Cornum Story.* Presidio, 1992.

Cummings, Missy. *Hornet's Nest: The Experiences of One of the Navy's First Female Fighter Pilots.* Writer's Showcase, 1999.

D'Amico, Francine, and Laurie Weinstein, eds. *Gender Camouflage: Women and the U.S. Military.* New York University Press, 1999.

Dean, Merrianne E. "Notes: Women in Combat—The Duty of the Citizen-Soldier." 2 *San Diego Justice Journal* 429 (1994).

De Pauw, Linda Grant. *Battle Cries and Lullabies: Women in War from Prehistory to the Present.* University of Oklahoma Press, 1998.

Ebbert, Jean, and Marie-Beth Hall. *Crossed Currents: Navy Women in a Century of Change.* Brassey's, 1999.

Feinman, Ilene Rose. *Citizenship Rites: Feminist Soldiers and Feminist Antimilitarists.* New York University Press, 2000.

Francke, Linda Bird. *Ground Zero: The Gender Wars in the Military.* Simon and Schuster, 1997.

Goldman, Nancy Loring, ed. *Female Soldiers—Combatants or Noncombatants? Historical and Contemporary Perspectives.* Greenwood Press, 1982.

Goodman, Jill Laurie. "Women, War, and Equality: An Examination of Sex Discrimination in the Military." 5 *Women's Rights Law Reporter* 243 (1979).

Holm, Jeanne. *Women in the Military: An Unfinished Revolution.* Presidio Press, 1982.

Katzenstein, Mary Fainsod, and Judith Reppy, eds. *Beyond Zero Tolerance: Discrimination in Military Culture.* Rowman and Littlefield, 1999.

Milko, James D. "Comment: Beyond the Persian Gulf Crisis: Expanding the Role of Servicewomen in the United States Military." 41 *American University Law Review* 1301 (1992).

Rogan, Helen. *Mixed Company: Women in the Modern Army.* Putnam, 1981.

Skaine, Rosemarie. *Women at War: Gender Issues of Americans in Combat.* McFarland, 1999.

Stiehm, Judith Hicks. *Arms and the Enlisted Woman.* Temple University Press, 1989.

———. *Bring Me Men and Women: Mandated Change at the U.S. Air Force Academy.* University of California Press, 1981.

———, ed. *It's Our Military, Too! Women and the U.S. Military.* Temple University Press, 1996.

Treadwell, Mattie E. *U.S. Army in World War II: The Women's Army Corps.* U.S. Department of the Army, 1954.

U.S. Congress. Hearings on H.R. 9832, 10705, 11267, 11268, 11711, 13729. *To Eliminate Discrimination Based on Sex with Respect to the Appointment and Admission of Persons to the Service Academies, and to Insure that Each Admission to the Service Academies Shall Be Made Without Regard to a Candidate's Sex, Race, Color, or Religious Beliefs, Before Subcomm. No. 2 of the House Committee on Armed Services.* 93d Cong., 2d sess., May 1974.

Weinstein, Laurie, and Christie C. White, eds. *Wives and Warriors: Women and the Military in the United States and Canada.* Bergin and Garvey, 1997.

Zeiger, Susan. *Battle Cries and Lullabies: Women in War from Prehistory to the Present.* Cornell University Press, 1999.

Zeinert, Karen. *The Valiant Women of the Vietnam War.* Millbrook Press, 2000.

Ruth Bader Ginsburg

Ellington, Toni J., Sylvia K. Higashi, Jayna K. Kim, and Mark M. Murakami. "Justice Ruth Bader Ginsburg and Gender Discrimination." 20 *Hawaii Law Review* 699 (1998).

Ginsburg, Ruth Bader. "The Burger Court's Grapplings with Sex Discrimination." In *The Burger Court: The Counter-Revolution that Wasn't.* Edited by Vincent Blasi. Yale University Press, 1983.

———. "Constitutional Adjudication in the United States as a Means of Advancing the Equal Stature of Men and Women Under the Law." 26 *Hofstra Law Review* 263 (1997).

———. "Employment of the Constitution to Advance the Equal Status of Men and Women." In *The Constitutional Bases of Political and Social Change in the United States.* Edited by Shlomo Slonin. Praeger, 1990.

——. "From No Rights, to Half Rights, to Confusing Rights." 7 *Human Rights* 12 (1978).

——. "Interpretations of the Equal Protection Clause." 9 *Harvard Journal of Law and Public Policy* 41 (1986).

——. "Men, Women, and the Constitution." 10 *Columbia Journal of Law and Social Problems* 91 (1973).

——. "Remarks on Women's Progress in the Legal Profession in the United States." 33 *Tulsa Law Journal* 13 (1997).

——. "Sex and Unequal Protection: Men and Women as Victims." 11 *Journal of Family Law* 347 (1971).

——. "Sex Equality and the Constitution: The State of the Art." 4 *Women's Rights Law Reporter* 143 (1978).

——. "Speaking in a Judicial Voice." 67 *New York University Law Review* 1185 (1992).

——. "Treatment of Women by the Law: Awakening Consciousness in the Law Schools." 5 *Valparaiso University Law Review* 79 (1971).

——. "Women at the Bar—A Generation of Change." 2 *University of Puget Sound Law Review* 1 (1978).

——. "Women's Work: The Place of Women in Law Schools." 32 *Journal of Legal Education* 272 (1982).

Karst, Kenneth L. "'The Way Women Are': Some Notes in the Margin for Ruth Bader Ginsburg." 20 *Hawaii Law Review* 619 (1998).

Merritt, Deborah Jones. "Hearing the Voices of Individual Women and Men: Justice Ruth Bader Ginsburg." 20 *Hawaii Law Review* 635 (1998).

The VMI Litigation

Amstein, Julie M. "*United States v. Virginia:* The Case of Coeducation at Virginia Military Institute." 3 *American University Journal of Gender and Law* 69 (1994).

Astin, Alexander. *Four Critical Years: Effects of College on Beliefs, Attitudes, and Knowledge.* Jossey-Bass, 1978.

Blair, Anita K. "The Equal Protection Clause and Single-Sex Public Education: *United States v. Virginia and Virginia Military Institute.*" 6 *Seton Hall Constitutional Law Journal* 999 (1996).

Fox-Genovese, Elizabeth. "Strict Scrutiny, VMI, and Women's Lives." 6 *Constitutional Law Journal* 987 (1996).

Gilligan, Carol. *In a Different Voice: Psychological Theory and Women's Development.* Harvard University Press, 1982.

Jacklin, Carol Nagy, ed. *The Psychology of Gender.* New York University Press, 1992.

Jaschik, Scott. "7 Women's Colleges Back VMI's Appeal to Retain All-Male Student Body: They Tell Supreme Court They're Threatened; Others Call Them Dupes." *Chronicle of Higher Education,* April 7, 1993.

Kayyem, Juliette. "The Search for Citizen-Soldiers: Female Cadets and the Campaign

Against the Virginia Military Institute." 30 *Harvard Civil Rights–Civil Liberties Law Review* 247 (1995).

Maccoby, Eleanor E., and Carol Nagy Jacklin. *The Psychology of Sex Differences.* Stanford University Press, 1974.

Mandelbaum, Sara L. "'As VMI Goes . . .': The Domino Effect and Other Stubborn Myths." 6 *Seton Hall Constitutional Law Journal* 979 (1996).

Miller, Emilie F. "Equal Access to Virginia Higher Education: Co-Education at VMI." *Lex Claudia* (summer 1990).

Soderberg, Jon Allyn. "The Virginia Military Institute and the Equal Protection Clause: A Factual and Legal Introduction." 50 *Washington and Lee Law Review* 15 (1993).

Vojdik, Valorie K. "At War: Narrative Tactics in The Citadel and VMI Litigation." 19 *Harvard Women's Law Journal* 1 (1996).

The Supreme Court Decision

Backer, Larry Cata. "Symposium: Practitioner's Guide to the October 1995 Supreme Court Term: Reading Entrails: Romer, VMI and the Art of Divining Equal Protection." 32 *Tulsa Law Journal* 361 (1997).

Bellman, Amy B. "Comment: The Young Women's Leadership School: Single- Sex Public Education After V.M.I." 1997 *Wisconsin Law Review* 827 (1997).

Brake, Deborah L. "Reflections on the VMI Decision." 6 *American University Journal of Gender and Law* 35 (1997).

Bowsher, David K. "Note: Cracking the Code of *United State v. Virginia.*" 48 *Duke Law Journal* 305 (1998).

Case, Mary Anne. "'The Very Stereotype the Law Condemns': Constitutional Sex Discrimination Law as a Quest for Perfect Proxies." 85 *Cornell Law Review* 1447 (2000).

Cowan, Jennifer R. "Distinguishing Private Women's Colleges from the VMI Decision." 30 *Columbia Journal of Law and Social Problems* 137 (1997).

Devan, William A. "Toward a New Standard in Gender Discrimination: The Case of Virginia Military Institute." 33 *William and Mary Law Review* 489 (1992).

Hurd, William Henry. "Gone with the Wind? VMI's Loss and the Future of Single-Sex Public Education." 4 *Duke Journal of Gender Law and Policy* 27 (1997).

Kovacic-Fleischer, Candace Saari. "*United States v. Virginia*'s New Gender Equal Protection Analysis with Ramifications for Pregnancy, Parenting, and Title VII." 50 *Vanderbilt Law Review* 845 (1977).

Kupetz, Karen Lazarus. "Note: Equal Benefits, Equal Burden: 'Skeptical Scrutiny' for Gender Classifications After *United States v. Virginia.*" 30 *Loyola of Los Angeles Law Review* 1333 (1997).

Lee, Allison Herren. "Title IX, Equal Protection, and the Richter Scale: Will VMI's Vibrations Topple Single-Sex Education." 7 *Texas Journal of Women and the Law* 37 (1997).

Levit, Nancy. "Separating Equals: Educational Research and the Long-Term Conse-
    quences of Sex Segregation." 67 *George Washington Law Review* 451 (1999).
Morgan, Denise C. "Anti-Subordination Analysis After *United States v. Virginia:* Eval-
    uating the Constitutionality of K–12 Single-Sex Public Schools." 1999 *University
    of Chicago Legal Forum* 381 (1999).
Nelson, Heather. "'Fatal in Fact'? An Examination of the Viability of Affirmative Ac-
    tion for Women in the Post-Adarand Era." 21 *Women's Rights Law Reporter* 151
    (2000).
Nemko, Amy H. "Single-Sex Public Education After VMI: The Case for Women's
    Schools." 21 *Harvard Women's Law Journal* 19 (1998).
Pyle, Christopher H. "Women's Colleges: Is Segregation by Sex Still Justifiable After
    United States v. Virginia?" 77 *Boston University Law Review* 209 (1997).
Saferstein, Bennett L. "Revisiting *Plessy* at the Virginia Military Institute: Reconciling
    Single-Sex Education with Equal Protection." 54 *University of Pittsburgh Law
    Review* 637 (1993).
Schneider, Elizabeth M. "A Postscript on VMI." 6 *American University Journal of Gen-
    der and the Law* 59 (1997).
Skaggs, Jason M. "Justifying Gender-Based Affirmative Action Under *United States
    v. Virginia*'s 'Exceedingly Persuasive Justification' Standard." 86 *California Law
    Review* 1169 (1998).
Stephenson, D. Grier, Jr. "The Future of Single-Sex Education: Virginia Military In-
    stitute Case." *USA Today* (January 1997).
Sunstein, Cass R. "The Supreme Court 1995 Term: Foreword: Leaving Things Unde-
    cided." 110 *Harvard Law Review* 6 (1996).
Vojdik, Valorie K. "Girls' Schools After VMI: Do They Make the Grade?" 4 *Duke Jour-
    nal of Gender Law and Policy* 69 (1997).
Widiss, Deborah A. "Re-viewing History: The Use of the Past as Negative Precedent
    in *United States v. Virginia.*" 108 *Yale Law Journal* 237 (1998).

Women at VMI and The Citadel

Brodie, Laura Fairchild. *Breaking Out: VMI and the Coming of Women.* Pantheon,
    2000.
Case, Mary Anne. "Two Cheers for Cheerleading: The Noisy Integration of VMI and
    the Quiet Success of Virginia Women in Leadership." 1999 *University of Chicago
    Legal Forum* 347 (1999).
Manegold, Catherine S. *In Glory's Shadow: Shannon Faulkner, The Citadel and a
    Changing America.* Knopf, 2000.

Index